The Silenced Drums:
A Review of Tribal Economic Development

The Silenced Drums:
A Review of Tribal Economic Development

Dr K.G. Karmakar

NORTHERN BOOK CENTRE
NEW DELHI

First Published 2002

ISBN 81-7211-122-3

Price : Rs. 750.00
$ 40.00
£ 20.00

Published by Northern Book Centre,
4221/1, Ansari Road, New Delhi 110 002
Phone: 3280295; Fax: 011-3252651

Laser typeset and Printed by
Paragon Enterprises, Ansari Road, New Delhi 110 002

This Book is Dedicated to the Tribal People of India who Continue to be Socially Marginalised and Economically Exploited in the Name of Development!

"We cannot allow matters to drift in tribal areas or just not taken interest in them in the world of today that is not possible or desirable. At the same time we should avoid overadministering these areas and in particular, sending too many outsiders into tribal territory. It is between these two extreme positions that we have to function. Development has to be ensured in various areas, such as communications, medical facilities, education and better agriculture".

Pt. Jawaharlal Nehru
09 October 1958

in Foreword to
"A Philosophy for NEFA"
by Dr. Verrier Elwin

एस. के. नायक
S.K. Naik
Tele : 3381652
Fax : 3073160

सत्यमेव जयते

Foreword

After five decades of planned development, around eight percent of the country's population, who are Scheduled Tribes (STs), still remains underserved. The human development indices of the ST population are still at a much lower level and the gap vis-à-vis the others is on increase. Faster and accelerated efforts towards development of STs are required with renewed vigour and in a more focused and holistic manner at this juncture when new concerns and challenges have emerged in the changed scenario of globalization and liberalisation of the national economy.

2. In this backdrop, a critical analysis of various welfare programmes implemented so far vis-à-vis their reach to the grass root level, using the policy research as a tool for analyzing various social, economic and political issues affecting the STs, assumes criticality. Efforts made in this direction are few and far between. The book authored by Dr. K.G. Karmakar is, therefore, a welcome publication. The indepth research and study of various aspects concerning tribal life in the state of Orissa would certainly be of immense use for the policy makers and the implementation machinery at the grass root level. The tribal economy predominantly based on procurement and sale of Minor Forest Produce (MFP), cultivation of medicinal plants, tribal art and crafts, availability of institutional finance, etc. has been comprehensively examined in this work. The suggested alternative policy prescriptions would be of utmost importance in ensuring timely corrective action.

3. In view of the commonality of concerns and critical issues effecting the tribal population, this work would be useful for socio-economic development of tribals outside Orissa as well. I am sure that the work of Dr. Karmakar would certainly interest the policy planners, implementers, scholars, NGOs and all those who share concern for the development of STs.

(S.K. NAIK)
SECRETARY TO THE GOVT. OF INDIA

Preface

A book on tribal economic development! Surely there are more interesting subjects to write on! And what is a city-bred man doing, writing on tribal people? The book may be well-meaning but won't sell! It is not fashionable anymore to write on tribal people! These were some of the articulated comments while the silence of others spoke many, more volumes! Has the nation given up on the development of tribal people? Are we trying to erase the presence of the tribal people by ignoring them? Do we just want to close our eyes and wish they would vanish forever alongwith their vanishing habitat—the forests?

Various poignant scenes flash on to my mind, jerked out from my memory banks! Whenever I think of tribals, I think about the lovely, dense forests teeming with birds and animals and the true kings of the forests, the tribal people. With strangers they are silent, morose, difficult to communicate with and deliberately try to avoid leaving any lasting impact and definitely give the impression that they would prefer to blend with the scenery and vanish! But if you could somehow earn their respect and are able to cross the threshold of the barriers created, then they are voluble, very knowledgeable in jungle-craft and survival skills and have lots of interesting experiences to speak about! Having trekked through many forests, hills and villages, all over the country both professionally and for leisure, I feel that we have failed miserably in our tribal development efforts and managed to marginalise and ignore them as people with definite wants and needs.

A colleague was conducting field visits for utilisation of loans in the late 1980's and had trekked for over two hours to reach an inaccessible tribal village which had a bad record of loan repayment. The branch manager who had accompanied him was cursing the tribal people and their repayment ethics, annoyed at having to abandon the jeep and walk all this distance for an exercise in futility. In one of the outlying huts, the borrower had died and the bank could not get repayment instalments from his wife, in spite of promises of repayment which were overdue for the last 3 years (a sum of Rs. 2,000 was due, including accumulated interest!). A young girl was outside the house, making dung-cakes for drying. The whereabouts of the mother were enquired and the girl said that she was inside, cooking and went in. Two or three shouts later, the woman did not emerge and the branch manager was furious at the delay for having to wait in the hot sun. After about 10 minutes, the woman emerged to a veritable barrage of abuses and threats from the branch manager for not having paid the loan instalments. The woman was downcast, very apologetic and said that the family was having a very hard time economically and yet promised to pay after the next harvest! While returning, he continued his tirade against the tribal people till my colleague asked him if he saw what the woman was wearing! The branch manager had not noticed that the mother was wearing the same saree which her daughter had worn earlier. There was only one saree to wear between the mother and daughter! The time taken to appear before us was spent in removing the saree from the daughter and wearing it herself. There was just no money for another saree!

At Thuamal Rampur in Kalahandi District, Orissa, alongwith Feroze of Antodaya at a tribal meeting, there was an impressive turnout. They said that I was the first-ever senior official they had ever seen and hence the turnout. Some men and a few women spoke up in the meeting which was remarkable, as tribal people rarely articulate their sufferings and deprivation before outsiders. It revealed the acceptance of the NGO and I particularly remember an old lady, very dignified and wise. She poignantly asked me if I could help them in enabling them feed their family during the monsoon months when there was little food available and they could not go to the forests in search of roots and edibles! I could only suggest a grain-bank scheme but I really had no answers for they needed a micro-watershed scheme and were willing to put in voluntary labour. Till date the project has not started.

In Simlipal, Orissa, the tribals live amidst threats of eviction from the forest officials as they are suspected of killing animals. The tribal people live without any amenities, refusing to leave their ancestral homes and are denied even roads and electricity by the forest officials who would want them to go elsewhere! (Where?). Yet their knowledge of medicinal values of different trees, shrubs and bushes, left me spell-bound! There was a treasure-trove of tribal medicinal practices, waiting to be tapped! At Gandhamardan (remember Hanuman bringing the Sanjivani herb along with the mountain in the Ramayan), in Sambalpur and in Keonjhar, the tribals were experts with their extensive knowledge of various medicinal herbs. But who has bothered to tap their skills or even exploit this knowledge?

At Islampur in Jannaram Reserved Forests, Adilabad, where I was involved in the Tiger Census 1997, there is no sign of the State! There is no road and after $2\frac{1}{2}$ hours of bullock-cart travel, the village is reached. There is no pump for water and the forest guards' hut is abandoned! A road was under construction and red Naxalite Flags (People's War Group) were everywhere. There was tension in the air but as there were two reports of tiger-sighting, we had to visit the village even though the forest guards did their best to dissuade us from going there. Finally, they accompanied us, minus official uniforms, and even in the village, we got little cooperation. Though we brought all rations, they grudgingly prepared our food (it was sufficient to feed 20 more people). And when we ventured into the forests, the drums spoke up, maintaining a continuous tempo, as long as we were in the forest, warning the 'anna-garus' (militants) of offical presence! It is only when we returned to the village after a futile three-hour search for the elusive tigers, that the drums stopped.

Let the tribal drums maintain their beats and the onward march to development. My silent prayer to the powers-that-be is that the tribal people should prosper and flourish and not be confined to the dustbins of history. Let them march ahead to their own drumbeats, at their own pace, unfettered and free in the lovely forests they inhabit. Let them be given a chance to survive, to find their moorings in the swiftly-changing and terrifying world where they are being exploited and let them develop and be educated to integrate into the rural economy.

Dr K.G. Karmakar

Acknowledgements

The publication of this book would not have been possible at all but for the constant encouragement and support I received from my wife and children in keeping me physically fit and mentally alert. She had been providing me the inspiration to complete the manuscript and I acknowledge all her efforts in making this mission successful.

I am thankful to Shri Pratap Vaish of Northern Book Centre, New Delhi and his staff for enthusiastically going through the manuscript and making valuable suggestions, and bringing out the publication in the present form in record time.

I also acknowledge the help rendered by Shri K.C. Mishra for liaisoning with the publishers and coordinating the entire work relating to the publication.

I have a special word of thanks for Shri Bhaskar Sen, Assistant General Manager, NABARD, New Delhi and a renowned painter for drawing a painting for the cover page of this book and giving suggestions for the designing of the cover page. I am also grateful to Smt. Uma Chandrasekhar and Shri D. Ravikumar from NABARD, Mumbai who helped me in typing the manuscript for publication.

Last, but not the least, I acknowledge the help rendered by my colleagues and friends from NABARD and their constant encouragement and suggestions for bringing out this book.

January 1, 2002 **Dr K.G. Karmakar**

Contents

Part–III
For Tribal People — A Framework for Sustainable Development

List of Tables

List of Abbreviations

AICRPE	—	All India Coordinated Research Project on Ethno-biology
AMCS	—	Artisans Multipurpose Co-orperative Societies
BAIF	—	Bharatiya Agro-Industries Federation
BCWS	—	Backward Classes Welfare Sector
BDO	—	Block Development Officer
CBFP	—	Community Based Forestry Programme
CCB	—	Central Cooperative Bank
CCF	—	Community Credit Facilitators
CDRI	—	Central Drug Research Institute
CF	—	Conservator of Forest
CFS	—	Contractual Farming System
CPIAL	—	Consumer Price Index for Agricultural Labourers
DCB	—	District Co-operative Bank
DCCS	—	District Credit Cooperative Societies
DCF	—	Deputy Conservator of Forests
DMS	—	District Marketing Societies
DPAP	—	Drought Prone Area Programme
DRDA	—	District Rural Development Authority
DRDs	—	Domestic Requirement Departments
EEC	—	European Economic Commission
ERRP	—	Economic Rehabilitation of Rural Poor
FCI	—	Food Corporation of India
FD	—	Forest Department
FGT	—	Foster Green & Thornbecke
FRLHT	—	Foundation of Revitalisation for Local Health Tradition
GATT	—	General Agreement on Tariffs and Trade
GBM	—	General Body Meeting
GCC	—	Girijan Cooperative Corporation
GDP	—	Gross Domestic Product
GDS	—	Grama-vikas Development Society
GOI	—	Government of India
ICAR	—	Indian Council of Agricultural Research
ICMR	—	Indian Council of Medical Research
IIFT	—	Indian Institute of Foreign Trade
IISS	—	Indian Institute of Social Sciences
IRDP	—	Integrated Rural Development Programme
ITDA	—	Integrated Tribal Development Agency
ITDP	—	Integrated Tribal Development Programme
JFM	—	Joint Forest Management
JRY	—	Jawahar Rojgar Yojana
KVIB	—	Khadi and Village Industries Board
LAMPS	—	Large Sized Adivasi Multi-purpose Societies
LDBs	—	Land Development Banks
MADA	—	Modified Area Development Approach
MFP	—	Minor Forest Produce
MSSRF	—	M.S. Swaminathan Research Foundation

MYRADA	—	Mysore Resettlement Agricultural Development Agency
NABARD	—	National Bank for Agriculture and Rural Development
NAFED	—	National Agricultural Federation
NBPGR	—	National Bureau of Plant Genetic Research
NBSC	—	National Bank Staff College
NCA	—	National Commission on Agriculture
NCAER	—	National Council of Applied Economic Research
NGO	—	Non-Governmental Organisation
NIRD	—	National Institute of Rural Development
NPA	—	Non-performing Assets
NTFP	—	Non-Timber Forest Produce
NWDB	—	National Wasteland Development Board
OAIC	—	Orissa Agro-Industries Corporation
OFDC	—	Orissa Forest Development Corporation
OHC	—	Orissa Handicraft Corporation
OMFED	—	Orissa Milk Federation
OSCMF	—	Orissa State Cooperative Marketing Federation
OSTSCS	—	Orissa State Tassar and Silk Cooperative Society
PACS	—	Primary Agricultural Credit Societies
PCCS	—	Primary Co-operative Credit Societies
PDS	—	Public Distribution System
PDs	—	Person Days
PHC	—	Primary Health Centre
PLDB	—	Primary Land Development Bank
PREM	—	People Rural Education Movement
RBI	—	Reserve Bank of India
RCMS	—	Regional Cooperative Marketing Societies
REC	—	Rural Electrification Corporation
RFO	—	Range Forest Officer
RIDF	—	Rural Infrastructure Development Fund
RRB	—	Regional Rural Bank
SAP	—	Seasonal Agricultural Produce/Surplus Agricultural Produce
SBI	—	State Bank of India
SC	—	Scheduled Caste
SCA	—	Special Central Assistance
SCBs	—	State Cooperative Banks
SCS	—	Service Co-operative Societies
SDO	—	Sub-Divisional Officer
SFDA	—	Small Farmers Development Agency
SFDC	—	State Forest Development Corporation
SHG	—	Self Help Groups
SGSY	—	Swarna Jayanti Gram Swarojgar Yojna
SLDB	—	State Land Development Bank
SMTD	—	Special Multipurpose Tribal Development
ST	—	Scheduled Tribe
STDC	—	State Tribal Development Corporation
SVP	—	Sisal Vikas Parishad
SWOT Analysis	—	Strengths and Weaknesses Opportunities and Threats Analysis
TAC	—	Tribal Advisory Council
TCMDFI	—	Tribal Cooperative Marketing Development Federation of India
TDB	—	Tribal Development Block
TDCC	—	Tribal Development Cooperative Corporation
TGCS	—	Tree Growers Cooperative Societies
THRTI	—	Tribal and Harijan Research Training Institute
TISCO	—	Tata Iron & Steel Company
TPC	—	Training-cum-Production Centre
TRIFED	—	Tribal Federation
TRYSEM	—	Training for Rural Youth for Self-employment
TSP	—	Tribal Sub-Plans
UMSB	—	Utkal Mahila Sanchaya Bikas
VA	—	Voluntary Agencies
VFMCs	—	Village Forest Management Committees
VFPMC	—	Village Forest Protection and Management Committee
WAS	—	Women's Advisory Sub-committee
WHO	—	World Health Organisation
WHS	—	Water Harvesting Structure
WTO	—	World Trade Organisation

Part–I
About Tribal People — An Overview of Development

CHAPTER I

The Tribal Way of Life

INTRODUCTION

The Imperial Gazeteer of India, 1911, defines a tribe as a "collection of families bearing a common name, speaking a common dialect, occupying or professing to occupy a common territory and is not usually endogamous though originally it might have been so". Another definition of a tribe by D.N. Majumdar is that "a tribe is a collection of families or group of families bearing a common name, members of which occupy the same territory, speak the same language and observe certain taboos regarding marriage, profession or occupation and have developed a well-assessed system of reciprocity and mutuality of obligations". A tribe is different from a horde or caste and is bound together by a tribal ethos of kinship, blood relations, culture and the need for protection against a hostile world.

The tribal people were the earliest inhabitants of India with four major tribes which together constitute the Indian people. They are:

(i) *The Austro-Asiatic Tribes* — In a very primitive form, they comprise the Mundas, the Khasis and the Nicobarees.

(ii) *The Mongoloids* — These belong to the Sino-Tibetian race inhabiting the sub-Himalayan regions such as the Nagas, Bodos and Kuki tribes.

(iii) *The Dravidians* — These are tribes which speak Dravidian tongues like the Gonds, Sauras, Oraons, *etc.*

(iv) *The Aryans* — These are represented by the Caucasian Tribes which came from the Caspian Seas and include the Shakas, Kushanas,

Huns and other tribes which invaded India at various times and were assimilated into Indian society.

The tribal people lived in a heavily forested country that was India and there was much internal movement due to varying periods of supremacy with the less powerful tribes being forced to occupy the farthest hills and forest regions, away from the fertile river valleys. Thus, from the earliest battles for supremacy even among the earliest Indo-Austric tribes, the defeated tribes were pushed into unoccupied areas.

In the medieval period, the Muslim rulers introduced the system of land grants or jagirs for services rendered by civil and military administration thus resulting in agrarian troubles for tribals. The Bhils, Gonds, Banjaras and Bodos had their areas of influence restricted during this period. The entry of the British into the Chota Nagpur area paved the way for the entry of exploiters like the forest contractors who felled massive forests, the money-lenders and the landlords (especially after the Permanent Settlement Act, 1789) as the system of tribal ownership was not acknowledged by the British. Various tribal uprisings continued to break out between 1772 and 1832 with brutal suppression of the tribal people who were oppressed. The great Kol revolt of 1832 led to the policy of isolation with the passing of Resolution XIII of 1833 and Chota Nagpur was declared a non-regulating area. The non-regulating system was extended over the years after the Khond uprising in 1846, the Santhal agitation in 1854 and the tribal rebellion in Dhanbad in 1869–70. This idea of isolating tribals was soon expanded into having separate districts exclusively for tribals. The Scheduled District Act, 1874 gave wide powers to the administration wherein the special arrangements for tribal isolation continued. However, tribal unrest continued with the Sardari rebellion (1887), the Birsa Munda agitation (1895), and the Tana Bhagat movement (1914), *etc.*, were all brutally suppressed. The tribals resented the changes which deprived them of their lands and forests, especially after 1850. The deprivation enforced by the rulers and the exploiters forced the tribal people to reach uninhabited areas like forests and hilly areas where they could live undisturbed and together face all challenges. The process of marginalisation which started during the medieval period continued with the Government of India Act, 1919 enforcing two types of exclusions, *viz.*, 'Wholly Excluded Area' and 'Area of Modified Exclusion'. By now, the tribals had got involved with the freedom movement. The Simon Commission (1928), suggested two types of exclusions and the Government of India Act, 1935 incorporated the "Excluded Areas" and 'Partially Excluded Areas', whereby reservations made for tribals (whether passed by the Federal Legislature or Provincial Legislature) would apply to tribally excluded areas.

During the colonial rule, another important development was the spread of Christianity as a result of conversions by Roman Catholic/Protestant missionaries. This did help in better educational and health facilities and large sections of the tribal population in the North-Eastern States and in the Chota Nagpur areas, got converted. But tribal societies got divided into tribal and tribal Christian societies. The religious conversions and the excluded area policy gave life to a separate tribal identity.

THE TRIBAL DIASPORA

India is one of the few nations in the world with a thriving tribal population in different parts of the country. There are 537 different tribal communities spread all over India. As per official data, there are 258 tribal communities speaking about 106 different languages notified as scheduled tribes. As per the 1991 census, the tribal population is 6.77 crore comprising about 8.08 per cent of the total population of the country. Madhya Pradesh has the largest tribal population with 1.54 crore, followed by Maharashtra with 0.73 crore and Orissa with 0.70 crore is the third (Annexure 1.1). About 82 per cent of the total tribal population is concentrated in central and western parts of the country whereas only 11 per cent is dispersed in small pockets in the Southern States.

The tribal population is increasing along with the Indian population but at a rate lower than the general population. This indicates that there is no systematic persecution though there may be exploitation. The growth in the tribal population during the last 100 years, has been set out at Annexure 1.2. The decennical growth rates are significantly lower than the average general population growth. This is a healthy sign as in most developed or developing countries, the indigenous people are being wiped out. The problems of the Indians in Brazil and the Gypsies in Eastern Europe, are well-documented.

The basic tribal occupations which are intertwined with their life-styles, need to be studied in some detail to have an idea of their way of life and their economy. It would be unwise to try and generalise about tribal life-styles as each tribe is unique and has its own system of coping with their multitude of problems relating to their environment, culture and practices, productive technologies and inclusive system of cooperation, non-monetised economy and their stubborn insistence on retaining their value-systems in a fast-changing world. If tribals are not to be marginalised further in a free-market economy without safety-nets, their strengths have to be studied and built upon.

TRIBAL OCCUPATIONS

I. Hunting, Collecting and Gathering Type

The tribes of this type, namely Kharia, Chenchus, Korwas, Jarawas, Rajis, Birhor, who live in the dense forests in the country, exclusively depend on forest resources for their livelihood by practising hunting, fishing, gathering and collecting. They live in tiny temporary huts made out of the materials found in forests. Under constraints of their economic pursuits, they live in isolated small bands or groups and with their primitive technology, limited skills and unflinching traditional and ritual practices, their entire style of life revolves around forests. Their world view is fully in consonance with the forest eco-system. The population of such tribes is numerically small, yet the impact of the ever-depleting forest resources upon them is very significant. Socio-politically, they have remained inarticulate and, therefore, have remained in a relatively more primitive stage and have been generally neglected as far as development is concerned. The settlements are small, comprising about 5–15 villages. The family members work in productive units while villagers join together and work in groups as an economic unit. Their way of life and food depends upon the forest and there is severe shortage of food during the monsoons. They live by hunting animals and birds, fishing, collecting roots, tubers, fruits, nuts and flowers. Leaves and fibres are used for ropes while bamboo is used for baskets and for huts. Honey and wax are also collected. Fishing by hand is common as is poisoning of ponds.

II. Cattle-herder Type

The rearing of domestic animals is widely prevalent among tribals for their utilitarian value. Goats, bullocks and buffaloes are common while cows are few in number in tribal villages. Each of them has various uses. The goat is slaughtered for its meat on festive occasions and is even sold in case of contingencies like sickness, death, *etc.* Many tribal people invest in cattle and their savings are 'mobile' though not very liquid. In times of need, cattle are sold in the cattle-markets. Bullocks are mainly used as draught power in agricultural practices, while cows are mostly kept for their dung and offsprings. Cows being reared for milk is a rare case in tribal villages. Buffaloes, mostly male ones, are kept for being used as draught power and for its meat. Moreover, buffaloes are cherished by tribals because of its resale value. The pastoral tribes like Gujjars, Todas, Gaddis, Nagesias, Rabaris and Lambadas live in various parts of India.

Feeding practices of these animals are simple. They are allowed to graze under the care of one person, most often in the case of goats, a girl. The health of the animals in tribal areas is relatively better when compared to that of the plains. However, common diseases like diarrhoea, stomach-ache, foot and mouth diseases are prevalent in these areas and are treated by indigenous medicines and practices. For example, in fracture cases, a medicine is prepared by adding to an equal quantity of milk to the paste of the roots of the 'Saura' tree which is applied over the fractured area and bandaged with bamboo sticks. For round-worm and foot and mouth diseases, the roots of creeper 'Gajapal' and the 'Kala Bhalia' seeds are respectively used.

Entrustment of Animals

Entrustment is common among the tribals and the phenomenon of entrustment is relatively predominant in villages close to the plains. A case study of Satgharia village, in Ganjam district reveals that bullocks followed by goats, cows and buffaloes are entrusted in order of priority. The poverty of the tribals, the need for draught power and their surplus work power drives the tribals to the practice of entrustment of animals from the farmers of the plains.

The farmers of the plains on the other hand readily entrust animals because they have surplus animals while having limited fodder resources. Moreover, they have the advantage of getting animals trained after a certain period of time without any investment and the difficulty of maintaining animals. For example, bullocks are entrusted to the tribals when they are just 2 years old under certain conditions. It is mandatory on the part of the tribals to feed the animals, train them to plough, to take care of their health and even sometimes to use them to plough the fields of the farmers. The bullocks are then to be returned after they become full-fledged young bullocks again under conditions which the tribals must fulfil. In case of each type of animals, the conditions differ. For instance, in case a goat is killed by whatever cause, its carcass must be produced before the farmer, otherwise, cash compensation should be met by the tribal. A benefit for the tribal is that the offsprings of goats are shared equally. For cows, the condition is that the tribal may keep the dung but sell the milk for the farmer. Offsprings of the cow belong to the owner. It is a sad fact that the farmer benefits so much from the entrustment that it amounts to exploitation of tribal labour.

Constraints for Low Animal Husbandry Activities in Tribal Areas

The tribal areas have a great potential for development of animal husbandry as they offer better grazing grounds and also surplus manpower, traditional knowledge and skills in rearing. However, popularisation of these activities is hindered by the following factors:

- *(i)* Animals in tribal areas depend on forests for their grazing. Access to grazing is essential, but this needs to be regulated and overuse of forests be stopped.
- *(ii)* Development activities become difficult in the tribal areas because the villages are small, scattered and are in remote/inaccessible areas.
- *(iii)* Most of the tribals are poor and face financial constraints even to buy a goat and provide necessary care.
- *(iv)* The fear of attack by wild animals remains as they live inside dense forest areas or close to forest areas.
- *(v)* Marketing of any products including animals is mostly controlled by middlemen. Tribals are unable to resort to alternative marketing strategies which can save them from exploitation.
- *(vi)* Shrinkage in pasture availablity due to rehabilitation of refugees in the tribal areas is another factor for slow the growth of animal husbandry activities.

III. The Simple Artisan Type

A number of tribes subsist on crafts and cottage industries like basket-making, tool-making (iron and wooden) and spinning and weaving, metal-work, *etc.* There is crafts-wise specialisation and the craftsmen are resident in the villages of other tribes under the 'jajmani' system of labour exchange. Handicrafts are a subsidiary occupation for most of the 'advanced' tribals who are proficient in matting, basket-making, bamboo-work, spinning, *etc.*, with about 2.5 per cent of the tribal working population being engaged as artisans.

The Orissa Mahali and Kol-Lohara, practise crafts, like basket-making and black-smithy respectively. The Loharas with their traditional skills and primitive tools manufacture iron and wooden tools for other neighbouring tribes and thereby eke out their existence. Similarly, the Mahalis earn their living by making baskets for other communities. However, both the tribes are now confronted with the problem of scarcity of raw materials and further, they are not always able to compete with others, especially in the tribal market where goods from the plains also come for sale, because of their primitive technology and inadequate resources.

The Khariars of Mayurbhanj are expert in bee wax and honey collections. In Mayurbhanj District, units of small scale industries are now manufacturing plates and cups of sal leaves. Basket-making is a household industry in Phulbani District. In Koraput District, the Khadi and Village Industries Board (KVIB) has now initiated cottage industries, based on forest products.

The tribals extract oil from mahuas, castor, neem and alasi seeds. For a change, the tribals of Nawarangpur manufacture fancy objects like chains and bangles. Lacquer coated boxes with beautiful art works are made. Lac processing, apart from brooms from broom grass and mat weaving out of mat seeds, are household industries in Kalahandi District.

The Bhuyans of Keonjhar are skilled in making mats and brooms and ropes. While the women weave the mats and bind broomsticks from datepalm trees, the men fashion the sabai grass into strong ropes. The manufacture of cups and plates out of sal leaves, is now in vogue among many tribal families. The Kondhs, Domas and Turis in Sundergarh District are skilled in mat-weaving and basket-making from bamboo and palm leaves.

These economic activities present the beautiful tribal arts and craft skills and culture. Now, all these traditional resources are badly affected, due to lack of technological innovations and marketing support.

IV. Hill and Shifting Cultivation Type

There are 3 main techniques such as *(i)* slash and burn cultivation, *(ii)* hoe and burn cultivation and *(iii)* terrace cultivation with natural/stored irrigation. These involve as many as 13 phases. Some of the cultivator tribals are the Garoas, Chakmas, Nagas, Birjias, Saoras, Kathiya Khonds and Maria

Gonds. About 11 million hectares of land is believed to be under 'swidden' cultivation done by over 4 lakh tribal families.

The practice of hill and shifting cultivation is very common in many tribal areas. In northern Orissa, the Juang and Bhuiyan and in southern Orissa, the Kandh, Saora, Koya, Parenga, Didayi, Dharua and Bondo practise shifting cultivation. They supplement their economy by food-gathering and hunting as production in shifting cultivation is low.

Shifting cultivation is essentially a regulated sequence of procedures designed to open up and bring under cultivation patches of forest lands, usually on hilly slopes. In shifting cultivation, the practitioners follow a pattern of cycle of activities which are as follows: *(i)* selection of a patch of hill slope or forest land and distribution or allotment of the same to intended practitioners, *(ii)* worshipping of concerned deities and making of sacrifices, *(iii)* cutting of trees, bushes, ferns, *etc.*, existing on the land before summer months, *(iv)* piling of logs, bushes and ferns on the land, *(v)* burning of the withered logs, ferns, shrubs, *etc.*, to ashes on a suitable day, *(vi)* cleaning of the patch of land before the on-set of monsoon and spreading of the ashes evenly on the land after a shower or two, *(vii)* hoeing and sowing of seeds with regular commencement of rains, *(viii)* crude bunding and weeding activities after sprouting of seeds, *(ix)* watching and protecting the crops, *(x)* harvesting and collecting crops, *(xi)* threshing and storing of corns, grains, *etc.*, *(xii)* merry-making and *(xiii)* selling of crops. In these operations, all the members of the family are involved in some way or the other. Work is distributed according to the ability of individual members. However, the head of the family assumes all the responsibilities in the practice and operation of shifting cultivation. The adult males, between 18 and 50 years of age, undertake the strenuous work of cutting trees, ploughing, hoeing and watching of the crops at night whereas cutting the bushes and shrubs, cleaning of seeds for sowing and weeding are done by women.

Shifting cultivation is an ecologically disastrous mode of production. However, it is not only an economic pursuit of some tribal communities, but it accounts for their total way of life. Their social structure, economy, political organisation and religion are all ,accountable to the practice of shifting cultivation.

Shifting cultivation has certain demerits. Wherever shifting cultivation is carried out on steep slopes, it invariably invites the agents of erosion and degradation. By deforestation, soil looses its water retention capacity and the sub-soil gets washed away to expose the rocks and boulders gradually. Slowly and steadily, the shifting cultivation process causes the streams down the hill to dry up. It also brings down heavy silts into the river basins, plains and valleys. The extensive deforestation affects rainfall, the life of animals and forest resources and it also leads to nomadic habits among the practitioners.

In the past, land in the tribal areas had not been surveyed and settled and the tribals, therefore, freely practised shifting cultivation in their respective habitats assuming that land, forest, water and other natural resources belonged to them. There were two traditional systems of land tenure. Among the tribes of northern Orissa, land and other resources were communally owned and the annual distribution of plots on the hill slopes for shifting cultivation was being done in a cooperative manner. But among the tribes of southern Orissa, all such land and other natural resources were under the control of the village (tribal) headman, who on approach, used to allot plots for use by individuals. However, since the evolution of the Indian Forest Policy in 1852 and survey and settlement of land in tribal areas, the traditional tribal land tenure system has dwindled. The tribals, therefore, now have limited land and forest resources for the practice of shifting cultivation and for carrying on hunting, collecting and gathering activities. The practice of shifting cultivation, however, continues unchecked and attempts made to wean away the tribals from shifting cultivation, have so far failed.

In certain hilly areas, terraces are constructed along the slopes and it is believed to be a step towards settled agriculture. Terrace cultivation is practised by the Saora, Kandh and Gadaba. The terraces are built on the slopes of hills with water streams. In terrace cultivation, the available hill slopes are fully used and the available water of hill streams are tapped for cultivation throughout the year as the water flows from one terrace to another in downward motion. The terrace walls are rivetted and packed with stones and boulders, which cannot be washed out easily. In terraces, paddy is mainly grown and the per-acre yield is quite high. However, the quantity of terrace land under the possession of a family is not much. The Saoras boast that not a single speck of soil is carried down from the top of the hill to the bottom of the valleys.

V. Settled Agricultural Type

About 70 per cent of the total tribal working population are cultivators, mostly of the subsistence variety. There are 3 types of land, upland, lowland and kitchen-garden varieties (mostly by women). There is total cooperation on a reciprocal basis during transplanting , sowing and harvesting of varieties of coarse grains as also rice, pulses, chillies.

Several larger tribes such as Santal, Munda, Ho, Khasis, Oraon, Tharus, Bhils, Gond, Koyas, Damarias, Savara, *etc.*, are settled agriculturists, though they supplement their economy with hunting, gathering and collecting. In general, they raise only one crop during the monsoon and, therefore, have to supplement their economy by other types of subsidiary economic activities. However, tribal communities practising settled agriculture suffer from various problems, *viz.*, *(i)* unproductive and uneconomic land holdings, *(ii)* land alienation, *(iii)* indebtedness, *(iv)* lack of irrigation facilities, *(v)* lack of power, *(vi)* absence of adequate roads and transport, *(vii)* lack of access to bank credit facilities, *(viii)* seasonal migration to other places for wage earning, *(ix)* lack of extension services, *(x)* lack of education and inadequate scope for modernisation of their skills.

VI. Industrial Urban Worker Type

A sizeable chunk of the tribal population in India have moved to mining, industrial and urban areas for a secured living through wage-labour. During the past three decades, the process of industrial urbanisation in the tribal belts in Bihar, Madhya Pradesh and Orissa has been accelerated through operations of mines and establishment of industries. Mostly persons from the advanced tribal communities, such as Santal, Munda, Ho, Oraon, Kisan, Gond, *etc.*, have taken to this economic pursuit in order to relieve pressure from their limited land and other resources.

In some instances, industrialisation and mining operations have led to uprooting of tribal villages and the displaced have become industrial nomads. They have lost their traditional occupation, agricultural land, houses and other immovable assets. They became unemployed and face unfair competition with others in the labour market. Their aspirations gradually escalated, although they invariably failed to achieve what they aspired for. Thus, the net result is frustration. Occasionally their disappointment has been reflected in unrest and agitation. The Jharkhand movement and Naxalite activists also capitalised on these issues. While it is neither possible nor desirable to halt the process of industrialisation, the authorities must contemplate built-in safeguards for all tribals who are affected by irrigation and industrial projects.

ANNEXURE 1.1

Statewise Distribution of Tribal Population in India—1991

[Figures in lakh]

Sl. No.	*States*	*Total population*	*Scheduled tribes*	*Percentage of ST to total*
	India	*8,463*	*677*	*8.08*
STATES				
1.	Andhra Pradesh	665	42	6.31
2.	Arunachal Pradesh	9	5	63.66
3.	Assam	224	29	12.82
4.	Bihar	864	66	7.66
5.	Goa	12	0	0.03
6.	Gujarat	413	62	14.92
7.	Haryana	165	—	—
8.	Himachal Pradesh	52	2	4.22
9.	Jammu & Kashmir	77	NA	NA
10.	Karnataka	450	19	4.26
11.	Kerala	291	3	1.10
12.	Madhya Pradesh	662	154	23.27
13.	Maharashtra	789	73	9.27
14.	Manipur	18	6	34.41
15.	Meghalaya	18	15	85.53
16.	Mizoram	7	7	94.75
17.	Nagaland	12	11	87.70
18.	Orissa	317	70	22.21
19.	Punjab	203	—	—
20.	Rajasthan	440	55	12.44
21.	Sikkim	4	1	22.36
22.	Tamil Nadu	559	6	1.03
23.	Tripura	28	8	30.95
24.	Uttar Pradesh	1,391	3	0.21
25.	West Bengal	681	38	5.59
UNION TERRITORIES				
26.	Andaman & Nicobar Islands	3	0.27	9.54
27.	Chandigarh	6	—	—
28.	Dadra & Nagar Haveli	1	1.09	78.99
29.	Daman & Diu	1	0.12	11.54
30.	Delhi	94	—	—
31.	Lakshadeep	1	0.5	93.15
32.	Pondicherry	8	—	—

Source: Census of India, 1991, Director of Census Operation, Orissa.

ANNEXURE 1.2

Names of Tribes in India
(According to 1981Census)

ANDHRA PRADESH

1. Andh
2. Bagata
3. Bhil
4. Chenchu, Chenchwar
5. Gadabas
6. Gond, Naikpod, Rajgond
7. Goudu (in the Agency tracts)
8. Hill Reddis
9. Jatapus
10. Kammara
11. Kattunayakan
12. Kolam, Mannevarlu
13. Konda Dhoras
14. Konda Kapus
15. Kondareddis
16. Kondhs, Kodi, Kodhu, Desaya Kondhs, Dongria Kondhs, Kuttiya Kondhs, Tikiria Kondhs; Yenity Kondhs
17. Kotia, Bentho Oriya, Bartika Dhulia, Dulia, Holva, Paiko, Putiya, Sanrona, Sidhopaiko
18. Koya, Goud, Rajah, Rasha Koya, Lingadhari Koya (Ordinary), KottuKoya, Bhine Koya, Rajkoya
19. Kulia
20. Malis (excluding Adilabad, Hyderabad, Karimnagar,Khammam, Mahabubnagar,Medak, Nalgonda, Nizamabad and Warangal Districts)
21. Manna Dhora
22. Mukha Dhora, Nooka Dhora
23. Nayaks (inthe Agency tracts)
24. Pardhan
25. Porja, Parangiperja
26. Reddi Dhoras
27. Rona, Rena
28. Savaras, Kapu Savaras, Maliya Savaras, Kutto Savaras
29. Sugalis, Lambadis
30. Thoti (in Adilabad, Hyderabad, Karimnagar, Khammam, Mahabubnagar, Medak, Nalgonda, Nizamabad and Warangal Districts)
31. Valmiki (in the Agency tracts)
32. Yenadis
33. Yerukulas

ASSAM

I. In the autonomous districts:
   1. Chakma
   2. Dimasa, Kachari
   3. Garo

4. Hajong
5. Hmar
6. Khasi, Jaintia, Synteng, Pnar, War, Bhoi, Lyngngam
7. Any Kuku tribes, inclding:
    (i) Biate, Biete
    (ii) Changsan
    (iii) Chongloi
    (iv) Doungel
    (v) Gamalhou
    (vi) Gangte
    (vii) Guite
    (viii) Hanneng
    (ix) Haokip, Haupit
    (x) Haolai
    (xi) Hengna
    (xii) Hongsungh
    (xiii) Hrangkhwal, Rangkhol
    (xiv) Jongbe
    (xv) Khawchung
    (xvi) Khawathlang, Kothalong
    (xvii) Khelma
    (xviii) Kholhou
    (xix) Kipgen
    (xx) Kuki
    (xxi) Lengthang
    (xxii) Lhangum
    (xxiii) Lhoujem
    (xxiv) Lhouvun
    (xxv) Lupheng
    (xxvi) Mangjel
    (xxvii) Misao
    (xxviii) Riang
    (xxix) Sairhem
    (xxx) Selnam
    (xxxi) Singson
    (xxxii) Sotlhou
    (xxxiii) Sukte
    (xxxiv) Thado
    (xxxv) Thangngen
    (xxxvi) Uibuh
    (xxxvii) Vaiphei
8. Lakher
9. Man (Tai-speaking)
10. Any Mizo (Lushai) tribe
11. Mikir
12. Any Naga Tribe
13. Pawi
14. Synteng

II. In the State of Assam excluding the autonomous districts:
1. Barmans in Cachar
2. Boro, Borokachari
3. Deori
4. Hojai
5. Kachari, Sonowal
6. Lalung
7. Mech
8. Miri
9. Rabha

BIHAR
1. Asur
2. Baiga
3. Banjara
4. Bathudi
5. Bedia
6. Bhumij (in North Chotanagpur and South Chotanagpur Divisions and Santal Parganas District)
7. Binjhia
8. Birhor
9. Birjia
10. Chero
11. Chik Baraik
12. Gond
13. Gorait
14. Ho
15. Karmali
16. Kharia
17. Kharwar
18. Khond
19. Kisan
20. Kora
21. Korwa
22. Lohara, Lohra
23. Mahli
24. Mal Paharia
25. Munda
26. Oraon
27. Parhaiya
28. Santal
29. Sauria Paharia
30. Savar

GUJARAT
1. Barda
2. Bavacha, Bamcha
3. Bharwad (in the Nesses of the forests of Alech, Barada & Gir)
4. Bhil, Bhil Garasia, Dholi-Bhil, Dungri Bhil, Dungri Garasia, Mewasi Bhil, Rawal Bhil, Tadvi Bhil, Bhagalia, Bhilala, Pawra, Vasava, Vasave
5. Charan (in the Nesses of the Forests of Alech, Barada and Gir)

6. Chaudhri (in Surat and Valsad Districts)
7. Chodhara
8. Dhanka, Tadvi, Tetaria, Valvi
9. Dhodia
10. Dubla, Talavia, Halpati
11. Gamit, Gamta, Gavit, Mavchi, Padvi
12. Gond, Rajgond
13. Kathodi, Katkari, Dhor Kathodi, Dhor Katkari, Son Kathodi, Son Katkari
14. Kokna, Kokni, Kukna
15. Koli (in Kutch District)
16. Koli Dhor, Tokre Koli, Kolcha, Kolgha
17. Kunbi (in the Dangs District)
18. Naikda, Nayaka, Cholivala Nayaka, Kapadia Nayaka, Mota Nayaka, Nana Nayaka
19. Padhar
20. Paradhi (in Kutch district)
21. Pardhi, Advichincher, Phanse Pardhi (excluding Amrell, Bhavnagar, Amnagar, Junagadh, Kutch, Rajkot and Surendranagar Districts)
22. Patelia
23. Pomla
24. Rabari (in the Nesses of the forests of Alech, Barada and Gir)
25. Rathawa
26. Siddi (in Amreli, Bhavnagar, Jamnagar, Junagadh, Rajkot and Surendranagar Districts)
27. Vaghri (in Kutch District)
28. Varli
29. Vitola, Kotwalia, Barodia

HIMACHAL PRADESH

1. Bhot, Bodh
2. Gaddi (excluding the territories specified in Sub-Section (1) of Section 5 of the Punjab Reorganisation Act, 1966 (31of 1966) other than the Lahaul and Spiti District)
3. Gujjar [excluding the territories specified in Sub-Section (1) of Section 5 of the Punjab Reorganisation Act, 1966 (31 of 1966)
4. Jad, Lamba, Khampa
5. Kanaura, Kinnara
6. Lahaula
7. Pangwala
8. Swangla

KARNATAKA

1. Adiyan
2. Barda
3. Bavacha, Bamcha
4. Bhil, Bhil Garasia, Dholi Bhil, Dungri Bhil, Dungri Garasia, Mewasi Bhil, Rawal Bhil, Tadvi Bhil, Bhagalia, Bhilala, Pawra, Vasava, Vasave.
5. Chenchu, Chenchwar
6. Chodhara
7. Dubla, Talavia, Halpati
8. Gamit, Gamta, Gavit, Mavchi, Padvi, Valvi

9. Gond, Naikpod, Rajgond
10. Gowdalu
11. Hakkipkki
12. Hasalaru
13. Irular
14. Iruliga
15. Jenu Kuruba
16. Kadu Kuruba
17. Kammara (in South Kanara District and Kollegal Taluk of Mysore District)
18. Kaniyan, Kanyan (in Kollegal Taluk of Mysore District)
19. Kathodi, Katkari, Dhor Kathodi, Dhor Katkari, Son Kathodi, Son Katkari
20. Kattunayakan
21. Kokna, Kokni, Kukna
22. Koli Dhor, Tokre Koli, Kolcha, Kolgha
23. Konda Kapus
24. Koraga
25. Kota
26. Koya, Bhine Koya, Rajkoya
27. Kudiya, Melakudi
28. Kuruba (in Coorg District)
29. Kurumans
30. Maha Malasar
31. Malakudi
32. Malakudi
33. Malayekandi
34. Maleru
35. Maratha (in Coorg District)
36. Marati (in South Kanara District)
37. Meda
38. Naikda, Nayaka, Cholivala Nayaka, Kapadia Nayaka, Mota Nayaka, Nana Nayaka
39. Palliyan
40. Paniyan
41. Pardhi, Advichincher, Phanse Pardhi
42. Patelia
43. Rathawa
44. Sholaga
45. Soligaru
46. Toda
47. Varli
48. Vitolia, Kotwalia, Barodia
49. Yerava

KERALA

1. Adiyan
2. Arandan
3. Eravallan
4. Hill Pulaya
5. Irular, Irulan
6. Kadar
7. Kammara [in the areas comprising the Malabar District as specified by Sub-Section (2) of Section 5 of the State Reorganisation Act, 1956 (37 of 1956)]

8. Kanikaran, Kanikkar
9. Kattunayakan
10. Kochu Velan
11. Konda Kapus
12. Kondareddis
13. Koraga
14. Kota
15. Kudiya, Melakudi
16. Kurichchan
17. Kurumans
18. Kurumbas
19. Maha Malasar
20. Malai Aryan
21. Malai Pandaram
22. Malai Vedan
23. Malakkuravan
24. Malasar
25. Malayan [excluding the areas comprising the Malabar District as specified by Sub-Section (2) of the State Reorganisation Act, 1956 (37 of 1956)
26. Malayarayar
27. Mannan
28. Marati (in Hosdurg and Kasaragod Taluks of Cannanore District)
29. Muthuvan, Mudugar, Muduvan
30. Palleyan
31. Palliyan
32. Palliyan
33. Paniyan
34. Ulladan
35. Uraly

MADHYA PRADESH

1. Agariya
2. Andh
3. Baiga
4. Bhaina
5. Bharia Bhumia, Bhuinhar, Bhumia, Bhumiya, Bharia, Paliha, Pando
6. Bhattra
7. Bhil, Bhilala, Barela, Patelia
8. Bhil Mina
9. Bhunjia
10. Biar, Biyar
11. Binjhwar
12. Birhul, Birhor
13. Damor, Damaria
14. Dhanwar
15. Gadaba, Gadba
16. Gond, Arakh, Arrakh, Agaria, Asur, Badi maria, Bada Maria, Bhatola, Bhimma, Bhuta, Koilabhuta, Kliabhuta, Bhar, Bisonhorn Maria, Chota Maria, Dandami Maria, Dhuru, Dhuwa, Dhoba, Dhulia, Dorla, Gaiki, Gatta, Gatti, Gaita, Gond Gowari, Hill Maria, Kandra Kalanga, Khatola, Koitar, Koya, Khirwar, Khirwara, Kucha Maria, Kuchaki Maria, Madia, Maria,

Mana, Mannewar, Moghya, Mogia, Monghya, Mudia, Muria, Nagarchi, Nagwanshi, Ojha, Raj, Sonjhari Jhareka, Thatia, Thotya, Wade Maria, Vade Maria, Daroi

17. Halba, Halbi
18. Kamar
19. Karku
20. Kawar, Kanwar, Kaur, Cherwa, Rathia, Tanwar Chattri
21. Keer (in Bhopal, Raisen and Sehore Districts)
22. Khairwar, Kondar
23. Kharia
24. Kondh, Khond, Kandh
25. Kol
26. Kolam
27. Korku, Bopchi, Mouasi, Nihal, Nahul, Bondhi, Bondeya
28. Korwa, Kodaku
29. Majhi
30. Majhwar
31. Mawasi
32. Mina (in Siroj Sub-Division) of Vidisha District)
33. Munda
34. Nagesia, Nagasia
35. Oraon, Dhanka, Dhangad
36. Panika (in Chhatarpur, Datia, Panna, Rewa, Satna, Shahdol, Sidhi and Tikamgarh Districts)
37. Pao
38. Pardhan, Pathari, Saroti
39. Pardhi (in Bhopal, Raisen and Sehore Districts)
40. Pardhi, Bahelia, Bahelia, Chita Pardhi, Langoli Pardhi, Phanse Pardhi, Shikari, Takankar, Takia ([in *(i)* Bastar, Chhindwara, Mandla, Raigarh, Seoni and Surguja Districts, *(ii)* Baihar tehsil of Balaghat District, *(iii)* Betul District, *(iv)* Bilaspur and Katghora tehsils of Bilaspur District, *(v)* Durg and Balod tahsils of Durg District, *(vi)* Chowki, Manpur and Mohala Revenue, Inspectors' Circles of Rajnandgaon District, *(vii)* Murwara, Patan and Sihora tahsils of Jabalpur District, *(viii)* Hoshangabad and Sohagpur Tahsils of Hoshangabad District and Narsimhapur District, *(ix)* Harsud Tahsil of Khandwa District, *(x)* Bindra-Nawagarh, Dhamtari and Mahasamund Tahsils of Raipur District)]
41. Parja
42. Sahariya, Saharia, Seharia, Sosia, Sor
43. Saonta, Saimta
44. Saur
45. Sawar, Sawara
46. Sonr

MAHARASHTRA

1. Andh
2. Baiga
3. Barda
4. Bavacha, Bamcha
5. Bhaina
6. Bharia Bhumia, Bhuinhar Bhumia, Pando

7. Bhattra
8. Bhil, Bhil Garasia, Dholi, Bhil, Dungri Bhil, Dungri, Garasia, Mewasi Bhil, Rawal Bhil, Tadvi Bhil, Bhagalia, Bhilala, Pawra, Vasava, Vasave
9. Bhunjia
10. Binjhwar
11. Birhul Birhor
12. Chodhara (excluding Akola, Amaravati, Bhandara, Buldana, Chandarapur, Nagpur, Wardha, Yavatmal, Aurangabad, Bhir Nanded, Osmanabad and Parbhani Districts)
13. Dhanka, Tadvi, Tetaria, Valvi
14. Dhanwar
15. Dhodia
16. Dubla, Talavia, Halpati
17. Gamit, Gamta Gavit, Mavchi, Padvi
18. Gond, Rajgond, Arakh, Arrakh, Agaria, Asur, Badi Maria, Bada Maria, Bhatola, Bhatola, Bhimma, Bhuta, Koilabjuta, Koilabhuti, Bhar, Bisonhorn Maria, Chota Maria, Dandami Maria, Chota Maria, Dandami Maria, Dhuru, Dhuwa, Dhoba, Dhulia, Dorla, Gaiki, Gatta, Gatti, Gaita, Gond Gowari, Hill Maria, Kandra, Kalanga, Khatola, Koitar, Koya, Khirwar, Khirwara, Kucha Maria, Kuchaki Maria, Madia, Maria, Mana, Mannewar, Modghya, Mogia, Monghya, Mudia, Muria, Nagarchi, Naikpod, Nagwanshi, Ojha, Raj, Sonjhari Jhareka, Thatia, Thotya, Wade Maria, Vade Maria
19. Halba, Halbi
20. Kamar
21. Kathodi, Katkari, Dhor Kathodi, Dhor Kathodi, Dhor Katkari, Son Kathodi, Son Katkari
22. Kawar, Kanwar, Kaur, Cherwa, Rathia, Tanwar, Chattri
23. Khairwar
24. Kharia
25. Kokna, Kokni, Kukna
26. Kol
27. Kolam, Kannervarlu
28. Koli, Dhor, Tokre Koli, Kolcha, Kolgha
29. Koli Mahadev, Dongar Koli
30. Koli Malhar
31. Kondh, Khond, Kandh
32. Korku, Bopchi, Mouasi, Nihal, Nahul, Bondhi, Bondeya
33. Koya, Bhine Koya, Rajkoya
34. Nagesia, Nagasia
35. Naikda, Nayaka, Cholivala, Nayaka, Kapadia Nayaka, Mota Nayaka, Nana Nayaka
36. Oraon, Dhangad
37. Pardhan, Pathari, Saroti
38. Pardhi, Advichincher, Phanse Pardhi, Langoli Pardhi, Bahelia, Bahellia, Chita Pardhi, Shikari, Takankar, Takia.
39. Parja
40. Patelia
41. Pomla
42. Rathawa
43. Sawar, Sawara
44. Thakur, Thakar, Ka Thakur, Ka Thakar, Ma Thakur, Ma Thakar

45. Thoti (in Aurangabad, Bhir, Nanded, Osmanabad and Parbhani Districts and Rajura Tahsil of Chandrapur District)
46. Varli
47. Vitolia, Kotwalia, Barodia

MANIPUR

1. Aimol
2. Anal
3. Angami
4. Chiru
5. Chothe
6. Gangte.
7. Hmar
8. Kabui
9. Kacha Naga
10. Koirao
11. Koireng
12. Kom
13. Lamgang
14. Mao
15. Maram
16. Mariang
17. Any Mizo (Lushai) tribe
18. Monsang
19. Moyon
20. Paite
21. Purum
22. Ralte
23. Sema
24. Simte
25. Sahte
26. Tangkhul
27. Thadou
28. Vaiphui
29. Zou

MEGHALAYA

1. Chakma
2. Dimasa, Kachari
3. Garo
4. Hajong
5. Hmar
6. Khasi, Jaintia, Synteng, Phar, War, Bhoi, Lynogngam
7. Any Kuki Tribe, including:
   (i) Baite, Biete
   (ii) Changsan
   (iii) Chongloi
   (iv) Doungel
   (v) Gamalhou
   (vi) Gangte
   (vii) Guite

(viii) Hanneng
(ix) Haokip, Haupit
(x) Haolai
(xi) Hengna
(xii) Hongsungh
(xiii) Hrangkhwal, Rangkhol
(xiv) Jongbe
(xv) Khawchung
(xvi) Khawathlang, Khothalong
(xvii) Khelma
(xviii) Kholhou
(xix) Kipgen
(xx) Kuki
(xxi) Lengthang
(xxii) Lengthang
(xxiii) Lhoujem
(xxiv) Lhouvun
(xxv) Lupheng
(xxvi) Mangjel
(xxvii) Misao
(xxviii) Riang
(xxix) Sairhem
(xxx) Selnam
(xxxi) Singson
(xxxii) Sitlhou
(xxxiii) Sukte
(xxxiv) Thado
(xxxv) Thangngen
(xxxvi) Uibug
(xxxvii) Vaiphe

8. Lakher
9. Man (Tai-speaking)
10. Any Mizo (Lushai) tribe
11. Mikir
12. Any Naga tribe
13. Pawi
14. Synteng

NAGALAND

1. Garo
2. Kachari
3. Kuki
4. Mikir
5. Naga

ORISSA

1. Bagata
2. Baiga
3. Banjara, Banjari
4. Bathudi
5. Bhottada, Dhotada

6. Bhuiya, Bhuyan
7. Bhumia
8. Bhumij
9. Bhunjia
10. Binjhal
11. Binjhia, Binjhoa
12. Bihor
13. Bondo Poraja
14. Chenchu
15. Dal
16. Desua Bhumij
17. Dharua
18. Didayi
19. Gadaba
20. Gandia
21. Ghara
22. Gond, Gondo
23. Ho
24. Holva
25. Jatapu
26. Juang
27. Kandha Gauda
28. Kawar
29. Kharia, Kharian
30. Kharwar
31. Khond, Kond, Kandha, Nanguli Kandha, Sitha Kandha
32. Kisan
33. Kol
34. Kolah Loharas, Kol Loharas
35. Kolha
36. Koli, Malhar
37. Kondadora
38. Kora
39. Korua
40. Kotia
41. Koya
42. Kulis
43. Lodha
44. Madia
45. Mahali
46. Mankidi
47. Mankirdia
48. Matya
49. Mirdhas
50. Munda, Munda Lohara, Munda Mahalis
51. Mundari
52. Omanatya
53. Oraon
54. Parenga
55. Paroja
56. Pentia

57. Rajuar
58. Santal
59. Saora, Savar, Saura, Sahara
60. Shabar, Lodha
61. Sounti
62. Tharua

RAJASTHAN

1. Bhil, Bhil Garasia, Dholi Bhil, Dungri Bhil Dungri Garasia, Mewasi Bhil, Rawal Bhil, Tadvi Bhil, Bhagalia, Bhilala, Pawra, Vasava, Vasave.
2. Bhil Mina
3. Damor, Damaria
4. Dhanka, Tadvi, Tetaria, Valvi
5. Garasia (excluding Rajput Garasia)
6. Kathodi, Katkari, Dhor Kathodi, Dhor Katkari, Son Kathodi, Son Katkari
7. Kokna, Kokni, Kukna
8. Koli Dhor, Tokra Koli, Kolcha, Kolgha
9. Mina
10. Naikda, Nayaka, Cholivala Nayaka, Kapadia Nayaka, Mota Nayaka, Nana Nayaka
11. Patelia
12. Seharia, Sehria, Sahariya

SIKKIM

1. Bhutia (including Chumbipa, Dopthapa, Dukpa, Kagatey, Sherpa, Tibetan, Tromopa, Yolmo)
2. Lepcha

TAMIL NADU

1. Adiyan
2. Arandan
3. Eravallan
4. Irular
5. Kadar
6. Kammara (excluding Kanyakumari District and Shenkottah Taluk of Tirunelveli District)
7. Kanikaran, Kanikkar (in Kanyakumari District and Shenkottah Taluk of Tirunelveli District)
8. Kaniyan, Kanyan
9. Kattunayakan
10. Kochu Velan
11. Konda Kapus
12. Kondareddis
13. Koraga
14. Kota (excluding Kanyakumari District and Shenkottah Taluk of Tirunelveli District)
15. Kudiya, Melakudi
16. Kurichchan
17. Kurumbas (in the Nilgiris District)
18. Kurumans
19. Maha Malasar

20. Malai Arayan
21. Malai Pandaram
22. Malai Vedan
23. Malakkuravan
24. Malasar
25. Malayali (in Dharmapuri North Arcot, Pudukottai, Salem, South Arcot and Tiruchirapalli District)
26. Malayekandi
27. Mannan
28. Mudugar, Muduvan
29. Muthuvan
30. Palleyan
31. Palliyan
32. Palliyar
33. Paniyan
34. Sholaga
35. Toda (excluding Kanyakumari District and Shenkottah Taluk of Tirunelveli District)
36. Uraly

TRIPURA

1. Bhil
2. Bhutia
3. Chaimal
4. Chakma
5. Garoo
6. Halam
7. Jamatia
8. Khasia
9. Kuki, including the following sub-tribes:
   - *(i)* Balte
   - *(ii)* Belalhut
   - *(iii)* Chhalya
   - *(iv)* Fun
   - *(v)* Hajango
   - *(vi)* Jangtei
   - *(vii)* Khareng
   - *(viii)* Khephong
   - *(ix)* Kuntei
   - *(x)* Laifang
   - *(xi)* Lentel
   - *(xii)* Mizel
   - *(xiii)* Namte
   - *(xiv)* Paitu, Paite
   - *(xv)* Rangchan
   - *(xvi)* Rangkbole
   - *(xvii)* Thangluya
10. Lepcha
11. Lushai
12. Mag
13. Munda, Kaur
14. Noatia

15. Orang
16. Riang
17. Santal
18. Tripura, Tripuri, Tippera
19. Uchai

UTTAR PRADESH

1. Bhotia
2. Buksa
3. Jaunsari
4. Raji
5. Tharu

WEST BENGAL

1. Asur
2. Baiga
3. Bedia, Bediya
4. Bhumji
5. Bhutia, Sherpa, Toto, Dukpa, Kagatay, Tibetan, Yolmo
6. Birhor
7. Birjia
8. Chakma
9. Chero
10. Chik Baraik
11. Garo
12. Gond
13. Gorait
14. Hajang
15. Ho
16. Kamali
17. Kharwar
18. Khond
19. Kisan
20. Kora
21. Korwa
22. Lepcha
23. Lodha, Kheria, Kharia
24. Lohara, Lohra
25. Magh
26. Mahali
27. Mahli
28. Mal Pahariya
29. Mech
30. Mru
31. Munda
32. Nagesia
33. Oraon
34. Parhaiya
35. Rabha
36. Santal
37. Sauria Paharia

38. Savar

ANDAMAN AND NICOBAR ISLANDS

1. Andamanese, Chariar, Chari, Kora Tabo, Bo, Yere, Kede, Bea, Balawa, Bojigiyab, Juwai, Kol
2. Jarawas
3. Nicobarese
4. Onges
5. Sentinelese
6. Shom Pens

ARUNACHAL PRADESH

1. Abor
2. Aka
3. Apatani
4. Dalfa
5. Galong
6. Khampti
7. Khowa
8. Mishmi
9. Momba
10. Any Naga Tribe
11. Sherdukpen
12. Singpho

DADRA AND NAGAR HAVELI

1. Dhodia
2. Dubla, including Halpati
3. Kathodi
4. Kokna
5. Koli Dhor, including Kolgha
6. Naikda or Nayaka
7. Varli

GOA, DAMAN & DIU

1. Dhodia
2. Dubla
3. Naikda
4. Siddi
5. Varli, Synonym, Halapati, Talavia Nayaka

LAKSHADWEEP

Inhabitants of the Laccadive, Minicoy and Aminidivi Islands who, and both of whose parents, were born in those Islands.

MIZORAM

1. Chakma
2. Dimasa, Kachari
3. Garo
4. Hajong
5. Hmar
6. Khasi, Jaintia Synteng, Phar, War, Bhoi, Lynogngam

7. Any Kuki tribe, including:
    - *(i)* Baite, Biete
    - *(ii)* Changsan
    - *(iii)* Chonglori
    - *(iv)* Doungel
    - *(v)* Gamalhou
    - *(vi)* Gangte
    - *(vii)* Guite
    - *(viii)* Hanneng
    - *(ix)* Haokip, Haupit
    - *(x)* Haolai
    - *(xi)* Hengna
    - *(xii)* Hongsungh
    - *(xiii)* Hrangkhwal, Rangkhol
    - *(xiv)* Jongbe
    - *(xv)* Khawchung
    - *(xvi)* Khawathlang, Khothalong
    - *(xvii)* Khelma
    - *(xviii)* Kholhou
    - *(xix)* Kipgen
    - *(xx)* Kuki
    - *(xxi)* Lengthang
    - *(xxii)* Lhangum
    - *(xxiii)* Lhoujem
    - *(xxiv)* Lhouvun
    - *(xxv)* Lupheng
    - *(xxvi)* Mangjel
    - *(xxvii)* Misao
    - *(xxviii)* Riang
    - *(xxix)* Sairhem
    - *(xxx)* Selnam
    - *(xxxi)* Singson
    - *(xxxii)* Sitlhou
    - *(xxxiii)* Sukte
    - *(xxxiv)* Thado
    - *(xxxv)* Thangngen
    - *(xxxvi)* Uibuh
    - *(xxxvii)* Vaiphei
8. Lakher
9. Man (Tai-speaking)
10. Any Mizo (Lushai) tribe
11. Mikir
12. Any Naga tribe
13. Pawi
14. Synteng

ANNEXURE 1.3

Tribal Languages in India 1961 Census

Dravidian Adivasi Languages	*Number of People Speaking*
Tulus	1,52,000
Kodagus	45,000
Kandhas	5,86,000
Oraons	10,38,000
Malto	71,000
Todas	600
Bodaga	67,286
Gadaba	54,454
Austric Family	
Santali	25,00,000
Mundari	6,50,000
Ho	4,50,000
Kharia	1,80,000
Bhumij	1,13,000
Savara	1,96,000
Korku	1,60,000
Khasis	2,34,000
Nicobarese	
Tibeto-Chinese Family	10,000
Lepcha	25,000
Kanauri	26,000
Kiranti	88,000
Magari	18,000
Murmi	43,000
Tharees	37,000
Bhotiyas	10,000
Newari	3,00,000
Mikirs	1,26,000
Nagas	3,49,000
Lushais	60,000
Manipuris	3,92,000
Meros	2,00,000
Khamptis	5,000

ANNEXURE 1.4

Percentage of Growth in Tribal Population

Sl. No.	*Census year*	*Nomenclature*	*Tribal population (in Crores)*	*General population (in Crores)*	*Percentage of total population*	*Percentage of growth in tribal population*
Pre-Partition						
1.	1891	Tribal Religion	1.60	23.6	6.7	—
2.	1901	Animists	1.60	23.6	6.7	—
3.	1911	Tribal Animists and Tribal Religion	1.60	25.2	6.3	4
4.	1921	Hill and Forest Tribes	1.60	25.1	6.3	—
5.	1931	Primitive Tribes	2.24	27.9	8.0	7
6.	1941	Tribes	2.47	31.9	7.7	3
Post-Partition						
7.	1951	Scheduled Tribe	1.91	36.12	6.23	10.5
8.	1961	Scheduled Tribe	2.99	43.91	6.80	32.7
9.	1971	Scheduled Tribe	3.87	54.79	7.06	0.27
10.	1981	Scheduled Tribe	5.10*	68.52	7.44	0.38
11.	1991	Scheduled Tribe	6.77	84.63	8.08	0.64

* Not estimated for Assam.

CHAPTER II

Tribal Economy: An Analysis

INTRODUCTION

On a cursory glance, the tribal economy appears to be very primitive and not worthy of a sustained study and being largely non-monetised, does not attract the research efforts of economists. Esoteric studies concentrate on sociological aspects and on tribal cultures and traditions. It is as if the tribal economy has been dismissed or written off. But a closer and incisive analysis will reveal that the tribal economy is environment-friendly, self-sustaining and not a wasteful one. Their lifestyle is one of struggles and a simple one, more attuned to their environment and tribals are largely free from the modern diseases which beset city-based persons. While this point is debatable, the tribal economy certainly deserves an in-depth and un-biased study. The tribal people are human beings with feelings, emotions, aspirations and needs. While these may not be articulated forcefully, nevertheless, they exist. And unless the tribal people are permitted their rightful place in the economy, today they risk being marginalised, perhaps forever!

While it is difficult to attempt a micro analysis, some broad patterns of the tribal economy are:

(i) The tribal economy is essentially forest-based with dependence on 'shifting' cultivation or on exploitation of forest products. Though 'shifting' cultivation is often termed as uneconomic, this is not true in the tribal context. With growing population and dwindling forests, the gap between two cycles of cultivation on the same patch of land which should ideally be around 20–25 years, has been

reduced to about 4–5 years. This prevents the land from recouping its regenerative capacity and destroys soil fertility. If no investments are made, the output is also low and hence not commensurate with the damage to the soil and the forest cover which should take about 50–150 years to regenerate, is not given a chance to recoup. More damaging is the stripping of forests, legally or illegally, using tribal labour which destroys forests.

(ii) The tribal economy is not systematically organised and, besides, is also largely non-monetised with 'jajmani' system of labour-sharing, being extensively followed in most tribal areas. In the absence of detailed data, it is expected that 70 per cent of the tribal economy is monetised while the non-monetised component of their economy is about 25 per cent. It is this non-monetised sector which gives rise to various types of exploitation as the tribals rarely get a good price for the forest-based products, they collect or make, due to lack of organised marketing outlets. Due to this exploitation, there is also no economic motivation for producing/collecting more produce for the market. Monetisation of the economy transfers purchasing power rights to the tribal people and will enable these people to shift easily from a primitive economy to a modern economy. This is yet to happen in most tribal areas.

(iii) There is virtually no end to exploitation of tribals as the tribal people require credit mostly for consumption and for various religious and social rituals. As there is no systematic and durable production base, the tribal people have little or no access to easy liquidity or cash. The tribal cooperative credit system is in total disarray and banks do not generally lend to tribals except under SGSY and other Government programmes. Their only resource is unofficial money-lenders like traders, shop-keepers, agents, *etc.*, who give them small loans for meeting religious expenses for marriages, death rituals and other rituals. It is these costly rituals which have forced many tribals to adopt Christianity, which does not encourage these rituals. Much of the tribal people's earnings are consumed in these rituals where a substantial amount of liquor and meat is consumed by the entire community. If these rituals are not followed, there is lack of status in the tribal society and ostracism. These rituals depress the economic conditions of the tribal people. In many tribal villages, scheduled castes who are better off relatively, function as money-lenders and charge high rates of interest. In recent times, clashes between tribal people and scheduled caste persons have increased due to the money-lending activities of the latter as also exploitation.

(iv) The tribal people have often retreated into dense, inaccessible forests and remote, hilly, areas so as to avoid contact with stronger elements of society. They live scattered in small villages having

> 5–25 households depending on available supporting infrastructure. This lack of contact with more developed societies, has ensured that the tribal people remain insular, insecure and terribly backward as far as technologies are concerned. Without aspiring for better economic status, progress is difficult. Gunnar Myrdal, the celebrated Swedish economist has stated that economic development depends on two factors, attitudinal change and institutional change. Unless these two interventions are brought about, economic development in tribal areas would be next to impossible. An awareness about their rights, their economic participation, their duties and responsibilities and their involvement in economic changes, has to be created through the tribal leaders. This dynamic leadership is slowly emerging due to better educational facilities. The changes must not be imposed from above but must evolve as a felt-need of the entire tribal community.

Thus, the socio-economic structure that has evolved among tribal people is based on simple technology that is eco-friendly and in keeping with their conservative outlook but is largely a marginal economy. The small-sized economy of the tribal community is a constraint as the 'economic' surplus is rare. The rate of innovation is low due to poor exposure or non-conformity with tribal needs. Another problem is the lack of marketable skills and less stress on individuals with more stress on community needs. The tribal notion of prosperity and well-being is related to expenditure and not to savings. Barter and exchange are important aspects of the tribal economy. The profit motive is largely absent and mutual sharing and obligations are important to the tribal people. Thus, collective endeavour and mutual cooperation are part of the tribal economy. The tribal family is a unit of both production and consumption while the entire community acts like a cooperative unit. Distribution is generally based on gifts in kind and ceremonial exchanges. There is a well-organised division of labour between all members of a tribal family, according to age and sex. The men generally concentrate on hunting and grazing of animals and search for honey while the women gather firewood, nuts, fruits and herbs. In farming communities, both men and women work in the fields. All these features of the tribal economy have had a unique effect on them.

FEATURES OF THE TRIBAL ECONOMY

A major portion of the tribal habitat is hilly and/or forested and as such, hills and forests form an indispensable part of the tribal economy. The secluded/alienated life led by the tribals over the years has led to the development of an economy with certain striking features/fundamental characteristics which distinguish the tribal economy from others. The striking features/fundamental characteristics encompass seven broad aspects as detailed below:

(i) Forest-based Economy. The structure of the tribal economy can be said to be in general, forest-based. The forest includes not only flora and fauna but also the sea fauna which caters to the economic needs of the coastal tribals. A close relationship exists between the economic life of the tribals and forests which are generally their habitats and which provide them edible roots, fruits, vegetables, flowers, honey, insects, fish, birds, monkeys, pigs and other flora and fauna. Forest degradation and forest protection have affected the tribal economy.

(ii) Simple Technology. The tribals use indigenously produced and very crude implements for hunting, food gathering and pastoral and agricultural activities. The use of such crude implements involves a considerable amount of manual labour and extensive waste of human energy, making it difficult even to fulfil the basic needs. Modern, low-cost agricultural implements would be useful.

(iii) Unit of Production, Consumption Pattern and Family Labour. The whole tribal family acts as the unit of production with cooperation from the individuals. There is a well-organised pattern of division of labour in a family which is based on age and sex alone. The males, females, boys and girls work according to their physical capacity. Males are usually engaged in hard work requiring physical strength such as hunting, fishing, *etc.* Women tend fields and attend to agricultural activities.

(iv) Absence of Profit in Economic Dealings. The economic relations and dealings amongst the tribals are mostly based on exchange/barter systems. The barter system fulfils the requirements but is devoid of any notion of profit. The profit motive in economic dealings is generally absent and this factor explains why bank lending in tribal areas has largely been a failure. Profits are rarely generated from economic activities to repay loans. Loans are often repaid from other sources of income.

(v) Periodical Markets. There are no permanent markets existing in the tribal communities. Only periodical markets exist which are held on a bi-weekly, weekly or fortnightly basis. The economic transactions take place in the form of barter for native goods and in cash for non-native goods. The 'haats' or weekly markets are a very important feature of the tribal economy.

(vi) Gifts and Ceremonial Exchanges. The tribal society is permeated by a constant give-and-take relationship for every ceremony, every custom, *etc.* Exchange of gifts exists as a part of economic relationship. Examples may be cited of the agricultural tribes like the Mundas and the Oraons who get their agricultural implements manufactured or repaired by Loharas who, in return, receive a customary annual payment in the form of cash or kind.

(vii) Absence of Capital Investment. As the wants of the tribals are very limited and their production is not market-oriented, the economy of the tribals is characterised by another feature, *i.e.,* absence of capital investments. Besides, due to location of tribal habitations in remote, inaccessible areas, there is lack of adequate infrastructure like irrigation, communication facilities, extension services system, *etc.* Hence, the tribal economy has also failed to induce capital investments as a mode of economic upliftment.

(viii) Mixed Economy. The tribal economy is generally subsistence-oriented and is based mainly on collecting, hunting and fishing (*e.g.* the Birhor, Hill Kharia), or a combination of hunting and collecting with shifting cultivation (*e.g.* the Juang, Hill Bhuiyan, Lanjia Saora, Kandh, *etc.*). Even the so-called plough-using agricultural tribes often, wherever scope is available, supplement their economy with hunting and collecting. This mixed economy uses different means for their sustenance and subsistence.

Quality of Tribal Lifestyles

Since 1947, an effort has been made to bring about qualitative changes in the tribal economy with socio-economic development of the tribal people. There is very little data on tribal households and their quality of life, based on human development aspects. The National Council of Applied Economic Research (NCAER) conducted a nation-wide sample survey, in 1994, of over 33,000 rural households spread over 1,765 villages in 195 districts of 16 States with the sample size of tribal people being 4,220. The rural Indian population is 74.3 per cent while 92.6 per cent of tribals live in rural areas but urbanisation of tribals has increased from 2.7 per cent in 1961 to 7.4 per cent in 1991, due to rising power of education and diversification of occupations leading to a change in life-styles.

Income Distribution

Inadequacy of income and accumulated wealth leads to deprivation in tribal quality of life and lesser well-being including starvation, poor education, poor health, *etc.* Household income analysis for tribals is rarely done and where done, has recorded the fact that tribal people are the poorest in the land (Table 2.1). The tribal people have the lowest average incomes and a larger proportion of people are in the lower income classes. There is also less income equality among the tribal people.

Incidence and Intensity of Poverty

Using the poverty-line as consumption of Rs. 2,444 per person per year, the assumption that for tribal people, income and consumption patterns coincide, the head count ratio is that 50 per cent of the tribal poor are below poverty level. This poverty index is based on calorie-intake and ignores shelter, clothing and medicines, all essential for survival. For other people, this is only 33 per cent. However, there is not much difference in per-capita

Table 2.1
Disparity in Income between Tribal People and Others

Income class (Rs. per year)	*All people*			*Tribal people*		
	Sample HHs	*Percentage of persons*	*Average income (Rs. per year)*	*Sample HHs*	*Percentage of persons*	*Average income (Rs. per year)*
750	997	3.5	512	154	4.2	515
751–1,000	913	3.1	880	152	3.9	875
1,001–1,500	2,759	9.1	1,271	482	12.3	1,270
1,501–2,000	3,595	12	1,758	581	14.7	1,758
2,001–2,500	3,352	10.7	2,251	555	14.3	2,240
2,501–3,000	3,092	9.4	2,739	428	9.8	2,737
3,001–3,500	2,680	8.1	3,240	339	7.5	3,234
3,501–4,000	2,234	7.2	3,753	258	6.3	3,756
4,001–4,500	1,936	5.6	4,256	214	4.9	4,256
4,501–5,000	1,522	4.6	4,744	167	3.6	4,759
5,001–6,000	2,442	6.8	5,475	248	5.7	5,480
6,001–7,000	1,706	4.7	6,481	143	3.1	6,466
7,000 +	6,002	15.2	13,290	499	9.7	12,498
Total	33,230	100	4,565	4,220	100	3,643
Ginni Co-efficient			0.43			0.42

Source: Estimated from data collected in the NCAER Survey, 1996.

Table 2.2
Estimated Poverty Parameters among Tribal People and Others in Rural India, 1994

Parameters	*All people*	*Tribal people*
Mean Income of the Poor*	1,595	1,600
Ginni Co-efficient among the Poor	0.19	0.19
Head Count Ratio	0.38	0.49
Sen Index	0.18	0.23
FGT Index	0.07	0.08

*Rs. per person per year.

Poverty line for 1973–74 estimated by Planning Commission have been updated by using the state specific CPIAL. (FGT—Foster, Green & Thornbecke, 1984; CPIAL—Consumer Price Index for Agricultural Labourers.)

Source: Estimated from data collected in the NCAER Survey, 1996.

income among the poor in India. Both the Sen Index and FGT index suggest that intensity of poverty is more severe among the tribal people than among others. (Details at Table 2.2).

Literacy and Education

For a better quality of life, knowledge, values, skills and attitudes are very important and education being a social resource, helps in reducing

Table 2.3
Levels and Trends in Adjusted Literacy Rates* in Rural India

Literacy groups	*Year*	*Population groups*		
		All	*SCs*	*STs*
Persons	1961	18.4	8.9	8.2
	1971	23.7	12.8	10.7
	1981	29.7	18.5	26.6
	1991	36.2	26.6	21.8
Males	1961	28.3	15.1	13.4
	1971	33.8	20	16.9
	1981	40.8	27.9	22.9
	1991	47.1	36.9	30.7
Females	1961	9.1	2.5	2.9
	1971	13.1	5.1	4.4
	1981	1.8	8.4	6.8
	1991	24.6	15.5	12.7

*Literates among all age groups.
Source: Computed from data in census of India, Series-1, Final Population Totals: Brief Analysis of Primary Census Abstract, 1961–91.

inequality. Growth of literacy rates are set out in Table 2.3. Education helps in better job placement, bettering of social status and acts as a catalyst. Disparities in literacy rates between Group '*A*' and '*B*' have been measured by a simple index as under:

$$\text{Disparity index } (A, B) = \frac{\text{Percentage literates in group 'A'}}{\text{Percentage literates in group 'B'}} \times 100$$

(Deprived group is '*A*')

Higher the value, lower is the disparity against group '*A*'.

Disparity in adjusted literacy among tribal people is set out at Table 2.4 and between males and females in Table 2.5. These disparities are declining over time and literacy among tribal people has increased at a slower rate, with literacy among females increasing at a rate faster than that of males. However, much more needs to be done, as effective literacy rates is low at 40.8 per cent as compared to 53.5 per cent to all Indians. The level of disparity is about 76.3 per cent. It has been estimated that non-attendance rate among tribals is higher as also the school discontinuance rate. There is also evidence to suggest that the percentage of tribal students completing beyond middle-level school and matriculation, is lower than that of all-India students.

Table 2.4
Disparity in Literacy between SCs, STs and All

(Per cent)

Literacy groups	*Year*	*Population groups*		
		All	*SCs*	*STs*
Persons	1961	100	48	45
	1971	100	54	45
	1981	100	62	50
	1991	100	73	60
Males	1961	100	53	47
	1971	100	59	50
	1981	100	68	56
	1991	100	78	65
Females	1961	100	27	32
	1971	100	39	34
	1981	100	47	38
	1991	100	63	52

Source: Computed from NCAER data.

Table 2.5
Female-Male Disparity in Literacy within Population Groups

(Per cent)

Population groups	*1961*	*1971*	*1981*	*1991*
All	32	39	44	52
SCs	17	26	30	42
STs	22	26	30	41

Source: Computed from NCAER data.

Health Care and Drinking Water

The estimated percentage of tribal villages without adequate health care facilities is higher than that of other villages (Table 2.6). The quality of drinking water is the poorest in tribal villages as about 77.5 per cent of the villages have unprotected water sources for drinking purposes (Table 2.7). The immunisation rates (Table 2.8) for tribal mothers and tribal children (Table 2.9) are the lowest. The percentage of tribal children born at home is also the highest showing that little trained medical help was available for mother and child (Table 2.10).

Table 2.6
Health Care Facilities by Type of Villages in Rural India, 1994

(Percentage of villages)

Type of villages	*Sub centre within village*	*No. of sub centre/hospital within 5 kms*	*Pharmacy within village*	*Anganwadi within village*
SC Villages	18.2	65.2	25.8	56.1
ST Villages	11.3	75	12.5	48.8
SC/ST Villages	25	60.4	31.3	52.5
All Villages	21.5	58.1	28.5	52.8

Source: Estimated from data collected in NCAER Survey, 1994.

Table 2.7
Major Source of Drinking Water by type of Villages in Rural India, 1994

(Percentage of villages)

Type of villages	*Major source of drinking water*			
	Piped water	*Hand pump*	*Other protected water*	*Unprotected water*
SC Villages	24.2	16.7	4.5	54.6
ST Villages	3.1	8.1	11.3	77.5
SC/ST Villages	8.3	16.7	14.6	60.4
All Villages	16.6	18.4	13	52

Source: Estimated from data collected in NCAER Survey, 1994.

Table 2.8
Percentage of Prospective Mothers Immunised by Social Groups in Rural India, 1994

Type of immunisation	*SCs*	*STs*	*All*
T.T. Immunisation	52.5	39.4	53
Iron Tablets	35	29.6	34.2
B.P. Check-ups	24.3	12.8	26.6

Source: Estimated from data collected in NCAER Survey, 1994.

Table 2.9
Percentage of Children Aged 12–23 Months Immunised by Social Groups in Rural India, 1994

Type of immunisation	*SCs*	*STs*	*All*
DPT (3 doses)	53.6	46.4	37.5
Polio (3 doses)	54.6	46.6	58.1
BCG (1 dose)	62.6	54.2	64.3
Measles (1 dose)	48.9	42.1	52.9
All (8 doses)	42.6	39.5	48.5

Source: Estimated from data collected in NCAER Survey, 1994.

Table 2.10
Distribution of Child Birth by Place of Birth and Type of Medical Attention Received among Social Groups

(Per cent)

Social groups	*Attended trained persons*	*Place of birth*		
		Hospital	*CHC/PHC*	*Home*
SCs	37.6	16.0	5.0	79.0
STs	31.9	7.6	2.6	89.8
All	40.0	17.9	5.5	76.6

Source: Estimated from data collected in NCAER Survey, 1994.

The above analysis indicates that tribal quality of life is still the poorest in spite of efforts to improve the quality of life, primarily due to the inaccessible tribal villages, poor communication and problems in implementation.

Deprivation in Tribal Villages

Of the tribal people in India, about 80 per cent live below the poverty line. Each tribal village is different from another and tribal people are different from each other. But the basic infrastructure for a tribal village remains the same. KIRDTI, an NGO in Pichalabela, Harichandanpur block, Keonjhar, Orissa, had prepared a list of the infrastructure, an ideal tribal village should have and has listed 37 elements such as,

1. Blacksmith
2. Tailor
3. Weaver
4. Potter
5. Village Doctor
6. Private Doctor
7. Dai or Traditional Birth Attendant
8. Carpenter
9. Educational Centre
10. College
11. High School
12. Drinking Water Well
13. Drinking Tubewell
14. Drinking Stream
15. Post Office
16. Cooperative Society
17. Anganwadi
18. Bank Branch
19. Hospital
20. Veterinary Centre
21. Milk Society/Centre
22. Public Health Centre

23. ANN Medical Centre
24. Fair Price Shop
25. Grocery Shop
26. Fertiliser Sale Centre
27. Nursery Plantation
28. Weekly Market (Hat)
29. Youth Club
30. Mahila Mandal
31. Gram Sabha
32. Electric Connection
33. Carpentry Centre
34. Telephone Booth
35. Rice Mill
36. Biogas
37. Solar Power/Source.

But as per a survey conducted by National Bank Staff College (NBSC), Lucknow in 1998, the maximum number of elements in any tribal village was 15 while a few tribal villages had 3 or 4 elements only (such as tubewell, dai (traditional birth attendant), *Mahila Mandal* and *Gram Sabha*). Most of the villages are in a state of grave deprivation even after 50 years of Independence. Rural Development has yet to percolate down to the tribal villages and there is poor pace of progress, as far as tribal people are concerned. Given the poor state of finances of all State Governments, it is difficult to envisage the creation of an adequate infrastructure within the next 10–15 years unless the tribal people join together and enrich the tribal economy adequately. Depending on the State to provide infrastructure, would be an exercise in futility.

Food Deficiency of Tribals

The food habits of tribal people are different depending upon the availability of food, wealth of forests, status of tribe, *etc.* An extensive study of the average food intake of the Pauri Bhuinya Tribe was carried out by the Tribal and Harijan Research-cum-Training Institute, Bhubaneswar, and the food deficiencies, recorded in Table 2.11.

Table 2.11

Comparison of Average Diet of Pauri Bhuinya with ICMR Recommendation

Sl. No.	*Foodstuffs*	*ICMR Diet (gm)*	*PB Diet (gm)*	*Excess/ Deficiency*	*Deficiency*
1.	Cereals	400	339	(61)	15.3
2.	Pulses	85	28	(57)	67.0
3.	Leafy Vegetables	116	64	(52)	44.8
4.	Other Vegetables	85	35	(50)	58.8
5.	Oils & Fats	28	5	(23)	82.1
6.	Milk & Milk Products	170	—	(170)	100.0
7.	Meat, Fish & Eggs	28	—	(28)	100.0
8.	Fruits & Nuts	57	—	(57)	100.0

ICMR Diet — Akroyd's Nutritive Value of Indian Foods and Planning of Satisfactory Diet.

The poor quality of food available to the Pauri Bhuiyas based on their average food intake is seen. But if the nutrients deficiency is studied then protein deficiency is 47 per cent, fat deficiency is 82 per cent while vitamin deficiency is around 65 per cent to 88 per cent. For 3–4 months (in the monsoons), the tribal people find it difficult to procure any food.

Educational Facilities

The tribal people have very little understanding of numbers and are easily cheated by traders and money-lenders. They do not understand financial intricacies or details of loans and interest payable thereon. Basic educational facilities should be made available and the facilities for educating children should be given.

Medical Facilities

The areas in which tribal people live are prone to malaria and other debilitating diseases which coupled with the lack of nutritious food, endanger the health of tribal people. Lack of modern medical facilities, especially for women and children, affects the general health standards severely.

Communication Facilities

Most of the tribal areas do not have metalled all-weather roads or rail facilities and the lack of motor communication is a severe handicap to the tribal economic development. Telephones too are rare (except in Himachal Pradesh where every village has telephone and electricity facilities including tribal villages). With little or no political clout, it is difficult to envisage tribal villages getting adequate communication and transport facilities soon.

The poor quality of infrastructure available for the tribal people is a severe handicap to their rapid economic development. With no voice of their own and none to expose their cause for more allocation of Government largesse and funds, the only way out is to create more wealth through conscious efforts at economic development.

Economic Changes

The various Government development programmes and State intervention in various economic sectors, have had a profound impact on tribal culture and the tribal economy. While the pace of change is slow, it has been felt. The tribal culture is slow to react to changes as changes are assimilated and then moulded into an acceptable framework. What does not fit into the tribal ethos, is rejected. An indicator of change could be the new economic activities which have emerged over the years and which have been able to add to earnings of tribal people. Another indicator could be the increased monetisation of the tribal economy. That the tribal cultures and economy are changing is a fact due to the following:

(i) rural roads
(ii) education
(iii) linking of tribal markets with urban markets
(iv) cooperatives (production and credit)
(v) public distribution system (food safety net)
(vi) commercial banks
(vii) labour unions
(viii) the Land Mortgage Act
(ix) savings and Self Help Groups
(x) consumption pattern shifts
(xi) emerging commercial aptitude
(xii) growth of tribal money-lenders
(xiii) cropping pattern changes from cereals to cash crops
(xiv) open sale of minor forest produce
(xv) reservation in Government jobs
(xvi) employment in police/armed forces
(xvii) religious conversions.

But these changes have not affected all tribes equally. Some tribes have adapted to changes more easily than most others. If droughts occur, many tribes migrate and try to survive. Some tribals stay put and many perish. This depends upon attitudinal factors and the impact of change on the tribal ethos and culture.

CHAPTER III

Exploitation of the Tribal Economy

INTRODUCTION

The tribal people have all along been subjected to a large scale exploitation by the non-tribals and even though a series of measures have been initiated since 1947 to ameliorate their economic condition, the degree of exploitation is on the rise instead of being reduced. The development of the tribal economy is seriously hampered by the lack of infrastructural facilities, such as, transport/communication facilities, organised/ monetised market system, adequate organisational base to cater to the needs of the tribals, *etc.* Large scale exploitation of the tribals by the non-tribals, money-lenders and traders, intensive industrial/mining activities in tribal belts, inefficiency/ callousness of the State-owned agencies as also the high degree of land alienation and indebtedness, have impoverished them.

Though the tribal people derive their income and livelihood by working on farmland, their land holdings are meagre and landlessness is the norm, among them. 90 per cent of tribal people are landless without productive assets or sustainable employment opportunities. 65 per cent of the land holder in the tribal category are small and marginal farmers (agricultural census 1990–91) while 36 per cent of the scheduled tribe men workers are labourers as against 31 per cent of others. 55 per cent of scheduled tribals are cultivators compared to 40 per cent of others, which comprise the forest people in Indian society. Fifty per cent of the scheduled tribes live below poverty line.

Land alienation cases in Andhra Pradesh, Bihar, Gujarat, Karnataka, Madhya Pradesh are increasing with thousands of cases filed in the courts involving lakhs of cases as can be seen in the Table 3.1.

Table 3.1
Land Alienation Cases filed in Courts

Sl. No.	*State*	*Cases filed in court No.*	*Area covered*
1.	Andhra Pradesh	65,875	2,87,776
2.	Bihar	86,291	1,04,893
3.	Gujarat	47,926	1,40,324
4.	Karnataka	42,582	1,30,373
5.	Madhya Pradesh	53,806	1,58,398

The number of atrocities per lakh of population for SCs/STs is highest in states like Madhya Pradesh, Rajasthan, Uttar Pradesh, Bihar and to some extent in Orissa, Gujarat and Maharashtra. States like West Bengal, Tamil Nadu, Karnataka have strong legislative movements and better avenues and to some extent Andhra Pradesh, Kerala and Punjab.

REASONS FOR TRIBAL EXPLOITATION

A brief account of exploitation of the tribals in Orissa is presented below:

1. Absence of Tribal Land Rights

Tribal land rights are almost a non-existent concept. The status of tribals with regard to land rights, is clear from the fact that in Government records, the tribal is an 'encroacher' of the land he has been occupying, through the ages. Whether he lives deep in the forest or in inaccessible hilly regions, he has no legal right over the land.

The 1991 report of the Planning Commission on land holding systems in tribal areas, with a special reference to Orissa, is revealing as it discovers the shocking state of affairs with regard to tribal land rights. The report records that, sometimes, not even one per cent of the land occupied by the tribals is recorded in their favour. Moreover, it points to the fact that the laws do not recognise the communal holdings of the tribals. Thus, the land the tribals use to meet their basic needs of food, fodder and fuel are actually the preserves of the State Revenue and Forest Departments on record.

The report makes another significant revelation. The 'value' of land is perceived in terms of market economy. So, often the land that is basic to the survival of the tribals is designated as wasteland in the records. Further, irregularities have reportedly been committed in settlement and survey operations, which have resulted in the transfer of large tracts of land, customarily held by tribals, to a new breed of non-tribal owners. Such abuses in settlement are a common phenomenon, given the collusion between the settlement officials and non-tribals, for mutual profit. Bribes, tampering of records, use of force and other methods are used to deprive the tribal of his land. This, of course, is a gross violation of the Land Alienation Act which explicitly declares that all land transfers from tribals to non-tribals, without the permission of the prescribed authority, are illegal and void.

A massive influx of coastal people to the uplands took place after the Bengal-Orissa famine of 1866–67 which took a toll of almost one-fourth of the population of the coastal districts of Orissa. This movement increasingly went up and continued till the end of the first quarter of the 20th century. The non-tribals called Ghatidinha (*i.e.*, crossers of Ghats) got settled there under the auspices of the feudal rulers and British-appointed agents for collection of land revenue and other taxes.

2. Land Holding Pattern

The land holding pattern prevailing in tribal dominated districts (undivided) in Orissa on the basis of the Bench Mark Survey conducted by Tribal and Harijan Research Training Institute (THRTI), Bhubaneswar, in 1978–79 is given in Annexure 3.1. While the landless and marginalised ST families constitute as low as about 30 per cent of the total tribal families in the district of Sundargarh, the same form as high as 72.5 per cent of the total tribal families in the district of Koraput. The position in other districts is 37 per cent in Phulbani, 39 per cent in Keonjhar, 44 per cent in Mayurbhanj and 64 per cent in Ganjam. The presence of lesser percentage of landless and marginalised families in the districts of Sundargarh, Phulbani, Keonjhar, Mayurbhanj is due to impact of opening of the areas into mining/industrial activities and spread of Christianity which checked the tribals from exploitation by the traders, money-lenders, *etc.*, as their degree of awareness increased. The 1961 census furnished information in respect of 1,00,411 tribal households which revealed the source of obtaining land. 80 per cent was owned or held by the Government (*i.e.*, tribals declared as illegal), 17 per cent belonged to private persons or institutions while only 3 per cent land was leased out to private persons. With growing indebtedness, the lands actually alienated, must be significantly high by now. As per 1961 census records, the land holdings of tribals and non-tribals (Table 3.2), are revealing:

Table 3.2
Tribal and Non-tribal Land Holdings

Particulars/ Land holdings	*Less than 1.0*	*1.0 - 2.4*	*2.5 - 4.9*	*5.0 - 7.4*	*7.5 - 9.9*	*10.0 - 12.4*	*12.5 - 14.9*	*15.0 - 29.9*	*30.0 - 49.9*	*Above 50.0*	*Un-specified*
1. Tribal land holdings	123.6	5.6	17.2	7.6	7.6	7.1	2.9	7.4	1.6	0.5	5.8
2. General land holdings	23.5	22.7	14.2	6.7	6.7	6.2	2.6	8.5	2.7	1.4	3.9

Source: 1961 Census Data.

It is obvious that compared to the general land holdings, the tribal land holdings are generally smaller. The prevalance of 'benami' holdings in the general land holdings to evade land ceiling laws exists but this phenomenon is absent among tribals. As the number of agricultural labourers and landless tribals are large (about 50 per cent of the tribal work force), land reforms and land availability for tribal people is an urgent necessity. The distribution of operational holdings among scheduled tribes is set out at Annexure 3.2.

3. Limitations of Forest Rights of Tribals

The drive towards better forest management and development had led the British Government and later independent India to enact stringent laws and policies, with regard to forests, thereby gradually enhancing and monopolising their power over it. Far from recognising the relationship of the tribals to the forest, these laws squarely blamed the tribals for its degradation. Moreover, instead of legalising existing rights and privileges of the tribals and forest dwellers over the forest, the laws deprived them of it. The legal position of the forest, however, remained fluid till the promulgation of Indian Forest (Orissa Amendment) Act, 1954, and finally the Orissa Forest Act, 1972. Tribals who enjoyed vast rights and privileges over the forest were limited in their use of it.

4. Exploitation and Land Alienation Caused by the Traders

A study made in 1975 by the National Institute of Community Development (now National Institute of Rural Development), Hyderabad, observes that in case of the tribal population in South Orissa, the non-tribal immigrants have become a dominant group, economically and politically. Land alienation and other forms of exploitation, such as debt bondage, money-lending at exorbitant rates of interest, are causing tribal unrest. However, the tribal communities in Northern Orissa appear to be careful and assert revivalism of their culture and nativism. Closely observing the economic activity of the tribals, it is found that their basic requirements are salt, kerosene, oil, onions, molasses, dried fish, cattle, goats, poultry and some pieces of clothes. Except the livestock, they get the rest of the items mostly through barter. Salt or a handful of onions or dried fish, for example, is procured in exchange of some good quality vegetable seeds or forest produce/products and often millets and other crops are exchanged for clothes. The traders take advantage of the simplicity and innocence of the tribal people and cheat them, using sub-standard weights and measures and resultantly, the tribals are getting impoverished, day-by-day.

In the pre-independence days, the merchants/traders used to come with their pack animals loaded with the daily requirements, such as salt, tobacco, onions, chillies, kerosene oil, cotton clothes, *etc.* By providing the tribals with these articles, they used to collect the dues in kind, at the time of harvest. The prices fixed by the merchants were always high and, therefore, the tribals always paid very heavily in kind. In many cases, the produce offered by the tribals was found insufficient for the prices charged by the merchants. This ultimately led to credit transactions which made the tribals heavily indebted to the merchants. The resources of the tribals being limited, their indebtedness increased day-by-day and finally situations arose when the tribals had to offer their land to the merchants for sale. The tribals had also to borrow in cash from the merchants to meet unforeseen expenditures on account of illness, death, religious rites, *etc.* Being unable to repay the loans received from the merchants, the tribals had to offer themselves as bonded agricultural labourers in the farms captured by the merchants from those very tribal people. Thus, bonded serfdom developed and reduced them to the status of landless serfs. Once a tribal family was trapped in this vicious circle of economic exploitation, it was an impossibility for them to escape, for generations.

In the post-independence days, the Land Alienation Act declared that any sale of land by a tribal to a non-tribal without the permission of the District Magistrate is illegal. Now, such powers have been delegated to the SDOs. Even though this Act is in force, the illegal transfer of land has been a routine one and prosecution and restoration has become difficult. The tribals who sell their land are reluctant to reveal their identity for fear of economic intimidation. The non-tribal buyers, do not get the land recorded in their name and hold it as a usufruct. Even though some cases have been investigated and decrees obtained to restore the land to the owners but the lack of follow-up action has rendered the court decrees infructuous. As a result, the non-tribal merchants continue to enjoy the benefits of the land which they acquire from the tribals and the latter are forced to remain impoverished as before or even worse. A study conducted by Indian Institute of Social Sciences, New Delhi, reports that about 18 per cent of the tribal land alienation is caused by the outsiders.

The Government-sponsored service cooperative societies and Grain Gola societies are intended to advance loans in cash and kind separately to the tribals at the time of their need. The community development study of National Institute of Community Development (now NIRD), Hyderabad, in 1975 reveals that "in practice, however, the cooperative societies are found to be rendering very little help to the tribal people as their management was in the hands of the local merchants who did not want to lessen their grip on the tribals. Also due to official red-tape, there was considerable delay in disbursement of loans, even if they were given. Thus, the very purpose of the loan was not served and whatever was received later on, was spent on something else. Under this circumstances, the tribals were left with no choice but to borrow either in cash or in kind, from the merchants with whom they maintained unbroken economic relationships. Further, the worst scenes observed were the corrupt practices the cooperative society officials were involved in. Even though the loan repayments were received in cash or kind, it was not being entered in the register and the debtor who had already cleared all dues, were repeatedly called upon to repay loans."

Another aspect of the tribal exploitation even in the post-Community Development stage is discerned by the economic studies conducted by different institutions. To protect the tribals from exploitation by the local merchants in purchasing agricultural and forest products the Government of Orissa has organised depots. But the local merchants have outwitted the authorities and are in no less stronger position as hitherto. The tribals collect the forest produce and take it to the nearest market centres for sale. More often than not, the merchants on the market days, would rush towards the tribal villages and before the tribals could reach the market places, they stop them either in the villages or on the way and take hold of the products, paying a very nominal price to them by adopting coercive methods. Even those few tribals who succeeded in bringing their products to the market centres, eluding the merchants on the way, are literally swarmed by the merchants. Here too, the tribals are deprived of their legitimate income. The tribals do not dare to hurt the feelings of the merchants lest they forego the financial help they get from them in times of their need, but inter-ethnic conflict is likely to emerge if this systematic exploitation is not stopped through immediate intervention of governmental agencies and education.

The extent of control exercised by the non-tribal money-lenders, traders may be assessed from the source and quantum of credit. The sources can be classified into two categories, *viz.*, official and non-official, the former comprising the commercial banks and cooperative banks/societies and the latter consisting of money-lenders, landlords, liquor vendors, petty businessmen, *etc.* It is estimated that the proportion of loans taken from the money-lenders and traders is higher, *i.e.*, about 55 per cent and that taken from the institutional sources constitute about 45 per cent.

5. Land Alienation Caused by the Process of Industrialisation

Ironically, the tribal belt of Orissa has been forging into a zone of intense industrial, mining and other activities in the recent decades because the tribal belt is not only rich in mineral resources but also provides strategic locations for dams. It is also known for rich flora and fauna which is either exploited or preserved by the Government. The Rourkela Steel Plant, Machkund Hydro Electricity Project, Talcher Coal-based Thermal Project, the NALCO, a host of ancillary industries, and a chain of mining complexes, as also sanctuaries have made their appearance in the tribal belts. An ancient agro-forest based traditional culture has been confronted with a modern sophisticated industrial culture. The abrupt confrontation has produced disastrous results for the tribals. There has been large scale alienation of tribal land in favour of the public and private sector industrial and mining complexes, townships, private enterprises, *etc.* Having lost the basic resource, the tribals have not been able to secure alternative sources of livelihood. The first generation has found it nearly impossible to imbibe the skills and culture of the industrial age. It would appear that the shock impulses generated on account of imposition of modern industries have been beyond the absorption capacity of the tribal communities. In fact, for the first generation, it has been an unmitigated disaster, as it has meant wholesale destruction of tribal values.

Detailed data on the extent of forest areas that has been destroyed for developmental projects and the number of tribal families that have been displaced by these projects are not available. However, some instances are cited in Table 3.3:

Table 3.3
Displacement of Tribal Families

District	*Name of the project(s)*	*Forest area covered (sq km)*	*No. of tribal families displaced*
Koraput	NALCO and other industrial projects	2,000	—
	Machkund Hydel Dam	—	1,500
	Balimela Project	—	2,000
	Upper Kolab Multipurpose Project	—	7,092
Koraput/ Kalahandi	Upper Indrabati Project	—	5,000
Keonjhar	Salendi Dam	—	965
Sundargarh	Rourkela Steel Plant	13,185	—
All Orissa	Sanctuaries (16)/Parks (12)	7,395	—
	Mining	950	—

Source: THRTI, Bhubaneswar.

The displaced tribals who are already a marginalised people are driven to the brink of acute poverty. Traditionally dependent on natural resources, which are the source of their sustenance, the tribals are unable to adapt themselves to the market economy into which they were suddenly thrown after being evicted from their old habitat. This has resulted in impoverishment and malnutrition. The study of Indian Institute of Social Sciences (IISS), New Delhi, reveals that about 15 per cent of the tribal land alienation has been caused by developmental projects.

6. Land Alienation Through Cash Crop Cultivation

The mono-crop plantations have not only displaced the tribals from their habitat, but also have given them little or no benefit as the government or the company concerned is at the receiving end of the profits. In 1960–61, cashewnut plantations were undertaken by the Soil Conservation Department, Government of Orissa, which was used by the tribals for grazing their cattle or collecting dry shrubs for use as fuelwood or even for cultivation. Similar were the disadvantageous situations created for the tribals by undertaking tea plantations in Keonjhar district.

7. Exploitation in Non-Timber Forest Produce (NTFP) Collection

Although separate agencies have been created to check the tribals from being exploited by the money lenders/traders and to ensure better remuneration for the forest produce collected by them due to inefficient functioning of the agencies and callous attitude of the government officials have contributed to worsening the economic condition of the tribals. The tribals are also subjected to exploitation by the State Government as regards the NTFP collection is concerned.

Kendu Leaf. Kendu leaf is one of the main NTFP items on which lakhs of tribals depend. Nationalised in 1973, the Kendu leaf trade has become the monopoly of the Forest Department, which has been entrusted with its collection and processing, while Orissa Forest Development Corporation (OFDC) has been entrusted with its marketing. As it is lucrative, the revenue from Kendu leaf has increased over the years from Rs. 3.31 crore in 1973 to Rs. 124.72 crore (estimated) in 1990–91. Nationalisation of Kendu leaf has not eased tribal exploitation, rather it has got firmly entrenched under the iron hand of government laws and policies. In 1979, the purchase price of Kendu leaf was Rs. 50 per quintal while its selling price was Rs. 350 per quintal fetching a 600 per cent profit to the government. Even in 1985–87, while the purchase price remained unchanged, the average selling price per quintal had risen from Rs. 972.61 in 1985 to Rs. 1,052.33 in 1986 and to Rs. 1,082.20 in 1987. Though the purchase price has now been revised to Rs. 500 per quintal, this is much less than the prices prevailing in other States.

Mahua Flowers. The nationalisation of Mahua flower is another instance of government encroachment and exploitation of tribals as the benefit of nationalisation has not reached the tribals. Though the government increased the purchase price to Rs. 3 per kg, it was never sincerely implemented. Apart from this, payment was not done quickly and it is reported that in 1991, the Tribal Development Cooperative Corporation had owed Rs. 1 crore to the tribals of Sundargarh for the forest produce collected from them. It is necessary to note that while the Government of Orissa has fixed the rate at Rs. 3 per kg, the Government of Bihar pays Rs. 5 to Rs. 7 per kg of Mahua to the tribals. The prices paid for certain other produce are also very less in comparison to the prices for the same given outside the State. Examples are as under:

Table 3.4
Sale Price of Minor Forest Produce (MFP)

Item	*Inside Orissa (Rs/kg)*	*Outside Orissa (Rs/kg)*
Kusum Seed	2	4.5
Kachada Seed	5	8.5
Karanj Seed	2	4
Char Seed	5	10

Thus, tribals are now being exploited by the Government also.

8. Deforestation due to Timber Felling/ Logging

Forests are the lifelines of the tribals and its destruction implies a direct threat for the very existence of these people. While to the industrial and commercial areas, forests are a source of abundant natural resources that are to be exploited and consumed at a frenzied rate, the resultant consequences are borne directly by the tribals and then all people around it. The State-owned Orissa Forest Development Corporation, whose major activity is timber-trading, not only sells timber for the paper mills, sawmills, manufacturers of furniture, *etc.*, but also leases out forests to various industries. For example, the Mangalam Timber Products has a lease of over 90 sq kms, in the Rayagada forest division. Straw Products Ltd., which is the only paper industry relying on the Forest Department for supply of wood, had a lease of 30 sq km, in 1989–90.

Bamboo nationalisation was another blow to the tribal economy. Used as a basic raw material for various artisan activities and as a construction material in all rural households, its nationalisation in 1988 has made it the exclusive monopoly of the State. Though the Corporation by way of policy is to supply bamboo to tribals/tribal artisans, this policy is observed more on paper. The most disturbing fact is that while the paper industries greedily swallow bamboo plantations, using unscientific methods of cutting, the bamboo reserves of the State are slowly being depleted and no attention is being given for the replacement of its stock.

9. Migration Trends Among Tribals

Mining, industrialisation, and exploitation of natural resources led to the impoverishment, socio-economic and cultural transformation among the Santhals and Mundas in the early part of the 19th Century. Correspondingly, the Santhals and Mundas are known to have begun migrating to the Assam tea gardens in the 1840s. Evidently, they were among the first recruits to the tea gardens. Historical records also show that the Santhals were among the founders (labourers) of the TISCO (Tata Industrial Steel Company) plant in Jamshedpur, Bihar, in the first decade of the 20th Century. By the 1930s, the Santhals of the adjoining Mayurbhanj district of Orissa, are known to have become regular migrants to the Assam tea gardens. From all accounts, migration has now become a way of life among these tribes.

The other major reasons for migration, besides the inducement techniques used by the contractors, were the natural disasters that struck often. For instance, the famines in 1886, 1921 were responsible for migration, and the migration increased from 19,407 in 1917–18 to 2,22,753 in 1918–19, to the tea garden areas. Tribals comprise a bulk of the tea garden labour even today. Most of these have settled in the gardens or surrounding areas.

In Orissa, the initial recruitment was primarily began in the Mayurbhanj and surrounding districts of the Bihar border, inhabited by Santhals and Mundas. 1943 saw a sudden opening up of new areas for recruitment. Among the new areas opened up in this year, the Parlakhemundi sub-division and the nearby district of Srikakulam in Andhra Pradesh were the important ones. Saoras were residing in these areas and though initially only the Hinduised plain land inhabitants of Srikakulam district in Andhra Pradesh joined the flow, this gradually spread to encompass Gumma, probably in the late 1950s, or early 1950s. The hill Saoras of Gumma were well known for their hard work and capacity to survive under adverse conditions. Besides this, Christianity functioned as a motivating factor. Christianity connected to converted tribal to the outside world and worked as a source of exposure to that world, thus providing the incentive for migration.

Development Issues — Then and Now

During the pre-independence era, nothing tangible had been done for the socio-economic progress of the tribals. Although the British trade and commerce created heavy inroads into the Indian economy, the British Government relied upon the policy of tribal isolation in view of the following considerations:

- *(i)* The task of administering the tribal areas was difficult and unrewarding due to lack of revenues.
- *(ii)* It was the desire of the British administration to quarantine the tribes from political infection so that tribal people may not form political fronts especially after the Santhal rebellion.
- *(iii)* A number of British Officers sincerely believed that the tribal people were better off and happier in their own traditional environment as they could not compete with more developed people.

After the independence, several efforts were made to revise the policy of isolating the tribals and measures were initiated to bring them into the mainstream of socio-economic life. However, the measures to assimilate and 'detribalise' them have not met with the desired success. In the process of civilising the tribals, they have been prone to economic exploitation by groups of unscrupulous traders/middlemen and their simple and trusting nature is usually taken advantage of. The post-independence developmental strategies adopted for the development of tribals and their impact are dealt with later.

In the context of economic backwardness, what can be done to improve the economic lot of the tribal people, most of whom are either unemployed or under-employed vide Annexure 3.3, needs to be explored seriously. The tribal people can contribute to the economy if they are given a fair chance. The tribal people are not separate entities and they have to be integrated and assimilated with others to enjoy the fruits of modern civilisation. No culture is exclusive, nor should it be made exclusive. The proposal to develop a separate pattern of economic development to maintain the integrity of tribal culture is not only undesirable, but harmful. They have to be a part and parcel of the Indian heritage. A broad pattern of development, keeping in mind the social environment in which they live, the subsistence economy in which they work and the resources and the skills that they possess, needs to be designed. If we implant a sophisticated model of development, the absorbing capacity will be negligible, leading again to exploitation of tribals by non-tribals. For improving the tribal life and increasing the economic well-being of the tribal people, a few proposals on the basis of a detailed study of inventory resources of different regions are set out below.

Tribal agriculture has to be improved. For a long time, agriculture will continue to be the main source of livelihood for tribals. But the units of their land ownership are extremely small. However, the tribal people have a cooperative attitude to their community. Gramdan movement has been successful in tribal areas only because they have not been exploited by the possession of private property. Private property generates greed and selfishness and creates anti-social attitude. As ownership rights of land among tribals are non-existent and alienation of land is common, tribal people are hardly attached to their property rights. This is the proper time when cooperatives can be organised among the tribals for deriving economies of large scale production. As many of them live in uneven and rocky areas, it will not be possible to provide irrigation everywhere. But whenever tribal people live in plain areas and there is scope for improvement of irrigation facility, irrigation should be provided to improve cropping pattern with modern inputs for increasing agricultural productivity and providing continuous employment opportunities. There should be demarcation of areas in different tribal regions with ground water survey for determining how much of irrigation facility can be provided. This should be done on a priority basis as irrigation is the foundation of modern agriculture.

But, where irrigation is not possible, dry land agriculture has to be developed on scientific lines. The Indian Council of Agricultural Research (ICAR) and Agriculture Universities have already evolved some dry land technologies. These can be applied in tribal areas. If rains are quite heavy, but confined to a few months, catchment areas have to be built up for water harvesting. The uneven lands are to be terraced with a view to preventing soil erosion and applying modern inputs for increased production. What is required, however, is to make a detailed study of each region so as to prepare comprehensive micro-plans, region-wise, as regards soil conservation, water harvesting, cropping patterns and input requirements, for agricultural development.

In agricultural development, horticulture assumes tremendous importance. These are the regions where fruit crops are grown in abundance. The tribals do not derive much benefit from these crops due to lack of marketing facility and preservation. Middlemen have been found to be exploiting them in all possible ways. Fruits of the trees are auctioned before they are ripe, for small loans and the tribals are called upon to watch the fruits till they are ripe, without any financial benefit. Dishonest middlemen exploit the honesty of the tribal people for securing exorbitant profits. If some fruit processing industries are located in these regions and fruit trees are nurtured on scientific lines, there will be a big economic advancement of the tribal people.

But only crop production will not change the tribal economy. Many of these tribal areas are not suitable for commercial crops. Some of the food crops that can be grown, are minor millets which cannot bring a fair return to the cultivator. Dairy farming, goat-rearing and poultry can be conveniently taken up in these areas. In view of the nearness to the forest areas, there will be no difficulty for feed or fodder. In other words, mixed farming and animal husbandry are essential for economic development in tribal areas.

But all the tribal people cannot be resettled in agriculture. There are many landless labourers who cannot be provided with land. Some landless labourers can be resettled in land wherever available. But unless some surplus people are diverted from agriculture to non-farm occupations, the tribal economy cannot prosper. There is plenty of scope for starting small scale industries in these regions on the basis of forest products and fruits. Only the technology has to be simple so that the tribal people can operate them efficiently and effectively.

For the development of agriculture-based industries, five factors are considered necessary:

(i) There should be suitable credit organisations to provide loans at a cheap rate and prevent exploitation.

(ii) A marketing machinery with credit links should be started so that the tribals can get a fair return for their produce.

(iii) There should be lease of land and settlement of colonies where modern farming can be done on irrigated land. Here both consolidation of holdings and cooperativisation have to be taken up to prevent alienation of land to secure economies of large scale production.

(iv) Improvement in organisations is necessary for effectively carrying out these programmes, managed by dedicated voluntary organisations with the participation of tribal people.

(v) An integrated area development approach has to be initiated so that all aspects of development in particular areas are taken up with a view to bringing about an all-round development of the region.

It has been said that tribal people require food, fodder, fuel, fruit and fair return. This can be done only when there is a concerted effort to achieve, simultaneously, all these in a particular region. An area approach has, therefore, greater relevance than a schematic programme. The entire programme of development has to be done on the basis of resource inventory of each region so that the micro-development pattern does not suffer from imbalance between supply of inputs and demand for inputs.

But no development can work if people are not interested to make it work. To prevent the isolation of the tribal people and make them an integral part of the economic process of the country, an awareness has to be created regarding their rights and duties, their responsibilities and involvements and the changing pattern which is envisaged for them and the work they have to do in bringing about such changes. All these can be done, provided they are sufficiently educated, both literally and functionally so as to understand the problems and challenges and to take up the management of their developmental programme with vigour and enthusiasm. A conscious and willing tribal community can invigorate tribal life and prevent exploitation much more quickly, than an ignorant and unwilling community. Productive education is, therefore, a vital link in the process of development.

ANNEXURE 3.1

Land Holdings in Tribal Districts* of Orissa

Districts/ Families	*Total land holdings in acres*	*Total families*	*Landless families*	*Percent of landless families*	*Below 1 acre*	*Percentage of families*	*Percentage of marginal families*
PHULBANI (Blocks-12)							
ST	1,50,315.8	51,118	7,622	14.91	11,450	22.39	37.30
SC	18,957.5	18,751	8,279	44.15	6,059	32.31	
OC	7,076.3	12,469	7,734	62.20	4,744	38.04	
KORAPUT (Blocks-41)							
ST	7,72,143.3	2,39,181	80,204	33.53	31,279	38.99	72.52
SC	1,25,613.1	57,272	27,528	48.06	6,159	10.75	
OC	3,30,969.0	1,04,063	41,442	38.82	10,025	9.63	
GANJAM (Blocks-7)							
ST	50,458.3	34,763	11,095	31.91	11,013	31.68	63.69
SC	4,095.4	7,397	4,904	66.29	1,233	16.66	
OC	30,603.6	38,869	9,450	24.31	4,271	10.98	
KEONJHAR (Blocks-17)							
ST	1,70,874.4	64,049	9,906	15.46	15,086	23.55	39.01
SC	17,568.0	9,661	3,367	24.50	2,765	28.62	
OC	1,56,886.9	38,529	4,654	12.07	5,770	14.97	
MAYURBHANJ (Blocks-17)							
ST	2,90,606.8	11,530	18,749	16.26	31,651	27.45	43.71
SC	14,300.0	12,760	4,689	36.74	4,615	36.16	
OC	1,71,228.4	54,835	6,360	11.59	12,857	23.44	
SUNDERGARH (Blocks-13)							
ST	2,77,335.1	78,004	12,388	15.88	11,230	14.39	30.27
SC	21,439.6	12,925	3,902	30.18	3,156	24.41	
OC	1,34,311.4	35,642	8,587	24.09	4,477	12.56	

* Only Tribal Sub-plan blocks are added together.

Source: Tribal Bench Mark Survey, 1978–79 by THRTI, Bhubaneswar.

ANNEXURE 3.2

Operational Holdings among Scheduled Tribes

(Per cent)

Sl. No.	States	No. 1980–81	No. 1990–91	Area 1980–81	Area 1990–91
1.	Andhra Pradesh	6.42	6.90	6.29	7.20
2.	Bihar	7.54	7.80	16.25	16.10
3.	Gujarat	10.92	11.00	8.05	9.10
4.	Karnataka	3.71	4.90	3.47	5.00
5.	Kerala	0.98	1.20	1.50	1.90
6.	Madhya Pradesh	25.11	24.70	24.84	25.40
7.	Maharashtra	6.02	6.70	6.08	7.70
8.	Orissa	27.58	26.60	29.90	28.70
9.	Rajasthan	15.36	15.40	8.35	8.40
10.	Tamil Nadu	0.67	0.80	1.01	1.20
11.	Uttar Pradesh	0.16	0.20	0.28	0.30
12.	West Bengal	7.08	7.30	6.59	7.00
13.	All India	7.71	8.10	10.20	10.80

ANNEXURE 3.3

Tribal Work Force as per 1991 Census

[No. of persons]

Sl. No.	*Particulars*	*Male*	*Female*	*Total*
I. Main Workers				
(*a*) Cultivators	Rural	11,72,794	2,51,569	14,24,318
	Urban	12,088	1,513	13,601
	Total	11,84,837	2,53,082	14,37,919
(*b*) Agricultural Labourers	Rural	5,91,911	4,62,274	10,54,185
	Urban	18,462	10,260	28,722
	Total	6,10,373	4,72,534	10,82,907
(*c*) Livestock, Forestry, Fishing	Rural	16,542	5,274	21,816
Hunting, Orchards and	Urban	2,230	487	2,717
other allied activities	Total	18,772	5,761	24,533
(*d*) Mining and Quarrying	Rural	24,903	11,514	36,417
	Urban	5,409	1,592	7,001
	Total	30,312	13,106	43,418
(*e*) Household Industry	Rural	21,957	22,939	44,896
	Urban	1,080	1,014	2,094
	Total	23,037	23,953	46,990
(*f*) Other than Household	Rural	20,686	8,205	28,891
Industry	Urban	15,914	2,654	19,568
	Total	36,600	10,859	47,459
(*g*) Trade & Commerce	Rural	13,222	4,812	18,034
	Urban	5,007	971	5,978
	Total	18,229	5,783	24,012
(*h*) Transport & Communication	Rural	8,715	672	9,387
	Urban	7,448	6,363	8,084
	Total	16,163	1,308	17,471
(*i*) Others	Rural	56,050	14,227	70,277
	Urban	25,779	8,923	34,702
	Total	81,829	23,150	1,04,979
Main Workers Sub-Total	Rural	19,26,735	7,81,486	27,08,221
	Urban	93,417	82,050	1,21,467
	Total	20,20,152	8,09,536	28,29,688
II. Marginal Works	Rural	48,736	5,86,712	6,35,448
	Urban	1,463	4,751	6,214
	Total	50,199	5,91,463	6,41,662
III. Non-workers	Rural	13,49,971	19,76,866	33,26,837
	Urban	92,569	1,41,458	2,34,027
	Total	14,42,540	21,18,324	35,60,864
Total Population	Rural	33,25,442	33,45,064	66,70,506
	Urban	1,87,449	1,74,259	3,61,708
	Total	35,12,891	35,19,323	70,32,214

CHAPTER IV

Sustainable Development and Tribal Innovations

INTRODUCTION

The tribal people consider their environment and habitat as a source of food, shelter and measures for survival, belonging to the entire community and recognise no restrictions on any member of the community to eke out his/her subsistence. Their freedom over exploitation of resources does not mean over-exploitation as the tribal people take from the environment strictly according to immediate needs. This type of utilisation is called sustainable subsistence. Centuries of dwelling in their native habitat, have developed a source of attachment to their habitat, giving shape to their cultural values and customs.

Most of the tribal people are in the process of being marginalised. Their environment is encroached upon by the immigrants, industries, mine operators *etc.* Even environmental restoration programmes like establishment of bio-sphere reserves and animal sancturies are acting against the interests of the tribal groups. Further, unimaginative developmental programmes aimed at helping this people have created more confusion and alienated them from their culture and habitat. The Chenchus of Andhra Pradesh are hunter gatherers are now unable to eke out a living as colonisation programmes have failed and the Srisailam Tiger Project has displaced a number of them. Expansion of agricultural communities has forced them into interior inaccessible places and they are now a minority in their own villages. Some have migrated to cities working as leaders, rickshaw pullers, rag pickers and beggars.

The entitlements of tribal communities should made known and then these communities should be empowered. They must understand the various developmental efforts being made and choose to be a part of these innovations.

The participatory development approach towards tribal groups is a must and they must not be forced to participate in their own colonisation, displacement and degradation of environment. These innovative approaches must be human centred and a minimum of four functions have to be performed—cognitive, social, instrumental and political.

Based on the tribal peoples cultural heritage and locally available resources, a different knowledge system has to be slowly built up, one step at a time. Failure of conventional strategies have to be met by promoting new alternatives so that tribal people pave the way for their own development. The right to choose their path to development has to be given to the tribal people.

INNOVATIONS IN DEVELOPMENT

All tribes have not responded equally to challenges faced by them. Today, there are three types of tribal communities in the country. The first type are those who have been assimilated into modern settlements and who depend on mines/factories for a living as wage-earners. In all major mines and factories in the entire Chota Nagpur belt, many tribal people have found employment and do not lead a communal existence (*e.g.*, Hos, Munda, Bhuiyas, *etc.*).

The second type of tribals have been exposed to modern trends and continue to lead a communal existence but with significant changes. Tribal lands have been parcelled off and land rights have come into existence. These tribals are exposed to the market economy and enjoy the benefits of both a tribal way of life and access to modern goods and ways of life. They have acquired necessary skills to adjust to the survival needs (*e.g.*, Sauras, Santhals, Gondas, *etc.*).

The third type of tribals have retreated to inhospitable and inaccessible areas to avoid modernising influences and they lead a lonely existence, safe and secure, away from a lifestyle they cannot comprehend. These primitive tribes have developed primitive skills which allow them to survive in their remote areas. Many avoid contact with modern man as a deliberate choice. Not much is known of their innovations due to their secretive lifestyle (*e.g.*, Hill Marias, Juangs, Baigas, *etc.*).

The effect of various innovations which tribals have introduced and some which have been introduced by others especially on the second type of tribals and changes induced in their lifestyles, are proposed to be discussed here.

Innovations that have helped Tribals

The tribal way of life has evolved over ages, attuned to the local environment. It would be a mistake to think that all tribal communities share a common way of life. Their simple way of life is subtly shaped by the environment and external influences and all minute changes in the tribal way of life are innovations which have been accepted and imbibed in their way of life. With the caution of an oppressed people who have been exploited and who have seen their world of forests ever-shrinking, innovations are treated with due caution and are accepted only if they are perceived to be an improvement over existing norms and practices. To look for quantum jumps in technologies for the tribals would be a mistake. The tribal people will not be able to assimilate technologies which are not improvements on the existing practices. To that extent, much of the innovations thrust upon them by the government officials, in accordance with various government-sponsored programmes, turn out to be failures. Under various credit-linked programmes, tribal people have been financed for wells and milch cattle for which they have very little use. Well-meaning interventions for the tribals are not easily assimilated into the tribal lifestyle. However, the tribal people are not averse to innovations. As long as the innovation does not alter their lifestyle and as long as it signifies a better method of doing something they have been accustomed to, the innovation has a definite chance of acceptance. Another significant factor is tribal taboos and beliefs which may hinder acceptance of innovative ideas. Thus, innovations in the tribal context appear to be "One step at a time". The tribal will not be pushed into innovative thinking and processes on hearsay. He has to see it and believe it and then only can he consider any innovation. It must be emphasised that tribal innovations are an essentially slow process if the ideas are implanted from extraneous sources and acceptance will be faster if it is possible to link up with the existing tribal ethos and way of life. A few examples of various innovations which have had an effect on tribal life in Orissa are discussed by way of examples of innovations and their effect on tribal development.

1. Shifting Cultivation among the Juangs–Keonjhar District. Swidden cultivation of 'Dongar-chas' or 'Podu-chas' are the terms used for 'slash' and 'burn' cultivation practised by tribals who are in the primitive stages of development and who may have taboos for plough cultivation. Shifting cultivation has been in existence since Neolithic times and can be defined as continuing agricultural systems in which temporary clearings are cropped in the forests for short periods. The problem is that the cropping gap which was in excess of 22 years has been reduced to less than 4 years, due to disappearance of forests and population pressure as also food needs.

The Juangs depend on paddy for their food obtained from shifting cultivation which is a way of life as it is established in tribal mythology that superior beings had taught these methods. Mango trees and jack-fruit trees are never cut as mango-kernel (crushed, roasted and made into paste) and jack-fruit seeds are a supplementary source of food apart from jungle roots and tubers which are collected by the women. However, during monsoons (3–4 months), food is in short supply and unless food is stored, starvation is rampant. In spite of hard work and constant supervison against depredation of wild animals, Juangs raise only an insufficient amount of crops for sustenance. Where cultivation under wells is possible, it is resorted to but there is little irrigated land available in the inhospitable hill-sides where the Juangs have been driven out by cultivators belonging to other communities.

To prevent further forest cover destruction, wet-land farming of valley bottoms may be encouraged for the tribals and land upto 30 per cent slope be brought under permanent cultivation, by giving land rights and title deeds to the Juang farmers. The various innovative methods used by the Juangs to harness hill streams to irrigate lands under permanent cultivation and to have perennial water source in the villages, are worth mentioning. Second year 'taila' on the same land is banned as it destroys soil fertility. Instead, the 'taungiya' system of horticulture is encouraged in lands between 12 per cent to 20 per cent slope and after 5 years gradually comes down to between 8 per cent and 12 per cent. In the first taila year, niger seeds are sown in July and after sowing is over, mango, jack-fruit, papaya and banana trees are planted before end of monsoons along the ridges so that they do not interfere with the cash crops but prevent further soil erosion. Thus, after 5 years, farming is restricted to 8 per cent to 12 per cent slope lands only. Terraced fields can be developed between 3 per cent to 8 per cent slope but the costs are heavy and the tribal wants immediate returns as he is unable to wait for 2–3 years. Land above 20 per cent slope is reserved for grazing and hill-top cultivation should be banned. These innovative techniques help wean away the Juang farmers from destroying their forest heritage and ensure that scientific land management principles are adhered to.

Some innovative methods which have helped Juangs are the creation of minor irrigation facilities such as dams and diversion weirs as also water harvesting structures which have transformed barren lands into paddy lands with private ownership. Sabai grass (Eulabopsis binate) brought from the Terai regions of the Himalayas has been large areas of Mayurbhanj and Keonjhar districts since the 1930s in badly eroded lands, to stop further erosion. The sabai grass is grown at virtually no expense, is hardy and besides it stops soil erosion and can be woven into beautiful ropes which are used for decorative articles, mats, furniture, *etc.* The grass clumps have an economic life of over 20 years and its introduction by the Maharaja of Mayurbhanj has been a boon for the tribals.

2. *Terrace Cultivation of the Lanjia Saoras — Gajapathi District.* Of the Saoras, the Lanjia Saoras are the most primitive but have small gardens on their homestead lands, and have developed excellent terraced fields but for additional income, also resort to swiddens on hill-slopes and hill tops. The terraced fields in which water flows throughout the year are reserved for paddy cultivation while the upper terrace which are dry, are used for cultivating beans, pulses and minor millets. The engineering skills of the

Lanjia Saoras are to be admired especially when it comes to designing the cultivable terraces. The terraces are built right upto the beds of the hill streams and extend many hundreds of feet down to the valleys from the hill-slopes and hill tops. The platform of each terrace is flat throughout and the fall of each terrace is stone-packed. The terraces are so constructed that no soil is carried down with the water that trickles down from the higher terraces to the lower. These innovative engineering skills deserve admiration as also the water management skills. Water-flow from one terrace to the other is controlled by channels and water ways which are provided in the ridges up the terraces. There is another way of facilitating water-flow from the higher terraces to the lower ones. Two or three pits are dug at the lower side of the upper terrace and these pits are packed with boulders. The water flows from these pits and trickles through the boulders, to the terrace below. The water management is so skilful that it avoids flooding of the terrace fields. In many places, water trickles level to level through stone facing and ultimately flows to lands in the plains. Neither the soil carried over with the water from the terraced fields nor any damage caused to the stone walls. These terraced fields, developed with considerable engineering ingenuity, are privately owned and handed down as valuable assets from father to son and are even mortgaged to local money/paddy-lenders in times of need but not sold. Another interesting innovation is that all agricultural activities are done on a cooperative basis called 'Ansir' whereby villagers work on other's land on the basis of reciprocity and mutuality of obligation but food is provided to the workers by the person on whose land they work. But this system is dying out and is being replaced by cash wages. Cattle are used as draught animals and also for payment of 'bride price' and hence are 'movable' assets. Swidden cultivation is being continued more as a habit or as a source of additional income.

3. Orange Plantations of the Saoras, Mahendragiri Hills—Gajapathi District. One of the most pleasing sights to a horticulturist are the lovely Mahendragiri Hills in Southern Orissa, covered with Orange trees. The initiator was a Saora Tribal who had worked in Burma and the Khasi Hills and came back with a handful of orange seeds over 60 years ago. These were carefully cultivated and the orange trees grew, both fruits and seeds were distributed free to other tribals who wanted to plant them. About 40 years ago, the Department of Agriculture also set up orchards and seed farms to propagate orange cultivation. Some of the innovative techniques used by the farmers are given below:

Fifteen feet spacing is to be maintained between trees which should be planted at the edge of the stone-packed walls of the terrace so that decomposed matter and litter flowing from the higher side of the slope could be deposited at the base of the plants for compost creation. Soil on the slope is not disturbed and shade trees present in the slope are not to be cut. No manure except the accumulated humus at the plant-base, is applied. Ginger and Turmeric are grown as inter-crops as the leaves on decomposition would add to soil fertility as also minor millets. For preparation of seedlings, seeds are extracted from well-ripened fruits in December and dried in the sun. When the reddish coat vanishes, the seeds are ready for dibbling. The seed bed is to be prepared close to a hill-stream and dried manure and water sprinkled over the bed when seedlings attain full growth (1 ft. height) they are removed from the seed-bed and planted in the hill slope. As for the fruit-borer pests, a pot of water is mixed with molasses and kept in different places in the orchard. The insects are attracted, fall into the water and are killed. However, today's tribal farmers have no knowledge of the traditional practices and lack even basic knowledge of important practices such as: *(i)* site selection, *(ii)* selection of plants and raising of seedlings, *(iii)* planting and after-care, *(iv)* plant protection measures, *(v)* manuring and orchard maintenance. The Dombs (SC community) purchase the entire orchard by auction, much before ripening of fruits and the farmers do not get much for their labour. Due to poor management practices, yields have reduced significantly and farmers spend time on other crops and 'jhum' cultivation and average productivity has reduced. Farmers are also not using improved plants due to bias against new ideas — 'As a foreigner cannot thrive in our villages, plants brought up under different conditions cannot survive local conditions and become sick and die when planted in the hills', has been stated by one tribal who has forgotten how the orange seeds travelled from the Khasi hills in Meghalaya.

4. Income Generation and Self-Help among Tribals—Samanwita Phulbani District. Samanwita is probably an unique institution, the only known NGO set up by State Bank of India to meet the needs of the tribals at G.Udayagiri. It was set up in an isolated part of Phulbani District with the assistance of the District Administration. The original scheme was to introduce sericulture (mulberry) amongst the tribal farmers and also with BAIF assistance to set up a cattle rearing and upgrading farm. Both schemes never took off but SBI continued to support Samanwita which took up health-care, welfare, medical activities along with income-generation activities such as selling spices (Cardamom, Turmeric processing, Pepper, Aonla, *etc.*) and manufacture of sisal mats, and ropes. Much stress is given on income generation and agro-processing activities and since 1994, on the creation of Self Help Groups (with the assistance from NABARD) using tribal facilitators who are from the villages in which the SHGs are located. Of the 60 SHGs set up, 13 have already been linked up with banks and income-generation activities have been initiated. The creation of SHGs in tribal areas has given a shot in the arm to the SHG movement especially in view of earlier failures by other NGOs, to successfully promote SHGs in tribal areas. Replication of SHGs in tribal areas are now being taken up only in areas where aid/subsidies have not reduced tribal people to the status of dole seekers. The SHG concept is being replicated in other areas/villages by Samanwita and other NGOs who have built up the SHGs in tribal areas. The innovative idea of building up SHGs with income generating activities with the help of trained local facilitators residing in the target villages, has been sought to be replicated in other tribal areas and villages.

5. Medicinal use of Animals. A study by the Zoological Survey of India (Joseph *et al*) in 1988, conducted in Madhya Pradesh and Orissa recorded the fact that tribals had discovered

- *(a)* 156 applications of mammals and products,
- *(b)* 33 applications of birds,
- *(c)* 30 applications of reptiles; and
- *(d)* 10 applications of fishes.

The blood and meat of pigeons are widespread in Orissa for treatment of paralysis. Derivatives of bear, tiger, wild boar, cow's urine, goat's liver, hen's eggs, honey, snake fat, earthworm flesh, elephant bones have been widely used but the exact scientific value of these medicines is not known but a large number of cures have been affected. More work needs to be done to find out the efficacy of these animal product cures.

6. Medicinal uses of Herbs and Plants — Simlipal Hills. Another study in Bihar, Orissa and West Bengal identified 120 herbal medicines. The tribal people are rather secretive about their customs and beliefs and their tribal medicines. A study conducted by the RRL, Bhubaneswar in 1988, revealed that 70 species in the Simlipal hills are available for commercial exploitation and are being used by a number of pharmacies manufacturing a number of compounds, ayurvedic/pharmaceutical medicines, tinctures and extracts. In addition, there were an additional 67 uses of vascular plants which had not been recorded in published literature before. The existence of such a large number of plants, with medicinal uses in a small portion of Orissa (*i.e.*, Simlipal Hills) raises the prospects of the existence of many more species which would be of benefit to mankind. A detailed study needs to be done of the medicinal properties of these plants. An interesting point to be remembered is that among some tribes, no plant will be removed entirely with its roots unless another one is planted in its place. This ensures that rare medicinal plants are not lost to posterity. A cure for cancer or AIDS may emerge from this research. Another rich area for medicinal herbs is the Gandhamardan Hills in Sambalpur District.

Innovations that Harm Tribals

1. Tasar Silkworm and Lac Worm Rearing — Keonjhar District. Tasar has had extensive success in Orissa as Tasar silkworms are exclusively reared by the tribals on Arjun, Sal and Asan trees which are leased out by the Forest Department to the tribals. As in the case of tasar, mulberry is increasingly being cultivated by the Tribals as it is being promoted as part of the Integrated Rural Development Programme (IRDP). But the gradual deforestation and the wholesale cutting of the host trees by tribals for monetary gains of non-tribals, is rampant and since 1990, tasar production has been dwindling. Also, as these are exclusively tribal products which have modern alternatives available, not much is being done to focus the problems of the tribal tasar/lac worm rearers. One of the main reasons for the setback to tasar production in the State has been partly on the inability on the part of officials and researchers to find solutions to technical problems. For tasar, 2 to 3 crops in a year are possible. A tasar-rearer takes the tasar worms and shifts residence to his 'adda' far from his home situated in the leased portion of the forest for rearing them on the branches of asan, arjun and sal leaves. He has to live the life of a hermit, following self-imposed religious restrictions and obligations as per customs and formalities. Having placed the worms on the tree leaves, he and other members of his family, sit under the trees with bows and arrows to scare off the birds and other enemies which eat up the silkworms. However, the problem is that tribal youngsters who are more aware of their talents and job opportunities, do not want to work as tasar rearers with poor income levels or lead a life of physical and economic hardship due to the small economic margins available for the growers. In lac too, the closure of the brood lac farm of the State Government has resulted in total dependence on brood lac procurement from Ranchi. Further, the survival rate of the brood lac is now only 20 per cent and hence lac production has been dwindling in recent years. Inadequate attention to backward and forward linkages and innovative alternatives, have succeeded in finishing off these tribal rearing skills and income avenues for tribals. These are two major areas of tribal income opportunities where emerging alternatives and changing lifestyles of tribals have posed a threat.

2. *Denudation of Forests, Cuttack — Khurda Districts.* From the Third Five Year Plan, an ambitious programme was set up by the State Government to plant cashew trees in areas which were once sal forests and which had been logged to such an extent that where mighty sal forests stood, only degraded scrub now remained. It was decided to plant cashew trees on a massive scale to reduce soil erosion and to enable better utilisation of the scrub forests. Targets were given and as is the case with 'top-down' planning efforts, targets go haywire and officialdom goes topsy-turvy. Securing opportunity or possibly, just to achieve targets, huge sal trees were cut and replaced by bad quality cashew plants, procured in a hurry. Another innovation which continues to cause misery is the humble bicycle. Every day, you will witness long lines of cyclists returning in the evenings to Cuttack, with loads of wood from the Athgarh Forests which will fetch them Rs. 100 daily in the market. Also, every morning, you will also see a line of cyclists emerging from Chandaka forests en route to Bhubaneswar. The humble cycle is now adding to denudation of forests.

3. *Grain Golas versus PACS — Koraput District.* In the early 1950s, after the Rural Credit Survey report was released, the Central/State Governments

needed to strengthen the Primary Cooperative Credit Societies (PACS). In the Western Orissa Districts, (Koraput, Kalahandi and Bolangir) revenue records reveal that 150 years ago, there was multiple cropping due to plentiful rains and vast forest areas. Today, forest cover has been destroyed and these districts face near drought situations in the non-monsoon months and lack of drinking water at times. To meet the recurrence of droughts and starvation deaths, the tribal communities had resorted to communal grain golas (or stores) into which excess paddy was stored by those tribal people during harvest times and in times of non-availability of food, these grain golas provided food-security and sustenance. People did not die of hunger or starvation or malnutrition. But this food security aspect was seen to come in the way of the formation of the Primary Agricultural Credit Societies as people kept their savings not in the form of deposits in PACS but in the form of paddy in the gramin golas. To promote the PACS, the grain golas were dismantled. Today, we have starvation deaths in plenty and selling of young children as their parents are unable to provide them food while the PACS/LAMPS which were supposed to help the tribals have ended up as yet another instrument for exploitation. Clearly, another innovation which has gone sour.

4. Traditional Irrigation Systems versus Water Harvesting Structures — Kalahandi District. In drought-prone Kalahandi District, under DPAP/ADAPT programmes, the Soil Conservation Department undertook to create 588 Water-Harvesting Structures (WHS) costing Rs. 8.57 crore, benefiting 6000 hectares. Without consulting the local people, the WHSs set up caused misery in a few places, by reducing water availability. At Sangadi, Khariar block, two perennial streams provided irrigation to 37 acre of land belonging to small and marginal farmers while the WHS subsequently created has hardly 3–4 feet of water and the natural sources are silted up due to the WHS construction. To compound to the misery, the Forest Department dug a trench just below the WHS which drained out whatever water passing through the seepage. Normally the land is at a higher level than the WHS and the water level does not reach the sluice level and hence there is no water for irrigation. At Dab, Boden Block, a single natural source was obstructed by the WHS. Clearly, the innovative WHS succeeded in bringing misery and not water for irrigation in a drought-prone district.

5. Mixed Orchards — Gumma, Gajapati District. In view of the natural farming abilities of the Saoras, the Department of Horticulture decided to build up mixed orchards comprising mango, cashew, guava, ber, *etc.*, with funds from ITDA/DRDA/JRY and after nursing plants for 3 years, handed the half-grown plants to the Saoras who promptly cut down all plants except mango and cashew and did gap-filling on their own with the same species. This was because the other fruit trees bear fruit and are harvested during the seasonal agricultural operations when the farmers work in the fields as casual labourers and hence they would be unable to protect the trees and their fruits during harvest time. When mango/cashew are harvested in April/May, they could afford to watch their trees. Further, cashew could also be stored for long periods after harvest to fetch better prices. Hence their terrible logic was to use only those fruit bearing trees which would fit into their scheme of things.

CONCLUSION

(i) The 11 case studies explained in this chapter reveal that innovations can do good and also harm to the tribal people. If tribal people are involved in the innovative changes being introduced, they will be able to comprehend, participate in decision-making and help in implementation. But if 'top-down' planning is resorted on the basis that Government knows best, the result is failure or misery. The tribals do not need charity but rather a sympathetic understanding of their way of life. Innovations should meet the tribal expectations and fit into their subsistence level economy. Food products which can be dried and stored for difficult days are preferred. Sustainable and low cost technologies are also preferred. For a tribal 'doing is believing' and this is the dictum for any innovation. The simple nature and low level expectations of tribals are unable to cope up with risky investments. Another important factor is that a steady daily income is more important than an income which will bring results after 4–5 months of labour and hence tribals are today themselves engaged in cutting down forests on behalf of others. The animal husbandry skills of the tribals are excellent in view of the good health of the scrub cattle they possess and the herbal remedies resorted to, in case of disease. But due to cost of maintenance of cross bred and heavier milch cattle, they persist with scrub cattle for manure and meat but not for milch purposes.

(ii) If innovative technologies are to be introduced, then it would be better to understand the present level technologies of the tribals and improve upon existing ones gradually rather than introduce a brand new concept without linkages to the existing technologies. The compulsion should be theirs and not that of 'outsiders' who have little knowledge or understanding of tribal needs or sensibilities.

CHAPTER V

Regulatory and Developmental Initiatives

INTRODUCTION

The policy of a Welfare State, which emerged after Independence placed a heavy responsibility on the Central and State Governments with regard to protection and advancement of the Scheduled Tribes. Article 46 of the Constitution laid down the directive principle to the effect that the State shall promote with special care, the educational and economic interests of the weaker sections of the people and in particular of Scheduled Tribes and Scheduled Castes and shall protect them from social injustice and all forms of exploitation. Since then, several measures have been initiated and programmes implemented through the successive Five Year Plans for the upliftment of the scheduled tribes to bring them on par with the rest of the population of the country.

The five fundamental principles advocated by Pandit Nehru (which were later on supported by the Dhebar Commission and the Shilu Ao Committee), have continued to influence the policy framework for development of the Scheduled Tribes. The principles were:

(i) The tribal people should develop along the lines of their own genius. Efforts should be made to avoid imposing anything upon them and their own traditional arts and culture should be encouraged.

(ii) Tribal rights on land and forests should be respected.

(iii) Efforts should be made to train and build up a team of their own people to do the work of administration and development. Some

technical personnel from outside will no doubt, be needed especially in the beginning, but introduction of too many outsiders into the tribal territory should be avoided.

(iv) The tribal areas should not be over-administered or overwhelmed with a multiplicity of schemes. Works should be undertaken through and not in rivalry to their own social and cultural institutions.

(v) The results should be judged not by statistics or amount of money spent, but by the quality of human character.

CONSTITUTIONAL SAFEGUARDS

Our leaders in the formative years of our country have always been concerned about the welfare of the tribal people. The five approaches that have evolved over the years are:

Policy of isolation	—	Favoured by the colonial British and continued by some of the administrators.
Policy of assimilation	—	Favoured by those who wished to end the policy of isolation and ensure some development for tribals.
Policy of revivalism	—	Sought to revive tribal culture and practices as a bulwark against rapid modernisation affecting tribal lifestyles and cultures.
Policy of integration	—	This was to ensure that the tribal society is integrated in the national mainstream gradually.
Policy of neglect	—	This policy is followed when initiatives have run out of steam and funds and the bureaucracy carries on unabashed.

The Indian Constitution has envisaged special provisions and safeguards for the tribal people. Article 46 of the Constitution states that the State shall promote, with special care, the educational and economic interests of weaker sections among the Indian population and in particular, of the Scheduled Tribes and shall protect them from social injustice and all forms of exploitation. Article 342 of the Constitution empowers the President of India to specify the community or communities to be designated as the Scheduled Tribes for the purpose of the Constitution. Article 244 provides for the administration of the 'Scheduled Areas' in accordance with the 5th and 6th Schedules. Articles 330, 332 and 334 provide for reservation of seats for the Scheduled Tribes in the Parliament and State Legislatures while Article 335 provides for reservation of jobs in various services under the Government and Public Sector Undertakings. Article 244 empowers the President to declare any area with a substantial tribal population as a Scheduled Area under Fifth Schedule as Tribal Area under Sixth Schedule.

Article 339 empowers the Central Government to give directions to the State for drawing up or execution of laws for welfare of Scheduled Tribe in the State. Article 275 provides for assistance to the States for the implementation of provisions of Constitution Scheduled Tribes. Article 15, 16 and 19 enjoin that tribal legislations on any matter for special conditions of tribals so as to safeguard their interests and way of life are taken into account. The Fifth Schedule gives enormous powers and lays certain duties on the Governor of every State that has Scheduled Areas.

The Fifth Schedule, Part B, Para 4 provides for compulsory setting up of Tribal Advisory Councils (TACs) in each State. These TACs have virtually no powers as they are only recommendatory. The Tribal Council in each tribal community was ignored. The District Councils too are of no consequence. Article 338 provides for a Commission of SCs and STs and was intended to be a link between the Constitution and the State Government.

TRIBAL DEVELOPMENT AND FIVE YEAR PLANS

The three main objectives of development, as envisaged by Michael Todaro, an eminent development economist are:

(i) the ability to provide the basic necessities of life,
(ii) to be a person with self-esteem; and
(iii) freedom of choice.

Tribal development is about ensuring and restoring the command over their resources which the tribal communities have lost. How much to develop and at what pace this micro-economic transformation should develop, should be left for the tribal people to decide. The development processes must aim at eliminating deprivation and restoring dignity and self-confidence in the tribal people. Development is not necessarily on the economic front, there ought to be progress on the social and cultural fronts too!

Several studies have shown that 80–85 per cent of all funds meant for tribal development are actually utilised for meeting the cost of maintaining a bureaucracy which is essentially non-tribal in character and outlook. In the years 1949–69, as many as six high-powered committees were set up by the Government of India:

(i) The Criminal Advisory Committee, 1949.
(ii) The Committee on Special Multi-purpose Tribal Blocks (Verrier Elwin Committee Report), 1960.
(iii) The Scheduled Areas and Scheduled Tribes Committee (UN Dhebar Committee Report), 1963.
(iv) The Committee on Tribal Economy in Forest Areas, 1967.
(v) Report of the Study Team on Tribal Development Programmes (Shilu Ao Committee Report), 1969; and
(vi) The Study Group on Tribal Labour, 1969.

The Verrier Commission Report, 1960, stressed on the participation and involvement of the tribals in the implementation of development programmes designed for them and recommended enactment of legislations to curb the exploitation of tribals by money-lenders and make provision of adequate Government funding for credit to tribals. It suggested measures to redeem tribals from chronic loans and discharge tribal bonded-labourers from unfair labour contracts.

The Dhebar Commission Report, 1963, stated that protective measures were sporadic and inadequate to solve complex tribal problems. The process of development in tribal areas was slow because of inadequate financial investment. It recommended that traditional tribal councils be involved for implementation of tribal development programmes.

The Shilu Ao Commission Report, 1969, felt that the tribal development blocks were inadequate to cater to tribal development. It noted that benefits of development did not percolate except to the most advanced tribal communities. Both the Dhebar and Ao Committees noted abject indigence, high incidence of indebtedness, chronic land alienation, educational backwardness, rampant exploitation and inadequacy of the communication system, as the major problems of tribals.

It is interesting to note that since 1947, many high-powered committees have been formed to study the problems of the tribal people and reports of study groups set up by the Planning Commission as part of the Five Year Plans. (Details at Annexure 5.1).

Development implies that all communities should move to a higher stage in the socio-economic scale and acquire characteristics of a modern social system which have different norms and mores of economic and social relationships. The programmes for socio-economic development of tribal people are based on the philosophy that these should be in response to tribals own urge for better standards of living in consonance with their culture. In order to ensure effective management of development of the tribal economy and culture, there have been a number of programmes designed by the Government of India as revealed in the respective Five Year Plans. (*Source:* Planning Commission)

The First Five Year Plan (1951–56)

Development of education, communication systems in tribal areas provision of medical and housing facilities were major programmes undertaken during the Plan. Thus, the Government of India spent an amount of Rs. 3.6 crore for economic upliftment of tribals and Rs. 6.5 crore towards development of roads and communication in tribal areas in Andhra Pradesh, Assam, Bihar, Orissa and Madhya Pradesh. During the Plan period, the Government established 4000 schools, 653 Forest Labour Cooperatives and 111 cottage industries, 312 multipurpose cooperatives were also formed in Orissa, Bihar and Madhya Pradesh for the economic development of tribals.

The Second Five Year Plan (1956–61)

The second Five Year Plan emphasised economic development in the fields of agriculture, cottage industries and forest cooperatives. The most important strategy of the Government was to establish as many as 43 multipurpose Tribal Development Blocks throughout the country as Central Sponsored Schemes. Besides, the Government of Andhra Pradesh established a separate agency, namely Girijan Cooperative Corporation for marketing tribal forest produce. Inspired by this, the States of Orissa, Bihar and Madhya Pradesh also set up Marketing Cooperatives for tribals in their States. During this Plan period, the Government of India spent an amount of Rs. 42.92 crore under various tribal development programmes.

The Third Five Year Plan (1961–66)

During this Plan, priority was given to the opening of tribal development blocks as overall units of development. The number of tribal development blocks was increased to 415 by the end of the Plan period. In addition, the various economic programmes were undertaken in the field of land reclamation, forest conservation, minor irrigation, supply of agricultural inputs and development of animal husbandry. An amount of Rs. 60.43 crore was spent on various programmes during this period.

The Fourth Five Year Plan (1969–74)

The Fourth Five year Plan envisaged that the tribal development blocks situated within a district should be grouped into one or more tribal development areas. Accordingly, six pilot projects known as Tribal Development Agencies were started as Central Sponsored Schemes to develop the tribal areas integrating various programmes implemented under the general sector. In 1971–72, six pilot projects were established in 4 States, *i.e.*, one each in Andhra Pradesh (in Srikakulam) and Bihar (in Singhbum), two in Madhya Pradesh (both in Bastar) and two in Orissa (Koraput and Ganjam). During the Plan period, Rs. 44 crore were released to the project.

The Fifth Five Year Plan (1974–78)

The strategy of the Fifth Five Year Plan was to ensure integrated tribal development programmes. The new strategy intended to cover two types of tribal areas, namely *(i)* Scheduled areas or other areas having more than 50 per cent of tribal population and *(ii)* Non-Scheduled areas with large but dispersed tribal population. The strategy for areas of tribal concentration culminated in the concept of Tribal Sub-Plans (TSPs) for these areas. The sub-plan of each State was divided into various Integrated Tribal Development Projects (ITDP). Out of Rs. 190 crore of the Plan outlay of the Central Government, only Rs. 112.35 crore was spent on the development programmes.

191, ITDPs were established in 17 States and 2 Union Territories. Moreover, 268 Modified Area Development Approach (MADA) pockets in

74 clusters were identified under the tribal sub-plan in respect of family-oriented income generating schemes. Special attention was paid to the development of Primitive Tribal Development under the TSP approach. Besides, there were group-based programmes like Large Sized Agricultural Multipurpose Cooperative Societies (LAMPS) for bringing the tribals into the cooperative movement and to eliminate money-lenders, middlemen and forest contractors. Thus, organisation of LAMPS were taken up in the Fifth Plan itself.

The Sixth Five Year Plan (1980–85)

The Plan envisaged a four-fold policy for the development of Scheduled Tribes:

(i) Integration of services at the delivery point of beneficiary,
(ii) Development of the service from the bottom upwards,
(iii) Development of skills to diversify occupations; and
(iv) Introduction of latest technology based on local material and local skills.

The Plan emphasised a three-dimensional approach to tribal development, namely

(a) Area approach	:	Development of natural resources and social infrastructure.
(b) Target group approach	:	Meant for those tribals who do not benefit from area approach.
(c) Economic approach	:	Programmes to be relevant without interfering in their traditional way of life and culture.

The Government of India spent Rs. 485 crores for tribal development programmes during the Sixth Plan period. More than 2000 LAMPS were set up with about 58 per cent tribal membership.

The Seventh Five Year Plan (1985–90)

The Seventh Five Year Plan focussed attention on the economic development of the tribal areas and tribal families. Development of skills, technology and exploitation of natural resources were the primary aspects of tribal area development. The TSP programmes were intended to uplift at least 30 lakh tribal families during the Plan period. Strengthening of LAMPS in tribal areas was one of the major tasks of the Seventh Plan. Much emphasis was laid in the coordination of Tribal Development Cooperative Corporation of various States. A national level body, *i.e.*, Tribal Cooperative Marketing Development Federation of India (TCMDFI) was established by Government of India in 1987 to provide market support by offering Scheduled Tribes, the best possible price for minor forest produce (MFP).

In addition, the National Scheduled Castes and Scheduled Tribes Finance and Development Corporation was also established. A sum of

Rs. 839.5 crore was released as Special Central Assistance for Tribal Sub Plan during the Seventh Plan.

The Eighth Five Year Plan (1992–97)

The Eighth Five Year Plan envisaged the following:

(i) TRIFED through the State Tribal Cooperative Corporations would organise collection and marketing of MFP in such a way as to ensure reasonable returns to tribals.

(ii) A new policy on Minor Forest Produce (MFP) in relation to the Scheduled Tribes was to be formulated. The cooperative structure in the field for this purpose would be suitably oriented and restructured.

(iii) The functioning of cooperative institutions including LAMPS in tribal areas would be reviewed with a view to meeting the genuine needs of tribal people in credit and marketing of MFP and supply of essential commodities.

In addition, cooperatives for different occupational groups amongst the Scheduled Tribes were to be formed. An important objective of the Eighth Plan was to provide increased access to credit from Banks and Cooperative Institutions by the tribals.

The Ninth Five Year Plan (1997–2002)

For the development of primitive groups, all the research institutions, NGOs and Self-Help Groups (SHGs) involved in the creation of awareness, confidence building, training of tribals in various skills would be given 100 per cent assistance. An 11-member Scheduled Areas and Scheduled Tribes Commission is being set up under Article 335 (1) of the Constitution and a National Institute for Training and Research in Tribal Affairs would be set up at New Delhi, as an apex body for the TRIs set up by State Governments. Rs. 250 crore would be earmarked for setting up 100 residential schools for tribals. Special incentives for tribal women and children in 136 districts in 11 States, have been given such as free land, school uniforms, free medical check-up and adult education for parents of girls. As a safety net against starvation and to check deaths of children due to starvation, village grain banks would be organised on a fully participative and community-based basis. Many Central schemes are on a 50 : 50 cost-sharing basis with the State Governments such as tribal education, medical facilities, vocational training, *etc.*, are being continued.

Government Interventions

The Central and State Governments have allocated funds for tribal development over the years so as to sustain their own development through economic activities. This interventionist theory is being increasingly challenged by economists and sociologists. These well-meaning efforts serve to point out the truth of the adage that the road to hell is paved with good intentions. The sad truth is that these tribal programmes launched with great fanfare and publicity are designed to help the tribal people, give marginal employment to more non-tribals and a few tribal people and ensures that the 'trickle-down' theory of development benefits some tribal people. But at what cost and for how many people ? Such 'doles' are not good for the tribal people as these programmes are designed by bureaucrats on the basis of the theory that 'the boss knows best'. The bureaucrat assumes that by virtue of his position and the doles that can be handed out, he can bring about tribal development. It is sheer arrogance of power and privilege that lets the Government officials get away with this line of thinking, year after year, for over 50 years! Bureaucrats rarely have the time, energy or the inclination to try and understand what is actually needed by the tribal people. Instead of grandiose schemes applied uniformly over all tribal areas all over the country, it would be better to have a few micro-area tribal projects, well-targeted and aimed at specific improvements in the tribal infrastructure which are needed by the tribal people. Rare is the bureaucrat who has the patience to try and understand what the tribal people really need. And rarer still is the bureaucrat who designs specific micro-plans to meet the tribal people's demands. The tribal people are being exploited in the name of development and all tribal development schemes are based on the 'top-down' planning approach. As tribal people are considered too primitive to know what is in their best interests, the bureaucrat has all the answers! This heavy-handed developmental approach has only marginally helped the tribal people. If this same money had been spent after involving the tribal people in participatory planning approaches, the rate of wastage of funds would have been lower, money siphoned off would have been much less and tribal development could actually have been a reality. And if (a very big if), the tribal people could have managed their own development, tribal development would have been on the road to sustainability. Any Government developmental initiative is basically an intervention or an innovation in the tribal system. Are these innovations or interventions necessary or are they harmful for the tribal people ? A study of various types of innovations is needed so that the right type of intervention emerges. These development interventions need to be self-sustaining and participative. The Government programmes are certainly not self-sustaining and if funding dries up, most of these programmes die a natural death. An inventory of the various planning fads and foibles over the past 50 years, will reveal that the Government programmes which were planned in splendid isolation are interpreted for implementation with dubious motives and die a natural death when funds are choked off or are diverted for yet another 'brilliant' tribal development scheme! This theory of 'tribal development plans' is still valid today. However, an interesting development is that while the earlier Government programmes have vanished, the bureaucracy spawned in its wake continues, sometimes in new forms, to proliferate and flourish. The tribals may not flourish but the tribal development bureaucracy does. Today, many

Government posts in tribal areas, especially those for teachers and doctors, are vacant for years as rarely do people serve in underdeveloped tribal areas and about 30–40 per cent posts remain vacant for years. This has been brought out in a Government report on the KBK district (undivided Koraput, Bolangir, Kalahandi) in Orissa by the Central team led by Shri JNL Srivastava, Joint Secretary, Ministry of Agriculture, Government of India, in 1997.

As all States have not taken uniform measures for the promotion and development of the tribal people, it would be instructive to study the regulatory and developmental initiatives taken in Orissa which has a large number of tribal people. Protective legislations enacted by some States for preventing land alienation are set out at Annexure 5.2 while those relating to debt redemption and money-lending are set out at Annexure 5.3.

The measures undertaken by the Government of Orissa for development of Scheduled Tribes in the State can be divided into two broad categories, *viz.*, *(i)* Regulatory and *(ii)* Developmental. As a result of stricter enforcement of the special regulatory measures, protection has been afforded to a great extent to the interests of the tribal people. Besides, implementation of special development programmes has to some extent improved the socio-economic conditions of these people. The details of the measures are given below:

Regulatory Measures

The following major regulatory measures have been taken for providing protection to the STs as well as the SCs against all forms of exploitation and conserving their assets for visible economic growth.

(a) Unlawful transfer of land belonging to Scheduled Castes and Scheduled Tribes has been prohibited under the Orissa (Scheduled Areas) Transfer of Immovable Property (by Scheduled Tribes) Regulation, 1956 and the Orissa Land Reform Act, 1964.

(b) Drastic amendments of the Orissa (Scheduled Areas) Money Lenders Regulation , 1967 and the Orissa Money Lenders Act, 1939 to liquidate the indebtedness of the SCs and STs.

(c) Eradication of untouchability and elimination of atrocities.

(d) Monetary relief to the victims of atrocities on members belonging to SCs and STs.

(e) Bonded Labour System (Abolition) Act, 1976.

(f) The Orissa Legal Aid to the Poor Rules, 1975 replaced by Orissa State Legal Aid Advice Programme, 1981 and Orissa State Legal Aid and Advice Scheme, 1981.

(g) The Orissa Reservation of Vacancies in Posts and Services (for SCs and STs) Act, 1975.

(h) Incentives for inter-caste marriages between caste-Hindu and Scheduled Castes/Scheduled Tribes to eradicate untouchability

from the Hindu Society and bring greater harmony and amity among them.

All these regulatory measures should have obviously tremendous thrust on the tribal societies to break the centuries old immovability, untouchability and stagnation deep seated on the tribal life of Orissa. But the big questions is how far the tribals of different denominations mostly inhabiting in the mountainous and forested parts of Orissa have been able to avail and enjoy the beneficial fruits of all these ameliorative provisions. The answer is partly negative and partly positive.

It is a fact that a high level of illiteracy is prevalent in the tribal areas and many tribals are not conversant with any of the languages in which documents are drafted. It has also been a fact that the tribal people are not well aware of the intricacies of the monetary system and the implications of documents. Further, in the remote forest areas, the traders and money-lenders are the only sources of credit to meet any eventuality. Resultantly, the regulatory measures have failed to create a tangible impact on the socio-economic life of the tribals, barring a few who are educationally advanced. There have been large scale transfers of tribal land consequent upon the undesirable activities of money-lenders, forest contractors and other exploiters. The reorganisation of forests and enunciation of new policies have resulted in the curtailment of their rights in forests and in fishing and hunting. The industrial and other developmental schemes have led to large-scale displacement of tribal people. There is need, therefore, for strengthening and in some cases, for reorganising the administrative set-up for scheduled areas, sensible policy decisions and careful implementation to protect the interest of the tribals on forest wealth. However, some achievements in implementation of the regulatory measures are furnished as under:

(a) Land Alienation. The Orissa (Scheduled Area) Transfer of Immovable Property (by Scheduled Tribes) Regulation, 1956, prohibits alienation of tribal land without prior approval of competent authority, in absence of which the property can be restored to the owner and any violation of the procedures will warrant initiation of proceedings. Upto the end of March 1993, 73,628 land alienation cases were initiated and 70,698 cases were finalised and 41,611.05 acre of land ware restored to 36,247 ST land owners.

(b) Release and Rehabilitation of Bonded Labourers. Since enactment of the Bonded Labour System (Abolition) Act, 1976, till the end of March 1993, about 49,824 bonded labourers have been identified of which 19,751 belong to ST categories and 13,351 to SC categories and the rest belong to other economically weaker sections of society. Out of the 49,824 identified bonded labourers, 48,912 have been released of which 19,641 belong to ST group and 12,945 SC group and the rest belong to other groups. Provision has been made for economic rehabilitation of the released bonded labourers by way of providing them avenues for gainful self-employment. From among the released bonded labourers, 46,781 have been rehabilitated of which 18,090 belong to ST category, 12,772 to SC category and 15,919 to other communities.

(c) Orissa Reservation of Vacancies Act, 1975. The Orissa Reservation of Vacancies in Posts and Services (for Scheduled Tribes and Scheduled Castes) Act, 1975, has been in force since 01 July 1975 which guarantees reservation of vacancies for ST and SC communities in initial appointment as well as in promotions, to all categories of posts at the rate of 23 per cent for ST and 15 per cent for SC candidates. Besides, for initial appointment, certain concessions like relaxation of upper age limit by 5 years, relaxation of experience wherever necessary by 2 years, exception of prescribed fees for competitive examinations and payment of journey fare for attending written tests and interview, *etc.*, are also given to ST and SC candidates at present.

Developmental Programmes

The developmental programmes aimed at achieving twin objectives, *viz.*, *(i)* area development in terms of provision of essential infrastructure like irrigation facilities, communication, health, promotion of education, development of horticulture and soil conservation, strengthening credit delivery structures, rural electrification, drinking water supply, *etc.*, and *(ii)* economic upliftment of individual tribal families by providing them income-generating durable assets under Integrated Rural Development Programme (IRDP), Economic Rehabilitation of Rural Poor (ERRP) supplemented by assistance from Special Central Assistance (SCA) and various sectors of the State Plan. The different developmental strategies adopted for tribal development after independence are as under:

Scheduled Areas. In order to give pointed attention to the needs of the tribal people, about 45 per cent of the State's area measuring 69,613.9 Sq.Kms and having concentration of tribal population has been declared as Scheduled Area under the Fifth Schedule of the Constitution.

Community Development. Soon after the beginning of the First Five Year Plan when the Community Development Programme was initiated, the tribal areas also received special attention and till the commencement of the Second Five Year Plan, the tribal welfare programme was more humanitarian and meant to ameliorate and extend medical and educational benefits to them. Community development approach in tribal areas was given a developmental orientation in the Second Five Year Plan by introducing Special Multipurpose Tribal Development (SMTD) blocks in a few areas predominantly inhabitated by the tribals. The working of the SMTD blocks was reviewed by the end of the Second Five Year Plan and subsequently, the concept of Tribal Development Block was evolved and under this, 75 TD blocks were carved out in the State out of 314 blocks. These Tribal Development Blocks continued till the end of the Fourth Five Year Plan.

Tribal Sub-plan Approach. A detailed and comprehensive review of the tribal problems was taken up on the eve of the Fifth Five Year Plan and the concept of Tribal Sub-Plan, as a strategy for development, was adopted in the year 1975 which is considered as a significant step in the history of Tribal Development. Under the TSP approach, various developmental projects, *viz.*, ITDP, MADA, Cluster, DTDP, micro projects were initiated for removal of the socio-economic and educational backwardness of the tribals living in compact as well as scattered areas. The same strategy with varied emphasis is continuing till now for achieving the following objectives:

(*a*) raising the productivity levels of the economic activities in which tribals are engaged with a view to enabling the targeted families to cross the poverty line,

(*b*) development of human resources and upgradation of education,

(*c*) elimination of exploitation of tribals especially as a result of land alienation, money lending, debt bondage, trade, *etc.*,

(*d*) development of critical infrastructure.

The Tribal Sub-Plan is termed as a plan within the State Plan and aims at all-round development of the tribals and tribal areas. It has been laid down in principle that funds should be earmarked by all departments for the development of sub-plan areas and the quantum of budgetary allocation must not fall short of the population equivalent to the scheduled tribe population. Central assistance for implementation of tribal development projects is available as an additive fund.

The various projects under implementation for development of the tribals are briefly discussed below:

(a) Integrated Tribal Development Projects (ITDP). The blocks having 50 per cent and above tribal concentration have been brought under the umbrella of Tribal Sub-Plan and Integrated Tribal Development Projects (ITDP) are being implemented.

The functions of the ITDAs are multi-pronged in nature and it functions not only as a nodal agency in terms of plan formulation, implementation of programmes and monitoring of progress but also implements specific programmes mostly out of Special Central Assistance (SCA). Each ITDA is manned by a whole-time Project Administrator assisted by a Special Officer of Class II rank. Besides, each ITDA has been given engineering staff consisting of one Assistant Engineer and two to four Junior Engineers for execution of small civil/minor irrigation works. In addition to the normal staff of the line Departments stationed in ITDA areas, Soil Conservation Assistant/Agriculture Extension Officers have been posted to ITDAs as a measure to strengthen the ITDAs. One Additional Welfare Extension Officer has also been posted to assist the BDO in identification of beneficiaries, processing of loan applications, sponsoring the same to financial institutions and to pursue sanction and disbursement of loans. Project level committees have been constituted for each ITDA of which the

Collector of the concerned district is the Chairman. The local MPs, MLAs, Chairmen of Panchayat Samitis, representatives of tribal women and all district level officers-in-charge of development programmes/departments are members. The Project Administrator is the Member Secretary and is fully responsible for formulation and implementation of plan programmes.

(b) Modified Area Development Approach (MADA). The concept of Modified Area Development Approach has been evolved towards the end of Fifth Plan when it was realised that quite a sizable tribal population was still outside the ITDP area and that they had to be brought under the specific development focus. Accordingly, beyond the ITDP areas, contiguous small areas having a population of 10,000 or more, with 50 per cent tribal concentration were identified under Modified Area Development Approach.

Both individual benefit oriented schemes and community benefit oriented programmes for the welfare of tribals are under implementation in these pockets out of Special Central Assistance. The Block Development Officer of the concerned block executes the MADA project and the MADA funds are released to the concerned Block Development Officer for utilisation. However, the programme is overseen by a MADA level Advisory Committee headed by the concerned Sub-Collector. An additional Welfare Extension Officer has been given to each MADA Block. There are also two special officers to oversee implementation of MADA programmes in undivided Kalahandi and Sambalpur districts where the MADA pockets are more.

(c) Cluster Approach. Beyond the MADA pockets, there were still small areas of tribal concentration remaining uncovered under the specific tribal development programmes. During the Seventh Five Year Plan, the cluster approach was adopted for contiguous areas having 5,000 population or more with atleast 50 per cent tribal concentration.

The administrative arrangement for the cluster is similar to that of MADA pockets except that no additional Welfare Extension Officer has been provided. The Welfare Extension Officer of the concerned block looks after the programme. For all-round development of tribals in these clusters, in addition to normal programme, SCA is provided for implementation of individual and community benefit oriented programmes.

The BDO of the concerned blocks execute the cluster programmes. There is a cluster level Advisory Committee in the pattern of MADA pockets to plan, review and oversee implementation of the programmes in cluster pockets.

(d) Micro Projects for Development of Primitive Tribal Groups. At the time of formulation of TSPs during the Fifth Plan, it was felt that among the tribal groups, there are a number of tribes which still continue to be in pre-agricultural stage or practising shifting cultivation and are at subsistence level of economy either dependent on forests or poor land. It

was further recognised that these tribal communities need special attention. Many of these tribes are scattered all over the country and their socio-economic conditions differ. In most cases, they are adversely affected by changes taking place around their habitat.

The criteria for identifying primitive tribes laid down by GOI are *(i)* tribes which still continue to depend on food-gathering, hunting or shifting cultivation, *(ii)* low literacy rate, *i.e.*, ranging from 0 to 5 percent, *(iii)* dwindling population because of special health problems and, lastly, *(iv)* as a group they are agricultural labourers.

The primitive tribes residing in the micro-project areas get hundred percent subsidy in individual family beneficiary-oriented schemes funded out of funds provided by the Ministry of Welfare. Development of core economic sectors like agriculture, horticulture, soil conservation, animal husbandry besides provisioning for drinking water, education, health, *etc.*, is also aimed at.

(e) Dispersed Tribal Development Project. The tribal sub-plan strategy has been further refined and extended to cover all the tribals including the dispersed tribals under beneficiary oriented schemes.

Various Corporations have been established by the States for providing financial assistance to scheduled tribe and also scheduled caste families living below the poverty line by way of arranging institutional credit for them for undertaking various income generating activities in agriculture, animal husbandry, fisheries, small and cottage industries, small business sectors. Besides, these Corporations implement several other developmental programmes, such as community irrigation projects like tubewell projects, river-lift projects, water harvesting structures, training programmes under TRYSEM, training in shorthand/typewriting and various other vocational activities. Besides, the National Scheme for Liberation and Rehabilitation of Scavengers and their dependents is being implemented with a view to rehabilitating the scavengers and their dependents in alternative vocations. The Corporations also provide margin money loans and subsidy to help SC/ST beneficiaries set up different income generating activities.

PLAN ALLOCATION AND UTILISATION DURING THE SUCCESSIVE FIVE YEAR PLANS: CASE-STUDY OF ORISSA

Quantification of funds from different sources for Tribal Sub-Plan area and fixing of physical targets to be achieved under different sectoral programmes for speedier development of the tribal areas and the life of the tribals, was the characteristic feature of the TSP approach. Prior to the Fifth Plan, no earmarking of funds out of State Plan resources for utilisation in the tribal areas was made. But under the Sub-Plan approach, quantification of funds from the State Plan resources for utilisation in the tribal areas in reasonable proportion became almost mandatory. Further, by providing quantified funds under a separate minor head in the budget of the concerned department, diversion from sub-plan funds to non-sub-plan area was prohibited.

Upto the Fourth Five Year Plan, special funds were provided under the Backward Classes Welfare Sector for the welfare of the scheduled tribes in addition to general development sector outlays which would normally accrue to the tribal people. It has not been possible to identify the portion of outlays under general sector that might have been utilised for the benefit of the Scheduled Tribes. Such investments are identifiable in financial terms only in case of Backward Classes Welfare Sector which as indicated above, is however supplementary to whatever provision is available for development of tribals and scheduled areas under general sector. The Table 5.1 would indicate the plan outlays and expenditure in the State from the First Plan to the Fourth Plan and share of the Backward Classes Welfare Sector (BCWS) during the corresponding period.

Table 5.1
Plan Outlay and Expenditure

[Rs. Crore]

Plan	*Total State Outlay*	*Outlays for ST under the BCWS*			*Expen-diture against Col. 2*	*Expen-diture against Col. 3*	*Expen-diture against Col. 4*	*Expen-diture against Col. 5*
		State	*Central*	*Total*				
1	2	3	4	5	6	7	8	9
First Plan (1952-53 to 1955-56)	20.07	—	—	2.01	18.42	2.02	—	2.02 (10.94)**
Second Plan (1956-57 to 1960-61)	99.99	3.18	2.87	6.05 (6.22)**	86.59	2.68	2.70	5.38 (6.05)*
Third Plan (1961-62 to 1965-66)	227.58	2.99	3.47	6.46 (2.84)*	224.89	2.84	3.05	5.89 (2.62)**
Annual Plans (1966-69)	126.06	0.96	3.32	4.27 (3.38)*	124.98	0.82	2.99	3.81 (3.05)**
Fourth Plan (1969-70 to 1973-74)	222.60	2.82	5.58	8.40 (3.77)*	256.00	3.14	5.20	8.34 (3.26)**
Total	696.30	9.95	15.24	25.19 (3.61)*	710.88	11.50	13.94	25.44 (3.58)**

* Share in percentage of outlay under BCWS in the total outlays.
** Share in percentage of expenditure under BCWS in the total expenditure.
Source: Unpublished Data from THRTI, Bhubaneswar.

It can be seen from the above that between the Plans, the growth rate in investment (outlays and expenditure) for the scheduled tribes under the Backward Classes Welfare Sector has been much less than the growth rate of investment under general sector. While the total State outlays has increased from Rs. 20.07 crore in the First Plan to Rs. 222.60 crore in the Fourth Plan, *i.e.*, by 11 times, the outlays under Backward Classes Welfare Sector for scheduled tribes has increased from Rs. 2.01 crore during the First Plan to Rs. 8.40 crore only, *i.e.*, about 4 times in the Fourth Plan. The rate of expenditure also indicates a similar record. Looking at it from another angle, it can be further observed that the rate of investment under BCWS for scheduled tribes has gradually diminished. While the expenditure on STs during the First Plan was about 11 per cent of the total plan expenditure, it has steadily diminished during the Second and Third Plan and has come down to about 3 per cent during the Fourth Plan.

The schemes undertaken till then for welfare of STs (such as payment of subsidies for cottage industries, supply of bullocks a few residential schools here and there) have not been effective in bringing about any perceptible change in their mode of life. This is mainly because the schemes were isolated and outlays meagre, whereas comprehensive measures in shape of packages of programmes with larger investments were called for. Such integrated programmes could not possibly be undertaken out of the limited resources of the BCWS which have always been treated as supplemental to the efforts of the general sector for improving the condition of the backward classes through their own programmes. But regrettably, the general sector resources that have flown to the backward areas or for the benefit of backward classes have fallen much short of the desired extent. Furthermore, past experience has often shown that wherever additional funds have been provided for tribal development under a special programme, there has been a tendency to reduce correspondingly the benefits accruing to the tribal areas from the normal programmes and provisions under the plans. Consequently, the supplemental efforts of the Backward Classes Welfare Sector have practically resulted in dilution of efforts and dissipation of resources leading to the widening of disparities and furtherance of regional imbalances. The statistical information as regards involvement of institutional finance during the above plan period is not available and hence, no assessment could be made possible about the quantum of credit flow for the benefit of the tribals.

Preparation of Tribal Sub-Plan was initiated at the beginning of the Fifth Plan after Sub-Plan approach was adopted as an effective instrument for tribal development. The implementation of TSP enhanced the flow of funds to the sub-plan areas out of the State Plan and other sources. The TSP approach envisaged the integrated development of the tribal areas in which all programmes irrespective of their sources of fundings would operate in unison to achieve a common goal of bringing these areas at par with the rest of the State and to improve the quality of life style of the tribals. The sources of investments in tribal sub-plan areas are as follows:

(i) State Plan
(ii) Central/Centrally Sponsored Schemes
(iii) Special Central Assistance

(iv) Institutional Finance.

At the time of finalisation of the sub-plan for the Fifth Five Year Plan (1974-75 to 1978-79), the Planning Commission had stipulated a minimum outlay of Rs. 127.35 crore out of the State Plan resources. But actually, the utilisation of State Plan funds in the sub-plan area during the above period was Rs. 141.67 crore which worked out to 24.07 per cent of the total State Plan outlay. During the Fifth Plan, the GOI in the Ministry of Home Affairs released a sum of Rs. 26.79 crore in the shape of Special Central Assistance (SCA) for implementing various programmes in the sub-plan areas. This was additive to the State Plan resources for supplementing the efforts of the State Government in the development of Sub-Plan areas. However, the utilisation was to the tune of Rs. 24.18 crore. Under Central and Centrally-sponsored schemes, against the projected outlay of Rs. 20.00 crore, a sum of Rs. 33.94 crore was utilised in the TSP area for implementation of various developmental programmes during the Fifth Plan. Thus, from different sources, a sum of Rs. 199.79 crore was utilised in TSP areas for implementation of various developmental programmes during the Fifth Plan. This does not, however, include the flow of institutional finance. Even though a sum of Rs. 21.00 crore was projected under this head, its achievement is not known.

During 1979–80, the plan outlay for the tribal sub-plan was fixed at Rs. 84.64 crore. As against this, the actual expenditure was of the order of Rs. 75.46 crore as detailed below:

Table 5.2
Tribal Sub-plan During 1979–80

[Rs. Crore]

	Sources	*Amount allocated*	*Amount utilised*
(i)	State Plan	64.75	55.65
(ii)	Central and Centrally Sponsored Schemes	11.09	11.09
(iii)	Special Central Assistance	8.80	8.72
	Total	84.64	75.46

Source: THRTI, Bhubaneswar.

One of the major achievements of the Sixth and Seventh Five Year Plans is the very substantial increase in investment in sub-plan areas from all resources, *i.e.,* from State Plan, Central and Centrally Sponsored Programmes and Special Central Assistance was to the extent of about Rs. 686.00 crore in the Sixth Plan and Rs. 1,442.00 crore in the Seventh Plan as against Rs. 199.00 crore in the Fifth Plan. The details of investment during Sixth and Seventh Plan were as under:

Table 5.3
Total Expenditure during the Sixth and Seventh Plan

[Rs. Crore]

	Sources	*Sixth plan expenditure*	*Seventh plan expenditure*
(i)	State Plan	521.82	998.63
(ii)	Central and Centrally Sponsored Schemes	107.67	352.53
(iii)	Special Central Assistance	56.59	91.17
	Total	686.08	1,442.33

Source: THRTI, Bhubaneswar.

The funds available from the State Plan for investment in tribal areas formed about 38 per cent and 31 per cent of the total State Plan outlays made for Sixth and Seventh Plan respectively. The involvement of institutional finance in TSP is estimated to be Rs. 26.54 crore.

The Seventh Plan was followed by two Annual Plans in 1990–91 and 1991–92. The flow of funds from different sources (except institutional finance) for the tribals during these two years is indicated as under:

Table 5.4
Expenditure on Tribal Development during 1990–92

[Rs. Crore]

	Sources	*1990–91*	*1991–92*
(i)	State Plan	269.02	381.86
(ii)	Central and Centrally Sponsored Schemes	22.60	25.62
(iii)	Special Central Assistance	93.78	173.44
	Total	385.40	580.92

Source: THRTI, Bhubaneswar.

The estimated flow of funds for the tribals during the Eighth Plan Period (1992–93 to 1996–97) aggregates to Rs. 3,543.37 crore, the details of source of which are as follows:

Table 5.5
Expenditure on Tribal Development during the Eight Plan

[Rs. Crore]

	Sources	*Amount*
(i)	State Plan	2,697.48
(ii)	Central/Centrally Sponsored Schemes	678.31
(iii)	Special Central Assistance	167.58
	Total	3,543.37

Source: THRTI, Bhubaneswar.

The share of funds flow to Tribal Sub-Plan areas out of State Plan outlay during the entire Eighth Plan Period and during 1992–93, 1993–94 and 1994–95 is worked out as under:

Table 5.6
State Sub-plan Outlay during the Eight Plan

[Rs. Crore]

Year	*Total state plan outlay*	*Flow to sub-plan*	*Percentage of flow of funds to TSP to total state plan outlays*
Eighth Plan (1992-93 to 1996-97)	10,000	2,697.48	27
1992-93	1,007.80	304.56	30
1993-94	1,209.15	367.01	30
1994-95	1,950.00	348.40	18

Source: THRTI, Bhubaneswar.

The allocation for the sub-plan during the year 1994–95 appears illogical as the same forms about 18 per cent of the total State Plan outlays *vis-a-vis* the tribal population which constitute about 22 per cent of the State's total population.

During the Seventh Plan period 1985-90 and Annual Plan 1990–91, SCA funds were utilised mainly for the family-oriented income-generating schemes along with development of critical infrastructure which is incidental or supportive to family-oriented schemes and the schemes relating to human resource development. Since the beginning of the Seventh Plan, allocation of SCA funds to different sectors/programmes was being done on the basis of the feasible proposals received from different line departments and ITDA's at the beginning of the year.

For speedy implementation and to ensure ITDA-wise proper allocation of funds, the State Government has changed the idea of placing funds with the departments from the year 1990–91. At present, SCA funds for ST are being kept in the Tribal Welfare budget and are being utilised through projects such as ITDA, MICRO, MADA, CLUSTERS and DTDP following the guidelines issued by Government of India. However, as far as possible, different sectoral departments are involved in the implementation of various income-generating activities.

ANTI-POVERTY PROGRAMMES

Scheduled tribes as well as the scheduled caste are mostly backward and they continue to live below the poverty line for many years. They are being assisted by several anti-poverty programmes like IRDP, ERRP, Rehabilitation of Bonded Labourers, *etc.*, to give a boost to their economic status. Besides, several income-generating schemes are also implemented through the ITDA's.

The coverage of scheduled tribe families so far (till 1992–93) under different anti-poverty/rehabilitation programmes in the State is presented below:

(a) Integrated Rural Development Programme (IRDP). The Integrated Rural Development Programme is an important anti-poverty programme launched by the Government in the year 1979–80 which aims at reduction of unemployment in rural areas and provision of inputs for creation of assets by the rural poor for enabling them to rise above the poverty line. The strategy for IRDP is to assist the target group of beneficiaries with the objective of creating income-generating assets by way of providing credits and subsidies and develop their skills to manage the same, so that they can supplement their family income.

Upto the end of the Seventh Plan Period as many as 11.04 lakh beneficiaries were covered with a total investment of Rs. 30,372.57 lakh. In 1991–92, Rs. 7,098.98 lakh was invested for assisting about 1.12 lakh beneficiaries. In the first year of the Eighth Plan, *i.e.,* in 1992-93, about 93,325 persons were benefited with an investment of Rs. 6,283.43 lakh. Out of the 11.04 lakh beneficiaries, upto end of the Seventh Plan, 27 per cent belonged to ST category. Similarly, the coverage of ST in 1990–91 was 32 per cent and in 1991–92 and 1992-93, the coverage was 31 per cent of the total number of beneficiaries assisted. The details are furnished as under:

Table 5.7
IRDP Covered during Plan Periods

Period	*Beneficiaries covered (families)*					*Investment (Rs. lakhs)*			*Expenditure per beneficiary*
	SC	*ST*	*OC*	*Total*	*Women*	*Subsidy*	*Credit*	*Total*	
Upto 7th Plan	258122	300306	546153	1104581	178259	12141.32	18231.25	30372.57	2765
1990–91	536501	48327	64784	149612	50337	3078.62	3253.19	6331.81	4232
1991–92	30429	34535	46748	111712	47360	3229.86	3869.12	7098.98	6354
1992–93	24849	28838	39639	93326	38587	2804.40	3479.03	6283.43	6740

Source: THRTI, Bhubaneswar.

(b) Training for Rural Youth for Self-employment (TRYSEM). The objective of the scheme TRYSEM is to provide technical and entrepreneural skill on selected trades to the poor rural youth within the age group 15–35 to enable them to take up self-employment programmes and thus it is a supporting component of IRDP. The trained youths are given credit facilities through banks for undertaking their own business/industry. The following table gives a picture of achievements under this scheme since its inception.

By the end of the Seventh Plan, out of 93,459 trained youths, STs accounted for 18.8 per cent. Similarly, out of 50,162 trained youths rehabilitated, 19.3 per cent belonged to ST category. During 1992–93, about 16,785 youths were trained of which 23.2 per cent belonged to ST category and out of the 15,072 rehabilitated youths, 32.4 per cent belonged to ST category. It may be marked that participation of the tribals in this programmes is marginally increasing over the years.

Table 5.8
Achievements of TRYSEM during the Plan Periods

Period	*Youths trained*					*Youths rehabilitated*				
	SC	*ST*	*OC*	*Total*	*Women*	*SC*	*ST*	*Others*	*Total*	*Women*
Upto end of 7th Plan	22944	17563	52952	93459	26812	13417	9670	27075	50162	12727
1990–91	3166	3001	6559	12726	5357	4279	4741	9042	18062	7575
1991–92	6517	5824	12853	25194	10213	5647	4936	10551	21134	9608
1992–93 (provisional)	4353	3902	8530	16785	7580	3778	4885	6409	15072	6282

Source: THRTI, Bhubaneswar.

(c) Indira Awas Yojana. The Indira Awas Yojana was launched for constructing low-cost houses for houseless SC, ST and released bonded labourers. By the end of the Seventh Plan, 22,033 houses were constructed with a cost of Rs. 2585.88 lakh. During the years 1990–91, 1991–92 and 1992-93, 9,041, 17,028 and 11,305 houses respectively were constructed for which the expenditure was Rs. 1,177.99 lakh, Rs. 2,099.51 lakh and Rs. 1,402.39 lakh during the corresponding years. 17,028 houses have been constructed with an expenditure of Rs. 2,099.51 lakh. Similarly, during 1992–93, 11,305 houses were constructed with an investment of Rs. 1,402.39 lakh. The share of ST people under the Yojana is not available.

(d) Jawahar Rojgar Yojana. This scheme being implemented from 1989–90 with the objective of generating gainful employment for the unemployed and under-employed persons in rural area, creating productive community assets for benefiting the families below poverty line and for strengthening rural infrastructure which will add to the rapid growth of rural economy and lead to steady rise in the income levels of the rural poor. The expenditure incurred and employment generated under this programme is furnished below:

Table 5.9
Achievements under Jawahar Rojgar Yojana during 1989-1993

Year	*Employment generated (in lakh man-days)*				*Total expenditure (Rs. lakh)*
	SC	*ST*	*OC*	*Total*	
1989–90	157.70	205.81	154.12	517.63	17,369.29
1990–91	102.62	127.42	111.93	341.97	12,845.26
1991–92	105.39	127.99	115.48	348.86	14,053.59
1992–93	96.92	119.73	109.74	326.39	13,067.15

Source: THRTI, Bhubaneswar.

(e) Drought Prone Area Programme (DPAP). DPAP has been in operation in 39 drought prone blocks in the State in 4 districts, *i.e.*, undivided Kalahandi, Phulbani, Bolangir and Sambalpur. This multisectoral programme aims at restoration of the ecological balance and drought-prone areas through harmonious management of land, water and other natural resources. Emphasis has been given on soil and water conservation, development of water resources, such as construction of Minor Irrigation Projects, Lift Irrigation Projects, Water Harvesting Structures, *etc.* Under Forestry Sector, plantations are taken up in the areas like degraded forest, Government wasteland and the cultivable wasteland to restore ecological balance. Under Animal Husbandry Sector, emphasis has been given for pasture development in the gochar and Government wasteland to meet the fodder needs of the locality. Under horticulture sector, plantation of species like ber, mango, papaya, pineapple, *etc.*, which can withstand dry spells are taken up in orchards. Availability of funds and expenditure incurred during the period beyond the Seventh Plan can be seen from the Table below:

Table 5.10
Financial Achievements under DPAP during 1990–91 to 1992–93

[Rs. lakh]

Year	*Funds available*	*Amount spent*	*Percentage of utilisation*
1990–91	832.49	545.48	65.5
1991–92	801.60	726.29	90.5
1992–93	480.32	563.41	117.3

Source: THRTI, Bhubaneswar.

(f) Rehabilitation of Bonded Labourers. As already reported, since the introduction of rehabilitation scheme in 1978, 48,912 bonded labourers have been released and 46,781 rehabilitated by the end of 1992–93 of which 38.7 per cent belonged to the ST categories.

(g) Distribution of Ceiling Surplus Land and Government Wasteland. By end of October 1992, about 1,10,011 acre of ceiling surplus land has been distributed among 47,644 ST and 43,606 SC landless families. Similarly, upto end of December 1992, about 5,09,847.00 acres of Government wasteland has been distributed among 198,890 and 89,489 landless ST and SC families respectively. By end of January 1993, about 18,435.00 acres of wasteland has been distributed among 1,86,263 ST and 1,56,797 SC families.

TARGET FOR EIGHTH FIVE YEAR PLAN

It has been targeted to cover 4,40,497 ST families under different poverty alleviation programmes during the Eighth Five Year Plan period keeping in view the basic objective as it was during the Sixth and Seventh Five Year Plans and the Working Group on Tribal Development. The programme-wise proposed coverage of families during the Eighth Plan is indicated below:

Table 5.11
Families Covered during the Eight Five Year Plan

Schemes/Projects	*No. of families*
IRDP	2,21,686
Assistance to small and marginal farmers	7,300
ITDA scheme	1,47,500
MADA/Clusters	22,000
Micro Projects	2,000
DTDP	25,000
Sericulture	2,500
Fisheries	2,000
Million Well Schemes/Soil	10,511
Conservation/Horticulture/AgricultureSchemes	—
Total	4,40,497

Source: THRTI, Bhubaneswar

Educational Development

Education is one of the most important input for rapid socio-economic development of the scheduled tribe and scheduled caste people. The rate of literacy among STs and SCs are only 22.31 per cent and 36.78 per cent according to 1991 census, in Orissa. The low rate of literacy is attributed to several factors like lack of communication, the age old social customs, habit and superstition, *etc.* Besides, they are unwilling to send their children to schools as they often depend on them for supplementing their family income. With a view to increasing retention of students in schools, residential schools have been opened from primary level to secondary level in the remote tribal areas of the State with provision of free lodging and boarding. These students are provided with facilities like scholarship, stipend, reading and writing materials, garments, *etc.*, to encourage them to continue their education without drop out.

Development of school education from primary level to secondary level in such areas is an indication of popularity of education among the ST and SC communities. There were 1,015 Shevashramas functioning in the State with 20,415 SC students, 54,681 ST students and 30,568 other students on their rolls during 1992–93. Besides, 105 Residential Shevashramas were functioning with 1940 SC, 7,136 ST and 1,631 other category students.

Medical and Public Health Care

For strengthening rural health services, efforts are being made to establish one health sub-centre for every 3,000 population and one PHC for every 20,000 population in the tribal areas. Besides, there will be one Community Health Centre for every 80,000 to 1.20 lakh population which will serve as a reference institution for four Primary Health Centres. Upto end of 1991–92, 2,298 health sub-centres, 296 PHCs/APHCs, 64 SHCs and 6 mobile health units, 156 ayurvedic dispensaries, 139 homeopathic dispensaries, 6 unani dispensaries and 148 allopathic dispensaries were providing health facilities in the tribal areas. During the Eighth Plan, it has been targeted to establish 60 PHCs, 59 CHCs, 70 ayurvedic dispensaries, 70 homeopathic dispensaries and 5 unani dispensaries in the tribal sub-plan areas at an estimated cost of Rs. 4,452.73 lakh.

Drinking Water Supply

Out of 19,204 villages in the tribal sub-plan area, about 17,148 villages have been identified as having no drinking water facilities. By end of the Seventh Plan, about 16,104 such villages have been provided with drinking water facilities by sinking tubewells and the rest 1,044 problem villages are proposed to be provided with safe drinking water during the Eighth Plan period. During 1990–91 and 1991–92, 653 villages were covered. In 1992–93 and 1993–94, 474 villages and 7 villages were provided with safe drinking water facility.

Rural Electrification

For the purpose of providing electricity to the ST and SC concentration villages, rural electrification programmes have been given high priority. Out of 19,204 tribal villages in the State, by the end of 1993–94, 9,860 villages have been electrified which account for about 50 per cent of the total tribal villages.

MONITORING AND IMPLEMENTATION OF TRIBAL SUB-PLAN

As per the existing arrangements, project level committees review the programmes periodically. At the district level, a District Level Review Committee on Tribal Development has been formed under the Chairmanship of the Collector. At the Department level (*i.e.*, Harijan & Tribal Welfare Department), the tribal development programmes are reviewed by the Principal Secretary on the basis of feedback received from the ITDA's/Micro Projects/MADA/Cluster pockets with the assistance of a small monitoring cell.

At the State level, there are two high level committees, one under the Chairmanship of Minister, Harijan & Tribal Welfare and another under the Chairmanship of Chief Secretary to oversee implementation of tribal development programmes. These committees specially review the flow of funds to Tribal sub-plan, its utilisation, measures to be taken to save tribals from exploitation, inter-departmental coordination, removal of bottlenecks, other related matters, *etc.* At the highest level, there is a committee under the Chairmanship of the Chief Minister to oversee, monitor and review the development programmes for the tribals.

Weaknesses of TSP Strategy

Though the TSP strategy has yielded results, these are not commensurate with both the expectations and the investments made so far. The common persistent allegations against implementation of the strategy are indicated as under:

(i) Allotments meant for tribals are spent otherwise for other purposes. The benefits do not reach the tribals.

(ii) No proper accounts about the utilisation of funds at the disposal of other Departments for expenditure on tribal development are maintained. No proper evaluation of programmes and schemes are undertaken. The effectiveness of the committees set up to review the development programmes leaves much to be desired. The reviews are done in a very casual manner and lack orientation and purpose.

(iii) The requirement of personnel for working in tribal areas, specially tribal welfare officers, technical specialists and field level workers has not been properly assessed and posted. There is reportedly chronic shortage of trained workers in the scheduled areas. Further, recruitment of personnel without a long-term view of requirements has proved unsatisfactory. The personnel who are to work in tribal areas must be oriented to the tribal way of life and appreciation of the special disabilities from which the tribal people suffer.

(iv) Development activities more or less conceived on the lines of non-tribal areas have generally failed to make adequate headway and impact on the tribal areas. There is need, therefore, for a larger effort through special institutions and otherwise for giving orientation training to personnel at various levels working in tribal areas. The tribal dominated blocks may be reorganised into smaller blocks so that the benefits of developmental programmes could reach the tribals quickly and conveniently.

(v) Deployment of suitable personnel in tribal areas is a vital factor for tribal development. Most of the tribal areas are inaccessible and unhealthy, characterised by lack of facilities for communication, health, education, entertainment, *etc.* The recommendations of the Maheswar Prasad Group on Administrative arrangements and personnel policy in Tribal Areas include grant of monetary and non-monetary incentives, creation of sub-cadres, lowering the minimum qualification to recruit local persons, training of the staff posted in tribal areas and setting up of special committees at the State, Division and District level for making selection of persons to be posted to these areas. Implementation of the suggestions needs a relook/review for the betterment of the tribals.

(vi) The TSP approach is interpreted as an area approach and, therefore, emphasis is laid on infrastructure development without corresponding emphasis on the development of the Scheduled Tribes. As per the estimate made by the Working Group on development and welfare of the tribals during the Eighth Five Year

Plan, investments on infrastructure development under Tribal sub-plan in Orissa is more than 50 per cent. As a result, even when the overall percentage of investments under TSP has shown positive signs of increase during every Plan period, the ground results do not reflect the achievements. Beneficiary-oriented schemes have received much lesser weightage in all these years.

(vii) In the sectoral allocations under TSP, the schemes under which quantification are made, do not reflect the felt needs of the tribals and do not create the desired impact.

(viii) Under the arrangements, till recently, for allocation of funds under TSP, the Tribal Development Department of the State had very little say both at the planning and implementation stage. Sectoral departments were implementing their schemes/programmes through their own set up in the districts over which the project level staff had no control. There was no earmarking of funds under the strategy of ITDPs. However, for speedy implementation and to ensure ITDA-wise proper allocation of funds, the State Government has changed the idea of placing Special Central Assistance (SCA) funds with other line departments from the year 1990–91. At present, the SCA funds for ST are being kept in the tribal welfare budget and are being utilised through projects such as ITDA, Micro, MADA, Cluster/DTDP following the guidelines issued by Government of India. As far as possible, sectoral departments are involved in the implementation of the income-generating schemes.

(ix) ITDPs were conceived under the TSP strategy as operational units for achieving administrative, organisational and financial integration with a view to promoting speedier development of scheduled tribes. But this integration under TSP strategy has not been possible because they have not been accepted as units of planning. As stated above, quantifications are made under the general schemes and are implemented without any adoption to the needs of the tribals and tribal areas.

(x) The State has, no doubt, enacted protective laws to provide protection to tribals from exploitation by non-tribals. But in actual implementation, this has not received priority. No prompt actions are taken against atrocities on STs in the State.

(xi) Officials have been exploiting or have been instrumental in exploitation of tribal people.

(xii) The non-tribals are mostly recruited (even against the posts reserved for STs) who take less interest in the development of the tribals.

(xiii) The Tribal Welfare Department has been politicised. The activities are politically motivated instead of being amelioration oriented.

(xiv) Senior officers do not visit the tribal areas to obtain first hand information from the grass-roots level and as a result the

equation of planning with the requirement of the tribals is found missing.

(xv) Lack of proper receptivity among tribals is a major obstacle for introducing or implementing any development activities for them. The only way to push them up is induced change through education which has been regarded as the key factor. But there has been large scale drop-outs of ST students and particularly the drop-out rate after Classes III and V appear to be very discouraging. The services of voluntary organisations with proven track records may be utilised for creating awareness among the tribals and ensuring their participation and involvement in the developmental programmes meant for them.

Strategy during the Eighth and Ninth Five Year Plans

No fundamental change in the Tribal Sub-plan strategy has been envisaged for adoption during the Eighth and Ninth Five Year Plans. Reportedly, steps are being taken to make the strategy more result-oriented and purposeful and emphasis is purported to have been on the following areas:

(i) Raising funds through 'pool system' and plan preparation by various developmental departments for implementation of such schemes and programmes as are having direct relevance and benefits to the tribals.

(ii) Development of irrigation, horticulture, crop diversification and improvement in the quality and spread of education with particular attention to women's education and reduction of drop-out rate among the ST students at primary level.

(iii) Formulation of special schemes for all-round development of the primitive groups and nomadic/semi-nomadic and other vulnerable tribes.

(iv) Provision of financial assistance to the tribals to raise their productivity levels and raise them above the poverty line.

(v) Constant monitoring and evaluation of the developmental programmes.

THE MAHARASHTRA MODEL FOR TRIBAL GOVERNANCE

All the various plan initiatives have remained implemented on paper only and are limited to achievement of financial targets while the physical targets achieved, compared to tribal targets, remain unfulfilled. The casual, unconcerned approach of the bureaucracy in the administrative departments. Yet the Maharashtra model seeks to cut through official lethargy and ensures flow of funds in a definite ratio (exceeding 8 per cent) to the tribal sub-plan such as from budget allocations, depending upon ratio of ST population. The guidelines were prepared by the Sukhtankar Sub-Committee of the State Planning Board, 1992 as under:

(i) Based on the State's Annual Plan, the tribal sub-plan outlay (9 per cent depending on tribal population proportion) is prepared by the Tribal Development Department.

(ii) 75 per cent of plan outlay is spent on TSP area schemes with the remaining in development of tribals in non-TSP areas.

(iii) Micro-planning at ITDP/block levels is done with inter-sectoral priorities fixed for TSP as a whole, depending upon problems, needs and socio-economic conditions of tribals. Effective training and orientation for officials is an integral part of the TSP.

(iv) In non-tribal areas, plans for benefiting tribals such as schemes for water and electricity supply, education, agriculture development, roads connecting to tribal habitations and for income-generating schemes for tribals.

(v) The TSP priority is for tribal-intensive projects such as minor irrigation works, soil and water conservation, drinking water, forest conservation, vocational education, women and child welfare, handicrafts, small bridges and roads, cross-drainage works with potential for tribal people.

(vi) The participation of NGOs in tribal development activities should be promoted.

(vii) Tribal people to be involved by Forest Department in regenerating and developing forests and traditional rights of tribals to minor forest produce, to be restored.

Since 1993–94, the funds allocation for tribal development has witnessed quantitative and qualitative changes with better funds outlays, utilisation and operational freedom as regards priorities. The review and monitoring mechanism has also improved with active participation of the people's representatives in scheme formulation and execution.

Replication of the Maharashtra Model

The success of the Maharashtra model has led the Government of India to insist on discussing the operational viability in various other States and Madhya Pradesh, Orissa, Himachal Pradesh, Gujarat, Karnataka and Rajasthan have accepted the basic framework with modifications and local adjustments. The Panchayat Act, 1996 extended to the Scheduled Areas, will enable tribal people's participation at the grass-roots level planning and ensure speedier execution of projects in tribal areas. Funds have never been a constraint in realisation of socio-economic justice for the tribal people and the dismantling of the bureaucratic functioning of the tribal development machinery and subsequent decentralisation of planning, will certainly improve development in tribal areas.

ANNEXURE 5.1

Reports of Committees/Commissions on Tribal Development

Sl. No.	*Committee/Commission*	*Chairman*	*Constituted in*	*Report submitted in*
1.	Backward Classes Commission	Kaka Kalelkar	Jan. 1953	Mar. 1955
2.	Scheduled Areas and Scheduled Tribes Commission	U.N.Dhebar	Apr. 1960	Oct. 1961
3.	Backward Classes Commission	B.P. Mandal	Jan. 1979	Dec. 1980
4.	Parliamentary Committee on Welfare of SCs & STs	A.C. Das	Dec. 1968	More than 180 reports submitted
5.	Joint Committee on SC/ST Bill, 1967	A.K. Chanda	Mar. 1968	Nov. 1969
6.	Advisory Committee on Revision of SC/ST Lists	B.N. Lokur	Jun. 1965	Jul. 1965
7.	Committee on Special Multipurpose Tribal Blocks & Tribal Affairs	Verrier Elwin	May 1959	Mar. 1980
8.	Special Working Group on Corporation for Backward Classes	M.P. Bhargava	Jun. 1961	Sep. 1962
9.	Committee on Tribal Economy in Forest Areas	Hari Singh	May 1965	Mar. 1967
10.	Study Group on Tribal Labour & Employment	L.P. Vidyarthi	Dec. 1966	Aug. 1967
11.	Working Group on Administrative Arrangements and Personnel Policies in Tribal Areas	Maheshwar Prasad	Oct. 1978	
12.	Working Group on Monitory Evaluation of Tribal Development and Development of Backward Classes	Dr. Bhupinder Singh	July 1978	July 1979
13.	Commission for SCs & STs		July 1978	Annually
14.	Committee on Forests and Tribals in India	B.K.Roy Barman	April 1980	Sep. 1982
15.	Study Team on Working Cooperative Institutions	K.S. Bawa	Dec. 1971	Sep. 1973
16.	Study Group on Relief, Indebtedness, Land Alienation and Restoration in Tribal Development Agency Areas	P.S. Appu	Dec. 1971	Oct. 1972

Sl. No.	Committee/Commission	Chairman	Constituted in	Report submitted in
17.	Committee on Orientation of Forest Education in India	K.M. Tiwari	Dec. 1982	Dec. 1983
18.	Committee on Forestry Programmes for Alleviation of Poverty	C.L. Bhatia	Mar. 1982	Oct. 1984
19.	Large Sized Multi-Purpose Societies (LAMPS) Cadre Management	B. Bandopadhyay	Oct. 1980	Sep. 1984
20.	Study Team on Social Welfare and Welfare of Backward Classes	Renuka Roy	Jan. 1958	July 1959
21.	Study Group on Welfare of Weaker Sections of the Village Community	J.P. Narain	Dec. 1960	Oct. 1961
22.	Study Group on Tribal Development Programmes	P. Shilu Ao	Oct. 1966	Sep. 1969
23.	Task Force on Development of Tribal Areas	L.P. Vidyarthi	April 1972	
24.	Working Group on Tribal Development during Medium Term Plans 1978-83	D.L. Mandal	Fed. 1978	July 1978
25.	National Committee for Development of Backward Classes	B. Sivaraman	Nov. 1978	June 1981
26.	Special Report on Development of Tribal Areas	B. Sivaraman	Nov. 1978	June 1981
27.	High Power Panel on Minorities, SCs and STs	Dr. Gopal Singh	May 1980	Oct. 1983
28.	Working Group on Tribal Development during Seventh Plan	S. Narayana-swamy	Oct. 1983	Dec. 1984
29.	Government of India Committee on Forests and Tribals	B.K. Ray Burman		1982
30.	Study Group on Land Holding System in Tribal Areas	R. Chaudhury		1986
31.	Report of the National Commission for Agriculture, Part IX	B. Sivaraman		1976

ANNEXURE 5.2

Land Alienation Laws in Various States

Sl. No.	*State/Union territory*	*Act/Regulation*	*Main provision*
1.	Andhra Pradesh	(*a*) The Andhra Pradesh (Scheduled Areas Land Transfer Regulation, 1959	Prohibits transfer of land to non-tribals whether the owner is tribal or nontribal. Authorises Government to acquire land in case a tribal purchaser is not available.
2.	Assam	The Assam Land and Revenue Regulation, 1886	Prohibits alienation of land in tribal blocks.
3.	Bihar	(*a*) Chota Nagpur Tenancy Act, 1908 (*b*) Santhal Pargana Tenancy (Supplementary Provisions) Act, 1949 (*c*) Bihar Scheduled Areas Regulations, 1969	Prohibits alienation of land of tribals and provides for restoration of alienated land.
4.	Gujarat	(*a*) Bombay Land Revenue Code, 1879 (*b*) Bombay Land Revenue (Gujarat Second Amendment) Act, 1980	Prohibits alienation of land of tribals and provides for restoration of alienated land.
5.	Himachal Pradesh	The Himachal Pradesh Transfer of Land (Regulation) Act, 1968	Prohibits alienation of land of tribals and provides for restoration of alienated land.
6.	Karnataka	The Karnataka Scheduled Castes and Scheduled Tribes (Prohibition of Transfer of Certain Lands) Act, 1978	Prohibits transfer of certain lands granted to persons belonging to Scheduled Tribes.
7.	Kerala	The Kerala Scheduled Tribes (Restriction of Transfer of Land and Restoration of Alienated Lands) Act, 1978 (Not yet enforced)	Prohibits transfer of certain lands granted to persons belonging to Scheduled Tribes.

(Contd.)

Sl. No.	*State/Union territory*	*Act/Regulation*	*Main provision*
8.	Madhya Pradesh	Madhya Pradesh Land Revenue Code, 1959	Prohibits alienation of land.
9.	Manipur	Manipur Land Revenue and Land Reforms Act, 1960	No transfer of land by a member of Scheduled Tribes to a non-member is valid without the permission of the Deputy Commissioner and District Council.
10.	Maharashtra	Maharashtra Land Revenue Code and Tenancy Laws (Amendment) Act, 1974 The Maharashtra (Restoration of Lands to Scheduled Tribes) Act, 1974	Prohibits alienation of land provides for restoration of alienated land.
11.	Orissa (within Scheduled Areas)	The Orissa Scheduled Areas Transfer of Immovable Property (Scheduled Tribes Regulations), 1956	Prohibits alientation of land provides for restoration of alienated land.
12.	Rajasthan	*(a)* The Rajasthan Tenancy Act, 1955	
		(b) The Registration (Rajasthan Amendement) Act, 1976	Prohibits alienation of land provides for restoration of alienated land.
13.	Tamil Nadu	The Revenue Board's Standing Orders	Land assigned to specified Hill Tribes shall not be transferred to persons not belonging to the same class without permission of divisional Officer.
14.	Tripura	*(a)* Tripura Land Revenue and Land Reforms Act, 1960	
		(b) Tripura Land Revenue and Land Reforms Act, 1974	Prohibits alienation of land and provides for restoration of alienated land.
15.	Sikkim	Standing Order of Government	

(Contd.)

Sl. No.	*State/Union territory*	*Act/Regulation*	*Main provision*
16.	Uttar Pradesh	Uttar Pradesh Zamindar's Alienation of Land Reforms Act, 1950 as amended by the UP Land Laws (Amendment and Ordinance, 1981) with regard to Section 157 and 211 of the Act (by insertion)	Imposed restriction on transfer of land by Scheduled Tribes to non-Scheduled Tribes without permission of the Collector.
17.	West Bengal	West Bengal Land Reforms Act, 1955—Chapter 11-A	Prohibits alienation of land.
18.	Dadra & Nagar Haveli	Dadra & Nagar Haveli Land Reforms Regulation, 1971	
19.	Nagaland	Bengal Eastern Frontier Regulation, 1873, and Assam Land and Revenue Regulation, 1886*	
20.	Arunachal Pradesh	Bengal Eastern Frontier Regulation, 1873	
21.	Lakshadweep	Lakshadweep (Protecting of Scheduled Tribes) Regulation, 1964	
22.	Meghalaya	Meghalaya Transfer of Land (Regulation) Act, 1971	
23.	Andaman & Nicobar Islands	Andaman and Nicobar Islands Protection of Aboriginal Tribes Regulation, 1956	

* Assam Land and Revenue Regulation further amended Section 162 vide Nagaland and Revenue Regulation (Amendment) Act, 1978.

ANNEXURE 5.3

Enactments/Regulations on Money-lending/ Debt Redemption in various States

State/Union territory	*Legislation in force*
Andhra Pradesh	*(i)* The Andhra Pradesh (Andhra Region) Scheduled Areas Money-lenders Regulation, 1960 (extended to Telangana area in 1963).
	(ii) The Andhra Pradesh (Andhra Areas Scheduled Tribes) Debt Relief Regulation, 1960 (extended to Telangana area in 1963).
	(iii) The Agency Debt Bondage Abolition Regulation, 1964.
	(iv) The Hyderabad Money-lenders' Act, 1938.
	(v) The Madras Agricultural Debt Relief (partially excluded Areas) Amendment Regulation, 1944.
	(vi) The Madras Debt Bondage Regulation, 1940.
Assam	*(i)* The Assam Money-lenders Act, 1934.
	(ii) The Assam Debt Conciliation Act, 1936.
	(iii) The Assam Rural Indebtedness Relief Act, 1975.
	(iv) The Mikir Hills District (Money-lending by Non-Tribals) Regulation, 1953.
Bihar	*(i)* The Bihar Money-lenders Act, 1938.
	(ii) The Bihar Money-lenders (Regulation of Transaction) Act, 1939.
	(iii) The Bihar Scheduled Areas Regulation, 1969.
Gujarat	*(i)* The Kerala Money-lenders Act, 1946.
	(ii) The Bombay Agricultural Debtors' Relief Act, 1947.
Kerala	*(i)* The Kerala Money-lenders Act, 1958.
	(ii) The Kerala Agriculturist Debt Relief Act, 1958.
Himachal Pradesh	*(i)* The Punjab Redemption of Mortgages Act, 1913.
	(ii) The Himachal Pradesh Debt Redemption Act, 1953.
	(iii) The Restitution of Mortgaged Lands Act, 1938.
	(iv) The Spiti and Lahaul (Relief & Indebtedness Laws Application & Amendment) Regulation, 1962.

(Contd.)

State/Union territory	Legislation in force
Madhya Pradesh	*(i)* The Madhya Pradesh Scheduled Tribes Debt Relief (Amendment) Regulation, 1963. *(ii)* The Madhya Pradesh Money-lenders Act. *(iii)* The Madhya Pradesh Usurious Loans Act, 1938. *(iv)* The Madhya Pradesh Protection of Debtors Act. *(v)* The Madhya Pradesh Anusuchit Jan jati Rin Sahayata Ordinance, 1966. *(vi)* Madhya Pradesh Anusuchit Janjati Sahukar Viniyam, 1972.
Maharashtra	*(i)* The Bombay Money-lenders Act, 1946. *(ii)* The Madhya Pradesh Money-lenders Act. *(iii)* The Madhya Pradesh Usurious Loans Act, 1938. *(iv)* The Hyderabad Money-lenders Act, 1938. *(v)* The Bombay Agricultural Debtors Relief Act, 1947. *(vi)* The Maharashtra Tribals Economic Condition (Improvement) Act, 1976.
Karnataka	*(i)* The Mysore Money-lenders Act, 1961. *(ii)* The Mysore Pawn Brokers Act, 1961. *(iii)* The Bombay Money-lenders Act, 1946. *(iv)* The Coorg Money-lenders Act, 1939. *(v)* The Madras Pawn Brokers Act, 1943. *(vi)* The Hyderabad Money-lenders Act, 1938. *(vii)* The Mysore Agriculturist Relief Act, 1928. *(viii)* The Mysore Debt Conciliation Act, 1937
Orissa	*(i)* The Orissa Money-lenders Act, 1939. *(ii)* The Orissa (Application of certain provisions) Regulation, 1950. *(iii)* The Orissa (Scheduled Area) Money-lenders Regulation, 1967 (regulation 2 of 1968). *(iv)* The Agriculturists' Loans (Orissa Amendment) Act, 1937. *(v)* The Orissa Debt Bondage Abolition Regulation, 1948.
Rajasthan	*(i)* The Rajasthan Relief of Agricultural Indebtedness (Amendment) Act, 1962. *(ii)* The Rajasthan Money-lenders Act, 1963. *(iii)* The Rajasthan Sagri System Abolition Act, 1961. *(iv)* The Rajasthan Cooperative Act, 1965. *(v)* The Agricultural Indebtedness Act, 1958.

(Contd.)

State/Union territory	*Legislation in force*
Tamil Nadu	*(i)* The Madras Money-lenders Act, 1937. *(ii)* The Madras Pawn Brokers Act, 1943. *(iii)* The Madras Debt Conciliation Act, 1936. *(iv)* The Madras Indebted Agriculturists (Repayment of Debts) Act, 1955. *(v)* Tamil Nadu Debt Relief Act, 1976. *(vi)* Tamil Nadu Debt Relief Act, 1980.
Tripura	*(i)* Tripura Agricultural Indebtedness Relief Act, 1979 (Tripura Act 8 of 1980). *(ii)* The Bombay Money-lenders Act, 1946, extended to Tripura under Tripura Money-lenders Rule, 1959.
Uttar Pradesh	*(i)* Uttar Pradesh Money-lenders Act, 1976. *(ii)* Uttar Pradesh Debt Relief Act, 1977.
West Bengal	*(i)* The Bengal Money-lenders Act, 1940. *(ii)* The Bengal Agricultural Debtors Act, 1936.
Andaman and Nicobar Islands	*(i)* The Andaman and Nicobar Islands (Protection of Aboriginal Tribes) Money-lenders Regulation, 1956. *(ii)* The Andaman and Nicobar Islands Rules, 1957. *(iii)* The Andaman and Nicobar Islands (Protection of Aboriginal Tribes) Rules, 1956.
Dadra & Nagar Haveli	The Bombay Money-lenders Act, 1946.
Laccadives, Minicoy and Amindivi Islands	The Laccadives, Minicoy and Amindivi Islands (Debt Conciliation and Grant of Loans) Regulation, 1964.

CHAPTER VI

Forest Laws and Tribal Rights

Most of the tribal communities live in and around forests. To the vast number of tribal people, the forest is their home, their livelihood and the source of their very existence. The forest provides them with edible fruits and leaves, honey and water, roots and tubers, wild game and fish and is a major source of food. It provides them with materials to build their homes and practise their arts and crafts. The lives of the tribal people are intertwined with that of the forests. About 50 per cent of the time is spent in agricultural activities followed by collection of Minor Forest Produce (MFP). About 50 per cent of the tribal income comes from MFP while the income from agriculture is estimated at about 50 per cent. The symbiotic relationship which exists between the tribal people and the forests is not confined to the economic sphere of activities only but also covers medicines, recreational activities, social, religious and cultural inputs of their life. This symbiotic relationship ensured the fulfilment of the physical needs of the tribal and protection of the environment. As tribal communities are almost landless or marginal farmers, they depend on the forests more for survival than on other sources of livelihood.

The varieties of trees and plants yielding valuable products and with food value are part of tribal survival skills. The different types of woods to be cut for building houses, for agricultural implements, for furniture and for crafts and artifacts. The thatching grass, rope-making fibres, cup and plate making leaves, seeds and bamboos for traps, poisonous ingredients for arrows and for poisoning fishes and numerous products are collected from forests. Their isolated existence in inaccessible areas in forests has compelled them to depend upon herbal medicines in time of illness and injuries. This symbiotic relationship depends upon the balance of their needs and the ecological needs of the forests. The mutual dependence ensures sustainable protection by the tribals towards all vegetation in the locality. The forests serve as the life support system for the tribals and they take all preventions against destruction of forest and forest wealth. The tribal people have developed over the years, a system of social culture, taboos and prohibitions, manner of utilisation of forest products. Their myths and legends remind them of the consequences of any harm done to the forests, their Mother and reinforce the symbolic relationship to their existence in peaceful harmony with nature.

The rights and privileges enjoyed by the tribal people in their use of the forest and forest produce, have undergone significant changes over the years! With the gradual extension of Government authority over the forests, when the British exploited India economically, the traditional rights of the tribals to the forests were disregarded. In 1894, rights and privileges existed which changed in 1952 to rights and concessions and later on were regarded only as concessions which could be withdrawn! A detailed study of the various forest policies is essential for an understanding of the denial of tribal people's rights and privileges.

FORESTS AND FOREST MANAGEMENT IN INDIA

Paleo-botanical evidences amply testify that India had dense forests 250 million years ago. Man developed only a million years ago in the Pleistocene age when Rajasthan and Punjab lay buried under swamps and other parts of India were covered with thick forests teeming with wildlife. The Dravidians and later the Aryans entered the country, cleared forests and built shelters for themselves. The chronicles of Megasthenes, Fa-Hieun, Hieun-Tsang and I-Tsing reveal the presence of protected imperial forests in the Indo-Gangetic plains. Right from Ashoka's times and continued by a long line of kings, emperors and chieftians, plantation of trees for avenues and roads, protection of animals and forests have been taken up till Shershah's times and even Jahangir's times in the 16th and 17th centuries. Indiscriminate cutting of forests and mass-hunting of animals for sport, however, began with the fall of Mughal rule due to lack of a strong central power. The British plundered the forests for teak wood for the British Navy and merchant ships and for other valuable wood for railway sleepers, especially for extending railway lines from the ports to the forests in the interior. But when it was realised that the destruction of forests was detrimental to the imperial British rule, there arose a consciousness and need to work the forest resources on a scientific basis.

Beginning of Forest Management

Indian teak has been found in ancient Babylon and Nineveh ruins. The entire Arabian peninsula used Malabar teak for building materials and even the Arabian dhows used to be constructed with hard-wood from the Western Ghats. The Portugese too used Indian teak to repair their ships.

The East India Company and the British Indian Government exploited the valuable timber from Indian forests, for commercial gains and for building ships. The naval demand for teak led the Bombay Government in 1805 to secure timber supplies for the Wadia shipyard in Bombay. In 1801, the Madras Government appointed the first Conservator of Forests for preserving forests and to supply good quality teak to the Navy. But the tribals resented this as their free access to the forests was disputed and this post was discontinued in 1822. Instead, teak plantations were set up by the British on the Malabar Coast and by 1888, over 3500 acre of prime teak plantations had been grown under professional forest management techniques.

Dr. Clegham was appointed as Conservator of Forests by the Government of Bombay in 1856 while Dr.Gibson was appointed as Conservator of Forests by the Government of Madras in 1857. The Madras Forest Act was passed in 1882. The lucrative forest income over the years led to increasing Government interference in forests and was increasingly resented by the tribal people, leading to tribal armed revolt and brutal repressions.

Forest Policy in Retrospect. The year 1855 was the beginning of a systematic forest policy. The then Governor General, Dallhousie issued a memorandum on forest conservation. In 1856, a German botanist Dietrich Brandis by name was appointed as the first Inspector General of Forests by the Government of India. It was under his guidance that the Forest Department was organised and the first Forest Act was enacted.

Forest Act of 1865. The Act was made to regulate forest exploitation, management and preservation. For the first time an attempt was made to regulate the collection of forest produce by forest dwellers. Basically, it was an attempt to regulate the practices of the local people under the force of law.

Forest Act of 1878. This Act was aimed at increasing the control of the Government over the forests. Under this Act the forests were divided into *(i)* Reserved Forests, *(ii)* Protected Forests and *(iii)* Village Forests. The people were required to record their claims over land and forest produce in the proposed Reserved and Protected forests. The practice of trespass and pasturing of cattle were prohibited. A duty on timber was imposed. Certain Acts were declared as forest offences and appropriate punishment prescribed.

Forest Policy Resolution, 1894. The Resolution declared that the sole object with which the State forests were to be administered, was the public benefit. On the whole the constitution and reservation of a forest involved the regulation of rights and restrictions of privileges enjoyed by the people in their neighbouring forest areas. The cardinal point was the emphasis laid on the advantages to be gained by the public limiting the rights and privileges of the individuals enjoyed by them as per customs and traditions.

The forests were divided into four classes:

(i) Forests, the preservation of which was essential for environmental protection,
(ii) Forests for the supply of valuable timbers for commercial purposes,
(iii) Minor forests; and
(iv) Pasture lands.

It was categorically specified that the claims of cultivation were stronger than the claims of forest preservation and that whenever any demand for cultivable land could be supplied from forest areas, it should be granted without hesitation. The resolution also stressed the need for raising finances from the forests.

Indian Forest Act, 1927. By decrees the Government of India gradually increased its control over the forests and the Forest Department was strengthened from time to time with a view to regulating people's right over forest lands and forest products. There was a steady increase of revenue obtained from the forest. The functions and duties of different forest officials were codified. Different forest products were listed. The items which were declared as forest produce under the Act are as follows:

Timber, charcoal, catechu, wood oil, resin, natural varnish, bark, lac, mahua seeds, myrobalan leaves, flowers and fruits, grass, creepers, reeds and moss, skins, tusk, horns, bones, silk, cocoons, honey, wax, peat, surface oil, rocks and minerals. Elaborate provisions were made to extend state control over forests. Provisions were also made for taking over the management of private forests in certain areas.

Government of India Act 1935. The British Parliament based on the Government of India Act of 1935, created Provincial Legislatures by virtue of which a dual system of Government came into operation. The subject of forests was included in the Provincial list under the Act. Thereafter several provinces made their own laws to regulate forests.

National Forest Policy, 1952. In laying down the National Forest Policy, 1952, the Ministry of Food and Agriculture enumerated the six paramount needs of the country:

(i) The need for evolving system of balanced and complementary land use under which there would be better production and less deterioration.
(ii) The need for checking
  (a) Denudation in mountainous regions.
  (b) The erosion along the treeless banks of great rivers.
  (c) The invasion of seas on coastal tracts.
(iii) The need for establishing treelands.
(iv) The need for grazing, small wood and firewood.

(v) The need for supply of timber and other forest produce.
(vi) The need for generating maximum annual revenue in perpetuity.

Under this new policy, the forests were classified into:

(i) Protected forests to be preserved for climatic consideration.
(ii) National forests to meet the needs of defence, communication and other general purposes of public importance.
(iii) Village forest to provide firewood, small timber and grazing.
(iv) Tree lands for protection of landscape.

The following statement made at the time of launching the National Forest Policy, 1952, clarifies the Government views regarding the relationship of tribals with the forests. "Village Communities in the neighbourhood of a forest will naturally make greater use of its products for the satisfaction of their domestic agricultural needs. Such use, however, should in no event be permitted at the cost of national interest".

While, therefore, the needs of local population must be met to a reasonable extent, national interest should not be sacrificed because they are not directly discernible, nor should the right and interest of future generation be subordinated to the improvidence of the present generation. The Scheduled Areas and Scheduled Tribes Commission, 1963, appointed by the President of India under the Chairmanship of Shri U.N. Dhebar reviewed the old 1894 policy and the new 1952 policy and studied the impact of these policies on tribal communities. The findings of the Commission in respect of differences between the two policies which affected tribal communities are as follows:

(i) The old policy envisages the release of forest land for cultivation subject to certain safeguards. The new policy withdraws this concession.
(ii) The old policy left margin for the supply of the needs of the villagers from the outlying areas in the reserved forests. The new policy decided that there should be village forests for this purpose.
(iii) The old policy did not touch the private forests of the tribals. The new policy applied to the same control to them.
(iv) The old policy did not touch free grazing in forest. The new policy sought to bring it under control.
(v) The new policy admitted that persuasive and not coercive measures should be used in a sort of missionary manner rather than in an authoritarian manner to attempt to wean the tribals from their traditional axe-cultivation.

The whole thing boils down to a situation whereby the tribals who were formerly enjoying considerable freedom in respect of their use of forest products turned into subjects placed under the Forest Department. Tribal villages were no longer an essential part of the forests but were merely on sufferance. The traditional rights of the tribals were no longer recognised as rights and the symbiotic relationship with the forest was clipped for good. In 1894, the tribals were enjoying several rights and privileges over the use of the forests but in 1952 these became rights and concessions.

National Commission on Agriculture (NCA), 1976. The Commission in its report on forestry has advocated commercialisation of forests at all costs and recommended regularisation of the rights of forest dwellers over forest produce. The Commission recommended a drastic reduction in people's rights over forests. It stated "Free supply of forest produce to the rural population and their rights and privileges have brought destruction to the forests and so it is necessary to reverse the process. The rural people have not contributed much towards the maintenance or regeneration of forests. Having over-exploited the resources they cannot, in all fairness, expect that somebody else will take the trouble of providing them with forest produce, free of charge". Thus, it shows that the Commission's recommendations were quite opposed to those made by the Scheduled Areas and Scheduled Tribes Commission, 1969.

Constitutional Changes. The subject of forests was included in the State list as per the VII Schedule of the Constitution of India. But it was changed in the year 1976 whereby the subject of Forests was transferred from the State list to the Concurrent list through the 42nd amendment to the Constitution of India. But by this change, the powers of the State were diminished and those of the Centre were enhanced over the forests. The Government of India promulgated the Forest Conservation Ordinance in the year 1980 prohibiting the State Government from allowing the use of any forest land for any other purposes without the prior approval of the Central Government. The ordinance was listed and converted into an Act in 1980.

The Indian Forest Bill, 1980. In accordance with the recommendations of the NCA, 1976, a draft forest bill was circulated in 1980 which curtailed the people's right over forest land and produce. However, this Bill was withdrawn because public criticism was mounted against it. A Committee was appointed to reconsider the present forest policy. The Committee which was appointed to reconsider the present forest policy, set up in 1980, emphasised the dependence of the tribal people on forests. Besides getting fuel, fodder, wood for house construction, the tribals also earned about one third of their income from the sale of MFP.

National Committee on the Development of Backward Areas. The Planning Commission constituted a National Committee for the development of Backward Areas in 1980. The Committee subscribed to the views expressed by the National Commission on Agriculture and recommended curtailment of rights of tribal communities over forest land and products.

The Committee also emphasised the importance of MFP in providing substantial income to tribal communities. It recommended removal of middlemen in all business transactions and stated that MFP should not be treated as a source of revenue to the State. It was of the opinion that the economic interest can be created in the mind of the tribal communities for maintenance of forest provided substantial income accrues to them regularly from the MFP. The tribal communities should be paid on the basis of the market price and not on daily wage basis for collection of any items of MFP. All leases for collection of MFP should be given exclusively to the cooperatives organised by the tribal communities.

The Review Committee on the Rights and Concessions in the Forest Areas. The Forest Department which was under the Ministry of Agriculture till 1984, constituted a Committee in 1981 to review the present status of rights and concessions obtaining in the forests administered by the Government and recommended steps for effective management consistent with the scientific management of forests. The report of the Committee was published in 1984. It recommended that exercise of rights and concessions should be restricted only to those tribals residing within a maximum distance of 8 kms, from the existing forests. It was also recommended that the beneficiaries should not be allowed to enter the forest and remove the products and that the supplies should be made through Departmental Depots opened outside the forest for this purpose. It also recommended that the barter and sale of forest produce obtained by the beneficiaries should be stopped.

National Forest Policy, 1988. The basic objective of the 1988 Forest Policy was oriented towards maintenance of environmental stability, conservation of natural heritage of the country, checking soil erosion and denudation of the catchment areas of the rivers, checking sand-dunes in the desert areas, increasing the forest-tree cover in the country, meeting the requirements of fuel wood, fodder, minor forest produce and small timber of the rural and tribal population, increasing the productivity of the forests and encouraging efficient utilisation of forest produce.

In regard to the rights and concessions, the policy was very much oriented towards the development of the tribal people. It stated that the life of the tribals and other poor living within and near forests revolve around forests. The rights and concessions enjoyed by them should be fully protected, their domestic requirements of fuel wood, fodder, minor forest produce and construction timber should be the first charge of forest produce. These and substitute materials should be made available conveniently, at reasonable prices. There is a section which gives a vivid picture of the tribal people *vis-a-vis* forests. What is stated under the Section 4.6 "Tribal People and Forest" is reproduced below:

> "Having regard to the symbiotic relationship between the tribal people and forest, a primary task of all agencies responsible for forest management including the Forest Development Corporations should be to associate the tribal people closely in protection, regeneration and development of forests as well as to provide gainful employment to the people living in and around the forest."

Forest-based Industries

For the first time, the resolution (National Forest Policy, 1988) tries to recommend something about the forest produce consumed by the forest based industries. It was laid down that forest-based industries should raise the raw materials preferably by establishment of direct relationship between the forestry and individuals who grow it. It is suggested that the forest-based industries should provide employment to the local people and also involve them fully in raising trees and raw materials. Natural forests should not be exploited to start new industries or to expand the existing forest-based industries. It is pointed out that the practice of supply of forest produce to the industries at concessional prices should cease. Industries should be encouraged to use alternative raw materials because the supply of forest produce to industries in the public and private sectors has been the main factor leading to destruction and over-exploitation of natural forests.

Withdrawal of Tribal Rights

The rich flora and fauna which is part of the rich botanical wealth of the country has existed for millions of years and the tribal people had been enjoying the freedom of the forests without any interference till the 1850's. The 1894 Forest Policy reflected the Government's authority to limit and regulate tribal rights. It claimed that "the sole object with which State Forests are administered is the public benefit. In some cases, the public to be benefited are the whole body of tax-payers, in others, the people of the tract with which the forest is situated; but in almost all cases the constitution and preservation of a forest involve, in greater or lesser degree, the regulation of rights and the restriction of privileges of users in the forest area which may have previously been enjoyed by the inhabitants of its immediate neighbourhood. This regulation and restriction are justified only when the advantage to be gained by the public is great; and the cardinal principle to be observed is that the rights and privileges of individuals must be limited, otherwise than for their own benefit, only in such degree as is absolutely necessary to secure that advantage".

With this, the foray into depriving the tribal people of their rights and privileges began and has continued since 1947. In the draconian National Forest Policy, 1952, tribals lost their statutory rights over forests but enjoyed certain concessions/privileges as under:

- *(i)* Right to take water for agricultural purposes
- *(ii)* Digging of wells and canals for agricultural purposes
- *(iii)* Free grazing in open forests (under passes)
- *(iv)* Removal of stones and earth for domestic or agricultural use
- *(v)* Removal of timber, bamboos, reeds, canes, *etc.*, for construction and repair of houses and for agricultural implements
- *(vi)* Collection of dead wood for domestic use
- *(vii)* Collection of grass for cattle and for covering their huts

(viii) Fishing and hunting excluding protected fauna
(ix) Cultivation of forest land.

However, these concessions vary from State to State without any uniformity. If at all privileges or concessions are given, these should be given on a uniform basis to all people. If privileges are to be taken away, this should be done only after creating informal public opinion and educating the tribal people. The lapse on the part of the administration coupled with the harassment and exploitation of the tribals by forest/revenue officials and private contractors, has created tension in forest areas.

The Forest Act has created an entire bureaucracy with very wide-ranging powers and the power to make laws! A forest officer without warning may arrest any person against whom a reasonable suspicion exists, and order a month's imprisonment! They can seize forest produce, cattle, tools, cart, *etc.*, if a forest offence has been committed. No civil suit can be lodged against them for acts in good faith nor can they be criminally prosecuted for offenses by mistake but not of law. Prosecution cannot be lodged without the approval of the Government. Such draconian powers have placed the tribal people under the oppressive power of the forest bureaucracy. And there are always unscrupulous officials who could exploit the hapless tribals. It is interesting to note that the tribal people are being paid to demolish forests and also despite the proliferating forest bureaucracy, the forests are dwindling day-by-day. Scientific Management of forests is far from being a reality in the Indian context. The stripping of forests continues unabated with the forest officials and the tribals unable to tackle the problems! Another problem is that forest officials claim large tracts as forest but on which no tree is left standing. There is a need to review the remaining standing forests and guard these zealously. On scrub forests, there is need to have replantation of quality trees and increase the percentage of forests to the desired 25 per cent from the level of 9 per cent, as is revealed by the remote sensing satellite images. The blame for the extensive deforestation lies generally on the contractors and the licence-permit raj system that has proliferated. Corrupt forest officials also exploit the tribals in various ways and often sell the minor forest produce collected by the tribals for their personal benefit.

The tribal is harassed by the highly cumbersome procedure of securing various permits, papers, licenses to avail of various concessions for exploiting the forests. Though fees or levy are not heavy, with their limited means and circumstances, rarely does a tribal get these official documents to exploit the forests. However, outsiders who are contractors, seem to have no difficulty in receiving these papers, permits and licenses. Contractors have become exploiters of national forests and with the help of the forest machinery are able to punish these tribal people who oppose them and get the tribal people framed under forest law infringements.

The Forest Department may be the custodian of the forests but would definitely want it minus its oldest inhabitants, the tribal people. The Dhebar Committee Report, 1963, has recommended, "The Forest Department as a branch of Government, should consider itself responsible in the development of tribals as well as forest areas. It should not think in terms of an exclusive obligation to trees or vegetation but should also accept an obligation to utilise the forest as much as possible from the angle of the economic development of the tribals residing in it. The Department should undertake the responsibility of giving adequate employment to the tribals living in and around the forest areas". Development priorities have to be reset and a framework for tribal development in-built into the Forest Department's priorities.

Changing Relationships

The forest-man relationship has been changing in recent years with grave and sometimes encouraging consequences.

(i) The Hunter — was one of the many animals and part of the eco-system, a food-gatherer and a hunter. He did not disturb the ecology.

(ii) The Planter — The food sources tapered off due to over-use and hence cultivation was taken up on the slash and burn type.

(iii) The Cultivator — was a development over the planter due to developments in technologies and settled cultivation due to soil fertility, but in small pieces of land with dependence on forest resources.

(iv) Large Farmers — Animal husbandry and development of large farms with settled agricultural practices prescribed. There was very little interaction with forests at this stage.

(v) Urban Settlers — With increasing specialisation and non-farm production, people stayed in urban areas and had no linkages with forests.

(vi) Industrial Man — The industrial and urban society has virtually no connection with forests and uses them as one more resource. Forests may be a source of recreation also.

Thus, man's relationship with the forest has been changing and is increasingly becoming distant. The ownership pattern of forests is also changing. From the communal ownership when man was a part of the forest eco-system to the point of evolution when forest areas got demarcated between tribal communities, to State ownership with the enactment of the Forest Act in 1855 and now the corporate ownership of forests when industries nurture forests for individual exploitation. The role of tribal people in these ever-changing patterns, if any, of ownership of forests, has to be examined afresh.

The effect of loss of communal ownership, new technologies and increasing, marginalisation of tribal communities, due to non-integration in the new economic order, leads to increasing tensions for the tribal communities. Is tribal development to be synonymous with forest development ? Or are these mutually exclusive terms ? There is no clear policy framework yet. One model will be to develop the forests with proper technologies and the tribal may be totally excluded from the forests and become unemployed lead us to mass immigration. In the Peoples' Development model, assimilated development by stages only is possible. This development will be a 'closed' one with minimal external inputs and carefully planned external links in the local economic development being the factor of development. What is more likely to happen is that the State will consolidate its position and the tribal economy will be disrupted and remain in a flux with migration or marginalisation of the tribal people, depending upon their genius and ability to adapt.

Plunder of Forest

The symbiotic relationship of the tribal people and the forests has been discussed earlier. But shrinkage of forests has been a major matter of concern for the tribal people as they have witnessed the disappearance of their forests before their very eyes. Many blame the tribal people for this deforestation. This is unfair because the tribal people depend on the forests for food, shelter, employment and safety from non-tribal people. Fuel, fodder, fruits, timber and a large source of minor forest produce, are available to them such as leaves, roots, mahua flowers, sal seeds, fruits like mango, guava, jack fruits and tamarind, broomsticks, lac and tassar cocoons, honey, resins and gums, *etc.* While some are consumed, most of it is sold for purchasing clothes, grains and other necessities. The tribals depend for their livelihood and existence on these forests and hence they try to preserve these forests. Their tribal culture, ethos and way of life is built around these forests but since the 1850's due to Government interference, they have become powerless to stop the vested interests such as contractors and the forest guards from plundering the forests! The receding forests cause implacable grief to the tribal people though they too use fuel, fodder and timber from the forests for their personal consumption.

The plundering of forests is done by the contractors as legal or illegal timber is being consumed by individuals, railways, defence forces, *etc.* The various development projects such as power (thermal and hydel), mines, irrigation projects and townships are preceded by extensive clearance of forests! The Narmada Valley Project is supposed to have involved a loss of 41,000 hectares of forests. All these major projects destroy forests and then do not bother to plant forests on other lands as the State does not monitor these lapses! The destruction of forest depletes land and water resources and causes faster rate of erosion of land in surrounding areas thus destroying the fragile tribal economy! Due to faster water run-offs in deforested areas, there is less charging of the underground water-table and leads to serious water shortages! With forest depletion, the collection of minor forest produce has dwindled in Madhya Pradesh, Orissa and Bihar.

In many reserved forests and animal/bird sanctuaries, the tribal people are being forcibly evacuated and no alternative land is being given to them except very little monetary compensation. It is the tribal land which is being appropriated for development projects while their land or even common village land is being appropriated by non-tribal predators in the garb of money-lenders, middle-men and land-grabbers! It is the commercial interests which are plundering the forests and even the Government connives by giving vast forest areas to timber/paper factories at ridiculously low prices! In the name of development, the tribal land which is the main economic asset base of the tribal people is under attack!

DEFORESTATION

Over-exploitation (academically called development) of natural resources like forests, leads to deforestation. It is estimated that continuous population pressure leads to loss of 15 million hectares of tropical moist forests annually, all over the world, including India. Satellite pictures have revealed the actual rate of deforestation over the years. The total tree cover of 55.52 million hectares in 1972–77 had reduced to 46.35 million hectares in 1980–82, *i.e.*, a loss of 9.17 million hectares over 7 years or 1.3 million hectares of forests per annum. The National Remote Sensing Agency has estimated a loss of 10.4 million hectares of closed forests, 63,000 hectares of mangroves and 1.29 hectares of good closed forest were converted into degraded forests. The States most affected by deforestation are Punjab, Haryana, Gujarat, Rajasthan and Delhi as also Madhya Pradesh, Orissa, Andhra Pradesh, Jammu & Kashmir and Arunachal Pradesh. The optimum forest cover at 33 per cent of total land mass as per the National Forest Policy, 1952, and National Commission on Agriculture, 1976, may not be achieved and is only about 9–10 per cent today. This will lead to environmental disasters, thereafter the tribal people's eco-systems and lead to non-availability of raw materials/resources for development of forest-based industries. The role of forests in maintaining the ecological balance in nature is set out at Annexure I. The optimal utilisation limit for forest exploitation has been exceeded and soil erosion due to inadequate tree cover, droughts due to loss of ground water shortage, floods due to run-off water and landslides due to deduction of hills are now common. It is estimated that 6,000 million tonnes of good quality top-soil is being washed away or blown off in India, every year. As top soil covers about 18 cms depth, this means a loss of about 2.4 million hectares of cultivable land every year when nature takes centuries to form an inch of valuable top soil. About 11 per cent of our tribal population consist of forest-dwellers with 70 per cent being tribals and totally dependent on the forests for food, medicines, sustenance, employment, fuel and recreation. The demand for fuel-wood which was 135 million tonnes in 1975–76, will be around 265 million tonnes in 1999–2000. To meet fuel-wood demand, manure will be burnt which would have been used as fertiliser to increase food production. Non-availability of fuel has been very hard on the rural women with women having to walk upto 20 km per day for collecting firewood! The sharp decline in Minor Forest Produce (MFP) availability due to loss of forest trees has caused economic loss to the tribal families who depended on MFP for survival. A large number of tribal families depending on shifting cultivation, have had to give up cultivation due to lack of trees.

Causes of Deforestation

The main reasons for extensive deforestation of our tree cover are due to;

(i) natural causes like diseases, parasites, termites, floods, wind, forest fires, *etc.*
(ii) increasing level of population depending upon forests for firewood
(iii) population increase leading to increasing demand for wood
(iv) industries taking to large-scale tree-felling for raw materials
(v) state governments which encourage tree-felling for increasing revenues
(vi) development projects for construction (rail, road, dams, major industrial projects, mines and power projects)
(vii) illegal felling of trees by vested interests
(viii) high-density cattle grazing resulting in soil erosion and poor regeneration of plants in Rajasthan, Madhya Pradesh, *etc.*

The deforestation can be tackled by better forest management and extensive re-generation of forests with species diversity and not by mono-culture. Apart from tribal people and NGOs/individuals who take up environmental issues, there are few people who are interested in regeneration of forests.

CONSEQUENCES OF DEFORESTATION

Wanton destruction of forests is not merely the disappearance of trees and bushes but the disappearance of the resource on which the tribal economy, culture, social life and religions depend, and indeed their very life support systems. The tribal people have traditionally depended on balanced utilisation of forests and have nurtured the forests. This relationship has been eroded due to population pressures and the contractors/vested interests who pay these tribals to denude vast tracts of forests for petty gain. The consequences of deforestation are:

(a) Cultural Alienation

The protection of nature and forests by tribal people and the just distribution of forest produce by the tribal people, is slowly dying out. The sacred forest groves or 'sarna' are also being cut down as are the sacred species of trees which was considered 'taboo' earlier. The poisoning of fishes in Tehri Garhwal and over-fishing in Goa, the deep cuts on chirpine in the Uttaranchal region for turpentine have succeeded in damaging the trees beyond repair and wanton killing of snakes by Jogis in Rajasthan for reptile-skin smugglers, are instances of tribal people being increasingly alienated from their culture and resource bases. The sharing of resources equally among their tribes, is also vanishing along with the forest resources. This gives rise to individualism as opposed to the tribal sense of solidarity. Lack of education and the change from a barter system to a monetised system, have enabled the tribals to be ruthlessly exploited, as also fostering competition for very minimal wages among themselves.

(b) Indebtedness, Land Alienation and Bondage

Loss of forests results in loss of MFP income which contributes to about 30 per cent to 50 per cent of a tribal family's income. Reduction of income leads to indebtedness for small loans which increases due to non-payment of interest at usurious rates of interest (exceeding 5 per cent per month due to the perceived risks by the money-lender). This leads to effective reduction of bargaining power during sale of MFP leading to land alienation or bondage for life or, even worse, generations to follow! Though officially the land continues to be registered as tribal land, its alienation is still prevalent. When money is lent, the loan agreement deprives the borrower of produce for about 9 years and as there is no income, further borrowings continue and the mortgaging of produce for more years, continues. The tribal thus becomes a bonded labourer producing crops for the money-lender on land that is legally his! The tribal can rarely break this vicious cycle of poverty. Migration of tribal people due to droughts, *etc.*, also lands these people in the clutches of labour contractors who literally enslave them and exploit them, for low wages.

(c) Displacement and Exploitation

Development projects such as minor irrigation/hydel schemes, power plants, *etc.*, come up in areas which are inhabited by tribals, leading to their forcible shifting and displacement to strange areas to which the tribal people have no bond or attachment. At times compensation only is given and this is often filtered away and the tribal family leads a life of utter poverty and starvation. Rehabilitation is given lip service and as tribals do not have land titles registered in their names, they often do not qualify for compensation. The sustained anti-Narmada agitation over the last 10 years, has ensured that compensation is adequate now. But, the rehabilitation authorities take into account only the 'land patta' or the lands cultivated are considered. They ignore the fact that about 30 per cent to 50 per cent of tribal family income is from MFP from surrounding forests. Land given for rehabilitation is rarely cultivable and even it were good cultivable land, the loss of income from MFP collection is not considered for compensation. Large dams have generally succeeded in displacing large number of the tribal population and in destroying their habitat.

(d) Physical Deterioration

With loss of income, surroundings and forests, the nutritional value of the food consumed by tribal people is reduced leading to increase in physical ailments and deterioration due to malnutrition with ailments like night blindness, dental cavities, anaemia, anoxeria, gum bleeding and stomach disorders. Also, traditional plant medicines are increasingly rare, leading the tribals to spend on modern drugs. For tribal women, the effect of felling forests is disastrous. The additional 3–4 hours of walking for firewood and MFP collection takes a toll with longer hours of walking and longer absence from home. Earlier when forests were nearer, the old women and children could join in MFP collection which is not possible now. Few women also use the primary health centres even though they get less nutrition than the tribal men. Pregnant women are forced to work till a few days before their delivery and return to work immediately after recovery from child-birth while old women also have to put in hard physical labour.

(e) Shortage of Raw Materials

There is competiton for raw materials like bamboo, timber, kendu leaves, mahua, and where the interests of the tribal people and the industrialists are in conflict, it is the tribal people who always lose out as they have rarely an articulative to voice their anguish and sorrow and their just demands. Some NGOs are taking up the cause of the tribals but the vested interests are just too powerful and the tribal people continue to be marginalised.

Shifting Cultivation

One of the major factors for deforestation is shifting cultivation or 'slash and burn' cultivation or 'jhum' or 'swidden' or 'podu-chas' or 'boofodo'. This is a very primitive form of cultivation with tribals felling a patch of trees, drying them and burning the same, so that the ash (high potash content) is used for fertilising the soil. The land is then ploughed, cereals/plants are planted for 2–3 years till soil fertility is reduced. Then the land is abandoned after the crops are harvested and this fallow period is long enough to allow forest cover regeneration. If the intervening fallow period is 18–20 years, shifting cultivation is most suitable in tribal lands with slopes of 15° or more. This fallow period is being shortened with disastrous consequences for the tribals and for the forests, such as low fertility and soil erosion. The fallow period which was an 18–21 years cycle in the early 1940's, became 15–18 years cycle in the 1950's and in the last 30 years, the cycle has reduced to 4–6 years only and both the tribal people and the land have suffered.

Shifting cultivation is practised by tribal farmers from 109 tribes in 233 blocks in 62 districts spread over 16 States. The land affected by shifting cultivation in a few States are as follows:

Table 6.1
Land Affected by Shifting Cultivation

Sl. No.	*State*	*Blocks*	*Area (in hectares)*
(i)	Arunachal Pradesh	33	92,000
(ii)	Andhra Pradesh	9	17,337
(iii)	Manipur	N.A.	83,200
(iv)	Assam	N.A.	69,000
(v)	Meghalaya	N.A.	70,000
(vi)	Orissa		37,084

Source: Unpublished material, NWDB, New Delhi.

However, about 13 per cent of these practising shifting cultivation are Scheduled Castes (9.47 per cent) and other castes. Some of the major tribes practising shifting cultivation are the Baigas in Madhya Pradesh, Naga tribes, Khasis in Meghalaya, Malayas in Kerala, Bondas, Saoras and Khonds in Orissa, *etc.* It must be remembered that shifting cultivation is practised in Sri Lanka, Korea, Africa, South-Central America, Pacific Islands besides India. The vicious cycle of smaller area available, deforestation, indebtedness and greater dependence of a larger number of families on shifting cultivation for survival, has continued the process of deforestation and deterioration of the socio-economic conditions of the tribal people. Greater pressure on less land (due to reserved forests) has reduced the cultivation cycle from 18 months to 6 years or even 3 years, and has prevented the regeneration of forests on this land causing soil erosion. The reduced fertility of the soil results in more pressure on the available land in order to meet minimal needs. From a constructive dependence, this has shifted to a condition of destructive dependence. Tribals living in forests have now shifted to a state of living on forests.

Wasteland Development

There is no such thing as a wasteland as all land has some use or the other. There is no land that is useless, no land that is waste but land can be neglected and land can be environmentally degraded. Out of a total area of 329 million hectares (mha) of land in India, data is available for 305 mha of land as regards land use.

As per these studies, area of wastelands is 79.5 mha while land that is productive but degraded is 95.5 mha. Land suffers from denudation and erosion, resulting in loss of top-soil through continued action of wind and water and water-logging resulting in soil salinity. Of the 175 mha of degraded wastelands, around 150 mha suffers from erosion of top-soil and its attended ills (floods and gully formation) and around 25 mha from wind erosion. This reveals that about 35 per cent of the land mass is badly degraded and half of our forests has very little or no growth. With their lifeline being connected to the health of forests, the tribal people who have virtually no lands registered in their names could be involved in wasteland development. This has been successfully done by the Madhya Pradesh State Government in Jhabua district

Table 6.2
Land Utilisation Data

Sl. No.	Type of Land	mha
(i)	Area under non-agricultural use	21.2
(ii)	Barren and uncultivable lands	19.8
(iii)	Net area sown	142.2
(iv)	Forest lands with good tree cover (45 per cent)	38.6
(v)	Miscellaneous tree crops and groves	3.7
(vi)	Forest lands with poor tree cover	29.3
(vii)	Cultivable wastelands	15.0
(viii)	Current fallow lands	13.8
(ix)	Old fallows	9.6
(x)	Permanent pastures and grazing grounds	11.8
	Total	305.0

Source: Unpublished material, NWDB, New Delhi.

and other district with the active involvement of the tribal people and it has been an astounding success. The MP model will be reviewed for replication elsewhere. But first it is essential to look at why earlier endeavours of wasteland development have failed! The National Wasteland Development Board (NWDB), set up in May 1985, has failed in its task of satisfying the needs of people dependent on it, in harmony with natural processes. The NWDB considered the wasteland development programme as essentially a joint effort of the various departments and the various State Governments.

At the implementation level, instead of a coordinated effort at implementation, it was the Land Development Department which cornered all funds and hence other Departments did not coordinate and the help of NGOs and local people including tribal people was never sought! The reasons for failure of the NWDB were that of a bureaucratic approach without any involvement of the affected people. Unless the tribal people and especially the tribal women are involved, any wasteland development programme will be a failure. But 'pattas' are not given to tribal women. All dedicated NGOs could be involved in the programme as Government departments and officials rarely have the inclination and compassion to deal with the tribal people. The tribal communities should also be involved in the effort with the micro-watershed treatment as the basis for all land treatment efforts. It has to be a collaborated effort on the pattern of the successful KFW-aided watershed project in Aurangabad/ Ahmednagar districts in Maharashtra. These projects are successful primarily due to extensive efforts by the NGO, to secure the active involvement and collaboration of all tribal people in the project.

The Madhya Pradesh Watershed Development Project

The livelihood security crisis results in a disturbed relationship between the local people and their natural resources. Employment oriented programmes were used to advocate a watershed-based plan for environmental management. The Rajiv Gandhi Watershed Development Mission was started in 1994 and is implemented in 7,827 villages with 30,344 user and self-help groups actively involved 5,304 women's thrift and credit groups have been operationalised. User groups have contributed over Rs. 3 crore for maintaining water harvesting structures which resulted in increasing groundwater levels in 3000 villages. The bureaucracy has been made very responsive and open in its working. Over two million trees have been regenerated due to the joint forest management programme as water conservation efforts have increased soil moisture and plant growth. The biggest benefit has been the rapid regeneration of grass which has increased fodder availability. The results in the Hathipalwa micro-watershed are given below:

Table 6.3
Income Parameters

Sl. No.	*Particulars*	*1995*	*1996*	*1997*
1	Grass Production (Tonnes)	160	360	480
2	Value of Grass (Rs. lakh)	3.2	7.2	9.75
3	Gross Productivity (Tonnes per hectare)	0.69	1.56	2.08
4	Gross Income per household (Rs. lakh)	3,048	6,957	9,286

Source: Anil Agarwal, Down to Earth, 31 December 1998.

143 percolation bunds have been built in 19 micro-watersheds (500–1,000 hectares). Irrigated area has doubled and agricultural productivity is increasing, while cropped area has increased by 7 per cent as also cropping intensity of cultivated land. There is a shift towards cash crops like soyabean and cotton. Food availability has increased and 313 grain banks have been established in the villages for availability of foodgrains on easy interest terms, in times of stress and drought.

Earlier, grass was purchased from Gujarat and seasonal migration was rampant. This has changed with export of grass-fodder due to watershed management. Better breed of cattle are being purchased and dependence on money-lenders has come down by 22 per cent. Grain banks have resulted in increased food security and distress migration has come down. All this has been done with an expenditure of Rs. 16.48 crore (till 30 June 1998) on watershed development of which Rs. 11.95 crore was spent on wages for watershed development programmes, while Women's Self Help Groups in the form of savings contributed Rs. 2.44 crore and money for maintenance of water harvesting structures was Rs. 0.48 crore. The money collected for all village funds was Rs. 0.42 crore while 17,297 members have deposited about Rs. 2.44 crore in deposits.

The success story of Jhabua can be replicated in other tribal districts in India. Here money has reached the beneficiaries in a very transparent manner and funds have not been siphoned off. The District Collector is the Mission Leader and is directly responsible for funds and project implementation. At the village level, there is an elaborate process of involving all sections of the village society. The work begins with a participatory rural appraisal exercise in which problems and solutions as also water-harvesting structures to be built, are identified by the village community. The plans are approved by the District Technical Group and funds for executing the programme are transferred directly to the Watershed Committee. For each structure proposed in the watershed development plan, a user group is created from the land-owners only. For the landless, Self-Help Groups are created for non-farming activities and women's groups are created for involving the women. The village watershed committees consist of the Chairpersons of the user groups, Self Help Groups and women groups with one-third being women members. In Jhabua, there are 1,256 SHGs involving 9,699 participants, 1,668 user groups with 13,947 participants and 1,748 womens groups with 25,506 participants. Thus, a committed administration can bring about a silent revolution in the tribal districts, if the active involvement of tribals and their views are taken into consideration. The tribal people can be involved in their socio-economic regeneration. The tribal people can certainly take care of their own future and the environment, provided they are given a chance! Let a hundred Jhabuas bloom so that tribal India can survive!

CHAPTER VII

Marketing in Tribal Areas

INTRODUCTION

The tribals observe a large number of traditional festivals during which they become quite frugal on other expenses but spend money lavishly, on food, drinks and clothing. Otherwise also, drinking liquor is a very common habit among the tribals which is the source of exploitation and is ruining their economic backbone. Taking advantage of this situation, the traders/middlemen provide them with needed commodities by resorting to advance trading for their agricultural or forest produce at throwaway prices or advance them money at very high rates of interest. The innocent tribals fall into their trap easily for early liquidity and in the process, get exploited. They themselves, however, do not realise to have been exploited as their wants are easily met at their door steps by these unscrupulous middlemen or traders.

Most of the tribal households are indebted to money-lenders because of this concealed socio-trading system to cover up their requirements of expensive festivals and rituals and heavy drinking. In spite of several stringent measures taken by the State Governments by promulgating several Acts and Rules and their rigid enforcement, exploitation is not significantly contained so far. A study of the marketing systems for tribal products and produce in Orissa would be an indicator for similar marketing set-ups in other States.

TRIBAL PRODUCE

The principal agricultural produce of the tribals are food grains like ragi, jowar, maize, rice, pulses and turmeric and oil seeds such as niger, mustard, groundnut and soyabean. The tribals also collect a large number of Minor Forest Produce (MFP) to eke out their livelihood / supplement their income. All forest products other than timber, firewood and bamboo are included under minor forest produce. The different types of MFP items collected by the tribals using very primitive methods are broadly set out as under:

Food and Beverage	Mangoes, jack fruit, kendu, tamarind, edible roots and tubers, green leaves, mahua, datepalm, salap juice and wild animals and rodents.
Oil seeds	Cashew nuts, sal, neem, mahua, karanj, kusum, char and others.
Medicinal herbs	Anantamool, chereita, dhunku, patal garuda, gaja pipal, ramdantan, bhuin nima, shekoy, dhakti flower, arrowroot, honey, wild onum, nux vomica.
Fuel wood	Brush wood and other woods.
Grass	Broom grass, sabai grass.
House-building and Agricultural material	Small timber, thatch grass, creepers and bamboo.
Household / Cottage Industries	Siali leaves, arrowroot, karanj seeds, green bark, tamarind seeds, sabai grass, broom grass, tassar cocoons, honey, wax and bamboo.
Produce of economic importance	Soap nut, honey and wax, tassar cocoons, mahua flowers, shikakai, kuchila, neem, nageswar, sal seeds, simul cotton, genduli gum, lac, char seeds, aswand, asok and sisal bark.
Fibres and Fossils	Sialifibre, simul cotton, jungle jute, kharma creepers, swan creepers.
Tan & Dye stuff	Myrobalans, fenfena bark, sunaribark, sialibark, kakala bark, datari bark.
Leaves	Kendu leaves, sal leaves, siali leaves.

MFP generates Rs. 300 crore annually and provides 70 per cent employment in the forestry sector. It generates 2 million man-days of work annually which can increase to 4.5 million man-days. After agriculture, the maximum income for tribal people is generated from MFP collection, processing and marketing.

Besides, a study of the Zoological Survey of India (Joseph, 1988) conducted in Madhya Pradesh and Orissa shows that the tribals have evolved to 156 applications of mammals and their products, 32 of birds, 30 of reptiles, 10 of fish, *etc.* The use of blood and meat of pigeons is widespread in Orissa for the treatment of paralysis. Derivatives of bear, bat, tiger, wild boar, cow urine, goat liver, hen eggs, honey, snake fat, flesh of earthworms, bones of elephants, *etc.*, are used for various diseases. While the exact 'scientific' value of these medicines is not known, the research reports a large number of cures effected by them. Another study conducted in Bihar, Orissa and West Bengal identified more than 120 herbal medicines. Out of around 1,000 persons treated, the medicines were successful in about 550 cases. Yet another study in Orissa and Madhya Pradesh (Fernandes, Menon and Viegas 1988 : 155–157) identified about 40 trees and more than 50 herbs used for medicinal purposes in these areas. This is obviously a lower estimate because it is not always easy to get secrets from the tribals.

MARKETING OF SURPLUS PRODUCTS

Weekly Tribal Markets

The 'haat' or tribal market, held on fixed days of the week in different locations, provides an inter-face between the tribal people and the outside world, sadly represented by exploitative traders and middlemen. Surplus grains, products and produce from the forests as also fish, poultry, honey, *etc.*, are sold by tribal people in these markets. Often they are not even allowed to come to the markets with their produce and they are chased by traders/middlemen and forced to part with their goods before they can reach the markets and naturally, the prices secured are less than what they would have got if they had sold the produce/products themselves. The sole major interaction with the non-tribal world is through the weekly '*haats*' as the limited food and other needs, are purchased here and their surplus available for sale, is sold here too. These markets are whole-day affairs and the entire layout of the market is interesting. All the tribal requirements for grain, hardware, clothes, groceries, *etc.*, are available in different sections. An important section is the '*handia*' or rice-beer which is the preferred intoxicant for relaxation. An important change is that some tribals are also selling their produce in these markets and getting better prices.

Collection of minor forest produce is one of the most important occupations of the tribal people with about 30 per cent to 50 per cent of their income derived from collection or value-addition after collection of minor forest produce. The State Governments generally try to eliminate the exploitative middlemen and pass on the monopoly purchase to State agencies. Due to sheer inefficiency, lethargy or competition, these agencies are not able to purchase all the surplus and often do not pay remunerative prices. More often than not, the traders and commission agents lend money to the tribal people during the monsoon when the tribal religious functions are held and then force the tribal people to sell their produce, at very low prices. As Government agencies are unable to purchase the tribal produce, it would be better if the Government agencies only regulate the market arrangements and ensure that the tribal people secure better prices. The elimination of traders/middlemen does not really serve the purpose and the inefficient functioning of the monopoly Government agencies, only serves to increase the woes of the tribal people. The barter trade system is another source of exploitation and the tribal people's terms of such barter trade are invariably weighed against them. The collection agents through Large Sized Adivasi Multipurpose Societies (LAMPS) are also exploiting the tribals, by not announcing purchase prices and fixing arbitrary quality standards. The tribal people are rarely aware of the fair prices fixed by the Fair Price Committees, on an annual basis.

The tribal weekly markets called 'shandies' or 'haats' are the major marketing outlets for tribal produce. It is basically an assembly of traders and people at a particular place on a specified day at least once in a week in order to bring and sell products and produce. Private traders visit 'haats' to purchase the produce and establish long-standing contacts with some villagers and visit these villages to purchase tribal produce. Tribal agents in the villages are also engaged in mediations or driving the tribal sellers to the traders. The tribal agents value commodities and arrange payments by the traders on the market day. The traders generally advance 40 per cent to 50 per cent of the produce value pledged to be sold and recovered at very low prices from producers for produce which is often under-priced or under-weighed. Some tribals prefer to sell to brokers because of personal contacts since long and also because of receipt of small loans in times of need or even due to fringe benefits like free tobacco or cigarettes, *etc.* The traders transport produce to major urban centres by carts and sell to the wholesale dealers. There are also 'bidari' traders who draw cash and kind loans from traders. While middlemen only purchase commodities, the 'bidari' tradesmen advance loans against commodities. These tribal markets are very important to the tribal people as they would otherwise have to walk miles for their bare necessities like grains, salt, oil, after selling their produce/products. The Government should open more such haats where necessary to the tribal people.

Government Agencies involved in Tribal Marketing

The tribal people are a well-knit and homogeneous social group. For that reason, the cooperative form of organisation, by and large, is considered suitable for them to bring about desired changes in their socio-economic status. The Social Welfare Team of the Committee on Plan Projects (1959) recommended in their report that "Commercial exploitation of forests be entrusted to cooperatives than to contractors". The Dhebar Commission (1961) recommended that "The sale and marketing of the produce and supply of tribal people's requirements at reasonable prices should receive special attention through cooperatives''. The Working Group on Cooperatives for Backward Classes (1961) attributed the slow pace of cooperative movement in tribal areas to structural weakness, faulty management, operational defects and adoption of wrong procedures and methods not suitable to the tribals. The Working Group suggested a separate organisation to provide such services as were being rendered by private traders. The Group further recommended the formation of ''Integrated Service Cooperatives'' at market level.

Against this backdrop, the State and Central Governments have organised/re-organised several agencies to provide an integrated marketing system in the tribal areas with an ultimate objective of weeding out the traders/middlemen and to ensure remunerative prices to the tribals for their produce both Seasonal Agricultural Produce (SAP) and MFP. The role/performance of LAMPS involved in the marketing of tribal produce are discussed below:

Large-sized Adivasi Multipurpose Cooperative Societies (LAMPS)

The Bawa Committee, 1972, recommended measures for improvement in the functioning of the cooperatives in the tribal areas, so as to provide multiple services such as credit, marketing and supply of consumer goods, *etc.*, to the tribals at a single contact point. In pursuance of these recommendations, the State Governments set up an integrated credit-cum-marketing tribal cooperatives at the primary level in the form of LAMPS, each society covering an average of 10,000 to 20,000 population in the tribal areas. In Orissa, there are 223 LAMPS operating in the tribal dominated areas.

The Tribal Sub-plan areas of Orissa consist of 21 Integrated Tribal Development Agencies (ITDAs) covering 118 Blocks inhabited largely by tribal people. These Blocks are in the undivided districts of Mayurbhanj, Keonjhar, Sundargarh, Koraput, Phulbani, Ganjam, Kalahandi, Sambalpur and Balasore. The LAMPS have been organised in the above 118 ITDA Blocks. While organising the LAMPS, the viability criteria on the basis of population and other factors were taken into consideration so that the area of operation of the LAMPS remained compact having 'haats' for procurement of produce, banking facility and potential viability. Out of these 223 LAMPS, 46 LAMPS cover a Block each in its area of operation whereas the rest of the LAMPS have been organised at the rate of 2–3 LAMPS per Block. LAMPS have been appointed as agents of State Marketing Agencies for procurement of agricultural produce and Minor Forest Produce (MFP) but the number of LAMPS participating in procurement operation are reducing as is value of produce handled. The LAMPS are given a commission of 2 per cent for MFP and 1 per cent in respect of agricultural produce handled on behalf of State Marketing Agencies.

The LAMPS have failed to achieve the objectives for which they were set up. A review of the functioning of the LAMPS leads us to identify the following structural limitations which need to be tackled on a priority basis:

(i) The large areas covered under LAMPS make them less effective to meet the demands of the tribals. The population is so scattered that quite often it takes a whole day for some members to come to the LAMPS on foot.

(ii) Heavy transporting expenditure is involved in carrying goods from purchasing centres to branch offices/head offices located in almost inaccessible and remote places in the hilly areas.

(iii) The financial condition of the LAMPS is very weak. They are unable to purchase required quantities of fertilisers in time to meet the demands of the farmers.

(iv) Most of the LAMPS are running under loss to such an extent that they are not in a position to meet even the salaries of the staff members.

(v) The transport charges paid by the Orissa State Cooperative Marketing Federation Ltd., is not sufficient to meet the expenditure incurred by LAMPS towards transportation of fertilisers.

(vi) Commission paid to LAMPS is not very encouraging. After deducting transport costs and handling charges, the margin left is negligible.

(vii) LAMPS incur loss as shortages of fertilisers occur in retail sales. Sometimes large shortages of fertilisers are incurred by LAMPS due to improper and prolonged storage. Most of the LAMPS have no improved godowns, which also results in damage to stocks during storage.

(viii) Quite often the official hours of operation of the LAMPS are not convenient to the tribals. As a result, both clients and business suffer.

(ix) The LAMPS are expected to be agents of STDCC in procuring Minor Forest Produce. But the STDCCs do not appoint all the LAMPS as its agents and all those appointed are not given permission to procure all types of minor forest produce. The tribals do not approach the LAMPS for sale of their produce for which they are primarily meant and organised. This is mainly due to lack of cooperation and coordination among LAMPS, TDCC and other cooperative agencies.

(x) Coordination and healthy organic linkage between the different tiers of the cooperative marketing structure (both horizontal and vertical) *viz.*, LAMPS, TDCC, RMCS, OSCMF, TRIFED, NAFED are lacking. Sometimes unhealthy competition among different cooperative organisations is discernible.

(xi) Management and supervision of advances/loans and their recovery need further streamlining.

(xii) Arrangement for linking credit with marketing of SAP and MFP needs to be strengthened.

(xiii) The share capital and managerial assistance is not adequate and hence most of the LAMPS borrow funds from the financing agencies to undertake consumer business. The financing agencies charge very high rates of interest to the extent of 13 per cent and above. Due to less margin and high managerial expenses, the LAMPS are not able to repay the bank loans and their viability is affected.

(xiv) The staff members of LAMPS do not belong to a single cadre. They are brought on deputation basis from Central Cooperative Banks, Cooperation Department, TDCC, *etc.* Even for the staff of the same ranks, different scales of pay are paid. The salary variations among the staff affect the work efficiency to a large extent.

Leasing Policies for MFP

The MFPs are categorised into 3 groups based on processes and methods:

(i) Non-nationalised MFP which is leased for collection to provide trade,

(ii) Nationalised MFP collected by government agencies as a monopoly (tendu leaf and malwa)

(iii) MFP commodities which are freely traded and collected.

The leasing system varies from State to State (Annexure 7.1) and depending upon local conditions, there is variation in collection systems. For non-nationalised MFP, the Forest Departments lease the right to collect for a season or for more seasons to the highest bidder through auction or tender system and is generally cornered by traders and commission agents, based on revenue maximisation principles and is against the principle of people's participation in MFP as the poor tribals cannot hope to challenge the traders lobby due to poor bargaining power and lack of market intelligence. The tribal collector is thus unable to form efficient collectives and as he is ignorant of prices, alternative markets and quality requirements, he is forced to sell for immediate and meagre cash to the traders. The monopoly STDCC organisations also do not give adequate purchase prices, besides cheating tribal people on account of 'sharp' practices, wrong weights, quality norms and low unit rates. Traders do not collect MFP unless market conditions are favourable while the tribal collector needs daily liquidity to purchase food and essential commodities and also due to past indebtedness which ensures that he is in perpetual need of cash. The MFPs which are freely found are also controlled by the traders. Cooperative societies like LAMPS and others, rarely succeed in securing leases from Forest Department as they are in poor financial health due to lack of marketing strategies, inadequate leadership, inefficient operations, malpractices and lethargy. These samitis are also expected to meet tax liabilities and abide by movement restrictions, such as for tree-borne oil-seeds. Thus the entire system that has evolved ensures that the tribal people manage to eke out a subsistence-level living in a buyer's market.

The nationalisation of MFP made through the State Forest Development Corporations (SFDCs) and State Tribal Development Corporations (STDCCs) ensures that the State retains monopoly over their trade and their method of price fixation ensures that overheads of these organisations are met, while the MFP collectors, the tribals, get only nominal amounts for their labour. The lack of village-level cooperatives has led to weaknesses in the entire cooperative network and have totally failed to evolve into dynamic organisations which assist the tribal people. Tribal Federation (TRIFED), the apex level tribal cooperative has a turnover of Rs. 100 crore and has also started exports to other countries. Their intervention or price support policies have also been nominal due to lack of efficient cooperation at the State level LAMPS at the grassroots level. While the list of MFPs nationalised is expanding, this has often resulted in tribal people being denied the right and access to market MFPs due to imperatives of state monopoly. This has restricted markets and potential buyers are kept out with only a few private traders exploiting the stagnant market. Thus, rather than protecting the interests of tribal MFP gatherers, nationalisation has provided a cheap and subsidised catchment area for raw material supply. Instead of tribal empowerment, the tribals have been badly let down by the inefficient government agencies. However, the Panchayat (Extension of Scheduled Areas) Act, 1996 has conferred ownership of MFPs to Gram Sabhas and Gram Panchayats in tribal areas and placed them in charge of marketing, but without proper means of doing so.

MFP Collection and Tribal Empowerment

With the liberalisation of the economy, further Government intervention can be safely ruled out. However, if the MFP policy is fine-tuned into an effective instrument of tribal empowerment, it would be necessary to take appropriate steps as MFP collection is an important economic activity for the tribal people. Appropriate cooperative organisations at the village level and revitalisation of existing structures for effective operations for MFP collection and procuring is a must. The use of NGOs and other informal groups like Joint Fund Management Groups, Self Help Groups, *etc.*, is necessary for improving the marketing arrangements for MFP. A uniform system of minimum prices, is a must. The Panchayats should also be able to play an effective role in collection, procuring and marketing of MFPs. There is also a need to reform and renovate all departments involved in tribal affairs such as Forest Department, Tribal Welfare, *etc.*, as this will facilitate tribal empowerment. The most important steps would be to facilitate village level cooperative institutions for MFPs on a cooperative basis with the Gram Panchayat as policy-maker. The steps to be taken are:

(i) Efficient marketing of MFPs.

(ii) Transparent system of operations.
(iii) Participation by all tribal people.
(iv) NGOs of proven capability with integrity to form SHGs.
(v) Dissemination of information among all tribal people.

This is a slow and painstaking process, by people who are able to win the tribals' trust and cannot be done overnight. The present system of control and nationalisation is not conducive for sustainable development of MFPs.

CONCLUSION

Despite the multiplicity of efforts of the State/Central Government to improve the marketing support for the tribal produce, there are frequent reports of exploitation of the tribals by traders, money-lenders and middlemen. Distress sales, collection of produce by traders at unremunerative/dictated prices, advance trading for crops, *etc.*, are still reported in different parts of the State. As already discussed, the situation is primarily due to lack of coordination/cooperation among the marketing agencies and their poor financial base, absence of production and consumer credit provisions for the tribals, lack of adequate processing facilities, engagement of traders in collection activities by the marketing agencies, *etc.* Under the circumtances, a detailed study on collection, processing and marketing of various tribal produce with reference to the operations of the credit and marketing agencies in the State is called for to streamline/improve the system. The tribal marketing set-up at the State level should be based on the following Table:

Table 7.1
Marketing Set-up Required for Tribal People

Sl. No.	*Particulars*	*Status*	*Action required*
1.	Role and Apparatus at State level for marketing	Inadequate and no initiative	Government of India (GOI) support required.
2.	Role and Apparatus at District level for marketing	-do-	-do-
3.	Market information availability on markets for tribal people	Very low/Not available	Support required/experiences of useful efforts to be shared.
4.	Professional Marketing Skills at State/District level	Absent	National efforts to streamline and ensure quality manpower.
5.	Existence of production and then marketing syndrome among State-level officials	Very high	Quality training programmes for re-orientation required.

(Contd.)

6.	Technology upgradation/ product modification efforts	Nil/Not Integrated.	National level stock and flow required
7.	Product Technology Information Collection and Transfer	Sporadic/Not Integrated	National Set-up Requirecd.
8.	Documentation in Marketing of Tribal Produce	Nil	Grassroots level required from NGOs.
9.	Policy Initiatives for Marketing of Tribal Produce	Lacks Clarity	Consolidated and Product-specific efforts to be made.
10.	Challenge to Poverty Alleviation from inadequate marketing infrastructure	Very High in Future	Setting up of National Marketing Support Agency is a must.

It is clear that without a top quality marketing set-up, the tribal produce, MFP and handicrafts products will not be able to withstand competition from machine-made products and mass-produced goods which benefit from economies of scale. This intervention should assist in creating a market niche and should not be perpetuated forever as it will make the tribals dependent on subsidised assistance.

ANNEXURE 7.1

Status of Procurement of MFPs in Different States

Sl. No.	States	Monopoly agency	Nationalised commodity	Collecting agency (if further appointed)	Price fixation method
1.	Gujarat	GSFDC	Tendu Leaves, Mahua flower, Mahua seeds and Doli, Gum Karaya	Village Panchayat	
2.	M.P.	MPMFP Federation	Tendu leaves, Gum Karaya, Myrobalan, Sal Seed	District Forest Union/ District MFP Union	Price Fixation Committee constituted by the Federation
3.	Orissa	M/s. Tribal Development Cooperative Corporation Ltd.	Tamarind, Hill brooms, Myrobalan, Nux Vomica, Siali Leaves, Harda, Amla Marking nuts, Soapnut, Gendigulum, Charagum, Dhawara Gum, Arrowroot, Honey, Cleaning Nuts, Kusum Lac, Thornbroom, R.S. Root, Sal Seed.		
		M/s. Agency Marketing Cooperative Society, Tikabali-kandamal	Tamarind, Hill brooms, Myrobalan, Siali Leaves, Harda, Amla, Marking nut, Soapnut, Gendigulum, Chargum Babul/ Outher Gum, Honey, Lac, Mahuwa Flower, Kara Seed.		
		M/s. Utkal Forest Product Limited	Mahua Seed, Bantulsi Seed, Chakunda Seed, Neem Seed, Kusum Seed, Karanj Seed, Char Seed Benachar, Bankulthi Seed, Gillo Seed, Gaba Seed, Indrozob, Shikakahai, Babul Seed Banhaldi Baidak Siali Leaves		

Sl. No.	States	Monopoly agency	Nationalised commodity	Collecting agency (if further appointed)	Price fixation method
		M/s. Orissa Forest Development Corporation	Tendu Leaves, Sal Seed		By High Power Committee
			Bankulthi Seed, Gillo Seed, Gaba Seed, Indrozob, Shikakahai, Babul Seed, Banhaldi, Baidak, Siali Leaves		
		M/s. Orissa Forest Development Corporation	Tendu Leaves, Sal Seed		By High Power Committee
		M/s. Markfed	Sal Seed		
		M/s. Kundli Lamps, Kundli Koraput	Tamarind Hill brooms		
4.	Andhra Pradesh	M/s. Girijan Cooperative Corporation	Adda leaf, Wild Broom, Hill Broom, Shikhakai, Amla Fruit, Cleaning nuts, Chironjee, Rock bee Honey, Apiary Honey, Kusum oil seed, Myrobalan, Mahua seed		Centralised commodities rates fixed by Chairman & MD of GCC.
		AP Forest Department	Mahua Flower, Marking nuts, Nux Vomica, Naramamidi Bank, Pongam Seeds, Sarapghandha Roots, (Rawlfiaserpencino) Soapnuts, Honey wax, Gum Karaya, Tamarind *(a)* Shell, *(b)* Seeded *(c)* Deseeded *(d)* Green *(e)* Seed, Teripods, Maredur, Gaddalu, Sugandhipala, Tendu leaves		Decentralised commodities rates fixed by the Divisional Managers of GCC.

Sl. No.	States	Monopoly agency	Nationalised commodity	Collecting agency (if further appointed)	Price fixation method
5.	Rajasthan	Rajasthan Tribal Areas Cooperative Development Federation	Gum karya (all kinds), Malkangani, Mahua Seed, Bichu Kanta, Dolma, Karanj Seed, Safed Musli, Ama, Soapnuts, Palas Seed, Honey, Chironjee, Giloy, Ratanjot, Dhatuni, Lal Arandi, Neem seed, Baheda Chaal, Amla Chaal, Chitrak Chaal, Shatavari, Puwad Seed, Bhilvaguda, Chatvor, Marodfali, Choti Kateri	LAMPS and own branches of RTADCF	By RTADCF on the basis of recommendation of District Collector. D.C. fixes the price on the basis of last year's sale and prevailing market rates in nearby mandies.
6.	Bihar	Territorial Circles of Forest Department	Tendu Leaves		
		M/s. Bihar State Forest Development Corporation	Sal Seed, Mahua Seed, Tendu Leaves and Myrobalan	M/s. Hanuman Minor Oil, Pvt., Lid., for Sal Seed	By High Power Committee at Patna for Sal seed, Tendu Leaves, Mahua Seed.
7.	West Bengal	M/s. West Bengal Tribal Development Cooperative Corporation	Sal Seed and Tendu Leaves	LAMPS	

Sl. No.	*States*	*Monopoly agency*	*Nationalised commodity*	*Collecting agency (if further appointed)*	*Price fixation method*
8.	Maharashtra	M/s. Maharashtra State Cooperative Tribal Corporation Ltd., Nasik	Mahua Flower, Mahua fruits, Gum, Hirda (Terminalia Chebula), Char, Awala, Baheda, Neem Seed, Karanj Seed, Amaltas Seed, Linn Seed, Tamarind Seeds, Palas Lac, Kusum Lac, Vanerand Seeds, Takada, Nirmali/Kapi, Guggul, Bapchi Seed, Kunchla Kari, Shikakari Ritha, Biba, Gunj seed, Broom grass, Mango Seed, Wavding, Baphali, Grass and fodder (excluding bamboo), Honey, Palas leaves, Sitaphal, Cashew nuts (except those grown by FDCM)	Through the network of its own office	The prices are fixed atleast once or twice in a week. The cost on four items, *viz.*, APMC cess, weighing charges, Hundi and Adivasi Cooperative Society commission are deducted from the basic price of APMC.
9.	Tamil Nadu	No MFP is nationalised and there is no restriction on trading of MFP.			
10.	Karnataka	No MFP is nationalised but the produce has to be traded in the regulated mandies.			
11.	Himachal Pradesh	H.P. State Forest Corporation Limited	Resin, Bamboo and Khair		
12.	North East States	State Government/ District Council	All MFP items		Mahul System on yearly basis

Source: Empowerment of Tribals and Sustainable Development of Non-Wood Produce, N.Ramji and A. Bhatnagar, Yojana, 15-17, April 2000.

CHAPTER VIII

Women in the Tribal Economy

INTRODUCTION

Living in remote, inaccessible and forested areas, the tribal people have learnt to depend on resources which are easily available locally. With the poor quality of available forest land and primitive technologies, every able-bodied person has to contribute to the tribal economy in a fight for survival in a subsistence economy. Young or old, male or female, all work for maintenance of the household, according to their capacities. In some tribal communities, women play a very important economic role, *viz.*, Koli women, Meitei women and Ho women. In traditional hunter communities, the men do the hunting while the women gather food and nuts, firewood and also tend small cultivated patches of land. They also have to look after their children, bring water and maintain households besides weaving cloth, *etc.* In many tribal communities, women have an equal economic role, attending to household duties, working in fields, construction sites, basket-making, running quarrying, weaving cloth and contributing to the family income. There is a distinction between the women in tribal, urban societies and those in rural areas. In urban areas, the males are more in number due to migration and factory labour (in Himachal Pradesh and Rajasthan) being examples of women continuing to live in rural areas while males migrate to towns for wage labour. While participation of urban males in labour work force is the same for tribals and non-tribals, in rural areas, it is 56 per cent for tribals and 53 per cent for non-tribals. But for women, only 11.64 per cent of non-tribal women are classified as labourers while 20.74 per cent are classified as labourers, as under:

Table 8.1
India: Labour Force (1981 Census)

(Per cent)

	Urban	*Rural*
Non-Tribal Women	8	12.38
Tribal Women	13	20.68

Source: 1981 Census data.

The high participation of tribal women in the work force is largely as cultivators and agricultural labourers both in urban and rural areas. The conclusion is that while the tribal male population is able to adopt new skills and technologies, the tribal women stick on to traditional occupations. This could possibly be due to lower levels of education among rural and urban tribal girls and women. In the 1981 Census, more than two-fifth of the tribal women were recognised as 'plain' or 'marginal' workers with a large proportion being engaged in agricultural activities.

Labour by Tribal Women

In tribal society, certain works are taboo for men while others are taboo for women. Certain specific roles have been assigned in tribal society for men, women and children (Annexure 8.2). The women's place in tribal society depends on various factors such as legal status, treatment meted out, her character and general behaviour in society. Hard work and contribution to family income have not helped to raise her status in society. The principles of social structure of a particular tribal society determines the tribal woman's status. The contribution of tribal women to economic development often exceeds that of the tribal men. Tribal women constituting 5.81 per cent of the total female population constitute 28.34 per cent of the female working population. Scheduled caste women and other women who form 22 per cent and 74 per cent of the total female population, constitute 24.6 per cent and 47 per cent of the women's working population, respectively. The tribal woman is thrice cursed *(i)* by being born as woman, *(ii)* by being born in an under-privileged class and *(iii)* lastly by having to survive in a hostile environment. However, tribal women have been assertive in groups and have organised several social initiatives *(i)* the Mothers' Movement in Manipur has sought to reduce drug-taking among youths in Manipur *(ii)* The Kaptapalli Samuhavikas (Self-Help Groups) in Nayagarh District Division have successfully stopped liquor production and sale in the village and later on in 22 surrounding villages. In many tribal villages, where the hunting role of the males has been curtailed, it is the women who work hard and cook food after collecting firewood, water, besides earning money, be sale of minor forest produce. But they continue to remain subordinate to men and have little role in family and community matters. This is where education could make a big difference. The education levels of tribal women are rising slowly, from 2.29 per cent in 1981 to 18.19 per cent in 1991. Educating the tribal women would certainly improve the health, hygiene and children's welfare as also the standards of tribal society. As per the 1971, 1981 and 1991 Census 92 per cent of the marginal workers are women, about 60 per cent are non-workers and 57 per cent are in the household industry and manufacturing process (Annexure 8.1). The percentage of tribal men workers has also been increasing from 26.8 per cent in 1971 to 43.7 per cent in 1991, implying that tribal women are being inducted into the work force. Literacy rates for women are also increasing. Tribal women have made their contribution as agricultural labourers, plantation labourers, construction workers and also as industrial workers. Women are a major economic force in tribal society besides being active on the home labour front. Besides various agricultural activities like sowing, weeding, transplanting and harvesting, the tribal women also collect minor forest produce such as leaf, gum, fruit seeds, herbal plants, brooms grass, oil seeds, *etc.*, used both at home and for selling in markets. Tribal woman have a major role in the construction industry as also in mining, mineral collection and other industrial operations, as tribal women are very hard-working, non-argumentative and obedient. It is a tragedy that land rights are never recorded in favour of tribal women except in matrilineal societies. A large number of tribal women in Bihar and West Bengal who own land, are being killed after being branded as witches so that vested interests/family relatives can possess their land. This is a social evil in which tribal society must ensure the rights of women. Most tribal women are rarely inactive. They are always busy at weaving, household chores, collecting and in wage-labour. Where the women are very hard-working, the tribal men have become lethargic mainly because of their loss of hunting rights. A mild segregation is visible as men take up activities such as hunting, fishing and felling timber for construction. In many cases, women exercise control not only over their own money but also money earned by the males who are prone to drunkenness. Women are also very knowledgeable about the type of soil, rainfall, climatic conditions while men and women have an equal say in crop-selection. Marketing decisions and decisions on children's education, are generally taken by women. In markets and *haats*, the tribal women actively participate in trade and barter negotiations and purchases or exchanges on farm, forest and animal produce for items of daily household use. In most tribal societies, women do equal labour as the men and in some, more than that of men. The Lhota Nagas and Lakher women perform hard physical labour as also among the Khasi and Garo women. Also, it is only the tribal women who save and earn money. The tribal males generally earn and spend, mostly on drinks and gambling. The setting up to micro-credit institutions called Self-Help Groups (SHGs), especially among tribal women, have helped them to harness their savings fruitfully, under the guidance of good NGOs. A few success stories of tribal women gathering together to harness their savings and mutual help, is set out in the following examples:

1. The Indira Gandhi Mahila Samiti, Kudamunda, Sambalpur

The poor can also exploit excellent business opportunities once they have money with them. This was proved by the SHGs formed by the women of Kudamunda village in Rengali block of Sambalpur district. After the linkage of the SHG with the Central Bank of India, Tamperkela, the SHG members who used to collect *Mahula* (Mohua flower, a forest produce) from the forest during their spare time, purchased around 750 kg of *Mahula* from others on payment of Rs. 2,055 (a portion of the loan was utilised for the purpose). After about 4 months, they sold the same to the collection agents and received an amount of Rs. 3,756 with a net surplus of Rs. 1,701 for the group. All the members of Indira Gandhi Mahila Samiti continued this for two seasons. They repaid the loan availed from Central Bank of India. They had a common problem, The Government-run primary school had only one teacher, and whenever he used to go on leave, the school remained closed and students used to enjoy unscheduled holidays. The SHG members approached other villagers and offered to partly finance the salary of an additional teacher from out of their profit if the villagers agreed to bear the rest of the expenditure. Finally, their children could get a second teacher. Next year, they got a loan of Rs. 10,000 from the bank which they wanted to utilise for creating an asset that would supplement their income. They opted for a goat-rearing scheme. Goats were purchased jointly and distributed among the members. To encourage them in their efforts, a he-buck was also supplied to the group by the Veterinary Department. Now the members of the group are proud owners of goats. Another problem faced by the members of the group related to non-availability of chemical fertilisers. In 1997–98, they considered bulk purchase and distribution of chemical fertiliser and directly from IFFCO. They borrowed Rs. 25,000 from the bank, purchased the fertiliser and distributed among the members as per their requirement. This helped in timely availability of fertiliser and that too at reasonable rates. The loan was repaid after the harvest of the crop. One will have to wait and see what ideas these enterprising ladies have for the future.

2. The Hill Broom Makers of Kalahandi

Poverty in an acute form exists in the tribal dominated district of Kalahandi. Distress sale of labour, land and produce in addition to the harsh economic environment, has led to the exploitation of the tribal inhabitants. Unforeseen and unplanned expenditure for religious and social functions left them in dire need without any savings for a rainy day. The money-lender and middleman, known as Gauntia, Charni Kalantar (those who charge 25 per cent interest per month) take away their agricultural and minor forest produce by giving nominal prices and the tribals in some areas go almost without food for 4–5 months every year during the monsoons. Lack of education, communication facilities and lack of awareness exposes them to exploitation by money-lenders, middlemen and businessmen. The main source of income is from cultivation and collection of minor forest produce. Antodaya, an NGO, helped in promotion of SHGs, whose members are engaged in procuring, processing and marketing of hill brooms. About 800 tribal women engaged in this activity, formed 35 SHGs and started saving small amounts on a regular basis. Initially, the tribals who collected the hill-brooms used to sell to middlemen @ Rs. 1 per kg as against Rs. 3 per kg offered by TDCC because of the presumable nexus between the middleman and the corporation staff. They did not have the right to process the raw material and TDCC used to collect the hill-brooms and sell these to businessmen from outside the State who process them into broomsticks. The NGO, through a Public Interest Litigation filed in the Orissa High Court, highlighted the plight of the tribal SHG members and provided them necessary skills to process the brooms and get a fair price through value addition. The SHG members had to travel to Bhubaneswar, the State capital and place their case before the authorities and the public through street plays and various other peaceful demonstration. But finally it had a marginal effect. This led to increase in procurement price of raw material by TDCC, but the SHG members are yet to legally get the right to process the hill broom.

3. The Santals of Mayurbhanj

DULAL, one of the leading NGOs has been working among the tribals of Labanyadeipur, Talia, Podadiha and Baripada and other areas of Mayurbhanj district. The tribals who have been encouraged to form SHGs are engaged in various activities such as Sabai rope-making, Khali leaf stitching and collection and marketing of various forest produce. The NGO is helping the group members to take up various income-generating activities such as poultry, goat-rearing, *etc.*

The NGO realised that it is very difficult to motivate the tribals to take up new professions as it is very difficult to change their style of living which is depend heavily on the forest for all their necessities which are, however, very limited. Poultry is one of the activities which has been adapted by the Santals as they raise and rear the birds for ritual sacrifice and cock-fighting which is one of the source of entertainment for Santals, especially on market days. Taking a cue from this, the NGO searched for an appropriate strain of poultry bird which can be reared in courtyards like the traditional variety while giving higher yield. They brought some new strains of one-day-old chicks from outside the State, inoculated and reared the birds for a month and sold them in lots of five to the SHG members. The members benefited out of this and repaid the loans to the Baitarani Gramya Bank.

The NGO also set up a training-cum-production centre for gem cutting with NABARD assistance and provided training to tribal women members of SHG. This created additional avenues for income for them. Now tribal women working at home can earn upto Rs. 150 per day instead of having to go deep into the forests in search of firewood at Rs. 75 a head-load.

4. Women Micro Entrepreneurs in Dhenkanal

Laxmi Narayana SHG in Dhenkanal district which started by saving and lending in kind rather than cash, subsequently switched over to cash savings in 1996. The group which consisted of 20 tribal women members, had been collecting savings @ 4 kg of rice per month per member and used to allow the needy members to borrow from the accumulated stock. The borrowing members used to repay whatever they had borrowed along with 3 kg of rice per quintal per month as interest. In 1996, they sold their stock for Rs. 7,000 and switched over to cash savings @ Rs. 25 per month per member. Subsequently, against the total savings of Rs. 10,000, the group availed a credit of Rs. 20,000 and the members borrowed from the group at 3 per cent interest per month. Many of the members of the group utilised the credit amount to increase the stocks of their own or husband's small shops. They could make a profit of 30–40 per cent from the extra stock created with the loan amount. They have plans to start a joint betelnut processing business with the involvement of the group members in the near future.

5. The Tribal Women of Kaptapalli SHG Fight against Liquor Consumption

Kaptapalli Gram Panchayat of Nuagaon Block in Nayagarh District (around 87 km from Bhubaneswar, State Capital of Orissa) has many Self Help Groups in Kahtapalli, Kersang. Godakabari and nearby villages. These SHGs have been formed with the intervention of an NGO named 'Samuhavikas' and have been maintaining their savings for the last 3 years and were linked to Bank of Baroda, Bandhabuin branch. The saving amount varies from Rs. 3 to Rs. 15 per month. Some of the SHGs have only male members whereas a few others have only female members. Most of the members who used to collect firewood from the forest and sell it in the market were persuaded by the NGO to organise into Thrift-cum-Credit Groups and take up various activities such as tamarind processing, paddy processing, trading in blackgram, leafplate making, processing of forest produce, *etc.* They provide loan for emergency as well as production purpose from SHGs.

Most of the SHG members are Kutia Kandhas (The Kandhas are the largest among 62 tribes in the State of Orissa with a population of 9.89 lakh as per 1981 Census. There are various sections among Kandhas—Dongria Kandhas of Koraput District, Kutia Kandhas and Desia Kandhas in Kandhamanal and nearby districts) who racially relate more closely to Proto-Australoid stock and speak the 'Kuli dialect. The Kandhas are basically agriculturist. the primitive groups, mostly the Dongria Kandhas of Koraput Districts are mainly engaged in shifting cutivation.

The Kandhas use both distilled and fermented liquor in their socio-religious affairs. Distilled liquor is largely consumed by Desia Kandhas. The primitive sections demand upon the local varieties like

Sagopalm juice (Salap) and date-palm juice (Tadi). Local herbs and roots are added to increase the alcoholic content. Sometimes Mahua flowers are collected and liquor is prepared to meet the requirement on special occasions.

Liquor is considered as food and at the same time a ritualistic food to satisfy dieties and spirits. It is considered as a social necessity by the Kandhas and, therefore, consumed by them irrespective of sex and age. It also affects them as they are exploited by the money-lenders and liquor vendors. At the time of marriage, among other gifts, 'Irpi-Kalu' or distilled liquor is exchanged between the two parties as a prestigious gift.

At the same time, in group meetings, the women folk used to discuss the ill-effects on their socio-economic life, especially its impact on their family life and family economy. It was a common consensus among the women folk that preparation and consumption of liquor has a shattering effect on their household which resulted in untold suffering for the women folk. Subsequent to the discussion among the women members of the Godkabari Mahila (Women) Self-Help Group on 26 February 1995, the consensus emerged that they will appeal in writing to the Village Committee for a long-lasting solution to liquor menace in their village. A village meeting was held on 26 March 1995 and the following decisions were taken:

(i) No villager will be allowed to consume liquor and disturb the peace in the household.
(ii) No one is allowed to prepare or sell liquor in the village.
(iii) For tribal rituals at the time of marriage and 'Sradha' Ceremony, permission of the Village Committee may be taken to prepare liquor at home.
(iv) A Committee was formed to implement this on whose report a person found guilty can be penalised, *i.e.*, imposition of fine amounting to Rs. 551 (Rupees five hundred and fifty-one only).

Similarly, on receipt of a written complaint by Kaptapalli Mahila (Women) Self-Help Group on 22 December 1995 the Kaptapalli Purusa (Male) SHG acted upon the complaint immediately and convened a joint meeting of all male and female members in the village on the same day and decided to stop preparation and consumption of liquor in their village, failing which the *Gramsabha* was authorised to take the help of the police.

Anti-Liquor Grama Yatra. The community pressure worked well for quite sometime and the drinking habit of the villagers came down. At the same time, there were a few instances of flouting the dictat of the *Gramsabha*. The determined tribal women were quite vigilant and as decided earlier, they unitedly intervened and broke the equipments, pots and the fireplaces, *etc.* The related issues continued to remain in their agenda in the group meetings. The collected mahua flowers was used as cattlefeed and the women members also helped in selling them outside. Even suggestions to cut all 'date palm' and 'sago-juice palms' trees were considered and rejected.

It was subsequently observed that the local addicts were coming from nearby villages to drink. The determined tribal women of the Self Help Groups decided to face this challenge initially by forming a joint committee of the villagers in three villages of Kaptapalli, Kersang and Godakabari. Later it was decided to cover all the nearby villages for anti-liquor *gramyatra*. On 19 May 1996, around 70 women and 30 tribal youths from different villages of Kaptapalli, Berhunbari and Bahadajhola Panchayats met at Kaptapalli village. A few NGOs also associated in creating consciousness against drinking and in participating in the *gramyatra*. They moved to Kersang, Gunamati and Phampuni villages where the participants were given a traditional welcome. In each village, meetings were organised where all the villagers participated and after thorough discussion in the *gramsabhas*, the host villagers agreed in writing to strictly practise prohibition in their own villages.

6. *Fisher Women of Gopalpur*

People Rural Education Movement (PREM), one of the reputed NGOs of the State, has been providing indirect support to the SHG movement in the State. It formed an organisation called Utkal Mahila Sanchaya Bikas 'O' Samaj Mangal Sangathan, (UMSB) for collection of small savings and promoting SHGs. Moreover, the major objective was to establish an alternative sustainable credit delivery system which was not usurious and would serve the poor at the time of their need. It would also help in organising local resources and optimising their use. During the past 10 years, people in and around 600 nearby villages had been discussing the basic problem of the present credit delivery system. In June 1992, they started their own method of savings to meet their credit needs, for assets creation. In Ganjam and Gajapati districts, UMSB has promoted around 800 SHGs with a total membership of 17,154 and savings of Rs. 19.47 lakh as on 31 March 1996. They have 17 area offices and only 308 groups had been linked to canara Bank, Berhampur with credit assistance of Rs. 18.86 lakh. With this, 4,835 members had been linked to bank credit. After the formation of SHGs during the last two years, which fostered various income-generation activities such as social forestry, community goat-rearing, fish vending, dry fish business, Kewda-leaf mat making, Agarbatti making, *etc.*, the SHG members have been getting regular income. The NGO provided skill to SHG members to make various useful artefacts out of kewda leaf which resulted in value addition from out of a product which till then had no value and was being wasted. Similarly, the fishermen folks in an around Gopalpur who formed SHGs and were earlier dependent on money-lenders for short term loans at exorbitant rate of interest for purchase of catamarans, nets, *etc.*, and used to sell their catch to them at a very low rate now could get small loans from the SHGs. This also encouraged the fisher women to start small business such as fish and dryfish vending with credit for SHGs. This is a step towards economic improvement of the poor, especially of woman and will lead to empowerment.

7. Tribal Women and Spices in G. Udayagari

Samanwita is a voluntary organisation operating in G. Udayagari area of Kandhamal District of Orissa. Formed in 1978, the organisation sponsored by SBI and the State Government and support by NABARD has been operating with the objectives of capacity-building of the tribals and downtrodden in the area which will, through socio-economic upliftment, bring about transformation in this backward area. One of the core activities pursued by Samanwita is empowerment of people through promotion of Self-Help Group besides various other activities such as Training-cum-Production Centre for turmeric and sisal fibre, sales promotion, *etc.*

Establishment of Samanwita has helped in creating awareness in adjacent villages. Eleven women came forward and formed Burupati Women's Self-Help Group. An account was opened in SBI, ADB, G. Udayagari with an initial deposit of Rs. 165 in August 1993. But, gradually the group members lost interest and deposits became irregular and group dynamics weakened. The bank provided loan directly to 3 individual members of the group but they were misutilised by the members.

In 1995, with NABARD providing support to Samanwita, a few training programmes were organised and it helped in survival of the groups with members. A training-cum-production centre was established at G. Udayagari. The group members who had a savings of Rs. 2,759 selected turmeric processing as a viable economic activity. Members got training at the TPC and started processing of turmeric with capital investment of Rs. 1,050. One quintal of raw turmeric was processed into 83 kg of turmeric power and a profit of Rs. 328 was earned on the first day. Members were visibly happy. They sat together and decided that each of them will take Rs. 20 towards labour and will reinvest the balance Rs. 128 in their group fund.

The process continues. Their capital has grown to Rs. 13,188.75 as on May 1997. The product range has covered mustard, ragi and black pepper. Products worth Rs. 33,176 have been processed and profit of Rs. 6,176 has been earned and 128 man-days of employment has been generated.

ECOLOGICAL DEGRADATION AND WOMEN

It is the poor tribal women who bear the brunt of the ecological degradation of the tribals. With more competition for ever-diminishing resources, women have to walk farther and farther away from home in search of safe drinking water, fuel-wood and other minor forest products. This leaves less time for attending to household duties and also adds to their physical burden whether they are old, young or pregnant. The tribal women are hardest hit of all rural women in view of the harsh environment. Availability of fodder, fruits, fuel, *etc.*, is closely linked to the quality of life of tribal women. Women as producers and carriers are wholly dependent upon the regenerative capabilities of natural system to provide the necessities of life. The close symbiotic relationship of women and forests, built up over the centuries is slowly breaking down.

The Aga Khan Rural Support Programme (India) in Netrang block, Bharucha, undertook a farm forestry programme in the teak forests which had been nearly degraded due to encroachment after illegal felling. The poor soil productivity added to the problem. The farm foresrty programme taken up among the male tribals did not work out. When the tribal girls and women were involved as Extension Volunteers (EVs), they selected fruit-bearing trees rather than the eucalyputs varieties thrust upon them earlier and tool enthusiastic interest in the programme. When women were involved in the project, their selection of tree varieties depended upon the following factors:

(*i*) ability of tree species for fuel wood
(*ii*) small wood for building shelters
(*iii*) fruits.

The men were more interested in quick growing varieties for monetary gains. Empowerment of women under this programme helped in halting the seasonal migration during dry seasons. Growth of village nurseries managed by women saw lower product mortality rates. The involvement of the tribal women not only encouraged them to be resource managers rather than resource-users, but also encouraged them to earn more and save for their families.

CONCLUSION

In this male-dominated tribal world, the recognition that the women too have a role to play, needs to be encouraged and replicated. Any development programme for tribals must necessarily be aimed at women first, if it is to succeed. The rural tribal women have been underestimated and discriminated against in all walks of life despite their substantial contribution to the household economy and in turn, the national economy. In India, women produce 30 per cent of all food commodities consumed but get only 10 per cent of the income and own less than 10 per cent of the property or wealth of the country. The provision of rights and protection from social irregularities in statute books, are not enough. Women in tribal society have been deprived of their economic status. The empowerment of tribal women and the improvement of their status and economic role, needs to be integrated into economic resources or employment opportunities that make them financially independent. Tribal women live in conditions that do not permit them to meet minimum food requirements. Even the money earned by them from hard physical labour is often not controlled by them. As tribal women have no property rights or mortgage to offer, bank credit is not available and they have to depend upon non-tribal money-lenders for their consumption needs. This entraps the tribal people in a vicious cycle of perpetual slavery and bondedness. A tribal woman's earnings are generally used for the family needs and also for clothing. By empowering tribal women, tribal economic development would be a reality sooner than later.

ANNEXURE 8.1

Tribal Work Force

Sl. No.	*Particulars*	*1971*			*1981*			*1991*		
		Ratio to total	*Male*	*Female*	*Ratio to total*	*Male*	*Female*	*Ratio to total*	*Male*	*Female*
1.	Population	100	50.38	49.62	100	50.43	49.57	100	50.28	49.72
2.	Literates	11.3	97.71	2.29	16.35	96.96	3.04	29.60	81.81	18.19
3.	Cultivators	22.80	80.15	19.85	23.15	74.55	26.45	24.38	70.65	29.35
4.	Total Men Workers	34.48	73.24	26.76	45.29	67.17	32.83	49.30	54.74	43.71
5.	Agriculture	12.87	60.36	39.64	13.20	53.61	46.39	15.74	56.80	43.20
6.	Household Industry and Manufacturing Process	0.38	65.75	34.25	0.60	59.55	40.45	0.69	49.03	50.97
7.	Other Workers	2.53	77.65	22.35	4.89	76.48	23.52	1.49	77.49	22.06
8.	Marginal Workers	—	—	—	7.26	10.24	89.76	9.91	7.82	92.18
9.	Non-workers	61.42	36.02	63.98	50.20	42.06	57.94	50.64	40.51	59.49

Source: Various Census Reports, 1971 to 1991.

ANNEXURE 8.2

Labour Division in Tribal Society

	Men	*Women*	*Children*
1.	Digging, channeling, making ridges, embankment.	Carrying loads, earth, supplying stones, gravel, earth for reparing dams and making ridges	Bird-catching and fowling, tending of cattle; Fishing in shallow water and carrying receptacle for fish.
2.	Manufacturing of musical instruments, bows and arrows, nets, traps, fishing implements.	Painting of mats, buckets making ropes, baskets, barter and sale of agricultural produce and marketing.	Collecting of baskets of Mahua, helping parents in agriculture and domestic works.
3.	Basket-making, making of leaf cups for final distribution.	Fishing drying and preserving fish.	
4.	Rope-making.	Making mud-walls, plastering and painting them. Weeding, threshing, husking rice and oil pressing.	
5.	Fishing, hunting and bird-marring.	Fetching water, collecting fuel, cooking, collecting mahua, drying and storing mahua and kusum, brewing wine, *etc.*	
6.	Cutting trees, bamboos, cart-driving, home-thatching, constructing wickets.	Sale of lac, collection of minor work, working as wage-earners in mines and in construction work, in construction workm digging, *etc.*	
7.	Ploughing, harrowing, winnowing, watching, planting of trees, propagation and collection of lac, cocoons. Tanning leather for use in musical instruments.		
8.	Cock-fighting, labour in mines and plantations.		

Source: D.N. Majumdar; A Tribe in Transition–A Study of Cultured Pattern: Longmans, Green & Co. Ltd., Calcutta, 1957.

Part–II
By Tribal People — Activities for Economic Development

CHAPTER IX

Collection and Procurement of Minor Forest Produce

INTRODUCTION

Forest resources consist of two types of products, namely *(a)* Major Forest Products and *(b)* Minor non-wood Forest Products. The Major Forest Products consist of timber, small wood and fuel-wood including charcoal. The Minor non-wood Forest Products include all products obtainable from the forests other than wood. Thus, Minor Forest Produce is composed of all products of vegetable, animal and mineral origin except those minerals which are under the control of the Mining Department.

The items of Minor Forest Products may be classified into the following categories:

1. Fibres and Flosses
2. Grasses, Reeds, Cane and Fodders
3. Essential or Volatile Oils
4. Tannins and Dyes
5. Gums, Resins and Oleoresins
6. Drugs and Medicines
7. Edible Products
8. Oil Seeds
9. Leaves
10. Animal, Mineral and Miscellaneous Products.

1. Fibres and Flosses

The fibres may be classified into three categories, namely *(a)* soft fibres like jute and flax which are derived from base of stems, *(b)* hard fibres collected from leaves of Manila hemps and Sisal and *(c)* surface fibres collected from the surface of stems, leaves and seeds like cotton. The fibres are used in textiles and also netting and cordage. These commercial fibres are of the types of cotton, jute, flax, ramie and hemp. There are plating and weaving fibres. These fibres are used for making baskets, straw hats, mats, chair seats, and other forms of wicker-works. Certain fibres are used as brush fibres, filling fibres and paper-making fibres and in the manufacture of natural fabrics. Generally these fibres are hard in texture.

The trees which give fibres from stems are many, but those which are easily available are Calotropis gigantica (Arakha), Acacia leucopholea (Ghoria), Bauhinia vahlii (Siali), Butea monosperma (Palas) giving fibres from young roots, Ficus bengalansis (Bara) giving fibres from aerial roots, Ficus religiosa (Aswatha), Sterculia Villosa (Kodala), Sterculia urens (Genduli) and Kydya calycina (Kapasia).

Fibres from Leaves. Plant leaves yield fibres. Some of the species whose leaves yield fibre are as follows:

Agave cantula (Baramasi) yielding fibres from the leaves which are extracted by the process of retting, Agave sisalana (Sisal fibre), Caryota urens (Salap) known as Indian Sagopalm of leaf fibre yielding plant.

Flosses. Flosses are used for a wide variety of purposes which include manufacture of life belts and as stuffing in mattresses, pillows and cushions. The most important floss yielding species found in forests is Bombax ceiba (Semul). Capsules of these trees yield a floss which is soft and strong, widely used for life-saving appliances at sea and also as a stuffing in mattresses and pillows. Calotropis gigantica (Arakha) is also another species of shrub type, the fruit of which give fine, silky, soft, glossy and resilient floss materials.

2. Grasses, Reeds, Canes and Fodders

The most important grass of great commercial value is Eulaliopsis binata (Sabai grass). This grass is extremely suited for manufacture of paper and pulp. It is also used for the making of ropes with which carpets are made. Another type of grass of commercial value is Thysanolaena Agrosta (Phuljhadu or hill brooms). This species is used as broom. Fodder grasses are of numerous type. Some grasses are exotic while others are native to different parts of India. Most of them grow wild and some of them are cultivated. The main fodder grasses are as follows:

(i) *Andropogon ascinodis.* It is a gregarious species growing in the hills of North-eastern India.

(ii) *Andropogon pumilis.* It is a gregarious annual grass. This species is a good fodder and preferred by cattle both in green condition and as hay.

(iii) *Bothriochloa ischaemum.* This is a fairly good fodder species found everywhere in the countryside.
(iv) *Chrysopogon aciculatus.* It is found in the plains and low hills and on village pasture lands.
(v) *Brachiaria mutica.* It is used for sillage, hay and grazing.
(vi) *Cenchrus ciliaris*
(vii) *Dichanthium annulatum*
(viii) *Panicum antidotale*

Fodder Trees

There are many tree leaves of which are relished by cattle and goats. Some of the common fodder yielding trees are Acacia catechu (Khaira), Acacia nilotica (Babul), Azadirachta indica (Neem), Bombax ceiba (Simuli), Butea monosperma (Palas), Dendrocalamus strictus (Baunsa), Ficus bengalensis (Bara), Ficus religiosa (Aswtha), Gmelina arborea (Gambhari), Lagerstroemia parviflora (Sidha) and Polyalthia longifolia (Debadaru).

Grasses used for Matting

There are a number of grasses which can be split and used for weaving mats. These include:

(i) *Cyperus corymbosus*
(ii) *Saccharum munja (Sarakanda)*
(iii) *Typha elephantina*

Grasses used for Making Ropes

The most important grass used for making rope is Eulaliopsis binata (Sabai) which has been already referred to above. The other types of grasses used for this purpose are Saccharum munja (Sarakanda) and Themeda arundinacea.

Grasses of various types may be used for other purposes such as manufacture of chairs, stools, baskets and screens, for khus-khus screens of aromatic scented mats and for house-brooms.

Canes

Over 350 cane species are found in India. They are the stems of climbing plants of the Genus Calamus and other related genera such as Ciratolobus korthalsia. The canes are used for a wide variety of purposes such as making of ropes and cables, for making furnitures, walking sticks, umbrella handles, and for making baskets. Canes are split into fine strips which are used for making seats, mats, baskets and other fine wicker works. Some of the important cane species are Calamus guruba, Calamus palustris, Calamus rotang and Calamus vaminalis.

3. Essential or Volatile Oils

Essential oils are volatile odoriferous liquids occurring in many plants. They evaporate when exposed to air. Different parts of a plant such as fruits, flowers, leaves, bark root, wood and seed yield such essential oils of aromatic smell. It is found out that over sixty families of Indian plants yield essential oils. Various methods are adopted for the extraction of essential oils from plants. Some of these methods are distillation, expression and extraction by solvent using enfleurage (extracted under ordinary temperature) and maceration (extracted from flowers such as rose).

The uses of essential oils are many. Some of such uses are listed below:

(i) Agarbattis
(ii) As solvents in the paints and varnish industries
(iii) As insecticides
(iv) Confectionery and aerated water
(v) Pharmaceutical and medicines
(vi) Toothpaste, scented tobacco, soaps, cosmetic and perfumes and flavouring essence used in candy and icecreams.

The essential oils can be classified on the basis of the parts of the plants from which it is extracted. The classification is as follows:

(i) *Grass Oils.* The important grass oils include *(a)* Citronella oil, *(b)* Ginger grass oil, *(c)* Lemon grass oil, *(d)* Palmarosa oil, *(e)* Vertiver oil.
(ii) *Wood Oils.* The important wood oils are *(a)* Agar oil, *(b)* Cedar oil, *(c)* Pine Oil, *(d)* Sandalwood oil.
(iii) *Leaf Oils.* The important leaf oils are *(a)* Camphor oil, *(b)* Cinnamon leaf and bark oil, *(c)* Eucalyptus oil, *(d)* Mint oil.
(iv) *Root Oils.* The important root oils are *(a)* Costus oil, *(b)* Khus-khus oil.
(v) *Flower Oils.* The important flower oils are *(a)* Champa (Michelia champaca) *(b)* Kewda, *(c)* Rose oils.

4. Tannins and Dyes

Tannins are secretions of plant tissues. They are used mainly to render the hides and skins resistant to decomposition and make them strong and flexible. The bark of many trees yield bark tans. Standing trees are not usually stripped off their bark to extract the tannins. Generally the barks are obtained from felled trees. The important species which yield bark tannins are as follows:

(i) *Acacia nilotica (Babul) and Acacia arabica.* The bark of these trees yield tannis of superior quality.
(ii) *Anogeissus latifolia (Dhaura).* The leaves of this species are used for extraction of tannins.
(iii) *Cassia fistula (Sunari).* The bark of this species gives tannin.
(iv) *Ceriops discandra.* Both bark and leaves of this species yield tannins.
(v) *Shorea robusta (Sal) and Terminalia arjuna (Arjun).* Barks of these trees produce tanning of reddish brown colour of good quality.

(vi) *Fruit Tans.* The fruits of many plant species give tannins which are used locally for commercial purposes. Some of the species giving tannin yielding fruits are as follows:

(a) *Terminalia chebula.* By far the most important of the myrobalan is the fruit of Terminalia chebula. Its fruits yield tannin,the trade name of which is chebula myrobaian. The best time for collection of fruits from the point of view of tannin content is January.

(b) *Terminalia bellerica.* Its fruits yield a tannin whose trade name is baleric myrobalan.

(c) *Emblica offianam.* This plant species yield tannin from its fruits, leaves and twig and stem barks.

Myrobalans are one of the important training materials of the Pyrogallol class producing brownish colour deposit on leather called bloom. The other speices yielding fruit tannin are Acacia nilotica and Caesalpinia coriaria. The pods of Acacia nilotica yield a tannin whereas the tannin extracted from other species is present in the tissue.

(vii) *Leaf Tans.* Leaf tans are generally used by local tanners. The species which yields leaf tans are Anogeissus latifolia and Carissa spinarum. Other well-known leaf tans are collected from Emblica oficinalis, Goruga pinnata and terminalia species.

Dyes

Many plant tissues secrete vegetable dyes. There are wood dyes, bark dyes, flower and fruit dyes, root dyes and leaf dyes. The plants which are included under Artocarpus family such as Artocarpus heterophyllus and Artocarpus lakoocha yield wood dyes. The wood is turned into powder which is boiled in water and extracted. By this process a bright yellow dye is obtained. The bark dyes are obtained from Acacia species and Terminalia species. The flower and fruits of many plant species yield valuable dyes which are more important than the dyes obtained from wood, bark and roots. The species which comes under Butea monosperma yields a bright yellow colour dye from its flowers. Similarly Crocus sativus is source of yellow colour dye collected from its flowers. The fruits of Malotus phillippensis (Kamalagundi) yield a red dye which is one of the most popular dyes of India. Kamala is the trade name of this dye. It is used for dyeing silk and other fabrics. It is used in colouring oil, soap, ice cream and drinks. The root dyes are obtained from certain plant species such as Berberis aristata, Morinda tinctoria, Onica granatum, The leaves of some plant species also yields dyes. Chlorophyll which is present in most plants is being used widely in the manufacture of foodstuff, soap, mouth fresheners and dental cream. One of the well-known species yielding leaf dyes is Lawsonia inermis. Its leaves yield an orange dye Henna.

5. Gums, Resins and Oleoresins

Gums and resins are exuded by plants mainly from the stem and also from roots and leaves. Those products are exuded as a normal process and also as a result of injury or disease to the bark or wood of the plant.

Gums are a sticky substance. They dissolve or are softened in water. They are known as true gums. Resin has a plastic consistency soluble in alcohol but unaffected by water. These are known as hard resins. Oleoresins are mixed with a fair percentage of essential oils. The gum resins are a mixture of gums and resins. There are also gum oleoresins which are composed of oleoresins with a small quantity of gum. There is also another product which is called balsam which contains certain liquid organic compound of aromatic acids with a small quantity of solid resin dissolved in them.

Gums

Gums are formed as a result of disintegration of plant tissue through a process called Gummosis. Natural gums emanate from plant as liquid which on exposure dries up into translucent amorphous flakes. These having the least colour and highest adhesive power are most valuable. These varieties are used for clarification of liqueurs, finishing of silk and preparation of quality water colours. Intermediate grades are used in confectionery, cosmetics, pharmaceuticals and printing inks and in dyeing. The cheaper grades are used in adhesives and in printing industries. Two kinds of gums are noteworthy for commercial purposes—Gum Arabic and Gum Tragacanth. The Gum Arabic is imported mostly from Sudan. It is collected from Acacia senegal. The Babulgum collected from Acacia nilotica can serve as a substitute for real gum Arabic. The gum collected from Anogeissus latifolia (Dhaura) which is known as Ghattigum can also be used as a substitute of real Gum Arabic. Gum Arabic which is imported from Sudan (about Rs. 1,000 per ton) is used for dyeing and block printing on fabrics.

Genduli gum obtained from Sterculia urens species or Gum Karaya, as it is called, is used as a substitute for the real Gum Tragacanth. The State which produces the largest quanity of Genduli gum (about 3500 tonnes) is Madhya Pradesh. It is used in pharmaceuticals, confectionery, cosmetics, textiles, *etc*. The technical know-how for processing the gum is lacking in India. Therefore, whatever quantity of gum is exported is all unproocessed and the countries getting the Indian gum get it processed to made it suitable for use and also for exporting to other countries. India holds the monopoly over production of gums. But it does not get full value of item because of its deficiency in knowledge about processing.

Further, due to defective methods of collection, cleaning, grading and packing, the produce does not fetch proper price. Research and extension in these aspects and training to the the collectors can add value to the produce. Indiscriminate tapping and clandestine cutting and felling have resulted in diminution of the gum yielding plants. Replenishment and plantation programmes are conspicuous by their absence.

The gums are exuded in the following manner:

(i) Spontaneous exudation in dry seasons.
(ii) Charred trees affected by forest fire exude gum.
(iii) Artificial incursion allows gum to flow out.
(iv) Heavy and intensive tapping causes gum to exude.

Many plants exude gum. Of them the trees account for a large portion. Some important species are *(a)* Acacia catechu, *(b)* Acacia modesta, *(c)* Acacia senegal, *(d)* Anogeissus latifolia, *(e)* Bauhinia retusa. There are various other gum-yielding species of secondary importance such as *(a)* Albizzia chineusis, *(b)* Anacardium occidentale, *(c)* Mangifera indica, *(d)* Spondias pinnala.

Resins

Resin secretes from cavities or passages in many plant species. When the resins exude from the bark they get hardened on exposure to air and sunlight.

Resins are used for a wide variety of purposes. Certain types of resins are melted and mixed with seed oil or turpentine oil to form oil varnish. Some resins are dissolved in alcohol to form spirit varnish. They are dissolved in alkali to form soaps. They are also used in medicine and pharmacy, for sizing papers, for incense and in the preparation of sealing wax.

The resins can be classified as follows:

Hard Resins

Some of the commerical hard resins are:

(a) *Copal*—It is a semi-fossil resin devoid of essential oils. It yields hard elastic varnish most suited for outdoor application.
(b) *Dammar*—It includes a group of resins used for varnishes.
(c) *Amber*—It is a brittle fossil resin used for making jewellery, beads, carving and varnish.
(d) *Lacquer*—It is a natural varnish and it is exuded from two and three species, namely Melanorrhoea usitata and Rhus virnicilua.
(e) *Sandarae*—It is light yellow soft resin used for making spirit varnish.
(f) *Mastic*—It is a very expensive and high grade resin used for coating metals and pictures.

Oleoresins

Oleoresins contain considerable amount of essential oil together with resin material. Some of the commercial oleoresins are:

(a) *Balsam*—Balsams are oleoresins containing benzoic or cinnamic acid. These are used in medicines and pharmacecticals and perfumeries.

(b) *Turpentine*—These oleoresins are obtained from coniferous trees.
(c) *Copaiba*—It is a natural oleoresin obtained from trees of the genus Copaifera which are native to tropical South America.
(d) *Elemi*—These are soft resins used for hardening varnishes.

Gum Resins

The gum resins are a mixture of both gum and resins. These gum resins are of great commercial value. Some types of gum resins are used for adding flavour to curries and sauces. One variety of gum resin is used as incense. Some others are used in medicines.

Some of the important hard resins, oleoresins and gum resins leading tree species are mentioned below:

(a) *Boswellia serrata*—Its trunk exudes gum oleoresin. It is used mainly as an incense and as medicine to get relief from rheumatism and nervous diseases.
(b) *Canarium strictum*—Its bark exudes resin. Resin flows from vertical incisions for six months yearly and this flow goes on for about 10 years. It is mainly used in the manufacturing of varnishes, bolting wax.
(c) *Shorea robusta*—The sal tree yields an oleoresin whose trade name is Laldhuma. The tree is blazed and the resin exudes out. Each mature tree can yield on an average 5 kg of resin every year. Resin also exudes naturally from injuries caused by sal heartwood borers. The main uses of laldhuma are: *(i)* It is aromatic and used as an incense and a disinfectant and fumigant. *(ii)* It is used in inferior paints, varnishes and caulking boats. *(iii)* It has certain medicinal properties and is used in the preparation of skin ointments.

6. Drugs and Medicines

The forests everywhere have numerous plants and trees, the parts of which yield important drugs and medicines. Man from the earliest times, has been using these medicinal herbs to get relief from various diseases. Roots, tubers, stems, barks, leaves, fruits and flowers of various medicinal plants are used as curative of diseases. The important MFP of medicinal importance which are collected from the forests are Amla, Baghanakha, Bahada, Baidanka, Banahaldi, Bana Kulthi, Bana Tulsi, Chakunda, Char Seeds, Chireita, Dhatuki Flower, Gaba, Harida, Indra Jaba, Kaincha, Kurchi, Kochila (Nux Vomica), Landa Baguli, Lodhra, Mankadakendu, Mahu (honey), Nageswar Flower, Palash, Pita Alu, Putrani R.S. Root, Sikakai.

There are many published works on medicinal herbs. These publications give names of the medicinal plants, their distribution, parts used and diseases for which plants are used.

7. Edible Products

Hundreds of edible forest products in the form of roots and tubers, fruits and flowers, pulps and seeds are available in different forest areas. These are known to the people and the tribal people in particular collect these edible products. Some of these wild edible products are eaten raw and some cooked at home. Due to the shortage of land in the tribal areas the crops grown in the lands are in short supply and therefore they are bound to depend upon hunting and food gathering from the forests in and around where they live. The starchy rhizomes, roots and tubers, green leaves are generally cooked and eaten. There are different types of fruit trees like Amba (mango), Panasa (jackfruit), Kendu, Bel, Kaitha, Tala (palm), Sitafala, Tentuli (tamarind) and Jamun, Barkoli, Khajuri (datepalm) and other varieties of plums are eaten either in the raw form or when ripe. Seeds of various fruits like Kaju, mango, jackfruit, sal, char, *etc.*, are relished very much by the tribal people. Saps tapped from many tree species like Salap (Sagopalm) and Khajuri (datepalm) quench their thirst for intoxicating drinks. Mahula flower is brewed to get a liquor which they are extremely fond of. Eggs of birds, larvae of insects particularly tasar (silkworm), white ants are a delicacy of tribal people. Collection of honey in which they have acquired great expertise is a favourite food stuff. These edible wild products are available in different seasons and therefore they are available to the tribal people round the year, particularly in the lean months starting from April upto the end of October.

8. Oil Seeds

Oil seeds are some of the most important items of forest produce. There are about more than 100 oilseeds-bearing trees in the country and many of them are found in the forests. Oil gives energy. Energy consumption in India is on the increase. The annual consumption of 649 million tonnes of oil equivalent in 1973 has increased to 2019 million tonnes of oil equivalent in 1992. Some of the important oil-yielding species are as follows:

1. Arakha (*Calatropis gigantica*)
2. Agara (*Argimone mexicana*)
3. Ashwagandha (*Withania somnifera*)
4. Bhalia (*Semicarpus anacardium*)
5. Cashew nut (*Anacardium occidentale*)
6. Jatropha (*Jatropha curcas*)
7. Karanja (*Pongamia glabra*)
8. Kusum (*Schleichera oeosa*)
9. Mahua (*Madhuca indica*)
10. Mango kernel (*Mangifera indica*)
11. Neem (*Malia azadirechta*)
12. Oil palm (*Elaeisa quinensis*)
13. Polang (*Calophyllum inophyllum*)
14. Sal (*Shorea robusta*)

15. Sirisa (*Albezia prosea*)

In addition to these species, there are plants, the seeds of which yield oil which is used for medicinal purposes. These are Ananta, Gilo, Bana tulsi, Banakulthi, Baghanakha, Charseeds, Chakunda, Babul, Morda, Baidanka seeds, Shikakai seeds, Palash and Indrajaba seeds. The oil extracted from these items are used for medicinal purpose as well as for making soaps.

The oils can be classified into three groups, namely non-drying oils, semi-drying oils and drying oils. The oil extracted from castor seeds and ground nuts (Which is a SAP) belong to the category of non-drying oil. The oil extracted from sesamum and cotton seeds fall into the category of semi-drying oil. The drying oils are those which are extracted from lin seeds and tung seeds.

Oils are used for a wide variety of purposes such as:

(i) For edible purposes as a cooking medium.
(ii) For the manufacture of soaps, cosmetics and toilet preparations.
(iii) For paints, varnishes and lubricants.
(iv) For heat and light.

9. Leaves

Like other MFP, leaves of many trees and plants occupy a very important position in the life of human beings. These are leaves which are used for medicinal purpose, leaves as edible items and leaves from which dyes are extracted. Leaves of certain tree species like Shorea robusta (sal) and palm are used as thatching materials to cover the roofs of houses. The leaves of Siali creeper, Sal and Kendu trees are of great economic value. Leaf utensils are manufactured from Sal and Siali leaves. Kendu leaves are used for making bidis. These items are in great demand in the rural areas and provide employment to thousands of people. The leaves of datepalm make good mats and this occupation keeps many women engaged in their own houses.

10. Animal, Mineral and Miscellaneous Products

A number of animal products are obtained from forests. Some of the products collected from the forest of Orissa include lac, cocoon, honey and wax.

Lac

This is a resinous matter secreted by the tiny lac insects Lacifer lacca, primarily as protective covering. It lives as a parasite on different plant species. The secretion from this insect forms encrustation over the twigs. Some of the host plants of the insect are Acacia nilotica (Babul), Albizia lucida, Butea monosperma (Palash), Cadjanus cajan (Kandula), Moghania strobilifers, Grewia serrulata, Leeasp, Schleichera oleosa. Shorea talura and Zizyphus mauratiana (Barakoli).

Only Kusumi lac is collected from the Orissa forests.

Silk

Tasar cocoons are either collected or cultivated in Orissa. The tasar silk-worm (Antheraea papila) feeds on leaves of Shorea robusta (Sal), Terminalia tomentosa (Asana) and Teminalia arjuna (Arjuna). The tribal people in different parts of Orissa are engaged in tasar silk-worm rearing from time immemorial. The women, in particular, play a greater role in this activity.

Honey and Wax

Bees collect nectar from many different flowers in the forests and store it as honey. Mainly two species of bees produce honey in the wild. They are rock bees (Apis dorsata) and Indian bee (Apis indica). A single comb may yield 2 to 4 kg of honey and round about 1 kg of wax. The tribal people are skilled in reaching the bee hives wherever they are.

Miscellaneous Products

There are some items which do not fall exactly into any of the classification of MFP. The cleaning nuts and soap nuts are some of the examples which come under miscellaneous category.

The pods of Acacia Concinna yield shikakai which contains saponins most useful for cleaning hair, washing silken clothes and woolen clothes. The fruits of sapindus trifoliatus known as Ritha contain saponin. It is widely used for washing silk, wool and delicate fabrics. The marking nuts procured from Senrecarpus anacardium contain corossive juice which is used for marking ink for clothes. There are cleaning nuts which are used for cleaning muddy water. A paste of these nuts is used in the inner surface of an earthen container containing muddy water. After sometime the mud in the water gets deposited at the bottom of the pitcher making the water clean. The seeds of Strichnus polatorum (Nirmala or Katak) serves this purpose.

There are various other MFP of the types of grasses beads, seeds which are used as ornaments and reeds which are woven into cloths in use among some of the primitive tribes of Orissa. Orchids of different types are used as decoratives.

SEASONALITY OF COLLECTION

The tribal people, irrespective of age and sex are engaged in collection of forest products both for their own consumption and for sale. The edible wild products like fruits, roots, tubers, green leafy vegetables are mainly collected as food items whereas other products such as seeds, honey, arrowroot, tamarind, hill brooms, *etc.*, are sold or are exhanged for their daily necessities like cereals, salt, kerosene, clothing and ornaments. Forest collection though not a main source of income for a majority of tribal people specially among the settled agriculturists and industrial workers or shifting cultivators it is a major supplementary source of income and provides scope for engagement almost round the year, particularly during lean period starting from April to the end of October.

Items like mango, sal seeds, ripe fruits, oilseeds, *etc.*, are collected by women and lac, honey, bark, gum, *etc.*, by men. Collection of honey is a difficult job and the honey collectors have to climb the hills with the help of rope to reach the bee hives. Therefore, it is exclusively done by men.

Annexure 9.1 shows the availability of different types of MFP on a month-wise basis. Very few items are available in the months of July to September after which the number of items increases and the largest number of items is available from January to May, the period conforming to the period of plenty and fiestas and festivals. The slack season begins from July till October when the growth of plants takes place and it is forbidden to interfere in the process by tapping the plants. This period coincides with the period of scarcity of food.

METHODS OF COLLECTION AND PRACTICE OF REPLENISHMENT

Fibres

The method of extraction differs from species to species. The process by which fibres are loosened from the woody plant tissues is called retting. The plant stems are kept under water for the fermentation to take place. The gummy substance is removed by water manually. Then the stems are broken and the fibres scrapped. Under-retting keeps some gummy substance attached to the stem whereas over-retting weakens the fibres. Not all species are required to be kept immersed under water, because in some cases the fibres become useless due to the application of water. Fibres from the leaf are separated by the same process of retting. The fibres which are extracted from the leaves are thoroughly washed and then dried in the sun. Grasses are collected manually and dried and then arranged into bundles.

Essential Oils

(a) Extraction by Distillation. The oldest and simplest method for getting essential oils is water distillation. Water is filled in copper stills and the plant materials are kept on grid immersed under water and then the water is boiled. Heat is supplied either directly or through a steam jacket. The essential oil evaporates and passes with the steam into a condenser. On pulling, the oil collects on the surface of water from where it is removed and filtered.

In the case of steam distillation, a separate boiler is provided for producing steam. With the help of a pipe, the steam is fed to the bottom of the still. The plant materials are kept in a stack of trays inside the still. The steam is blown through the still. Thus the volatile oil which comes after the material passes with the stream is recovered after filtering the water in the condenser.

(b) Extraction by Expression. When the essential oil is extracted on a small scale, the pressure is applied manually. But when large scale extraction is

required, mechanical devices are used for the application of pressure. The method of expression is used in such cases where there is a likelihood of heat destroying the odour of the essential oil. Normally the peels of citrus fruits are subjected to pressure for extraction of essential oil.

(c) Extraction by Solvents. There are two ways by which extraction of essential oil can be done. One is extraction by non-volatile solvents. Two processes are involved in the case of extraction by non-volatile solvents. One process is called Enfleurage and the other is called maceration. The process of enfleurage is adopted for obtaining oil from flowers. A fatty greasy base is smeared on glass plates arranged in tires one above the other. This base absorbs the essential oils present in the flowers. The flowers sticking to the fatty base are left for a couple of days. These are again replaced by another set of fresh flowers. After this process is repeated a number of times, the fatty base saturated with perfumes is removed. It is washed with alcohol to extract the perfume.

In the case of maceration process which is used for extraction of essential oil from roses, the bruised flowers are immersed in a bath of olive oil which is maintained at a temperature of about 70 °C by water bath. Fresh flowers are added from time to time to get the desired concentration of the perfume.

As regards the volatile solvent, the procedure is the same as that of maceration. Petroleum is used in this case as volatile solvent. essential oil is extracted from various substances and the oils which are extracted are of different qualities and types. Some of these types are mentioned below:

Grass oils — Citronella oil, Ginger oil, Lemon grass oil, Palmarosa oil, Khus oil.

Wood oils — Agar oil, Sedar oil, Pine oil, Sandalwood oil.

Leaf oils — Camphor oil, Cinnamon leaf and bark oil, Citrodora oil, Eucalyptus oil, Mint oil.

Root oils — Costus oil, Indian valerian oil. No such oil is extracted anywhere in Orissa.

Flower oils — Keora oil—This oil is obtained from the flowers of Pandanus tectorius (Kia). The essential oil is obtained from the white or cream colour layers of lowers by distillation method. No water is used in this process.

Tannins and Dyes

Wood Tan. No standing tree is stripped of its bark to extract tannins. Rainy season is avoided. The stripped off bark is dried in the sun for some days and these are put in a wooden vat to which steam is applied for extraction of tan liquor from the bark. the liquor is purified and mixed with other substances to give the desired quality and colour to the leather. Such species as cassia fistula (Sunari), Acacia nilotica (Babul) and Acacia catechu (Khaira) supply barks to extract wood tannin. Tannin is also extracted from leaves. A mixture of green leaves, red leaves and petals are collected. These are dried and grind to a fine powder from which tan substances are extracted.

Dyes are extracted from different parts of the trees like bark, flower and fruit. In some cases the wood of certain species is grind to a powder or broken into piece and then boiled in water to get wood dyes. Ripe fruits are collected in gunny bag and beaten and shaken till the red powder separates. This process is applied to Mollotus Phillippinensis (Kamala gundi). The trade name of the dye which is extracted is known as Kamala. Sometimes fruits are soaked in water and then dried and then stirred to get the dye.

Gums, Resins and Oleoresins

Gums. Gums are obtained in various ways. Some of the methods are mentioned below:

In some cases the gums exude spontaneously in hot summer month and in other dry seasons. Gums exude from those trees which are charred by forest fire. The gums are collected by hand. Large lumps are broken into pieces. Foreign bodies like bark, stems, leaves, sands, *etc.*, are removed by hand as far as possible. Some grading is also done manually. Gathering and grading are done in dry season when the yield is more.

Gum is collected by artifical incisions, but heavy and repeated tapping causes damage to the tree and sometimes death to the tree. In Orissa, gum is extracted from Acacia nilotica (Babul), Acacia catechu (Khaira), Anogeissus latifolia (Dhaura) and Sterculia urens (Genduli) Amta, Terminalia balerica (Bahada) and Char.

Acacia catechu does not give any gum during the rainy season. The gum begins to ooze out freely during the dry seasons, usually from the injured areas on the bole and branches or from incisions. These trees can be tapped heavily for a couple of years after which they are felled for extraction of catechu.

Anogeissus latifolia yields gum which is called Ghatti. The gum oozes out naturally fom the wounds during the summer months.

Bauhinia retusa (Kanchana) gives gum of superior quality. A blaze is made of 7 cm × 15 cm × 2 cm, with the help of a sharp knife. The width is slowly increased to about 35 cm. The gum oozes out from the blaze during hot season. A tree is tapped for four to five years and then given some rest.

Sterculia urens (Genduli) is the source of Gum karaya. The gum which exudes from the tree is of 4 grades. The finest grade is either white or colourless, the second grade is either pinkish or dirty white. The third grade is black in colour. The fourth grade is dust-like. The main properties of gum karaya are: It is white or intense rubbery in colour and solidifies to large roundish tears. It is not soluble in water, but swells into jelly-like mass. It is adopted as a substitute for gum tragacanth. It is widely used in the textiles, food processing, cosmetics and other industries.

Resins. Resins of different types are collected from different species,. Boswellia serrata (Salai) gives gum oleoresin whose trade name is Salai gum. A piece of bark is shaved from the trunk of fully-grown tree at a certain height from the ground. By this process the Phloem containing resin candlea and ducts is exposed. The blaze is freshened after every 4th or 5th day. The first collection is made after two weeks. Freshening is done from time to time and the original blaze is widened. Salai gum exudes from the blaze in 5 cm. to 8 cm. long tears. It hardens after about 4 days and retains its golden colour and transparency. The tapping season lasts for 8 months starting from November to July until the monsoon sets in. The Salai gum is used as incense and as a cure of rheumatism and nervous disorder. It is also used for lighting fires.

Shorea robusta (Sal) is a source of oleoresin whose trade name is Sal or Laldhuma. Resin exudes out from the blaze on the tree trunk and solidifies quickly on exposure. Freshening is done from time to time by scrapping hardened resin from the blaze. A fully-grown tree yields upto 5 kg of resin in a year. Blazes which are freshened in every two weeks rather than every month.

Edible Products

Hundreds of edible wild plants occur in the forests. Different parts of different plants are edible. Some edible items are eaten raw, some are baked and some other are cooked. Many fruits are eaten when they are unripe and some other fruits are eaten ripe. Many types of edible roots and tubers are collected by digging them out from the underground with the help of digging sticks or sharp pointed iron crowbar. Leaves of many plants are plucked and cooked. Pulp of fruits is eaten without cooking them. Kernels like mango kernels are dried, made into powder with which cakes are prepared by baking.

The tribal people acquired adequate knowledge regarding seasonality of various items of wild edible products. For example when the leaves of many tuberous plants turn yellow, it is ready for digging. Arrowroot which is very common wild edible product is dug out from the ground when its leaves turn yellow.

Harida, Bahada, Amla, tamarind, *etc.*, are collected using a uniform method. For collection more than one person is required. Generally a family consisting of three to five members is employed in the job. Gunny bags, baskets, broom sticks, bamboos are required for collection. Sometimes, some people climb up and shake the branches so that the fruits fall on the ground. These fruits are heaped in a particular place with the help of broomsticks and thereafter brought home by filling them in gunny bags.

The seeds and roots of Bauhinia vahlii (Siali) are eaten. The seeds are eaten raw or fried. The roots are boiled and eaten as a substitute for potato.

The fully-grown plant yields edible parts. Roots are dug by crowbar and the seeds are collected when the fruits are ripe. Some plant species contain delicious sap which is tapped by incision. Cariota urens (Salap) is a kind of sago palm which gives refreshing juice collected from the flower stock which ferments into toddy or palmwine. Palms having an age of more than 15 years are tapped and a palm tree of full growth yields about 15 litres of juice in 24 hours. Datepalm also yields juice which is drunk fresh or after it is fermented. The juice is boiled to yield jaggery. A good quality sago is obtained from the pith of the stem. The sago is dried and pulverised to make cakes out of it. Dendrocalamus strictus (a variety of bamboo) yields seeds which fall on the ground. These seeds are picked up by hand. These are eaten either raw or after making a gruel out of seed flour. Diosoyros melanoxylon *(Kendu)* bears fruit containing sweet pulp which is relished by the tribals. These fruits are either plucked or collected from the ground. Ficus glomerata (Fig) is found in the forests. Its fruit is eaten in the form of vegetables when they are ripe. The fruits are plucked by climbing up and collecting them in bags or baskets.

Oil Seeds

The oil seeds which are collected from the forests are Kusum, Neem, Karanja, Mahua, Banatulsi, Narda, Nageswar, Gillo, Banahaldi, Banakulthi, Chakunda, Babul, Polanga, Mango kernel and Sal seeds. Mainly two methods are used for extraction of oil—*(i)* Expression and *(ii)* Extraction. The method of expression involves the following steps.

The seeds are cleaned and all impurities are removed. The kernels are separated from the outer shells either by crushing or running a heavy roller over the seeds. Oil is extracted by cold-pressing or by hot-pressing. In latter case the crushed seeds are boiled and kept in two containers which are placed one upon the other, face to face. These containers are placed on a wooden plant kept horizontally at a height above the ground and with another plank one end of which is fixed to a tree trunk, the containers are pressed by lowering the free-end of the upper plank to touch the end of lower plank.

Besides this traditional method of extraction, oil presses (ghani) are used to extract oil. The oil press is operated by harnessing bullocks to rotate the beam which presses the oil seeds in the Ghani.

Extraction by Solvent Method

This method involves the use of volatile solvents to recover the fixed oil from the oil seeds. The oil seeds are cleaned to remove the impurities. Then the kernels are separated from the shells and crushed. Thereafter these are placed in extractors to which solvents are pumped in a continuous flow. As the extractor works the solvent containing fixed oil comes out. It is distilled and again pumped into the extractor. The fixed oil which is thus extracted is led to a tank to settle down and thereafter it is purified. Solvents like petroleum, Ethal, Carbon disulphide, *etc.*, are used for this purpose. There are only a few solvent extraction units for extraction.

Leaves

Previously it has been mentioned that leaves of many different species are used as edibles. Besides, there are leaves from which dyes are extracted. There are also leaves of different plants which are of medicinal importance. In addition to these uses of the leaves, there are leaves of great commercial importance. Kendu leaves, for example, from which Orissa and Madhya Pradesh collect revenues, are used for rolling bidis. The State Governments get millions of rupees as royalty out of the sale proceeds of the Kendu leaves. Similarly Sal and Siali leaves are of great economic value. These products fetch millions of rupees to the State exchequer out of the commercial use of these products. All these leaves are plucked manually by thousands of labourers employed for this purpose. These are dried and kept in bundles in stores maintained by lease-holders.

Animal Products

Mainly three items are worth mentioning in this section. These are lac, honey and wax and cocoons.

Lac

This is a resinous matter secreted by the tiny lac insect Lacifer lacca primarily as a protective covering. It lives as a parasite on different plant species both in the wild and in cultivated conditions. the secretions from these insects for encrustations over the twigs.

Only kusumi lac is collected by the tribals. There are two crops of kusumi lac, one crop called "Aghani" and the other is called "Zethwi". The kusumi crops are mostly grown from the tree called Kusum (Schleichera Oleosa) and with kusum brood lac on a few host plants. Some of the host plants are Acacia nilotica, Cadjanus cajan. In kusumi strain inoculation for Aghani crop is done in July and harvesting in January and February, and for Zethwi crop inoculation is done in January and February and harvesting in June and July. The Zethwi supplies brood for the major kusumi crop. Since the period of development of the Zethwi crop falls entirely in summer months, it very often undergoes failure because of the extreme heat.

The figures of last two years show that in the year 1993–94 the quantity collected was of the order of 209.04 quintals whereas it has increased to 280.00 quintals in the following year 1994–95. There was a time when the State was producing 1381 MT half a century ago (1947–48). Almost two decades ago, Orissa was producing on an average almost 300 MT of kusumi lac every year. The present average production as stated by the Study Group on Lac sponsored by NABARD in 1988 is about 80 MT. But the procurement of lac today is only about 25 MT.

It shows that the production of kusumi lac has suffered a great setback. The reasons for the fall in production are many. There is non-availability of brood-lac. Although a few brood farms are maintained, the quantity of brood lac production is insignificant. In the lac-growing districts of the country, intensive cultivation is slowly dying out.

Besides the shortage of brood lac, adverse climatic condition and price fluctuation, dominance of intermediaries, continuous traditional method of cultivation, inadequate extension services and restrained availability of credit all taken together have been working adversely against the lac cultivation.

Honey and Wax

Honey. Many tribal people collect honey mainly for sale. The Hill Kharias of Mayurbhanj district are expert bee-wax and honey collectors. In a dark night, the Kharias climb trees or hills where beehives are traced out. The hives of hills are usually found in the precipitous side of the hill which cannot be reached on foot. A ladder fixed to a tree at the top of the hill is lowered upto the hive. A man comes down with the help of this ladder upto the hive and moves a torch emitting smoke around the hive to scare away the bees. He pokes at the comb with a stick and breaks it so that honey and pieces of hive fall into a basket which is held at the bottom of the hive. One hive yields about four to six litres of honey and one to 2 Kg of wax.

Honey is usually collected from January to April, and wax is collected as byproduct of beehive. After honey is squeezed out, the hives are boiled in water. This mixture is poured into a gunny bag placed on a pit dug in front of the house. This strained material is poured into a pan placed over a pot of boiling water. By this process, the water content is steamed out and the wax deposited as a sediment. thus the wax is made ready for sale.

Tasar Cocoons

Tasar cocoons are collected from the forest and also cultivated near the village sites. The tasar silk-worm moth has been identified as Antheraea paphia. The cocoons which form the source of the silk are locally called Bobei and Nadia. The insect is a denizen of the forest inhabited by tribal communities. The tasar silk-worm feeds on such food plants as Asan, Arjun and Sal.

The seed cocoons are collected from the forests during the months of June and July. They are sold during August and September to the rearers as seeds. The moths emerge during the period from August to October and the laying are collected and retained for rearing. The newly-hatched larvae of August and September spins cocoons in the branches of host plants by the end of October or early November. Two crops can be obtained in a year. Sometimes three crops are possible, if the moths are bivoltine or trivoltine in character.

It is a practice that forests are leased out by the Forest Department in the tasar tract to the rearers in the interest of the industry. A moderate fee is collected from the rearers as Dalkati (cutting of the twigs). The Adapahis (a tasar-growing plot having hundreds of host plants) are under cultivation since time immomorial and adapahi of one person is not trespassed by any other person. The trees are topped each year to get fresh leaves for the rearing next year.

A rearer temporarily shifts his residence to his Adda from his home. He leads a life of a hermit following self-imposed religious restrictions and obligations as per custom and tradition. the rearer and his whole family sit under trees with bows and arrows to scare away the birds and other enemies who eat up the moths.

The silk worms crawl out to the leaves of the trees in which the packets containing hatched eggs are placed. The worms grow larger and larger, and spin cocoons in the tree. From the colour of the cocoons the termination of spinning by the silk worms is indicated. After 8 to 10 days the cocoons are harvested and sold out in the weekly market or to the Tasar Growers Cooperative Societies. In Orissa generally the cocoons are steamed so that the silk worms inside the cocoons are killed. These steam-stifled cocoons are sun-dried and later stored in bags for sale.

PERSPECTIVES

It is observed that the tribal people who are closely linked with the forest and whose life pivots around the forests are employed as daily labourers for which they are paid daily wages not in terms of market price of the produce which they collect. Except the nationalised items private trading is in vogue in respect of most of the items. Even in the case of nationalised items, the real growers or rearers who are mostly tribals do not turn up to compete with other bidders and ultimately the non-tribal merchants succeed in the auction sale and enjoy the profits and the tribals are expropriated from such benefits.

Massive amount of money is realised from different agencies towards royalty payable to the Government. A portion of its proportionate to the quantum of collection area wise of MFP should go to the Tribal Sub-Plan for utilisation in development of tribal people. The main objective of setting up Cooperative bodies was to eliminate private trading and middlemen and involve tribal people in the business for their gain. But it is hardly fulfilled. Various agencies which have been given lease or entrusted with the task of collecting MFP engage at places local private traders in the work of collection and buy the produce from them as well as sell them to the same traders, thereby the tribals were largely eliminated instead of private traders.

Very little processing of any MFP is undertaken by the private collectors to add value to the MFP in the interest of the tribal people. In fact, the entire marketing and whatever little processing is done is taken care of by the wholesalers. The study shows that preliminary processing of most of the items of MFP can be done by the tribals at their door steps, because no complicated process is involved at the primary stage of processing.

The whole analysis boils down to the fact that the procuring agencies have not tried to involve the tribal communities in the preliminary processing due to shortage of manpower and financial resources needed for this purpose. Of all the negative factors the will to take up the exercise on a trial basis is wanting. The foremost concern of agencies is to achieve bulk procurement and make payment of revenue to the state exchequer. In this situation charged with anxiety to obtain revenue for the forest department, the collecting agents are made to deliver the commodities to purchasing agents and the payment obtained from the latter is passed on to the Forest Department, thus, leaving no scope for processing. In other words, there is no plan at any level to have an infrastructure for tribal development throughout the process of collection and marketing transactions relative to MFP.

There is a great need for training and guidance to the tribals in respect of methods of collection and processing of items in the simplest way such as the elementary steps of tapping, blazing, drying, grading and packing, *etc.* The institutes like Tribal Research Institutes and Social Forestry, Training and Research Institute can be entrusted with the task of organising training courses for the tribal communities and other collecting agencies.

ANNEXURE 9.1

Seasonal Availability of Minor Forest Produce

Sl. No.	*Minor forest produce*	*Availability by months*											
		Jan	Feb	Mar	Apr	May	June	July	Aug	Sep	Oct	Nov	Dec
1	Seeded Tamarind	*	*	*	*	*							
2	Deseeded Tamarind	*	*	*	*	*							
3	Hill Broom	*	*	*	*								
4	Myrobalan (Harida)	*	*	*								*	*
5	Honey		*	*	*	*	*	*	*				*
6	Siali Leaves	*	*										
7	Nux Vomica	*	*										*
8	Marketing Nut	*	*	*								*	*
9	Cleaning Nut	*	*								*	*	*
10	Antudi Flower				*	*							*
11	Dhatuki Flower	*	*	*									
12	Swan Climber	*	*	*	*	*							*
13	Thorn Broom	*	*	*									*
14	Genduli Gum	*	*	*	*								*
15	Dhauna Gum	*	*	*	*								
16	Amta Gum	*	*	*	*								
17	Bahada Gum	*	*	*	*								
18	Other Gum	*	*	*	*								
19	Char Gum	*	*	*	*								
20	Lac	*	*			*	*	*	*				
21	Nageswar Flower	*	*										
22	Sunari Bark				*	*							
23	R.S. Root				*								
24	Siali Fibre				*	*							
25	Mushroom (Edible)							*	*	*	*		
26	Bhalia Koli				*	*	*						
27	Fenfena Bark			*	*	*							
28	Simuli Cotton			*	*	*							
29	Bhuin Neem									*	*	*	*

(Contd.)

Sl. No.	*Minor forest produce*	*Availability by Months*											
		Jan	Feb	Mar	Apr	May	June	July	Aug	Sep	Oct	Nov	Dec
30	Khilua Creeper				*								
31	Bahada	*	*	*								*	*
32	Amla	*	*	*								*	*
33	Broom Grass	*								*	*	*	*
34	Sal Seeds					*	*						
35	Soap Nut					*	*						
36	Tamarind Seed				*	*							
37	Thatch Grass	*	*										
38	Cane					*	*						
39	Mahua Seed					*	*						
40	Karanja Seed		*	*									
41	Kusum Seed					*	*						
42	Char Seed				*	*	*						
43	Babul Bark					*	*				*	*	
44	Resin (Sal)			*	*	*	*						
45	Patala Garuda	*									*	*	*
46	Shikakayi		*	*									
47	Fenfena Fruit									*	*		
48	Ashoka Bark												*
49	Mushroom (Poison)									*			
50	Kendu Leaves				*	*							
51	Arroroot			*	*	*							
52	Arjuna Bark	*	*										*
53	Sal Leaves	*	*								*	*	*
54	Mango Kernal				*	*	*	*					
55	Mahua Flower		*	*									
56	Pita Alu										*	*	*
57	Chireita	*	*										
58	Mankada Kendu Fruit					*	*						
59	Rohini Flower		*	*	*								
60	Bee Wax				*	*	*						

CHAPTER X

Tribal Art and Handicrafts

INTRODUCTION

Man seeks to express his inner self in various art forms and all art is lively, compelling and is imbued with a sense of purpose and creativity. But repeated use of this expression of art with no conviction and no compelling tone is dull and many experts are of the opinion that handicrafts are dull. This needs to be studied in some detail as little attention has been devoted to a serious study of tribal art and handicrafts. The various tribal art forms are:

- *(i)* carving
- *(ii)* metal casting (brass)
- *(iii)* terracotta sculpture and pot-making
- *(iv)* painting on walls
- *(v)* cloth-weaving and dresses
- *(vi)* bamboo and grass weaving
- *(vii)* tribal music and dance
- *(viii)* ornaments and body tattooing
- *(ix)* tribal songs, stories
- *(x)* tribal implements and weapons.

VARIOUS TRIBAL ART FORMS

Tribal arts and skills vary from tribe to tribe and can range from superb technical skills to clumsiness and from utter simplicity to confusing complexity. Much of tribal art flows from the tribal religion, with its affinity to nature and is almost always inter-linked with nature. The tribal people are in their true elements when surrounded by nature and their native art forms decay and atrophy when removed far from their natural surroundings. Tribal art forms draw their sustenance from nature. Tribal art and handicrafts are an essential part of daily life and is inspired by religious beliefs and spiritual experiences. The tribal craftsman is not ashamed of his creations and does not bother about the effect his art has on others. He seeks to recreate based on his experiences and reproduces his feelings, faithfully. Generally, skills are passed down in the family from father to son and from the mother to daughter. The various tribal art forms and handicrafts are described briefly below:

1. Carvings

The preferred medium is wood but horn and stone are also used. The tribal people rarely worship idols and statues and their tribal Gods are rarely represented in carvings. The Nagas, the Santhals, the Saors, the Gonds, the Bhils generally represent their deities by stones, lumps of earth, unchopped bits of wood and their shines are generally empty. Images are generally offered to the Gods and most carvings made by tribals represent animals/birds which are supposed to be offerings/sacrifices to the Gods. These are all statues of demons, animals and products of fantasy. The workmanship is vigorous rather than crude and the finish is rough and does not boast of any polish or smooth finish. Carvings of elephants and horses are common as also birds. Some tribes work exclusively on horns.

2. Metal Casting

The tribal people are very good observers and their art reflects their environment and the birds and animals. The brass castings are exclusively of animals such as horses, elephants, cocks, peacocks, deer, fish, scorpion, *etc.* The quality of these metal castings using wax and clay moulds is remarkable, though the finish may be somewhat crude.

3. Clay Artefacts

Since Mohanjo-daro, clay figurines and terracotta sculptures and tiles, have been in vogue and in tribal villages, under sacred trees and sacred groves, heaps of these clay figures may be seen as offering to their Gods in memory of various memorable incidents in their lives. Depending upon the individual skills and styles, these artefacts of clay are unique. Pots are also ornamented sometimes.

4. Paintings

Some tribal people have excellent painting traditions and their painting is exclusively on walls. These wall paintings are not merely decorative but are made in honour of the dead, to drive away evil spirits and disease, to ensure crop fertility and also for celebrating tribal festivals. The tribal paintings are supposed to be inspired by dreams and the Warli tribals in Thane, Maharashtra and the Saora paintings in Ganjam, Orissa, are now nationally famous due to the exceptional quality and abstraction. On marriages, intricate and complex patterns with a riot of colours are drawn on the ground, presumably to ward away evil spirits. The marriage crowns for the bride and bridegroom and the site of marriage are beautifully decorated. The Santhals also make very beautiful 'palkis' for the newly-wedded couple to be carried from house to house. Even the rituals in death ceremonies have an artistic touch in tribal society with the Marias, Phems and Konyals excelling in grove effigies. While some tribes merely paint or carve the scenes that were of interest to the deceased person, some tribes believe that all beautiful things created by the deceased person should be buried forever along with the person. It is as if the creative urge should be stilled with the person's death! It is not unusual to find on the bamboo platforms for the dead, a great variety of ornaments, clothes, baskets, weapons, traps, *etc.*, and not awry due to exposure and is a tragic waste.

It must be remembered that the expensive funeral ceremonies have impoverished and driven into indebtedness many tribal families. The breaking of all pots and pans and baskets, the ceremonies and the feasts are a very costly affair indeed!

5. *Weaving*

The artistic taste of the tribal people finds true experience in the simple and elegant clothes they wear, their body decoration and their decorated houses. In the North-eastern tribal communities, weaving is a compulsory skill for all women and among the Nagas, each tribe has its distinct decorative motifs, for identification. Though they are mostly vegetable dyes and their colour type is limited to yellow, red, blue, green and black, the clothes woven are very colourful and give full expression to the tribal personality.

6. *Bamboo and Grass Weaving*

The true artistry of the tribal is reflected in the beautiful household objects they make with their strips of bamboo and various grasses like sabai, sisal, *etc.* The baskets, traps and other household objects of everyday use made of bamboo are a work of art, especially in the North-East. The Nagas especially make beautiful drinking mugs and spoons out of wood and bamboo. In Cuttack, golden grass and in Kerala, Kewda leaves are also used for making beautiful mats.

7. *Tribal Music and Dance*

The tribal people enjoy their dances and their music is attuned towards communal dances and merry-making. They have a long tradition of music and dancing and these vary from tribe to tribe. The music is relatively simple on the 1-2 beat system and instruments used are relatively simple, including stringed instruments and percussion instruments. A few dances are also harvest-related such as Bihu and Gauri dances.

8. Ornaments and Body Tattooing

Both men and women in tribal society love to adorn themselves and the women are especially colourful with hairpins and combs of wood, bamboo and lone, flowers, cowries, beads and ribbons are used to decorate their hair and bodies while jewellery made of white copper, lead, bronze, beads, nuts, straw, grass are also used. Huge bangles, bronze anklets, necklaces and jewellery are worn on special occasions and market days. The head gears of the Oraons and Marias and the North-eastern tribes are very elaborate and truly works of art. The body tattoos of the Bhils, Banjaras, Murias and Maria women are also works of art and are done to attract men, on various parts of the body including face. The men generally tattoo only on their arms or wrists. Bone decorations are done by the Tibetans, Nagas and also North-eastern tribes who depend on hunting and the bones are used to make decorative articles for the house.

9. Tribal Songs and Stories

The oral tradition is very strong among tribals as the written word is rarely used. Their philosophy and their life styles are set out in their myths and folk tales. Many relate to their origins and are often contradictory. Many relate to various tribal cultures and the punishments meted out by supernatural forces for not obeying these taboos. The forests, animals and vegetation are the major themes for these myths. The folk tales are not only imaginative but also meant for entertainment and the supernatural, and ghosts predominate. They are also acquinted with lullabies, romance rhymes, prayers, marriage songs, harvest songs, love lyrics and epics in ballad form. Their Songs are mostly in solo, duets or choruses along with riddles, proverbs and epigrams.

10. Tribal Implements and Weapons

The martial tribes like the Nagas decorate their weapons and the human heads are used as trophies. The bows and arrows are also artistically designed, especially the arrows by the Bhils while the Manipuris decorate their spears. Articles of daily use are also of decorative. Stools, chairs, cots are suitably engrossed as are totemic poles and emblems. Baskets are also beautifully decorated.

TRIBAL HANDICRAFTS

With such a rich tradition of arts, the role and importance of handicrafts in the tribal economy are understood in the context of the total tribal economy. A study of 384 tribal communities and their occupations was made by Shri A.K. Danda in 1973 (Tribal Economics and their Transformations, Indian Council of Social Science Research, New Delhi) and the results, set out below, are revealing:

Table 10.1
Frequency Distribution of Occupations of Tribals of India

Levels of Involvement	*Economic pursuits*									
	Collection of forest products	*Hunting*	*Fishing*	*Animal husbandry*	*Shifting cultivation*	*Terrace cultivation*	*Settled agriculture*	*Handicraft & allied jobs*	*Trade & commerce*	*Labour work*
I	39	19	7	15	84	11	139	49	7	40
II	51	49	13	23	16	5	29	33	13	90
III	41	30	24	20	6	1	13	28	14	31
IV	13	20	20	8	5	1	4	17	11	8
V	—	3	5	4	—	—	1	—	1	2
VI	—	—	—	—	—	—	—	—	1	—

Note: 6 points have been assigned to each entry for 1, 5 points to II, 4 to III, 3 to IV, 2 to V and 1 to VI levels of involvement.

Ref.: Danda, A.K. 1973: Tribal Economics and their Transformations. Indian Council of Social Science Research, New Delhi.

The primary occupations of the tribal people is shifting cultivation along with their handicrafts and allied activities. A study reveals the level of involvement in handicraft activities are given tribe-wise (Annexure 10.1). The tribal handicrafts include *(i)* religious magic, *(ii)* articles of daily utilisation, and *(iii)* decorative objects. In tribal societies, entire tribes rarely follow a particular craft unlike the scheduled castes/other castes who follow traditional occupations like iron-melting, basket-weaving, *etc.* The tribal craftsmen generally make handicrafts to cater to the needs of their own community. The settled tribes have more complexity in their handicrafts as seen in the following table:

Table 10.2
Region-wise Dependence on Handicrafts

Region	*Levels of involvement*					
	1	*2*	*3*	*4*	*5*	*Total*
North Eastern	5	16	10	4	—	35
Himalayan	3	1	1	2	—	7
Central	29	8	14	8	2	61
Western	22	6	8	4	1	41
Southern	15	10	5	2	2	34
Islands	—	—	—	1	—	1
Total	**74**	**41**	**38**	**21**	**5**	**179**

Source: A.K.Danda, 1973: Tribal Economics and Their Transformations, ICSSR, New Delhi.

The Central and Western Indian tribes have a greater dependence on handicrafts. An interesting aspect of the tribal economy is that tribes rarely follow the occupation exclusively and the economy of most tribes is a mixed one and handicrafts is the most important subsidiary occupation.

The raw materials for these handicrafts are mostly sourced from local supplies or are grown locally and hence the handicrafts are generally determined by the availability of raw materials. Very rarely will tribal people move outside their area of operations to source raw materials. However, though these handicrafts have a limited market, they have tremendous economic potential for the tribal economy, especially in the context of renewable resources. While tribal people may not be able to attend exclusively to handicraft production. As a means for supplementing their income, these handicrafts have a great demand and the income from their sale would be able to make the income more stable.

Development of Tribal Crafts

When the tribals lived in their forests in isolation, their crafts not only served their own community but also served other local people to some extent. The advent of British made goods destroyed the rural economy of India, including the tribal economy. The British restrictions on forest exploitation by tribals created a scarcity of raw materials which were sourced mainly from the forests. The National Forest Policy has continued the policy of restricting use of forests for handicrafts, which resulted in acute shortage of raw materials, increasing their prices and hence reduce their profit margins. Forest species are being planted for industrial or commercial purpose and thus reducing the raw material supply. The interests and needs of the tribal people are deemed as secondary to the needs of commerce and industry and there is a need to change tree planting priorities, if tribal handicrafts are to survive. Many species of bamboo have ceased to exist and this is to the detriment of tribal handicrafts which depend a lot on cane and bamboo raw materials.

Limited Production

Tribal handicrafts are very different from village industries or small scale industries as these are highly individualistic with several complicated processes being carried out in a sequential manner by the same craftsmen. The tools are also simple and mass-production is ruled out for the present. This affects the question of viability. Credit is another constraint and money-lenders, traders and landlords provide this at high interest rates, which squeeze the borrowers. Often tribal craftsmen are forced to work on a daily wage basis. The marketing is generally done by the traders and not by the tribal people and hence the real benefits go to the trader and not to the craftsmen. Various tribal cooperatives have been set up but as these are controlled and managed by non-tribals, the tribal people rarely benefit from such ventures. These cooperative ventures are rarely operational and are not being set up nowadays!

CONCLUSION

If tribal handicrafts are to become more profitable for the tribals, certain drastic measures needs to be undertaken:

Faster Production. Better tools and sourcing of raw materials, needs to be supplied besides, craftsmen getting together and working on a mass production basis.

Better Designs. Age-old designs are rarely improved upon or designs changed to meet modern needs. Therefore more research in design to be undertaken alongwith marketing.

Seasonal Demand. Due to lack of credit facilities, stockpiling of products, especially baskets and other bamboo products, have not been possible as the tribal craftsmen have no capital.

Marketing Infrastructure. The lack of adequate marketing infrastructure, limits the area of sale and hence their real market value is reduced and middlemen or traders benefit. Efforts should be made to market these handicrafts in cities and for exports.

Credit Availability. Various types of credit packages should be evolved such as production credit facilities, marketing credit facilities, *etc.*, through LAMPS.

Source of Raw Materials. Forests are the source of raw materials for the tribal people for handicrafts. With vanishing forests and restrictions, raw material sources are drying up or are becoming costlier. Social forestry programmes which can provide raw materials for the tribal craftsmen, should be implemented.

Development of tribal crafts is not an easy task for tribal people as the tribal arts and crafts are intricately interwoven with their society and cultural traditions. However, the tribal arts have to be rescued and should be revived with all-out efforts of the State Governments and NGOs.

ANNEXURE 10.1

Tribal Handicrafts and Allied Occupations

Sl. No.	*Name*	*Distribution*	*Levels of involvement*				
			1	2	3	4	5
1.	Abor	Nagaland, Arunachal Pradesh				1	
2.	Agaria	MP, UP, Maharashtra	1				
3.	Angami	Manipur				1	
4.	Ao Naga	Nagaland				1	
5.	Baiga	Bihar, Orissa, WB, MP		1			
6.	Bamcha	Gujarat	1				
7.	Banjara	HP, Bihar, Orissa Karnataka	1				
8.	Barda	Gujarat, Karnataka, Maharashtra			1		
9.	Bedia	WB, Bihar			1		
10.	Belalhut	Tripura	1				
11.	Baria	Madhya Pradesh			1		
12.	Baria Bhumia	MP, Maharashtra			1		
13.	Bharwad	Gujarat			1		
14.	Bhimma	Maharashtra, MP	1				
15.	Bhoi	Meghalaya		1			
16.	Bhuiya	Orissa, Bihar, MP			1		
17.	Bhata	Maharashtra, MP	1				
18.	Bhautia	Punjab, WB, HP, Tripura			1		
19.	Birhor	Bihar, WB			1		
20.	Chik Barik	Bihar	1				
21.	Chiru	Manipur			1		
22.	Dafla	Arunachal Pradesh			1		
23.	Deori	Assam	1				
24.	Desua Bhumij	Orissa	1				
25.	Dhoba	MP, Maharashtra, Gujarat, Karnataka		1			
26.	Dholia Bhil	Maharashtra, Gujarat, Karnataka	1				
27.	Dhulia	Madhya Pradesh	1				
28.	Dhurwe	Maharashtra, MP				1	
29.	Dimesa (Kachari)	Nagaland, Assam			1		
30.	Gadaba	Orissa, AP, MP				1	
31.	Gait	Maharashtra, MP	1				
32.	Garo	Assam, WB, Tripura, Meghalaya, Nagaland			1		
33.	Gatti	Maharashtra, MP	1				
34.	Gorait	West Bengal, Bihar				1	
35.	Hasalaru	Karnataka		1			

(*Contd.*)

Sl. No.	*Name*	*Distribution*	*levels of involvement*				
			1	2	3	4	5
36.	Ho	WB, Bihar, Orissa				1	
37.	Jaintia	Assam	1				
38.	Kabui	Manipur	1				
39.	Kachari	Assam	1				
40.	Kaikari	AP, Maharashtra	1				
41.	Kalbelia	Rajasthan, HP, Assam					
42.	Kamar	Maharashtra, MP			1		
43.	Kammara	AP, Kerala	1				
44.	Kandra	Maharashtra, MP			1		
45.	Kaniyan	Tamil Nadu, Karnataka		1			
46.	Karmali	West Bengal, Bihar	1				
47.	Kathera Gadaba	AP, MP, Orissa,		1			
48.	Mampti	Arunachal Pradesh			1		
49.	Karwar	MP, Bihar, WB, Orissa, Maharashtra				1	
50.	Khasa	Uttar Pradesh			1		
51.	Kisan	Bihar, Orissa, WB			1		
52.	Koila Buta	Manipur		1			
53.	Koireng	Maharashtra, MP		1			
54.	Kolcha	Gujarat, Maharashtra, Karnataka, Dadra and Nagar Haveli		1			
55.	Koli Dhor	Maharashtra, Karnataka, Dadra and Nagar Haveli		1			
56.	Koraga	Kerala, Karnataka, Tamil Nadu	1				
57.	Korema	Karnataka		1			
58.	Kota	Kerala, Karnataka, Tamil Nadu		1			
59.	Kukna	Gujarat, Maharashtra, Karnataka	1				
60.	Kuli	Orissa, Andhra Pradesh	1				
61.	Kullia	Orissa, Andhra Pradesh	1				
62.	Kurumba	Kerala, Karnataka, Tamil Nadu		1			
63.	Kuruman	Kerala, Karnataka, Tamil Nadu		1			
64.	Lakher	Assam		1			
65.	Lohra	Bihar, WB	1				
66.	Lishai	Nagaland, Assam, Manipur		1			
67.	Mabli	WB, Orissa, Bihar	1				
68.	Mala Vettuvan	Kerala				1	
69.	Maler	Bihar				1	
70.	Malis	Andhra Pradesh		1			
71.	Malivans	Kerala			1		
72.	Maliga Savara	Orissa		1			
73.	Man (Tai-speaking)	Assam		1			

(Contd.)

Sl. No.	*Name*	*Distribution*	*Levels of involvement*				
			1	2	3	4	5
74.	Mankidi	Orissa		1			
75.	Matya	Orissa			1		
76.	Meda	Karnataka	1				
77.	Mikir	Assam, Nagaland, Arunachal			1		
78.	Miniyong	Arunachal Pradesh		1			
79.	Mizo	Assam, Arunachal, Mizoram, Nagaland, Manipur	1				
80.	Moghya	MP, Maharashtra	1				
81.	Momlea	Arunachal, Nagaland	1				
82.	Monpa	Arunachal			1		
83.	Munda	Bihar, WB, MP, Orissa, Tripura		1			
84.	Munda Lohar	Bihar	1				
85.	Minga Mahali	Bihar	1				
86.	Nagarchi	MP, Maharashtra			1		
87.	Nagesia	Maharashtra, MP				1	
88.	Naikda	Karnataka, Gujarat, Maharashtra, Dadra and Nagar Haveli		1			
89.	Nat	Madhya Pradesh	1				
90.	Nayady	Kerala	1				
91.	Nicobarese	Andaman & Nicobar Islands				1	
92.	Ojha	Maharashtra, MP, WB, Bihar, Orissa	1				
93.	Oraon	Maharashtra, Tripura					1
94.	Paiko	Andhra Pradesh		1			
95.	Pando	Madhya Pradesh		1			
96.	Panika	Madhya Pradesh	1				
97.	Pardhan	AP, MP, Maharashtra			1		
98.	Pasi	Arunachal		1			
99.	Pawra	Gujarat, Karnataka, Maharashtra	1				
100.	Phans Pardhi	Gujarat, Maharashtra		1			
101.	Phar	Meghalaya, Assam		1			
102.	Pomla	Gujarat, Karnataka, Maharashtra	1				
103.	Rathia	MP, Maharashtra				1	
104.	Rengma Naga	Nagaland				1	
105.	Saonta	MP, Maharashtra	1				
106.	Sapera	Bihar, MP	1				
107.	Saroti	Madhya Pradesh	1				
108.	Saur	Madhya Pradesh		1			
109.	Sema	Nagaland		1			
110.	Sherdukpen	Arunachal Pradesh		1			
111.	Sherpa	West Bengal				1	

(Contd.)

Sl. No.	Name	Distribution	Levels of involvement				
			1	2	3	4	5
112.	Shikari	MP, Maharashtra			1		
113.	Sonphari	Maharashtra, MP	1				
114.	Sonr	Madhya Pradesh		1			
115.	Sonwal	Assam	1				
116.	Swangla	Punjab	1				
117.	Tadvi Bhil	Gujarat, Maharashtra	1				
118.	Takankar	MP, Maharashtra	1				
119.	Takia	MP, Maharashtra	1				
120.	Tangkhul	Manipur		1			
121.	Tangsa	Arunachal Pradesh		1			
122.	Thakur	Maharashtra					1
123.	Thatia	MP, Maharashtra	1				
124.	Tota	West Bengal				1	
125.	Urali Kuruman	Kerala			1		
126.	Uridve Gowdalu	Karnataka					1
127.	Valmiki	Andhra Pradesh	1				
128.	Vitalia	Gujarat, Karnataka, Maharashtra	1				
129.	Yerukala	Andhra Pradesh	1				
130.	Zemi Nagar	Nagaland		1			
	Total No. of Communities		48	33	28	17	4

CHAPTER XI

Tribal Forest-based Products

INTRODUCTION

Spice production is a traditional economic activity pursued by the tribals in hill districts of Orissa. Human sacrifices which are now restricted to bovine sacrifices, attached with spice yields and quality, are a reflection of the economic dependence of tribals on income generated from spices. As a nation, India has made rapid progress in spice trade in terms of productivity, exports, value addition, processing, *etc.* However, the fruits of development have so far eluded the tribal growers in Orissa due to a skewed marketing system wherein there is no incentive for higher production or for better quality of products. This in turn resulted in continuing with low yielding/poor quality varieties, traditional methods of cultivation, crude methods of processing, *etc.*, thereby sacrificing the competitive edge of Orissa in the domestic/international spice trade.

Turmeric, Ginger, Tamarind, Garlic and Chilly are the major spices cultivated in districts of Phulbani, Kalahandi, Koraput, Gajapati, Mayurbhanj, Sundergarh, *etc.* The area under production of these spices in Orissa *vis-a-vis* the country are given in Table 11.1 which amply reveals the State's contribution to spices.

However, spices are traded in the name of places located in Southern India, *viz.*, Guntur Chilli, Alleppey Turmeric, Sangli Turmeric, Madras Turmeric, Cochin Ginger, Calicut Ginger, *etc.*, and thus the advantages of branding are not harnessed by the State. In Orissa, the tribal cultivators mostly sell off the products of their spice fields on area basis during October-November itself (just before their cereal harvests) much before the

Table 11.1
Area and Production of Spices during 1991–92

(Area in lakh hectares Production in lakh MT)

Spices	*India*		*Orissa*		*Position of the state*	
	Area	*Production*	*Area*	*Production*	*Area*	*Production*
Chilly	7.95	5.85	0.94	0.74	IV	II
Ginger	0.53	1.70	0.09	0.14	II	IV
Turmeric	1.16	3.21	0.23	0.48	II	II
Garlic	0.91	3.46	0.19	0.59	II	IV
Coriander	3.49	1.58	0.21	0.10	V	V

Source: Department of Agriculture, Government of Orissa, Bhubaneswar.

actual harvest (February-March), thus is almost no incentive for higher yields/better quality. The well-known system of local traders advancing small loans to tribals at the time of dire need in lieu of the future produce which is always priced low, continues.

Remotely located production centres, low yields, small tradable lots, crude processing facilities/practices which result in poor quality, traditional varieties (with low levels of spicy content) and above all the simplicity of producers, has resulted in multi-layer market systems and poor remuneration to the primary producers. A silver lining to this gloomy condition is that the 'Organic way of spice production' practised in Orissa, which if harnessed, would fetch better returns to the farmers. A multi-pronged approach is detailed below for long term development of spice trade in the State ensuring a few rupees more to the tribal producers.

APPROACH

If we agree on the "Tribal-first" approach for development of the spice sub-sector in Orissa, the following steps can individually and collectively contribute to the income of tribal spice producers, who develop the spice sector in the State.

1. Increasing Productivity

Research has shown that the productivity of spices in the State could be increased by replacement of traditional varieties with high-yielding varieties, besides following proper time for planting, mulching, pest and disease control through phytosanitary methods and regular prophylactic sprays, and application of chemical fertilisers, *etc.* By considering the relative contribution of each factor towards yield and the adoption levels of these technologies by the tribals, it is suggested to concentrate on replacement of varieties (Turmeric-Suroma, Ranga, Rasmi, Roma, Ginger-Suprabha, Suruchi, Suravi), proper mulching, seed treatment and planting during first half of May. These technologies are incidentally low capital intensive and the risk involved is very low with minimal demand on expertise.

2. *Improving Quality*

Factors contributing to quality of spices are high yielding varities harvesting time, proper cooking, hygiene during processing (cooking, drying, polishing, storage, *etc.*), grading and storage. Harvesting turmeric/ginger at full maturity (March) and cooking in double jacketed drums with addition of baking soda (0.2 per cent) (cooking in clean water for exports), polishing and drying on black polyethylene sheets, is suggested. Awareness-creation and supply of "double jacketed drums made from locally-available materials", "black polyethylene sheet", "locally made wooden polishing drums" at subsidies prices on individual or community basis, are also suggested. Popularising "underground storage" of turmeric/ginger is another important factor for not only improving quality but also the holding capacity of the tribals.

3. *Bargaining Power of the Producer*

Bargaining power of the tribal spice producers in Orissa is dependent on the following factors and conditions:

- Financial strength of producers
- Marketable surplus in a locality
- Holding power of producer
- Market intelligence/information
- Storage facilities
- Nearness to the end-user (processor)
- Availability of production/marketing credit
- Self-help through cooperation

Making available the consumption/emergency credit to tribals in times of need, which is presently being met by local traders should be the first step in breaking the vicious circle of poverty/exploitation. As the formal credit delivery systems are too inflexible to accommodate their emergency credit needs, promotion of 'Self Help Groups' or 'Thrift Societies' may be an answer to break the dependency of producers on traders. SAMANWITA's efforts in this direction in Phulbani district, Orissa, are commendable.

Once the tribal producer's credit needs are met, they will not be under any obligation to sell the produce before it can be harvested or sell in terms of a limited area under cultivation of spices. This can be the first step in transforming the trade from 'area basis to quantity basis'.

Marketing of small quantities of produce is another service offered by the local traders. As the marketable surplus is small for each individual tribal farmer and within a compact area, it would be uneconomical for the end-user to procure directly from the producers, a number of layers of agents/traders come to exist who invariably take a major chunk of the final price paid by the consumer. Lack of holding power of tribal producers is also exploited by the traders. In order to meet this challenge, creating a marketable surplus and increasing the holdings power of producers till better prices are obtained, is the next step in increasing the income to producers. Organising the producers in an area, through Self Help groups/Cooperatives can serve the function of pooling of produce. As the producer does not require the entire value of his/her produce, the group can extend a part of the value to them immediately after pooling and the remaining as and when the produce is sold. The line of credit available to Self-Help Groups from banks (through 100 per cent refinance) without any preconditions or procedures, can be gainfully employed to supplement the resources of the group.

Creating common storage facilities (godowns/underground storage structures) is essential with Government support for facilitating the pooling and marketing operations by the producers themselves. Marketing Credit/Pledge Loan is another facility available from the banking sector.

For facilitating the above, a committed organisational network is required whose role is to ensure human resource development and transfer of technology. Special project on spices being implemented by DRDA, Phulbani and NGO's like SAMANWITA are a few examples in this direction.

Reducing the number of market layers is one way of reducing the marketing costs whereby prices could be paid to the primary producers. This could be achieved by three ways:

1. Facilitate a few local traders as spice exporters.
2. Promote a few processing units to open their procurement centres locally.
3. Promote a few processing units in the areas of raw material source.

It would be successful only if the quality and quantity of spices produced is improved to meet the domestic/international standards.

4. *Value Addition*

Various ways of value addition available in spices includes grading, sterilised spices for exports, preparation of spice powders from sterilised spices, value-added spice mixtures, extraction of oleoresins, spice oils, preparation of ginger candies, *etc.* AVT McCormick Ingredients Ltd., Aluva, Cochin, is one of the major exporters of sterilised spices in the country. Export-oriented spice processing units being highly capital intensive (Rs. 20–30 crore), initially it is suggested to facilitate opening of their procurement centres in Orissa. In addition, value-addition units like making dried powders (turmeric, ginger, chilly, *etc.*), spice mixtures, batch method of oleoresin extraction units are suggested in the State.

5. *Product Branding*

Spices being food additives, intrinsic quality determines the value realisable. Quality being more a subjective one, brand promotion is important to fetch good prices. In domestic and international markets, whole spices are traded in the name of the place where it is generally traded like Guntur Chilly, Alleppey Turmeric, Sangli Turmeric, Madras Turmeric, Cochin Ginger, Calicut Ginger, *etc.* In spite of the fact that Orissa is a major producer with surplus for trading in other markets, it is hardly traded in the name of Orissa, which means part of the State's production is traded in other names. On lines with the India brand promotion at international level by Spices Board, local efforts are needed to promote some Orissa brands like Khandamal, Berhampur, *etc.* This would be possible easily if we develop a big trading centre for spices within the state. Branding facilitates investment from other States/countries in production and processing within the State and also creates awareness of the scope for spice development in the State.

Organic Spices. The demand for organically produced spices is increasing worldwide and the price realisable is 4.5 times that of intensively cultivated products. Spices Board is promoting a few farmers in Southern India to shift to organic cultivation and Ferguson is one successful example. The production system of spices by tribals in Orissa is truly organic and thus better prices could be obtained if Orissa spices are promoted under the brand of organic spices. Certification is an expensive affair in this regard. As the entire production of spices is under organic conditions, the Government may invite the certification agency from Germany and facilitate premium prices for the local produce.

Product Branding. In Orissa, spice brands like Ruchi, Gruhasthi are well-established and many more such brands need to be supported so that they will have a positive fallout on the price realisable by the tribal producers.

6. *Financial Support*

Financial support from banking sector can come in the following ways:

- Crop loans for regular cultivation including changing of variety.
- pledge loan to hold the stocks.
- Matching loans to Self-Help Groups for their marketing operations.
- Term loan for supplementing processing facilities (individual/group) *e.g.,* Cooking, Polishing, Drying yards/Polyethylene sheets, Storage units, *etc.*
- Term loan for setting up of processing facilities.
- Export credit (pre-shipment/post-shipment credit) for spice exporters.

Besides, these credit supports, financial assistance is also available from DRDA/APICOL/JRY, *etc.*, both for production, marketing and processing of spices.

SAL-LEAF PRODUCTS AND END-USERS

Products

Generally the dining plates, tiffin plates and cups of different sizes are made from sal-leaf. The size of plates varies according to the choice of the end-users, which differs from State to State. For domestic consumption in Orissa, small-sized plates are manufactured while bigger plates for export to States like Gujarat, Maharashtra and Rajasthan.

Traditionally, the dining plates are flat with a raised brim. In recent times dining plates with small depressions for accommodating various items of food are being manufactured according to the demand. The demand for cups is about three times that of plates and hence the ratio of their production is 3 : 1.

End-users

Leaf plates and cups are used for taking food, prasad, *etc.* Major demand comes from cities, tourist places and religious places like Varanasi, Ujjain, Tirupati, Puri, Baroda, Calcutta, Mumbai, Ahmedabad, Agra, *etc.* Hotels, Chat shops, festive sites are major consuming centres, besides temple-cities.

POLY-PLATE MAKING

Sal leaves collected from the forests are dried by local tribals. Raw plates are stitched from the leaves with 2 patha (leaves), 3 patha, 5 patha and 8 patha. 8 patha are needed for making dining plates, 5 and 3 patha for tiffin plates and 2 patha for cup-making. Leaves are generally collected from June to February. In between two such raw plates a small piece of polyethylene is kept and hot pressed in the poly-leaf making machine. It is a simple pedal-operated machine with a die and a heating element. It is run with electricity and a single-phase meter is sufficient. Die becomes hot with heating element and the raw leaves are pressed manually, with a pedal, between the base plate and die so that the raw leaf plate acquires the shape of the die. Because of the heat, the polyethylene piece kept between two leaves melts and on cooling sticks the two leaves tightly. After 5 plates are pressed, boarders are cut with a pedal-operated knife attached to the mold are cut so that even-sized plates/cups are formed. Plates are counted and bundled before disposal. Electricity is consumed for heating the die only, whereas other operations like pressing and cutting are pedal-operated.

Grades

Poly-plates are graded according to size, colour of leaves. Green colour leaves without much blemishes, burning spots fetch better prices in the market.

MARKET CHANNELS AND PRACTICES

Poly-leaf industry is run by 4 sets of people, namely *(i)* sal leaf collectors, *(ii)* people involved in hand-stitching for making raw plates, *(iii)* poly plate, cup-making and *(iv)* traders dealing in local or export marketing.

Sal leaf collection and hand-stitching is done in places like Thakurmunda, Bisoi, Keonjhar, Midnapur (West Bengal). These raw plates are supplied to plate-making units mostly located in Betnoti, Bijatola and Karanjia in Mayurbhanj district. Similarly, leaf plate making is going on in Bastar area of MP. The product is collected by traders mostly located in Betnoti, Karanjia and stock it for exporting to wholesale traders in consumption centres. Some of the wholesalers/stockists in Betnoti, Baripada, *etc.*, finance poly-leaf makers by supplying machines, molds and raw materials and the recovery is made from the supply of end-products. This way the stockists keep a control on regular supply for onward sale to final consumers.

Poly-leaf makers train local youth in leaf pressing on their machines and the wages are made on number of pieces made. This way efficiency is rewarded and the owner need not supervise closely the production.

Wholesale traders in turn sell to retailers who either operate on credit or cash basis. In some cases the traders employ sellers at pilgrimage points where the commission is given on sales and the unsold stock is returned.

ECONOMICS OF POLY-LEAF MAKING

Investment in poly-leaf making mainly include a set of machines, different sized molds and electric connections. Generally units are fixed in a separate shed in the home so that supervision is easy. Besides working space for machines a storage space is also important to store the raw materials and end-product.

During our visit, the team visited a poly-leaf making unit financed under IRDP at Betnoti. The entrepreneur has started the unit with two machines and over a period of two years he has expanded it to five besides repaying the loan and repair of his house. In Betnoti and nearby places, this is a flourishing industry which is done as a cottage industry.

A model scheme of three-machine unit of poly-leaf making is given below:

Poly-leaf making from sal leaves is a household industry in Mayurbhanj supplying plates to distant places in the country. This activity gives employment for people involved in leaf-collection, preparation of katcha leaves by hand-stitching, poly-leaf makers, wholesalers and retailers.

Marketing

Sal leaf collection and hand-stitching is done in places like Thakurmunda, Bisoi, Keonjhar, Midnapur (West Bengal). These raw plates are supplied to plate-making units mostly located in Betnoti, Bijatola and Karanjia in Mayurbhanj District. Similarly, leaf plate making is going on in Bastar area of MP. The product is collected by traders mostly located in Betnoti, Karanjia and stock it for exporting to wholesale traders in consumption centres. Major consumption centres include cities, tourist places and religious places like Varanasi, Ujjain, Tirupati, Puri, Baroda, Calcutta,

Mumbai, Ahmedabad, Agra, *etc.* Hotels, chat shops, festive sites are major consumers besides temple-cities.

Project Details

Investment in poly-leaf making mainly includes a set of machines, different sized molds and electric connections. Generally units are fixed in a separate shed in the home so that supervision is easy. Besides working space for machines, a storage space is also important to store the raw materials and end-product. A three-machine unit along with capitalised working capital for two months costs Rs. 52,550.

Assuming a margin of 15 per cent, the bank loan can be Rs. 44,650. The rate of interest is decided by the bank as per the RBI guidelines. The loan can be repaid in 5 years.

Table 11.2
Project Cost (Three-machine Unit)

Items	*Price (Rs.)*	*No.*	*Amount (Rs.)*
A: Plant & Machinery			
1. Cost of machines	2,000/machine	3	6,000
2. Cost of plate die	1,400/dice	2	2,800
3. Cost of cup die	600/dice	2	1,200
4. Cost of tray die	1,800/dice	1	1,800
5. Cost of tiffin plate die	1,000/dice	1	1,000
6. Electrification			500
B: Shed (Work Shed and Storage)			
Asbestos roof shed:			
Machine Room (15′ × 10′)	Rs. 75 per sq ft.		18,750
Storage Room (10′ × 10′)			
Total capital cost (A + B)			**32,050**
C: Recurring Cost (2 Months)			
(3 : 1 Ratio of Cups and Plates)			
Work output:	3,000 cups/md/machine		
	2,000 plates/md/machine		
One shift per day; 25 working days per month			
10 per cent wastage of leaves while plate-making			
1. Dipata for cups	1,000/lakh	6.6	6,600
2. 8 pata for plates	4,000/lakh	2.2	8,800
3. Polyethylene sheet			100
4. Labour charges	Cup 9/1,000		2,700
	Plate 14/1,000		1,400
5. Electricity			200
6. Machine maintenance			100
7. Packing and transportation			600
Sub-Total			**20,500**

D: Project Cost (A + B + C)	**52,550**
Promoters' contribution/subsidy (15 per cent)	7,900
Bank loan	44,650

E: Income for 2 Months

Items	*Production (Lakhs)*	*Sale price (Rs. 1000)*	*Income (Rs.)*
Cups	3	30	9,000
Plates	1	170	17,000
Total			**26,000**

F: Net Profit for 2 Months	5,500
Net Profit for 1 Year (8 Months)	**22,000**

G: Repayment Schedule

Year	1	2	3	4	5
Loan O/s	44,650	35,720	26,790	17,860	8,930
Interest (13.5 per cent)	6,028	4,822	3,617	2,411	1,206
Instalment	8,930	8,930	8,930	8,930	8,930
Total Repayment	14,958	13,752	12,547	11,341	10,136
Gross Surplus	22,000	22,000	22,000	22,000	22,000
Net Surplus	7,042	8,248	9,453	10,659	11,864

Assumptions

1. 25 Working days per month.
2. At least one shift of 8 hours per day is operated.
3. 8 months of working per year.
4. Trained machine operators are available.

CONCLUSION

Price is the most powerful tool for ensuring a commerical outlook with the farmers. Farmers, especially the tribal spice producers in far-flung areas of Orissa, are living with a number of input, infrastructural and market constraints, which act as a disincentive for them to enhance the production/productivity unless the returns are made attractive with as less a dependence on the external inputs and less risk in production. A stepwise approach for improving the income of spice producers is more a practical one rather than attempting for an abrupt shift from subsistence agriculture to the high input agriculture which is logically associated with high risk. The technology and development package should therefore have a "producer-first" approach which brings an incremental income to the tribal spice producers. The promotion of tribal spice products as organically produced, after due certification from concerned agencies, needs to be explored so as to get better prices in the competitive European markets. This requires determined marketing efforts as also financial and other credit support to develop local brands as also quality improvement with polyethylene sheets for mats for drying and better cooking drums and polishing drums. Technology transfer of spice oil/spice oleoresin from turmeric, ginger and chillies for local entrepreneures may be done. A special package for market intervention in tribal areas of Orissa is necessary to wean away the tribal producers from the exploitative marketing network.

CHAPTER XII

Grass-based Products

INTRODUCTION

Sabai grass is a perennial grass from the Terai regions of the Himalayas growing in the forests of Mayurbhanj District. Traditionally, the grass collected by local tribals from forests is being used for making ropes. Realising the economic importance of the Sabai grass and its utility in soil binding, Soil Conservation Department has promoted its cultivation on Government wastelands, farmers' lands and village commons. ITDA and DRDA also fund the Sabai grass cultivation @ Rs. 1800 per acre. It is estimated that about 21,635 hectare of land is under Sabai grass cultivation in the district. In recent years, this grass has been introduced for cultivation in other districts but Mayurbhanj is still the major producer in the State with over 21,500 hectares of Sabai grass under cultivation. The area brought under Sabai grass cultivation with ITDA/DRDA funds is given in Table 12.1, which clearly indicates that there is a sustained interest among farmers and growth in the size of the industry.

Table 12.1
Area brought under Sabai Grass Cultivation

Year	*Area (acres)*
1986–87	997
1987–88	2,450
1988–89	1,535
1989–90	1,605
1990–91	1,983
1991–92	2,250
1992–93	1,133
1993–94	1,579
1994–95	1,650

Source: DRDA, Mayurbhanj, Orissa.

Elders believe that Sabai grass is the gift of God to this tribal district and starvation deaths are unheard of in this otherwise-underdeveloped district, because of the regular income generated from Sabai industry.

Sabai Products and End-users

Sabai grass is used for making different products like:

(i) *Sabai rope of different thickness twisted out of grass.* Sabai rope is being mostly consumed by paper industry for tying bamboo bundles at the time of harvest from the forests. Sabai grass found favour with paper industry because it is pulpable and hence the bamboo bundles as such can be fed into chipper, besides the cost of rope is partially recovered from the pulp it contributes. It is estimated that about 35–40 per cent of the demand for rope comes from this sector.
Major end-users are:
M/s. J.K. Corps, Rayagada, Orissa
Orient Paper Mills, Sambalpur, Orissa
BILT, Chowdwar, Jaypur, Orissa
A.P. Paper Mills, AP
ITC Bhadrachalam Paper Mills, AP, *etc.*

(ii) *Decorative and utility items.* Other major use of the Sabai rope includes weaving of cots (Charpai) in Bihar, UP and other Northern Indian States. This sector accounts for about 50–60 per cent of the rope consumed. The rest 10–15 per cent is locally consumed besides using it for making value-added products like decorative and utility items.
Commonly made decorative and utility items include:
Doormats, Carpets, Toys (Birds, Animals), Wallhangings (Konark Wheel), Crocodiles, Coconut Trees, Cottage, *etc.*
Sofa sets, Stools, Cots, Vanity bags, Modas, Baskets, *etc.*

(iii) *Paper-making.* Emami Paper Mills, Balasore is a bulk buyer of rough grade Sabai grass for making paper.

Rope-making

Rope-making is a household activity practised by entire family including women and children. It is a common sight in the district that a woman involving making rope as well as attending to children on one side and cooking on the other side. This amply indicates the level of skill they have acquired and rope-making has almost become an involuntary activity. According to the grade of rope to be made, 2–6 blades of grass are twisted with hand followed by further twisting with a locally-made twister. After sufficient quantity of rope is twisted and dried, they are polished by rubbing against three trunks or branches and bundled as per the standard weight (approximately 1 kg). Twenty such bundles are tied together in a 20 kg. bundle.

District Industries Centre, Baripada attempted to introduce Sabai Yarn Twisting machines from Chennai. These machines are pedal-operated and two people are required to operate the machine. It is claimed that the efficiency of rope-making is doubled. However, the machine did not find favour with locals because of the following:

(i) The twisting is anti-clockwise with the machine while the traditional one is of clockwise direction, thus there was reluctance on the part of the people.

(ii) It constantly requires two persons working in synchronisation whereas in traditional method, individuals at leisure are making ropes.

(iii) Additional financial burden.

(iv) Fine rope could not be made with the machine in which case it would have at least served that segment of the market.

In view of the above, hand-twisting of Sabai is only being recommended. Besides, the objective of the industry is labour deployment and not labour replacement.

Sabai grass is graded on the basis of length and colour. Usually long and mature grass is used for rope-making and short, over-mature grass goes for paper-making. Sabai rope is graded according to the thickness, which ultimately depends on the ply number (number of the grass strings used in rope-making). Common grades of commerce include:

i. Super fine	Two ply	(1 + 1)
ii. Fine	Four Ply	(2 + 2)
iii. Rough	6–8 ply	(+)

Sabai grass once planted can give yield for about 10 years. The first harvest is expected after 8–9 months of planting. However, commercial harvest starts from second year only. 2–3 harvests per year is possible. Peak seasons of production are as follows:

i. August-September	:	30 per cent yield
ii. December-January	:	50 per cent yield
iii. May-June	:	20 per cent yield

Market Channels and Practices

Sabai Grass. Individuals with their own Sabai cultivation sell the grass to local traders/rope-makers, leaving their own requirement of grass with them. Traders stock the grass purchased in the season and sell to rope-makers either on credit or on cash payment or buyback-of-rope basis. To a major extent, grass is also transacted in the village weekly markets (*haats*) or Betnoti and Baripada weekly market. People who make decorative items from Sabai grass also purchase from *haats*. The bulk buyers of grass, namely M/s Emami Paper Mills, Balasore, collect grass in bulk from weekly *haats* through their agents.

Sabai Ropes. Sabai rope produced by individual tribal families finds its way to big traders in Betnoti, Baripada through village level traders/weekly markets. Sometimes, credit is advanced to rope-makers for purchase of grass or consumption needs in which case the price of rope is pre-determined and sold to the lender only. Major part of the transaction of ropes occurs at village *haats*. Betnoti Sabai Grass Manufacturers' Cooperative Society is engaged in trading of grass and Sabai rope.

Decorative and Utility Articles. Decorative articles are not made on regular basis and the products are mostly sold on festive occasions in and around Mayurbhanj and a couple of melas in Calcutta, Bihar and Bhubaneswar. Occasionally, traders in Baripada also place orders with artisans based on their prior orders. Artisans' Multipurpose Cooperative Societies, promoted by KVIB in the district, are also involved in manufacture of decorative and utility items for which the marketing support is given by Orissa Handicrafts Corporation. Unfortunately, the Corporation's sales are mostly in exhibitions and thus there is irregular lifting of the produce from these societies. In some cases, they return the unsold goods to the Societies. A few NGOs, namely Bharatiya Janakalyan Kendra, Mahatma Gandhi Club, *etc.*, are involved in training artisans and marketing of their products.

Utility items like sofa sets made out of Sabai grass on bamboo/cane frame are made by prisoners at Baripada, AMCS and women groups working in Balasram, Baripada.

Economics of Sabai Products

Sabai Rope. Three grades of Sabai rope commonly traded along with their average prices are given below:

Table 12.2
Grades of Sabai Grass

Sl. No.	Type	Market (Rs. per Kg.)	Trader (Rs.)
1.	Super Fine	14	12
2.	Fine	10–12	9–10
3.	Rough	7–8	6–7

80–85 per cent is the recovery of rope from dry grass. The price differences among various grades is mainly due to the labour component of the rope-making. On an average 5 Kg, rope is made per day per head. Assuming a grass price of Rs. 3 per Kg labour charges, one earns by making fine rope is Rs. 32 per day. The output of super fine rope is only 2–3 Kg, per day and labour charges comes to Rs. 25 per day. Assuming an output of 6 Kg per day and grass price of Rs. 2 Kg, the labour charges comes to

Rs. 30 per day in case of rough rope. On an average, Rs. 25–30 per day is earned per head (adult).

Because the demand for super fine quality rope comes from handicrafts which is very small and irregular besides low rope output and labour charges realised, the availability of this grade rope is slowly becoming limited.

Decorative Items. For production of one cottage (a decorative item), the following items are required:

Table 12.3
Scheme Costs

Items	Rs.
Sabi grass (200 gms.)	0.60
Fine thread (4 reels)	4.00
Fevicol	1.00
Thick thread	2.00
Cardboard	2.00
Total Cost	**9.60**

One trained person can make one cottage per day and selling price of each cottage is about Rs. 40. Hence the labour charges/profit one can earn is about Rs. 30.

Similarly the economics of few other decorative items is given below:

Table 12.4
Economics of Some Decorative Items

Product	*Material cost*	*Output/ day (no.)*	*Price*	*Labour & profit/day*
Small house	5	2	25	40
Coconut tree	5	1.5	25	30
Cottage	10	1	40	30
Konark wheel	60	0.5	120	30
Vanity bag	3	2	15	24
Manchi	12	3	25	39
Mat	4	3	15	33

Another set of furniture that is made of sabai grass which has a good market on account of the good quality and finish of the products. This is set out in the Table 12.5.

Table 12.5
Sabai Grass Furniture

Items	*Quantity*	*Rate*	*Amount*
Rope (Fine Quality)	22	12	264
Cane	150 ft.	2 per ft.	300
Frame making			150
Miscellaneous			36
Total			750
Sale price			1,400
Profit & Labour charges			650

One Sofa set can be woven by two people in 10 days. Here labour charges are paid on piece basis and on average, Rs. 450 is paid per set. If the weavers themselves sell the set, the labour and profit per day comes to Rs. 32.50.

Prospects and Problems in Marketing

There is a ready market for rope in the local haats and the demand from end-users like paper mills and cot-makers is quite high for the sale of the Sabai rope produced in the district. According to traders the demand for Sabi rope is increasing every year and they are not in a position to meet the entire demand and hence the supply needs to enhanced.

As regards use of Sabai grass in paper-making, presently, only one paper mill, namely Emami Paper Mills, Balasore, purchases grass. A handmade paper-making unit has been set up at Danthamahala, Baripada block with the financial assistance from KVIB with the primary objective of making handmade paper from Sabai grass. In addition to the usual machinery like pulp beater-cum-washing drum, hydraulic press, calendering unit, paper cutting machine, a digestor is needed for pulping Sabai grass. The pulp recovery is only 35–40 per cent whereas from hosiery waste (a commonly-used raw material), it is 95 per cent. As Sabai grass has a natural brown colour, it is difficult to bleach the colour. Therefore, only coloured paper can be made. Even in this case the amount of colour needed is very high. Hence the Units' experience is that Sabai grass is not an economical raw material for handmade paper unit.

Sofa sets made of Sabai grass are very attractive and elegant besides being durable if protected from damp conditions. However, the trade in sofa is limited by high transportation cost (it is a high-volume low-value product) and competition from other products in the market. Even the Handicrafts Corporation is not able to provide counter/godown space for sale of this product because of the more space occupied compared to the price. Thus, the market is limited to the exhibitions and local use.

It is suggested that the sofa making can be promoted like in cities where demand is high, while the rope and Beni making can be promoted locally in Mayurbhanj district. This way the employment can be created and the product can be popularised. In view of the ready market available for Sabai rope, the value-added products-making can be encouraged only if a strong marketing support is extended to the products.

Replicability

Commercial cultivation of Sabai grass is promoted western districts of Orissa, which are tribal-dominated and with hilly terrain. In these districts, alternative land use is limited to subsistence agriculture and soil conservation is promoted, besides encouraging Sabai grass cultivation and rope-making to promote economic activity among the tribes. As this activity provides income on a regular basis, the pressure on forests for fuel wood collection could be reduced by employing tribals in this regular income-generating activity. Additional employment generation in Sabai industry can be done from:

1. expansion of Sabai grass cultivation and rope-making
2. by further value-addition by making items of utility like modha, sofa sets, *etc.*

Model schemes for 'Integrated Sabai Cultivation and Rope-making' and Unit for manufacture of decorative items are given in Annexures 12.1 and 12.2 respectively.

IMPORTANCE OF SISAL

Sisal (Agave sisalana), a xerophytic crop native to South America was introduced in India during 15th Century and is now extensively grown in the districts of Koraput, Keonjhar, Phulbani and Mayurbhanj in Orissa. Orissa has the maximum area under sisal cultivation in the country. As this crop can adopt to wide-ranging climatic and soil conditions, the Soil Conservation Department of Orissa, some twenty years back, had taken up plantation of this crop as mostly a soil conservation measure in the degraded areas. At present, more than 6,000 acre of wasteland/degraded land is under sisal cultivation.

Over the years, sisal has gained economic importance as raw material for its fibre and for multifarious usages ranging from manufacture of marine and industrial ropes, agricultural and commercial twines and other forms of ropes and cables. They are also utilised for padding, upholstery, matting bags, sacks, fishing nets, various types of brushes and brooms. Besides, this fibre is used for making a number of quality handicraft items. While quality of fibre from sisal is one of the best natural fibres, the yield of sisal fibre in Koraput district in particular is more under the prevailing agro-climatic conditions as compared to other districts.

As per the estimates of Indian Institute of Foreign Trade, the requirement of sisal fibre in India is around 40,000 tons by 2,000 AD whereas production at present is around 2,500 tons thereby leaving a huge gap in demand and supply, and the demand is met largely by imports from South American countries, involving valuable foreign exchange.

Besides fibre, other byproducts are sisal pulp, wax and chemicals like Hecogenin (a raw material for synthesis for cortisone drugs), mallic acid, *etc.*, for use in pharmaceutical and cosmetic industry.

Employment Opportunities

Sisal generates a three-tier system of work opportunities for work force, in the field during the stage of sisal crop production which goes on for 12 years for a single plantation, secondly in the sisal fibre extraction stage and thirdly in manufacture of ropes and other small scale and cottage industries and handicrafts.

Substantial employment can be generated by making utility and handicrafts items from sisal fibre. If a proper strategy is adopted by the concerned agencies involving Government Departments, bankers with participation of NGOs and people themselves, sisal plantation can improve the impoverished economy of people by generating primary as well as supplementary incomes/employment opportunities.

Government Efforts

The existing plantations in Koraput covering more than 6000 acre by the Department of Soil Conservation to counter soil erosion, are exploited for extraction of fibre to a very limited extent. 3–4 fibre extraction units are being run by the Soil Conservation Department itself whereas, another 4 units are being run by "Sisal Vikas Parishad", a voluntary agency floated in 1989 with District Collector as Chairman and Project Officer, District Rural Development Authority (DRDA), and General Manager, District Industries Corporation (DIC), *etc.*, as members. While large amount of this fibre is lifted mostly by Calcutta-based traders through State-level auctions conducted by the Soil Conservation Department, local use is very limited due to lack of infrastructure and clear-cut policies by the Government although one or two privately run units in the district are doing good business. The policy of the Soil Conservation Department/District authorities for leasing the plantation has been a major deterrent factor for private entrepreneurs to come up in large scale for fibre extraction. With large untapped existing captive plantations by the private entrepreneurs along with extraction units may not be an attractive proposition, as the short-term prospects are poor. Growth and processing of sisal by tribal people and their assured market at attractive prices by entrepreneurs with extention units, appears to be a better avenue for both tribal farmers and entrepreneurs.

DRDA Programme

It is learnt that the DRDA authorities of Koraput have recently submitted an Integrated Project with Sisal Plantations, fibre extraction and rope-making components. The Project envisages a sisal plantation on another 1000 hectare of wasteland and high intensity soil erosion areas like catchment areas of river valley projects through Soil Conservation Department and integrating fibre extraction and rope-making units for every 100 hectare of plantation. The project to be implemented by Sisal Vikas Parishad aims at generation of 36,34,000 of man-days over a period of 12 years involving a projected outlay of Rs. 2.6 crore. Formation and involvement of Self-Help Groups in the project villages for making handicrafts and other utility items from fibre would also greatly supplement the rural economy. Marketing has been envisaged to be done through the District Marketing Societies. While the project appears to be a very ambitious programme, if planned and properly implemented, it can go a long way in mitigating the poverty of the tribal people in the district.

Banks' Involvement

While sisal is still at a nascent stage of development despite having good growth potential in the district, the involvement of formal credit from banks' to the sisal related schemes has been confined to a few women's groups engaged in rope-making and handicrafts. Moreover, lack of more bank sponsored schemes in sisal development is largely due to the lesser involvement of the banks.

The activities related to sisal which have commercial potential and can be explored for bank financing are:

(i) Plantation of sisal
(ii) Fibre extraction units
(iii) Rope-making units
(iv) Handicrafts units.

Integration of some of the above activities can also be taken up.

Plantation of Sisal

NABARD has already prepared the unit cost for sisal plantations. Sisal plantation requires high investment (Rs. 32,000/hectare over 5 years) due to large plant population per hectare and the refractory nature of sites where sisal plantations are normally taken up.

As sisal plantation is a high cost activity, this would reduce the economic viability of the processing models, leaving less margin for risk-taking. The model schemes are prepared specifically for development of tribals, who have low risk-taking capacity.

Thus, the following model schemes have been prepared for implementation by the tribal people:

(i) Scheme for fibre extraction unit — Annexure 12.3
(ii) Model Scheme for Sisal Fibre Handicrafts — Annexure 12.4.

Fibre Extraction Unit

A fibre extraction unit can be taken as a stand-alone scheme wherever existing plantations are available. It is envisaged that the State Government would provide usufructory rights to ST/SC societies/Cooperatives/ groups allowing them to harvest leaves from the plantations at a very nominal rent (Rs. 100 per hectare per year). The responsibility of replanting and maintenance can also be shifted to the group.

A fibre extraction unit can be set up with a total financial outlay of Rs. 2,01,000, a part of which shall be met through bank loan. The unit will be employment-intensive with each unit generating around 9000 man-days per year. Each unit would need a minimum of 100 acre of existing sisal plantations.

At present, due to high demand of sisal fibre in bulk, marketing does not seem to be a problem. Agents from traders in Calcutta approach the current producers of sisal fibre for bulk purchase. Smaller markets like one existing rope-making units and proliferation of sisal handicraft units also exist. In case sisal handicraft-making can be popularised within the district, an assured market for sisal fibre within the district can be created.

Handicrafts Unit

Sisal-fibre can be used to make decoratve and utility items as is being done from jute. As sisal fibre is much stronger and has a better luster, slowly items made of sisal fibre are gaining popularity. In Koraput, handicraft items are mainly prepared by women's groups under the DWCRA programme. Due to the availability of sisal fibre with the Sisal Vikas Parishad, the DRDA has held a number of training programmes by Master Crafts Persons from West Bengal and Andhra Pradesh. The major items being prepared now are doormats along with items like shoulder bags, sikka, dining mats, paper stand, *etc.*, besides some decorative items.

CONCLUSION

While it is necessary to mention the need of coordinated efforts of various Government agencies, Banks and NGOs for promoting sisal processing, the following suggestions are made:

(i) The State Government/District authorities may issue policy guidelines regarding granting usufructory rights to the SC/ST Societies/Cooperatives/ Groups or NGOs on their behalf, allowing them to harvest and extract sisal fibres from such plantation. As per the model scheme, each fibre extraction unit needs about minimum 100 acre of sisal plantations. The lease rent should be waived off altogether or a nominal amount of upto Rs. 100 per acre per year may be charged. Any higher amount would lead to viability problems. The lease for usufructory rights should be of at least 10 years and preferably for a longer period.

The responsibility of maintenance and replantation should also be given to the groups and DRDA may consider providing small grants to the groups for the purpose in case they can not take it up from their own funds.

(ii) New plantation of sisal should be taken up in cluster basis with the dual objective of soil conservation and sisal fibre extraction. This implies an emphasis on the planning of sisal plantation along with communities which are interested in taking up sisal fibre extraction and related activities. Any new sisal plantation should plan for an SC/ST group-run fibre extraction plant linked with it. DRDA may also consider intensifying funding of sisal plantation with an aim of establishing forward linkages.

(iii) NGOs/VAs can play a vital role by taking up activities related to sisal development. There should be a conscious effort to involve NGOs for sisal development in their operational areas.

(iv) Banks may consider financing viable schemes on sisal processing, specially by tribal groups/societies, supported by Government agencies or NGOs.

(v) Sisal Vikas Parishad should be developed as a resource centre for sisal development. It should try to develop its role in marketing of sisal products as well as product design for handicrafts and utility item. The district level coordination on matters and issues related to sisal should also be handled by Sisal Vikas Parishad. For this, the district administration may consider professionalising its management. Restructuring of the SVP may be considered to make it a federal structure of SC/ST groups/societies involved in sisal processing.

(vi) Natural, non-synthetic dyes need to be introduced for the sisal handicrafts as only these dyes are acceptable in the competitive export market.

ANNEXURE 12.1

Integrated Scheme of Sabai Grass Cultivation and Rope-making

1. Introduction

Sabai grass is traditionally grown by tribals in Mayurbhanj District. This grass is very hardy and even can be grown on laterite, gravely soils with few inches soil depth. It has excellent soil-binding property and, therefore, controls soil erosion. Because of its economic utility and soil-binding nature, the Department of Soil Conservation is promoting its commercial cultivation in the district with financial assistance from DRDA, ITDA, *etc.*

2. Rope-making

Sabai grass is used for rope-making which has good demand from paper mills and cot makers in Northern India. Rope-making is undertaken by every member of a family. It is frequently seen that the women of the family will be attending to household work while making rope. After manual twisting of rope, it is twisted by locally-made twisting wheel. This follows polishing by rubbing against tree branches. About 5 kg., rope can be made by a member by working for 8 hours a day. 80–85 per cent is the recovery of rope from dry grass.

3. Cultivation

The crop can be grown either by seed or slips and slips are more commonly used by farmers. The land is ploughed after receiving the initial monsoon showers and planting is done with the onset of regular monsoon. Slips are planted at a spacing of 75 cm × 75 cm. Two cartloads of FYM is added at the time of planting. At the time of planting chemical fertilisers (@) 10 kg nitrogen and 8 kg potasium 205 per acre should be band placed at a distance of 10–15 cm from the slips. In the second year, another cartload of FYM should be added followed by one howing or ploughing through interspaces to control weed and facilitate sprouting of more tillers. Application of 10 kg nitrogen per acre is recommended from second year onwards.

After 8 to 9 months of planting the bushes are cut back in the first year to obtain a better and uniform growth in the second year. Grass can be harvested from second year onwards and can be continued for about 10 years. Commercial yield of grass is expected from second year and it gradually increases in the subsequent years and yield stabilisation is expected in fifth year. The following yields are expected from 1 acre of Sabai grass field:

Year	*Yield (q/ac)*
2	4
3	9
4	12
5–7	14
8	12
9	10
10	7

Unit cost for cultivation of lac is given in Annexure 12.3.

4. Assumptions

The scheme assumes a family size of 3 and the output of 10 kg rope per day. Rope-making is undertaken for 270 days a year. One acre land will be brought under cultivation of Sabai grass. The yield of grass even at peak age is only 12 q/ac. There is no grass yield in the first year. With the above assumptions of rope output, one acre Sabai field cannot meet the grass requirement of a family and the difference is to be purchased from the market. In the scheme grass requirement for two months is capitalised. The maintenance cost of plantation can be recovered from the income generated from rope-making. Cost of the twisting wheel @ Rs. 300 is also provided.

5. Maketing

Sabai ropes have ready-made demand from paper industry and cot-makers in Northern India. Rope is sold in the weekly *haats* in Mayurbhanj District, most important being Betnoti, Baripada, *etc.* Local traders also purchase the rope from tribals and supply to the end-users through middlemen/whole sellers.

6. Project Cost

Sl. No.	*Particulars*	*Rs.*
1.	Cost of raising Sabai grass (1 year)	1,825
2.	Cost of twisting wheel	300
3.	Cost of grass required for 2 months @ Rs. 3 kg, for 600 kg	1,800
4.	Family labour for 1 month @ Rs. 30 day	900
	Total	4,825

7. Financial Assistance

The unit cost of Rs. 4,800 should be provided as bank loan. No margin money should be collected from the beneficiary as the amount is less than Rs. 10,000 as per RBI guidelines. Since the loan is less than Rs. 5,000 no mortgage/collateral security is needed by the bankers as per RBI guidelines.

8. Profitability

The borrower will be able to produce 2,700 Kg of rope per year by employing entire family. By assuming a modest price of Rs. 8 per Kg of rope, the family can earn about Rs. 3,000 besides earning about Rs. 8,100 per annum towards own labour. The loan can be repaid in four years with one year grace period on principal.

Unit Cost for One Acre Sabai Grass Cultivation for year

Sl. No.	*Items*	*Cost (Rs.)*
1.	Ploughing (2) 6 Plough days @ Rs. 40 per Plough day	240
2.	Cost of Slips (7,200 Slips = 8Q) @ Rs. 30 per Quintal	240
3.	Labour for uprooting slips	300
4.	Fencing	200
5.	Transportation of slips to site	100
6.	Manure 2 cartloads @ Rs. 30 per cartload	60
7.	Fertilisers 10 : 8 : 0	135
8.	Digging of pits and planting	450
9.	Weeding and intercultivation	100
	Total	1,825
	Maintenance Cost in Subsequent Years	500

Financial Statement

Items	*Years* 1	2	3	4	5
A. Cost					
Cost of plantation	1,825	500	500	500	500
Cost of Twisting Wheel	300				
Rope output/year (kg)	2,700	2,700	2,700	2,700	2,700
Grass utilised (kg)	3,105	2,705	2,205	1,905	1,705
Grass field from own source (kg)	—	400	900	1,200	1,400
Grass purchased from market (kg)	3,105	2,705	2,205	1,905	1,705
Cost of grass purchased (Rs. 3/kg)	9,315	8,115	6,615	5,715	5,115
Labour Cost (of family @ Rs. 30/day)	8,100	8,100	8,100	8,100	8,100
Total Cost	19,540	16,715	15,215	14,315	13,715
B. Income Rope @ Rs. 8/kg	21,600	21,600	21,600	21,600	21,600
C. Surplus Income	2,060	4,885	6,385	7,285	7,885
D. Repayment Schedule					
Loan outstanding	4,800	4,800	3,600	2,000	
Loan instalment		1,200	1,600	200	
Interest on loan (Rs. 5,100) @ 12 per cent	576	576	432	540	
Total Repayment	576	1,776	2,032	2,240	
E. Surplus with Farmer	1,484	3,109	4,353	5,045	

The unit cost can be modified if more land can be brought under cultivation. A plantation of 1 hectare can meet the grass requirement of a family (3 members) from fourth year onwards.

ANNEXURE 12.2

Scheme for Making Decorative and Utility Items from Sabai Grass

Introduction

Mayurbhanj district is well-known for Sabai rope-making which is widely used in paper industry and for cot-making. Besides these traditional uses of Sabai grass, about 5–10 per cent of grass produced is used for value added products like decorative items and utility items. These products are progressively becoming popular and its demand is rising. DCIO is promoting this value-added segment of Sabai trade. The value-addition will generate additional employment and income to tribals.

1. *Products*

The commonly-made decorative and utility items include:

Doormats, Carpets, Toys (Birds, Animals), Wall hangings (Konark Wheel), Crocodiles, Coconut trees, Cottage, *etc.*

Sofa sets, Manchi (stools), Cots, Vanity bags, Modas, Baskets, *etc.*

2. *Product Making*

Manufacture of various decorative and utility items is a skilled job. It mainly involves weaving of Sabai rope with or without a wooden frame. Major inputs involve the wooden/cane frame wherever required, different grades of ropes, thread, colour, Sabai grass, *etc.*

3. *Skill Development*

DCIO is imparting training in preparation of value-added Sabai products at their Training-cum-Production Centres (TPCs) which are manned by IPOs. Training is also imparted under TRYSEM. Master craftsmen are employed for imparting training. New designs are also given to the entrepreneurs. NGOs are also involved in imparting training.

4. *Marketing*

At present, there is no organised marketing system for these products. These are mostly sold on festive occasions in and around Mayurbhanj and a couple of fairs in Calcutta, Bihar and Bhubaneswar. Occasionally, traders in Baripada also get order from metros and employ artisans for manufacturing the items as per the specification of the buyer. Artisans, Multipurpose Cooperative Societies, promoted by KVIB, are also involved in marketing of the products. Recently, ORMOS has started its district centre at Baripada which will give regular market support to the Sabai products.

5. *Assumptions under the Scheme*

In the existing scheme, it is designed to employ 5 artisans round the year. The promoter would either be an artisan himself or only organiser of the production and marketing of the products. The product range will depend on the market demand. For the purpose of the scheme, commonly-produced items are taken into consideration and the quantum of their production is as per the existing demand. This may change as per the market demand. Wages to the artisans is per-piece basis. They work either at their home by taking raw material or work at a common place as per convenience. The promoter will arrange for marketing directly or through Government agencies, *etc.*

6. *Project Details*

The project envisages a workshed, equipment, capitalised working capital for two months and one month stock of Sabai grass. The project cost comes to Rs. 15,610. Being a small farmer category, the margin the entrepreneur has to bring in is @ 5 per cent. Bank loan can be Rs. 14,800. The rate of interest will be guided by RBI guidelines. The scheme can employ 5 people directly. The project generates a surplus of about Rs. 8,000 per year. The loan can be repaid in 5 years.

Scheme for Making Decorative and Utility Items

Production Schedule

Sl. No.	*Items*	*Production per month*	*Output MDs/Piece*	*Average MDs required*
1.	Sofa sets	2	20.00	40.0
2.	Papauch	50	0.33	16.5
3.	Manchi	40	0.33	13.2
4.	House	15	0.50	7.5
5.	Coconut Tree	15	0.67	10.05
6.	Cottage	15	1.00	15
7.	Vanity Bags	25	0.50	12.5
8.	Konark Wheel/Wall Hangings	10	2.00	20
Total		172		134.75

Sl. No.	*Items*	*Cost of material per piece*	*Labour charges per piece*	*Material cost per month*	*Labour charges per month*	*Total cost*	*Sale price per piece*	*Sale proceeds (Rs.)*	*Net income per member*
1.	Sofa sets	750	450	1,500	900	2,400	1,400	2,800	400
2.	Papauch	4	5	200	250	450	15	750	300
3.	Manchi	12	8	480	320	800	25	1,000	200
4.	House	5	12	75	180	255	25	375	120
5.	Coconut Tree	5	12	75	180	255	25	375	120
6.	Cottage	10	20	150	300	450	40	600	150
7.	Vanity Bags	3	6	75	150	225	15	375	150
8.	Konark Wheel/ Wall Hangings	60	30	600	300	900	120	1,200	300
	Total			3,155	2,580	5,735	1,665	7,475	1,740

A: Project Cost:	Rs.
1. Working Shed (Thatched Roof) 15 × 15 @ Rs. 35/ sq ft	7,875
2. Material cost for 1 month	3,155
3. Labour charges for one month	2,580
4. Rope stock 1Q @ Rs. 10/Kg	1,000
5. Tools and equipment	1,000
Total	15,610
Margin/Subsidy @ 5 per cent	780
Bank Loan	14,830
B: Income per Month:	1,740
Management and Selling Costs	750
Net Surplus per year (8 months) (Rs. 1740-750)/Month	7,920

C: Repayment Schedule:

Items/Years	*1*	*2*	*3*	*4*	*5*
Loan O/S	14,800	11,840	8,880	5,920	2,960
Interest @ 12 per cent	1,776	1,421	1,066	710	355
Loan Instalment	2,960	2,960	2,960	2,960	2,960
Total Repayment	4,736	4,381	4,026	3,670	3,315
Gross Surplus	7,920	7,920	7,920	7,920	7,920
Net Surplus	3,184	3,539	3,894	4,250	4,605*

* This surplus is in addition to the managment cost of Rs. 750 per month kept aside.

Assumptions

1. The unit will employ 5 craftsmen.
2. The range of items and quantities produced is only illustrative and it is as per demand.
3. Regular market arrangement is made either with traders in cities/ORMAS/NGO/any agency.
4. The craftsmen are trained under Government programme or by promoter.

ANNEXURE 12.3

Scheme for Fibre Extraction Unit

Extraction of sisal fibre from sisal leaves is an employment-intensive commercial activity which can be taken up with bank finance. In the context of Koraput District, the major objective of a scheme for fibre extraction unit would be employment generation for the weaker section.

The major requirements for a sisal fibre extraction unit is a simple machine for extracting sisal fibre called raspador/decorticator. It is run through a 5–6 HP motor. The process for fibre extraction is:

(i) Harvesting of sisal leaves
(ii) Transportation of sisal leaves to extraction unit
(iii) Extraction of fibre by decorticator
(iv) Washing the fibre
(v) Drying the fibre
(vi) Beating the fibre tc remove the foreign material
(vii) Baking and storage
(viii) Marketing.

(i) Harvesting of Sisal Leaves

Sisal leaves can be harvested from the plantation from October/November to May, *i.e.*, excluding the rains. From each sisal plant, all the leaves from below excluding 10–12 leaves on the top can be harvested. Since in each hectare of plantation around 5,000 sisal plants are planted, considering mortality (due to lack of pupa case) one may assume an existing healthy plant population of 3,500 which can produce around 12 leaves per plant per annum. For one unit as proposed in the model, around 100 acre of sisal plantations would be needed. The main equipment required is a chopper for cutting the leaves clearly.

(ii) Transportation of Sisal Leaves to Extraction Unit

The existing sisal plantations sufficient for one unit may be in compact patches or scattered over a larger area. The transportation from the plantation to the extraction can be done on headloads, carts or tractors. The extraction units (decorticator and motor) can also be made mobile (with wooden foundation blocks) so that they can be rotated to the various plantation sites.

(iii) Extraction of Fibre by Decorticator

The decorticator is made up of a blade down rotating against a stationary shaft with adjustable gap. The leaves are fed in between this gap manually, the front half of the leaf is decorticated and pulled out and then the rear end of the leaf is fed between the blades and pulled out. This separates the fibres from the wet pulp. The decorticator needs two persons with reasonable level of skill.

The decorticator fibre is washed to separate the pulp and dried in the sun (preferably off the ground on suspended ropes or wires). After drying, they may need to be beaten to separate the dried pulp sticking to the fibre. Thereafter, they are tied up into bales for storage and marketing.

The model scheme provides for two decorticators and three 5–6 HP diesel motors for each unit. The reason behind providing more than one decorticator and motors is that these tend to breakdown, disrupting the whole extraction process. It is envisaged that in the worst eventuality at least one decorticator is run by a motor to provide continuous employment by way of uninterrupted operation. More than one mobile set also implies flexibility in exploiting dispersed plantations.

The other major investment are purchase of land (if needed), construction of a small godown with asbestos roofs and construction of temporary sheds. The working capital components mainly consists of labour payments for harvesting, decortication, transportation, washing, drying, baling, *etc.*, besides costs of fuel (diesel) and lubricants. For non-IRDP scheme by society/cooperative, a position for the one supervisor is provided for. This is optional and may be availed of, if needed.

The total capital investment works out to Rs. 1,49,600. The working capital cycle is assumed to be for two months and the working capital for first two months is capitalised. The total financial outlay works out to Rs. 2,30,250 and the term loan is Rs. 2,07,225. The repayment of the loan can be done in 3–4 years.

Institutional Arrangements

It is visualised that the unit would be run by a society/cooperative society/informal group formed of members from within an SC/ST community. The society/group would get the sisal plantation on nominal lease for long term (at least five years) from competent authorities. This arrangement is proposed from the view point of development of weaker sections (SC/ST) and from the same perspective, financing of such units based on plantation of public land to individuals/corporate sector should be discouraged.

The unit can also be financed as group financing under IRDP to persons from the same/close by village communities. An assured usufructory rights on sisal plantation to the extent of 100 acre should be available.

The question of leasing/giving usufructory lease of sisal plantations on Revenue Lands to a society/cooperative society/group of IRDP beneficiaries may need policy decision at State level.

Marketing

The major market of bulk sisal fibre is Calcutta. Sisal fibre is mainly (as bulk commodity) used in marine shipping sector and by the handicrafts sector.

The largest producer of sisal fibre in Orissa is the Soil Conservation Department which holds a central auction at Bhubaneswar once a year. The rates of sisal fibre are more or less decided by the price trend at the auction. Locally, Patra Industries is manufacturing sisal ropes at Koraput. Sisal Vikas Parishad is also a major producer of sisal fibre in Koraput district.

It is assumed in the model that the bulk sale shall be done to traders from Calcutta or to local industry, whoever offers better prices. Sisal Vikas Parishad can be asked to provide guidance and support in marketing. It is also assumed that a part of the production shall be sold to the various DWCRA and other artisan groups making handicrafts from sisal fibre.

Scheme Economics
Sisal Decortication (Fibre Extraction) Unit

A. *Technical Parameters*

(i)	Daily Output of Wet Fibre	350 kg
(ii)	Wet Fibre/Leaves	40 gm
(iii)	Leaves/Day	8,750
(iv)	Assumed Leaves/Plant	12
(v)	Plant Population Hectare of Existing Plantation	3,500
(vi)	Leave Production Hectare	42,000
(vii)	Running Months	8
(viii)	Days per Month	25
(ix)	Days per Season	200
(x)	Leaves Required per Season	17,50,000
(xi)	Area Required Under Leave/Unit	42 ha = 104 Acre
(xii)	Working Capital Cycle	2 Months

B. *Fixed Assets*

(i)	Godown	Asbestos Roof and Brick Walls	300 sq ft	Rs. 90 sq ft	Rs. 27,000
(ii)	Temporary Sheds	Thatched Roof	100 sq ft	Rs. 40 sq ft	Rs. 4,000
(iii)	Land		0.5 Acre	Rs. 10,000 Acre	Rs. 5,000
	Total				**Rs. 36,000**

C. *Machinery and Equipments*

(i)	Decorticators	Rs. 16,000 unit	2	Rs. 32,000
(ii)	5 HP Diesel Motor	Rs. 16,000 unit	2	Rs. 32,000
(iii)	Other Equipments	Lumpsum		Rs. 10,000
(iv)	Other Expenses	Lumpsum		Rs. 10,000
(v)	Contingency	5 per cent		Rs. 6,000
	Total			**Rs. 90,000**
	Grand Total			**Rs. 1,26,000**

D. *Working Capital Requirement for one Month*

(i)	Output per month Wet Fibre	8,750 kg Equivalent to 3,500 Dry Fibre 2,18,750 Leaves per Month	
(ii)	Cutting, Transportation and Stocking Charges	Rs. 0.07 per leaf	Rs. 15,313
(iii)	Extraction Cost (Labour)	Rs. 250 per day	Rs. 6,250
(iv)	Cleaning, Drying, Baling cost per day	Rs. 150	Rs. 3,750
(v)	Diesel (4 Lt. per hour)	10 Litres	Rs. 8,000

(vi) Lubricant and Grease	Lumpsum	Rs. 1,000
(vii) Repair and Maintenance	Lumpsum	Rs. 500
(viii) Office Expenses	Lumpsum	Rs. 200
(ix) Travel and Transportation	Lumpsum	Rs. 500
(x) Salary of Supervisor		Rs. 2,000
Total		**Rs. 37,513**

E. *Financial Analysis*

(i) Cost of Production/Year		Rs. 3,00,100
(ii) *(a)* Lease Rent	Rs. 100 per Acre	Rs. 10,417
(b) Maintenance of Plantation	Rs. 400 per Acre	Rs. 41,667
(iii) Interest on Working Capital Loan	18 per cent	Rs. 9,003
Total		Rs. 3,61,186
(iv) Sale of Sisal Fibre	Rs. 16 per Kg — 28,000 Kg	Rs. 4,48,000
(v) Operating Surplus		Rs. 86,814
(vi) Depreciation on Building	5 per cent	Rs. 1,550
(vii) Depreciation on Machinery	10 per cent	Rs. 9,000
(viii) Interest		Rs. 76,264

F. *Financial Parameters*

Year		*1*	*2*	*3*	*4*	*5*
Capital Cost		12,600				
Recurring Cost		3,61,186	3,61,186	3,61,186	3,61,186	3,61,186
Total Cost		4,87,186	3,61,186	3,61,186	3,61,186	3,61,186
Total Benefit		4,48,000	4,48,000	4,48,000	4,48,000	4,48,000
Net Benefit		39,186	86,814	86,814	86,814	86,814
Gross Surplus		1,61,839	86,814	86,814	86,814	86,814
IRR			219.41 per cent			
BCR	15 per cent		1.14			
NPV	15 per cent		1,81,448			

G. *Repayment*

TFO			2,01,025			
Loan	90 per cent		1,80,923			
Margin			2,01,03			
Rate of Interest	16.0 per cent					
Year		*1*	*2*	*3*	*4*	*5*
Principal		1,80,923	1,30,923	1,02,923	70,923	3,4923
Interest		28,948	20,948	16,468	11,348	5,588
Interest O/S		0	0	0	0	0
Repayment—Interest		28,948	20,948	16,468	11,348	5,588
Repayment—Principal		50,000	28,000	32,000	36,000	34,923
Gross Surplus		1,61,839	86,814	86,814	86,814	86,814
Net Surplus		82,891	37,866	38,346	39,466	46,304

ANNEXURE 12.4

Model Scheme for Sisal Fibre Handicrafts

The availability of sisal fibre from the Sisal Vikas Parishad and Soil Conservation Department have been used by the DRDA to promote small handicraft units. A group of women can be financed for the tools and equipment as well as sisal fibre after training in making utility and decorative items from sisal fibre. A number of training programmes through master craftswomen/men from West Bengal and Andhra Pradesh have been arranged by DRDA and a pool of trained women for sisal handicrafts are available.

The sisal handicrafts are slowly becoming popular because of the luster and strength of the sisal products. A number of innovative products like doormats, bags, sikka, dining mats, sitting mats, paper stands, *etc.*, are already being produced in Koraput by DWCRA groups. A number of other products like carpets, wall hangings, baskets, *etc.*, can be made if training is given.

A small group of 8-10 women can be organised into a group production process. The major inputs are one or two rope-making machines, frames for making doormats (rectangular and round), dyeing container, *etc.* A small shed for storing material and furnished could be provided for.

Skills

Some amount of skill is necessary for the workers to make sisal handicrafts/utility items. The strategy which had been followed by the DRDA has been to get master crafts person to conduct training programmes for selected women from DWCRA groups, who would in turn share and teach the skills to the women in group. Till now skills have been imparted for making the items mentioned above. Training for products like carpets needs to be imparted.

By this time, a number of skilled women are available in the district which can provide training for new groups.

Marketing

Handicraft items from sisal are new products which are yet to make out a niche for themselves. It was observed that sisal items, specially doormats, are gaining popularity even in the local markets (Koraput and Jeypore). The major advantages of sisal items are the strength and durability as compared to items made of Jute and Coir. It is also moisture/water resistant. Even though the items are costlier due to higher cost of fibre, with a little promotion, the products would be popularised in the urban handicrafts markets.

One NGO, Prajwala, based in Chittoor, Andhra Pradesh, has been exporting handicrafts items of sisal fibre through a Chennai-based export house. According to their representatives, the major requirement of export, apart from good design, quality and finish, is the use of non-synthetic, environment-friendly dyes. The DSMS and Sisal Vikas Parishad are trying to introduce natural dyes with the help of Prajwala.

Assumptions under the Scheme

Each unit would consist of around 10 women. It is assumed that making handicrafts would not be a full time activity, and each woman is assumed to put around 12–15 person-days per month over the year—they may put in less time during the agricultural season and more time during the slack season. Thus a group of 10 women are expected to put in around 125 person-days (PDs) per month. Therefore, 125 PDs per month has been used to work out the production schedule. The production schedule includes items such as bag, dining mat, paper stand, sitting mat, sikka and doormats. Depending on market demand and skills this combination can be varied.

Within one group, two rope-making machines shall be given on a collective basis, five sets of doormat frames (round and rectangular), dyeing containers and one small storage godown are included. The working capital cycle is taken as one month, on the basis of down payment by the DSMS for products. The wages/remuneration to each worker could be on price basis—this may be left to be decided within groups.

A. Scheme Economics

Sl. No.	*Items*	*Unit Cost Rs.*	*No.*	*Rs.*
(i)	Rope-making Machine–Per Machine	2,300	2	4,600
(ii)	Doormat Frame		5 Sets	
	(a) Rectangular	290		1,450
	(b) Round	460		2,300
(iii)	Dyeing Container with Lid (50 Litres)	550	2	1,100
(iv)	Needles, Scissors, Combs	200		200
(v)	Workshed/Godown (Thatched)	40 per sq ft	75	3,000
	Total			12,650
	Contingency	10 per cent		1,265
	Grand Total			13,915

B. Recurring Costs for one Month (One Working Capital Cycle)

Sl. No.	*Items*	*Rate*	*Quantity*	*Rs.*
(i)	Sisal Fibre	16	64.22 kg	1,027.52
(ii)	Dyes	500	0.5 kg	250
(iii)	Cloth/Thread/Other Material	Lumpsum		200
(iv)	Labour	25	125	3,125
(v)	Repair/Maintenance	Lumpsum		100
(vi)	Contingency	10 per cent		470.252
	Total			5,172.772

C. Capital Cost 13,915
Capitalised Working Capital (one month) 5,173
Total Financial Outlay 19,088
Loan 90 per cent 17,179
Margin 1,909

D. Production Schedule

Sl. No.	*Items*	*MD Required per Piece*	*Prod. per Month*	*MD per Month*	*Sisal Fibre (GM)*	*Cost of Fibre (Rs.)*	*Cost of Labour (Rs.)*	*Sale Price (Rs.)*
(i)	Bag (With Inner Cloth)	2.00	15	30	7,500	120	750	90
(ii)	Dining Mat	0.63						
(iii)	Paper Stand	1.00	20	20	6,000	96	500	60
(iv)	Sitting Mat	1.50	10	15	7,500	120	375	75
(v)	Sikka	0.60	20	12	4,000	64	300	35
(vi)	Doormat	1.00	28	28	19,600	314	700	55
		6.725	124	125	64,220	1,028	3,125	345

E. Item Costing

Sl. No.	*Items*	*Sisal fibre required (grams)*	*MD required per piece*	*Cost of fibre*	*Labour cost*
(i)	Bag (With inner cloth)	500	2.00	8	50.00
(ii)	Dining Mat	150	0.63	2.4	15.63
(iii)	Paper Stand	300	1.00	4.8	25.00
(iv)	Sitting Mat	750	1.50	12	37.50
(v)	Sikka	200	0.60	3.2	15.00
(vi)	Paonpocha	700	1.00	11.2	25.00

F. Sale/Month 6,500
Recurring Cost/Month 5,173
Annual Sale 52,000 (The handicrafts unit is assumed to operate for 8 months in a year)
Annual Recurring Cost 41,382

Financial Parameters

Items/Year	*1*	2	3	4	5
Capital Cost	13,915				
Recurring Cost	41,382	41,382	41,382	41,382	41,382
Total Cost	55,297	41,382	41,382	41,382	41,382
Total Benefit	52,000	52,000	52,000	52,000	52,000
Net Benefit	– 3,297	10,618	10,618	10,618	10,618
Gross Surplus	13,882	10,618	10,618	10,618	10,618
IRR 321.00 5 per cent					
BCR 1.18					

Repayment

TFO	17,179
Loan 90 per cent	15,416
Margin	1,718
Rate of Interest	12.5 per cent

Items/Year	*1*	2	3	4	5
Principal	15,461	12,369	9,277	6,184	3,092
Interest	2,474	1,979	1,484	990	495
Interest O/S	0	0	0	0	0
Repayment—Interest	2,474	1,979	1,484	990	495
Repayment—Principal	3,092	3,092	3,092	3,092	3,092
Gross Surplus	13,882	10,618	10,618	10,618	10,618
Net Surplus	8,316	5,547	6,041	6,536	7,031

CHAPTER XIII

Medicinal Plants Cultivation

INTRODUCTION

Over 10,000 wild plants are used by tribals for various uses with about 8,000 of them used for medicinal purposes with at least 2,000 plants warranting detailed scientific scrutiny. From a large number of edible plants only four species are used for stable food—rice, wheat, maize and potato. Research in edible plant species could lead to more and generation of income for tribals without damaging ecosystems. The tribals use plants species for fibre, cords, fodder and pesticides, besides dyes, resin, perfumes and incense. Wild Plant species which are used for edible purposes are over 4,000 with 800 hitherto undiscovered and minimum of 250 can be developed as alternative sources of food in the near future. 600 wild plant species are used for making fibre and cords with about 80 having potential for commercial exploitation. Out of 500 wild plants, over 80 can be commercially exploited for fodder purposes. Out of 325 wild species used by tribals as pesticides, 180 could be developed into safe bio-pesticides. Almost all plant species from which grass, resin, dyes, incense and perfumes are extracted, have commercial use. A large number of endangered plant species have also been identified by the All India Coordinated Research Project on Ethnobiology by the ICAR from 1982 to 1997.

The intensive study revealed that tribals used

(i) 55 per cent of plant species for medicinal purposes
(ii) 28 per cent of plant species for edible uses
(iii) 4 per cent of plant species for fibre and cords
(iv) 3 per cent of plant species for fodder

(v) 3 per cent of plant species as pesticides
(vi) 2 per cent of plant species as pisticides
(vii) 1 per cent of plant species as incense and perfumes
(viii) 4 per cent of plant species for socio-cultural/miscellaneous purposes.

About 250 cultivators like millets of inferior and wild varieties (Kondon, Kudki, *etc.*) are in use and could yield rare genetic foods for future plant breeders, have also been depicted in the National Bureau of Plant Genetic Research, New Delhi. The nutritional constituents of 200 wild edible plants have already been evaluated and shown rich proteins, amino acids, lysine and minerals. Photochemical and biological investigation of over 600 wild plants for medicinal purposes by tribals have indicated discovery of new therapeutic agents of industrial value. The AICRPE study revealed that tribal communities have unique knowledge of many wild plants. Such ethno-medicinal information of wild plants is very cost-effective for drug-hunters in finding new bio-dynamic drugs.

The Indian herbal drug market has a turnover of Rs. 2,300 crore in 1999–2000 and is expected to increase to Rs. 4,000 crore in another two years. The 8,000 species of plants used for medicines are spread over 4,600 tribal communities for human and veterinary health care. In Ayurveda, 1,700 species of plants are fully documented with biological properties and actions. Over 10,000 herbal drug formulations based on these plant species are recorded for various health conditions. The All India Coordinated Research Project (AICRPE) was initiated in 1982 under a UNESCO programme and is under the Ministry of Environment and Forests with over 27 national level institutions participating, including the Botanical Survey of India and the Central Drug Research Institute, until 1998 when the project concluded.

There is a need to investigate the scientific and medical properties of each plant and a monograph is prepared to find out the raw materials used for formulation, based on morphology, habitat ecology, storage; collection, preparation, posology, therapeutics, maturity, chemical content, substitutes, adulteration and their uses. The therapeutic content varies with area and similar-kind of plants have different therapeutic values. Thus, fingerprinting the drug formulation will be the first step at standardisation. China's herbal drug market is about Rs. 23,000 crore annually because the stiff conditions set by the drug administrators have been met. Around 300 plants are used in Western bio-medicine, modern perfumery and food processing industry. Some important medicinal plants of economic value are listed at Annexure 13.1.

A majortiy of the medicinal plants are flowering plants. One-third are trees and another one-third are shrubs with the remaining one-third being herbs, grasses and climbers. 70 per cent of these medicinal plants are found in tropical forests (dry and moist decidious forests) while only 30 per cent are from temperate and higher altitudes. As per WHO estimates, the value of trade in medicinal plants in India is around Rs. 5.5 billion per year while the world trade is around $ 55/60 billion and is growing. India's share in the global export trade is only 0.5 per cent for medicinal plants. Enhancement of exports by Rs. 5,000 crore annually can provide sustainable productive employment and income to 20 million tribal families. 95 per cent of the medicinal plants are collected from the wild and only 20 plant species are under cultivation while over 4,000 species are in industrial use. Over 70 per cent of plant collection involves destructive harvesting of roots, bark, wood, stem and entire herbs. There is a threat to the genetic stocks and to the diversity of medicinal plants. Thus, the only alternative is to take up extensive cultivation of medicinal plants. This can be done by tribal farmers, ensuring income and an assured market and could major drug manufactureres under contract farming system.

MARKET DEMAND FOR MEDICINAL PLANTS

The tribal domestic market for crude herbal drugs and extracts is around Rs. 3 billion as under:

	(Rs. in billion)
(i) Requirement for over-the-counter products including aromatics and cosmetics	1.20
(ii) Requirement for ethical formulations	0.60
(iii) Requirement for clinical formulations	0.60
(iv) Requirement for traditional Vaids (doctors)	0.40
(v) Requirement for home formulations	0.20
The same demand can be considered as under:	
(i) Crude Drugs	1.28
(ii) Essential Oils, Gums and Resins	0.56
(iii) Herbal Extracts	0.64
(iv) Condiments and Food Additives	0.40

Source: AICRPE, GOI, Ministry of Environment & Forests, New Delhi.

80 per cent of sales come from 147 medicinal plants. The export turnover is around Rs. 1.1 billion for herbal extracts and essential oils while Rs. 1.45 billion is for drugs.

The total export turnover of herbal products is approximately Rs. 23 billion, with allopathic drug formulations contributing Rs. 12 billion, Ayurvedic ethical commodities Rs. 6.5 billion and Ayurvedic clinical formulations contribute Rs. 4.5 billion. Sale of medicinal plants is only Rs. 2.4 billion, *i.e.*, 10.5 per cent of the total turnover. The export market is fast increasing at a rate greater than the domestic market. The quality of medicinal plants depends on the geographical origin, time and stage of growth when collection is done and the post-plucking, bundling completed. Collection is done by tribal people mostly from the forests and plants are collected without paying attention to the stage of maturity, dried on the ground and stored in adverse conditions and the quality of collected material is often poor. There is a vast secretive and largely unregulated trade in medicinal plants due to involvement of petty traders and exporters. There is a tremendous adulteration and substitution of other plants, similar in nature, in this trade. Use of tribal people merely for stripping off forests for their medicinal herbs, harms the biological diversity of our country. With low prices, it would be difficult to grow medicinal plants unless the trade is regulated and tribal farmers working under contract farming terms, could be persuaded to take up this activity as it promises a daily income, from small land plots.

Need for Medicinal Plant Conservaton

Medicinal plants are a national resources, growing under different ecological conditions. These plants can only be conserved in the wild, under viable breeding conditions or they run the risk of extinction. Medicinal plants have distinct and large areas of distribution while there are endemic species confined to a few pockets. There is a need for a National Medicinal Plant Conservation Policy with a network of scientists ensuring the cultivation of these plants, retaining their therapeutic values and genetic variations. This can be ensured only through a network of regional and sub-regional ethno-medicinal plants known to the various tribal communities, all over India. The recording of tribal medicinal uses of plants and animals was taken up by the ICAR in 1982 till 1998 under the All India Coordinated Research Project on Ethno-biology (AICRPE). There are also about 50 medicinal plant gardens ranging from 1 acre to 40 acre, set up between 1987–92. Another 15 gardens have been set up in Southern India under the Foundation of Revitalisation for Local Health Traditions (FRLHT) with only one managed by the Kerala State Government, and the others by NGOs. Private Ayurvedic medicine manufacturing companies have also set up herbal gardens as also several agricultural universities.

However, there is no organised nursery network for supply of quality planting materials of medicinal plants. The cultural practices of about 25 species of medicinal plants (list at Annexure 13.2) have been standardised by ICAR and supply of quality planting materials of about 40 species of aromatic and medicinal plants are available in the ICAR/CSIR network.

FRLHT has set up a network of 55 supply nurseries which raise medicinal plants for

(i) primary health care
(ii) for industry
(iii) endangered species
(iv) institutional gardens

There is a need for a countrywide chain of medicinal plant nurseries which will multiply all region-specific plants used in traditional tribal medicines. These nurseries should become the primary sources of supply of plants and seed materials that can be subsequently multiplied by the tribal people in small herbal gardens. There is no need for credit subsidies (either of principal or interest), if a contractual farming system can be set up by the 15 major drug manufacturers with the help of the NGOs/State Governments and the tribal people. NABARD has announced in 1995, a policy for financing cultivation of medicinal plants while in 1996, the World Bank was considering investing funds on 'medicinal plants' as a special sub-sector in its agricultural programmes. The agricultural universities also need to take up systematic research on cultivation of medicinal plants.

Cultivation of Medicinal Plants

The world trade in medicinal plants is expected to touch about US $ 5 billion. Demand till now has been from wild sources. Entire species will be wiped out if investment in commercial cultivation of medicinal plants is not taken up immediately. This can easily be taken up by tribal farmers who could be trained to cultivate various species of medicinal plants which they use or are familiar with. As tribal people are aware of the uses/potentials of these plants, they will be easily motivated to cultivate them if backward and forward linkages can be set up under the contractual farming system. Standardised agronomic practices and quality planting materials as also buy-back systems should be undertaken. Today, of all the numerous species of medicinal plants in traditional Ayurvedic, Unani, Siddha, Tibetan and Chinese medicines, only about 20 medicinal species are being cultivated. A gene bank needs to be established to deposit seeds of wild medicinal plants and evaluate the genetic variation of these medicinal plants. There are at present only 3 gene banks at New Delhi, Lucknow and Thiruvananthapuram. Considering the low value of many medicinal plants in a raw form, there is a need to promote community level enterprise by tribals for value-addition to medicinal plants through simple techniques like drying, cleaning, crushing, powdering, grading, packaging, *etc.* This will increase the stake of tribal communities in conservation of medicinal herbs and plants.

ANNEXURE 13.1

A List of Important Medicinal Plants of Economic Value

I. Plants with Culinary, Aromatic, Religious and Commercial Use

	English name	*Common name*		*English name*	*Common name*
1.	Vetiver	*Usheer*	13.	Valerian	*Tagar*
2.	Rose	*Gulab*	14.	Crocus	*Kesar*
3.	Sandal	*Chandan*	15.	Banyan	*Vata*
4.	Shirish	*Siris*	16.	Pipal	*Aswathama*
5.	Marigold	*Genda*	17.	Grass	*Doorva*
6.	Olive	*Jaitom*	18.	Lotus	*Pankaj*
7.	Camomnils	*Babuna*	19.	Lemon Grass	*Bhootrins*
8.	Geraniums	*Laljabi*	20.	Camphor	*Karpoor*
9.	Henna	*Madhyantica*	21.	Zedoary	*Karchoor*
10.	Rudraksha	—	22.	Mimusops	*Bakul*
11.	Rosemary	—	23.	Gaultheria	*Gandhpura*
12.	Hibisas	*Jaba*			

II. Plants Used in Food or Food Additives

	English name	*Common name*		*English name*	*Common name*
1.	Pepper	*Marich*	11.	Ferugreen	*Methi*
2.	Ginger	*Shunthi*	12.	Chicory	*Kaasani*
3.	Ajowan	*Yavani*	13.	Catechu	*Khadir*
4.	Cloves	*Lavang*	14.	Garlic	*Lasun*
5.	Asafoetida	*Hingu*	15.	Nutmeg	*Jaiphal*
6.	Dill	*Shatousha*	16.	Mace	*Jayatri*
7.	Fennel	*Saunf*	17.	Onion	*Pulandu*
8.	Cumin	*Jeera*	18.	Coriander	*Dhanyaka*
9.	Coram	*Jajode*	19.	Cinnamon	*Dalchini*
10.	Turmeric	*Haridra*	20.	Kokum	*Vrikshamla*

The high-volume demand comes from about 50 plants.

III. Medicinal Herbs with Export Value

	English name	*Use*		*English name*	*Use*
1.	Tulsi	Anti-bacterial	8.	Shathi	Eosinopeanic
2.	Nirgundi	Analgesic/ Anti-inflammatory	9.	Kutki	Hepatsopic
3.	Kushtha	Anto-bacterial	10.	Vidhkandh	Anabolic
4.	Manjistha	Dematological use	11.	Bhringraj	Hepatits/ Hair Tonic
5.	Mahashringi	Anti-asthmatic	12.	Tagar	Memory-booster
6.	Mandukurpani	Neurotropic	13.	Kadrer	Anti-cancer/ Anti-inflammatory
7.	Neem	Immuno-modulator	14.	Madhunashi	Anti-diabetic

IV. Aramo-therapy and Cosmetic Use of Plants

	Common name	English name		Common name	English name
1.	*Kumari*	Aloe	6.	*Jaba*	Hibirues
2.	*Tarunj*	Rose	7.	*Nagkesar*	Mesua Terrea
3.	*Bahuna*	Camomile	8.	*Marigold*	Calendula SP/ Tagetes crecta
4.	*Tulsi*	Ocimum	9.	*Ustakhuddus*	Lavendula stoechas
5.	*Mehndi*	Lawsonia inermis	10.	*Pudina*	Mentha arvenis

ANNEXURE 13.2

Medicinal Plant Species which can be Cultivated

Sl. No.	*Botanical name*	*Local name*	*Uses*
1.	Aegle marmelos	*Bel*	Root is an ingredient of Dasmool. Fruit pulp treats diarrhoea, leaves treat diabetes.
2.	Andrographis paniculata	*Kalmegh*	A bitter tonic, and as a febrifuge and used in liver diseases.
3.	Asparagus racemosus	*Shatawar*	Extensively used as nutritive tonic and in various formulations
4.	Azadirachta indica	*Neem*	A biopesticide and used in many diseases.
5.	Bacopa monnieri	*Brahmi*	Brain tonic in nervous disorders such as insanity, epilepsy, neurasthenia and nervous breakdown and memory enhancing.
6.	Berberis aristata	*Berberis*	Roots, stem bark and Rassaut or Rasanjan are used in conjunctivities, enlargement of liver and spleen, jaundice, urinogential disorders and ulcerative condition.
7.	Catharanthus roseus	*Periwinkle*	Contains more than 100 alkaloids. Used for treatment of leukaemia.
8.	Cassia angustifolia	*Senna*	Leaves and pods are purgative and laxative.
9.	Celastrus paniculatus	*Malkangni*	Decoction and oil of seeds are stimulant for the neuromascular system and are given in rheumatism, gout and paralysis. Also used as brain tonic and sharpens memory.
10.	Chlorophytum tuberosum	*Safed musli*	Used as demulscent, wholesome tonic alternative nervine. Roots are highly priced drugs.
11.	Commiphora wighti	*Guggul*	Used in urinary infections, piles, fistula, arthritis, rheumatism and in lowering cholesterol.

(Contd.)

Sl. No.	*Botanical name*	*Local name*	*Uses*
12.	Emblica officinalis or Phyllanthus emblica	*Amla or Aonla*	Fruit is used as laxative, in hair oils, and as general tonic.
13.	Ephedra geradiana	*Ephedra*	Used in asthma and hay fever.
14.	Gloriosa superba	*Gloriosa or Kalihari*	Rhizome is extensively used to induce the abortion and for painless delivery.
15.	Gymnema sylvestris	*Gurmar*	It has anti-diabetic properties and for controlling the body weight.
16.	Hydnocarpus kurzil	*Chalmogra*	Oil is used in treatment of leprosy.
17.	Mesua ferrea	*Nagkeshar*	Used in bleeding piles, dysentery, cough, *etc.*
18.	Narodostachys grandiflora	*Jatamansi*	Used in hysteria, palpitation of heart, menopause and various nervous diseases.
19.	Ocimum basilicum	*Tukmaria*	In unani used as anti-dysenteric, anto-diarrhoel and aphrodisiac drug.
20.	Plantago ovata	*Isab or Psyllium*	Seed and husk are used in treatment of chronic constipation, control of diarrhoea and dysentery.
21.	Picrohiza kurroa	*Kutki*	Used in the treatment of dyspesia, respiratory disorders, jaundice and anaemia.
22.	Rauvolfia serpentina	*Sarpagandha*	Used as desdative in insanity; it is hypotensive and tranquilizers.
23.	Swertia chirayata	*Chirayata*	It is a tonic, febrifugal, laxative, stomachic, antithelmintic and anti-diarrhoeal.
24.	Santanum album	*Chandan*	Oil used in various formulations.
25.	Withania somnifera	*Ashwagandha*	It is sedative, alterative, anti-inflammatory tonic and rejuvenative.

CHAPTER XIV

Projects for Tribal Development

INTRODUCTION

The tribal areas in the country have been endowed with vast natural resources in the form of rich forest, minerals, tourist potential, traditional arts and handicrafts, culture, *etc.* The large tribal communities of these areas have continued to remain isolated from the mainstream of developmental processes, dogged by stark hunger, poverty, illness and illiteracy. Despite the efforts made, by the Central/State Governments and NGOs with various developmental strategies, and also generous assistance from banks and creation of infrastructural facilities, the necessary impetus for sustainable development continues to be elusive possibly because of the inaccessibility of the areas, bureaucratic hurdles, large scale illiteracy and continued alienation of natural resources from forests from the indigenous tribal population. While it would be presumptuous to suggest that formulation of appropriate credit packages with necessary linkages, would be able to extricate the tribal people from the hungry clutches of traders and money-lenders and sundry exploiters, it is necessary to launch a coordinated series of micro-plans, taking small progressive steps, to enable the 'forgotten' tribal people to reap the fruits of development. In the new millennium, there is an impatience to forge ahead and there is a possibility that the tribal people are left to fend for themselves, without access to the natural resources and forests which have sustained them over the centuries. Grandiose schemes over vast areas with impressive targets and funds attached have been formulated in the past and have been consigned to the dustbins of history, without a trace as these have not been centred around the tribal needs and sensibilities. The need for relevance and a tribal-centred approach for a series of interventions at the micro-level, cannot be over-emphasised.

DEVELOPMENT AND TRIBAL PARTICIPATION

The tribal people need assistance and sometimes intervention, not as charity but to achieve sustainable development and attain economic independence from the clutches of traders and money-lenders. Good intentions are not always the best guidelines for development. The three stages for tribal development are:

(i) subsistence stage
(ii) take-off stage
(iii) sustainable stage.

It would be erroneous to try and attain the third stage of development which is ideal without getting to the first and second stages. In the first and second stages, NGOs and SHGs would be necessary while in the third stage, banks would be useful in providing credit for individual requirements. While designing an appropriate programme, sound financial principles as also clear social objectives must be kept in mind. However, the problem is not in achieving these objectives, which can often be debatable, but to ensure the participation of the tribal people in these development programmes. In addition to enhancing individual incomes and community prosperity, there have to be specific activities that enhance inputs of production like *(i)* natural resource management, *(ii)* human resource management, *(iii)* rural infrastructural development and *(iv)* savings and credit-related programmes. These objectives can be secured only if the tribal people participate willingly in their poverty alleviation process. The four kinds of participation are:

(i) Participation in decision-making, in identifying problems, formulation of alternatives, planning activities and allocating resources.
(ii) Participation in implementation in carrying out activities, managing and operating programmes and partaking of services.
(iii) Participation in economic, social, cultural or other benefits, individually or collectively.
(iv) Participation in evaluation of the activity, its outcome, which should provide feedback into the first three kinds of participation.

Individually, a tribal person tends to be erratic, uncertain in his behaviour. The community membership and participation smoothens such rough edges making them more reliable. Individuals feel exposed to all kinds of hazards and require guidance and advice from people they know and trust. Membership in a tribal group gives a feeling of protection and the benefit of collective perceptions, decision-making and implementation of programmes for common benefits. The approach towards poverty alleviation has to be one of self-help and should enable the tribal community to benefit from their own exertions and should encourage them to help themselves. Self-Help Groups are one of the many answers to tribal development. But there is no single approach to tribal development. What is needed is a series of micro-development efforts, leading to the final goal of tribal development. Obviously, such an approach requires dedicated administration, planners, bankers and NGO volunteers who are committed to tribal empowerment, tribal participation and tribal development. There can be no textbook approach and ideally, various institutions have to be considered and whatever succeeds in taking the tribal people one step at a time towards the final goal, should be encouraged. What should be discouraged is dependence on textbook theories and circulars on project formulation. Bureaucrats and bankers should be trained in preparing specific micro projects based on exploiting available natural resources, tribal expertise and skills.

Preparation of Bankable Schemes

There are a large number of schemes which are implementable and which assist in tribal economic development. It may be recalled that during the implementation of the Integrated Rural Development Projects being implemented by the State/Central Governments, due to pressure to attain targets, unsuitable projects were forced on the tribal people which were not viable when implemented in tribal areas. Dairy schemes for tribals and goat-rearing schemes flopped because the tribals love meat and the animals were promptly dispatched to the cooking pots! Implementation of such schemes only indebted the helpless tribal people. In its new incarnation, the Swarna Jayanti Swarojgar Yojna, it is hoped that the scheme implementation is more attuned to tribal needs and actually succeeds in helping the tribals towards economic empowerment. There is a need to encourage processing of minor forest produce without too much technology, which would not be understood by the tribal people. The simple processing of a few minor forest produce into products for sale, would enable the tribal people to earn more, without much risk or capital and ensure that they get a better return on the minor forest produce. Product profiles of a few such products and the projected financial returns would enable the preparation of area-specific or product-specific projects which could be implemented in tribal areas and benefit them economically. The project profiles are:

(i) Sal Seed Processing
(ii) Mango Kernel Processing
(iii) Hill Broom Products
(iv) Gum Extraction and Refining
(v) Lac Collection and Processing
(vi) Tasar Silk-worm Rearing.

These are projects which have been handled by tribals themselves, right from the collection stage to the processing and marketing stages and have the necessary know-how. Without going into huge production facilities and power, water and technical/technological processes, the tribal people are able to manage various processes traditionally and a slow stage-by-stage process development, for greater economy and profits. Though there may be more technically efficient ways for processing minor forest produce, these may not be implementable by the tribals yet. It would be better to introduce technological upgrading as and when the tribal people need such upgradation.

(i) Sal Seed Processing

Sal seeds are used as food by the tribal people but with the seed containing oil (13–15 per cent hard fat) which can be extracted by various processes, the tribal people have a ready source of income from sale of sal seeds. Sal seeds are used in soap-making while sal fat is used for adulterating ghee while defatted sal cakes are used as cattle or poultry feed. Solvent extraction is essential for efficient extraction of sal fat. Refined bleached sal is substituted for cocoa in chocolates. Sal seed cake contains 30 per cent starch and is used in the textile industry as a tannin material. Sal seed cakes contain 14 per cent tanin and is used in the leather industry. After starch and tannins are removed from the cake, it is used as manure. The rate is now around Rs. 2 per Kg of sal seed. There is a 7 year cycle with 1 very good year, 4 medium years and two poor seed years. Fruits ripen in May and fall on the ground and are then collected and dried in the sun. The wings are burnt or removed manually and decasticated seeds are sold with 100 Kg of sal seeds yielding 60 Kg of kernels with collection continuing upto June till the onset of monsoons. The tribal people extract fat from the sal kernels by traditional methods. The kernels are pounded, boiled in water and the fat skinned off the surface and forms a hard ghee on cooling. This fat is edible and also used for lighting LAMPS.

Value-Addition

(a) Cost of sal kernal	— Rs. 2,000 per ton
(b) Price of sal fat	— Rs. 10,000 per ton
	8 per 100 tons of fat — Rs. 280 per Kg of fat
	$10{,}000/1{,}000 \times 280$ = Rs. 2,800
(c) Cost of processing	— Rs. 700 per ton of fat
	Rs. 200 per 280 Kg
Value-addition	= $b - (a + c)$ = Rs. 600 per ton of sal kernel
Sal butter per ton costs Rs. 18000	

In addition, tannin extraction and use of oil cakes as manure, have additional yields.

(ii) Mango Kernel Processing

Mango kernels form 61–83 per cent of stones which have an oil content of 6–14 per cent. Hand or power-operated decortication are available for separation of kernels from the stones. Drying at storage of kernels, extraction, refining and oil-utilisation as also meal used as manure, have been studied and processes developed. Mango kernel fat contains desaturated triglycerides (30–45 per cent) and stearic acids (36–41 per cent) and is valued as a cocoon butter substitute for exports and is also used as vanaspati and soap-making.

Value-Addition

		Rs.
(a)	Dried Mango Kernel (1 ton mango seed = 600 Kg of kernel)	1,700 per MT
(b)	Cost of extraction	1,400 per MT
(c)	Fat — 8 to 9 per cent (90 Kg of fat per ton of kernel) Cost of refining @ Rs. 2,000 per ton Loss in refining — 25 per cent = 67.5 Kg of refined fat	180
(d)	Price of refined fat for 67.5 Kg	1,800
(e)	De-oiled kernel — 86 per cent Price for 800 Kg	3,500
(f)	Total Price of fat and meal	4,800
(g)	Total Cost $(a + b + c)$	3,680
(h)	Total Profit $(f - g)$	1,120

However, solvent extraction units will employ tribal labourers as processors and women as gatherers of mango kernel.

(iii) Hill Broom Products

Hill broom stalks are collected exclusively by tribal women and is a major income earner as these brooms sell all over the country and are an export-earner also. Hill broom stalks grow wild on the hills and can earn Rs. 5–7 per Kg, for the tribal women. But if the hill brooms are manufactured by the women themselves, with a little better finish and tying with wire, nylon or cane, and packing in polythene, the prices shoot upto Rs. 8 per broom! Individual processing and packing is less economical than joint processing, due to economics of scale and not much skills are required for training tribal women to produce good quality hill brooms.

Value-Addition

Cost of Raw Materials

		Rs.
(a)	Cost of 454 quintals of hill brooms Rs. 700 per quintal to get 400 quintals for processing	3,17,800
(b)	Forest Royalty @ Rs. 170 per quintal	77,180
(c)	Purchase Tax — 8 per cent of royalty	6,164

(d)	Incidental expenses @ Rs. 20 per quintal towards transportation, *etc.*	9,080
(e)	Cost of cane-binding 1,60,000 hillbrooms @ Rs. 1.50 per broom 1 Kg to per	2,40,000
(f)	Cost of G. I. Pipes for binding 1,60,000 nos of hillbrooms @ Re. 0.30 per pipe	48,000
(g)	Labour charges for 1 labourer @ Rs. 1.50 per broom	2,40,000
(h)	Packing/Binding @ Rs. 15 for 50 pieces	16,000
X	**Total Costs**	9,54,224
Y	Sale Price @ Rs. 8 per broom for 1,60,000 brooms (including sales tax, octroi, *etc.*)	12,80,000
	Surplus (X – Y)	**3,25,774**

This will be divided among 120 women for broom-making and 200 women for broom collection, for about 3 months in a year.

(iv) Gum Extraction and Refining

There are two varieties of edible gums—Gum Arabic from Acacia trees (Babul) and the Gum Karaya from Genduli/Kartira. Gum Karaya is used in pharmaceuticals, confectionary, cosmetics, textiles and for sizing. Indiscriminate tapping for gum extraction can ruin the trees while the proper collection of gum with cleaning of impurities (bark, sand, mud, grit), grading and packing enhances gum value. Gum is generally collected from Genduli, Char, Bahada, Dhaura trees and is not separated or graded but are mixed together.

Value-Addition

		Rs.
(a)	Average price of ungraded gum per ton	2,600
(b)	Loss of quantity in grading 1 ton of graded gum = 1/0.7 ton of ungraded gum = average price/0.7	3,714
(c)	Value added by grading of gum	1,121

(v) Lac Collection and Processing

The lac insect (Lacifer lacca) leaves resinous incrustation on the twigs of trees such as Kusum (Schlevicher oleora) and Palasa (Butea monorperma). Twigs of a tree having deposits of crowded larvae are tied to the twigs of a host tree (Arjun or Asan trees) to be brought under cultivation. Such lac sticks having mature female insects are called brood lac. Insects are gradually hatched from the larvae and crawl out to feed on the sap of the host tree and in the process, a thick resinous fluid which exudes from the body of the insects, forms a hard incrustation of lac over the whole twig with kusum lac fetching maximum price. Good quality brood lac is not available and what is available from Ranchi has 80 per cent mortality. There are 2 lac crops, one in hot summer and the other in winter. Lac cultivation requires intensive operation such as pruning, harvesting, inoculation, *etc.* The two lac forms are Avi, cut from the host plant and Phunki, collected from the brood lac. Lac removed for the sticks is known as stick lac which is then dried, crushed and winnowed to free the substances from grit, wood, sand, *etc.* Storage over a long period causes deterioration. Lac is washed to remove colouring matter, insect bodies and then graded according to quality and is now called seed lac and costs about Rs. 250 per ton and can be done by the tribal people themselves. Seed lac is converted into shel lac by heat process costing Rs. 1,000 per ton and the yield is 55 per cent of stick lac by weight. Fresh Kusumi seed lac yields the most lac while solvent extraction process gives the best quality of lac.

Value-Addition

		Rs.
(a)	Stick lac price	3 per kg or Rs. 3,000 per MT
	Conversion charges into seed lack	250 per MT
	Total	3,250 per MT
(b)	1 ton of stick lac	550 to 600 Kg of seed lac
	Price of seed lack	8,000 to Rs. 10,000 per ton
	Value added @ Rs. 8000 per ton of seed lac	Rs. 4,400 to Rs. 5,500 = Rs. 1,150 per ton of stick lac
(c)	Conversion into shellac	1 ton of seed lac yields 550 Kg of shellac
	550 Kg of seed lac yields	= 550 × 55 = 303 Kg of shellac
	Price of hand-made shellac	16,300 per ton
	Cost of 303 Kg of Shellac	16,300 × 0.303 = Rs. 4,938
	Conversion cost of 550 Kg of seed lac to shellac	550
	Total cost = Rs. 3250 + Rs. 550	3,800
	Value Added = Rs. 4,938 – Rs. 3,800	**1,138**

(vi) Tasar Silk-Worm Rearing

Of the four forms of silk worm rearing, *viz.*, mulbery, eri, muga and tasar, the tribal people take to tasar silk worm rearing as it is entirely a forest product plantation of host plants, rearing of silk worms and for spinning of silk fibres general employment. The tasar silk worm (Antheraea mylitta) is reared only on forest trees like Sal (Shorea Robusta), Asan (Terminilia tomentora) and Arjun trees (Termimilia arjuna). It provides employment to a large number of tribal families, who collect the natural grown cocoons or rear it on forest trees as in Mayurbhanj in Orissa. The indiscriminate cutting of Arjun and Asan trees in recent years has proved to be disastrous for the tasar silk industries and to the tribal people.

Value-Addition

(Economics of rearing host plants having 300 Arjun/Asan trees in 1 hectare)

Cultivation 1-5 years

		Rs.
(a)	Raising seedlings	6,000
(b)	Seedlings plantation	50,000
(c)	Maintenance cost (Rs. 2 per plant/dig well for 4 years)	28,000
(d)	One dug well	50,000
(e)	One diesel pumpset	20,000
(f)	Diesel and maintenance costs (Rs. 2,500 × 5 years)	12,500
(g)	Guards during crop cycle (2500 × 5 years	12,500
(h)	Seeds	1,000
(i)	Implements and accessories	20,000
(j)	Overheads and miscellaneous expenses (5 years)	7,200
	Total	2,07,200

Arjun trees yield from the fourth year while Asan trees yield from the sixth year.

The Tasar silk worm is bi-voltine with two crops—the seed crop and the commercial crop. A tri-voltine crop is now introduced and a third crop possible in October–December with drier climate and better yields with less larval damage. The yield is available from 4/6 year till 50 years, if plants are provided fertilisers, irrigation and pesticides.

Yield Status

	1st harvest (July–Aug.)	*2nd harvest (Sep.–Oct.)*	*3rd harvest (Oct.–Dec.)*
Period (days)	40	50	70
Yield (cocoons)	6,400	6,400	12,800
Rate (Rs.)	1,600	2,000	6,000

Thus, a tribal breeder gets Rs. 9,600 from 16 Kahans (1 Kahan = 1,600 cocoons) in addition to fuel worth Rs. 400 which gives an annual income of Rs. 10,000 from 3,500 Asan trees.

CONCLUSION

A few projects have been discussed in this chapter. Many more such projects of this type can be prepared by banks, depending on the needs of the tribal community. Unfortunately, officials depend on circulars sent by the Head/Regional Offices and they rarely are trained to prepare area-specific projects which may be useful for the tribals. One time projects help tribal where a large number of micro-loans are required. What is more important is how the scheme makes a difference in tribal life. A few suggestions on tribal-specific development schemes or credit packages are mentioned below:

(i) need for timely credit,
(ii) need for minimum documentation,
(iii) need for low interest rates,
(iv) need to explain terms on which development aid/credit is given,

(v) obligations of tribal people to service/repay loans to be clearly specified,
(vi) need to have daily income which may be small but regular,
(vii) need to inculcate savings through tribal SHGs; and
(viii) need for monitoring visits for verifying end-use of loans.

The tribal borrower is usually wary of taking loans from individual lenders. There is need to have tribal credit facilitators who can assist or educate the tribals about procedural formalities and monitor end-use of loans besides loan recovery, as there are few branches in tribal areas.

Part–III

For Tribal People — A Framework for Sustainable Development

CHAPTER XV

Food Security and Self Help

INTRODUCTION

In a country like India which has witnessed famines periodically since centuries, the cyclical processes of drought, deprivation, hunger and starvation deaths, are not uncommon alongwith forced sale of assets, cattle and sometimes even children, ultimately leading to mass-deaths or forced migration to cities, in an effort to keep body and soul together. However, the incidence of famine after 1947 causing loss of millions of lives, was last witnessed in free India during 1958-61. Since then, there have been incidences of severe drought conditions and localised famine like situations in Bihar (1967), Maharashtra (1973), West Bengal (1979) and Gujarat (1987). But drought situations in the central belts of Rajasthan, Gujarat, M.P., Maharashtra, A.P. & Orissa, have continued over the years and starvation deaths, though not acknowledged as such by the State Governments, have also continued over the years. With food grains production exceeding 203 million tonnes in 2000-01 and overflowing godowns unable to stock food grains (estimated at around 65 million tonnes), it is distressing to learn of starvation deaths in many parts of the country. With tonnes of foodgrains rotting in FCI godowns, these starvation deaths are not due to any lack of foodgrains but due to lack of proper distribution systems and non-availability of foodgrains at affordable prices.

FOODGRAINS DISTRIBUTION SYSTEM

Since Independence, the State and Central Governments have tried to cope up with the need to provide food to the huge present-day population of over a billion people. After the drought years of 1965-67, the strategy has been to concentrate on enhancing production of foodgrains which were input-intensive such as wheat, rice, *etc.*, to the exclusion of traditional foodgrains such as jowar, bajra, ragi, *etc.* The Green Revolution emphasised water availability, fertiliser intensification, improved seed variety *etc.* all of which were input-intensive and reduced foodgrains diversification and equitable food distribution. The input-intensive programme of foodgrain production has endangered food security. The increase of foodgrains year after year due to generous agricultural subsidies (and no income taxes), has created an illusion of foodgrains availability while playing down the breakdown of the local food security systems. The massive foodgrains distribution at skewed prices, built up under the public distribution system (PDS), led farmers to produce for commerce rather than for self-consumption. The pressure to increase yields through expensive inputs and subsidy-oriented culture, destroyed the rich bio-diversity of Indian agriculture. Despite record growth in agricultural production, hunger is prevalent over much of rural India.

The PDS has become corrupt and inefficient with high price and poor quality foodgrains and utter lack of concern for local preferences. While the betteroff sections of the rural and urban population have access to foodgrains of their choice, the poorer sections have only the PDS to full back upon and with an inefficient supply system. The poor are often deprived of the foodgrains under the PDS, especially in the tribal areas. Thus, in areas where food security is badly needed, it is those very people who are let down. Thus, the starvation deaths are basically due to the inefficiencies of the PDS.

Efficient Foodgrains Storage and Distribution

The problem of storing foodgrains needs an urgent solution and the Government seems to have run out of ideas. The Centre has suggested that State Governments manage their own procurement and distribution system for foodgrains, but the State Governments refuse to do so on grounds of insufficient money. Even if they agreed to do so, the PDS would not be more efficiently run. The State Governments are unable to improve efficient storage and effective distribution of foodgrains and also would not be able to meet the larger social purpose of getting it to the really needy people in time to avert starvation deaths. The only effective method would be to do away with the existing methods of centralised foodgrains collection and distribution, maintain the buffer foodgrains stock at around 20 million tonnes rather than the unmanageable 65 million tonnes available today and build up a grain bank movement at the village level.

The FCI is unable to meet the requirements of food for needy people as their cost of management is a staggering 30 per cent which makes the entire operation uneconomical and a huge drain on resources. Also, the minimum support price at which procurement is made is higher than the market price! The Government's decision to export foodgrains at the price fixed for people below poverty level under the public distribution system (but at prevailing international prices) is also being criticised!

The advantages of a grain bank scheme being low cost technologies makes this effort an affordable one and as grain quantities handled are smaller, these grain banks would be manageable and would lead to less wastage than the 10 per cent being managed by FCI!

Grain banks would also serve the purpose of targetting the really needy tribal and drought prone villages which are difficult to reach. The Government's record in foodgrain management and distribution is at best patchy and it seriously needs to come out of the huge foodgrains subsidy mess by reducing its role in food distribution, storage and management. Recent experiments have proved that village level efforts at providing local resources such as fuel, fodder and water have been very successful and better food availability/management could be based on innovative models of self-governance.

CONCEPT OF GRAIN BANK

The grain bank or 'grain gola' is a concept that is rooted in times immemorial amongst primitive tribal communities of Orissa like Garba, Paraja, Bhumiya, *etc.* It is prevalent in tiny villages as a hedge against food scarcity and starvation. The tribals contribute the grain bank by contributing to the common village fund of cereals, mainly paddy and ragi and this villages-based grain storage system was called 'Kotha Panthi' or 'Kutumba Panthi' which means community fund. However, this did not really flourish due to various reasons, management failure being the major cause. However, the concept of a common pool of foodgrains survived in many tribal villages till the State Government rooted out these grain banks, in an effort to popularise primary agricultural credit societies (in 1950's) which were later converted into Large Sized Adivasi Multipurpose Societies (after 1972). The present day grain bank initiatives by various developmental agencies are merely the revival of the old 'grain golas'! During the harvests, the village community members contributed a small portion of their harvested cereals such as paddy, ragi and maize to establish the village grain bank on a collective basis and draw grains therefore for a period of about 100 days between mid-June to end-September every year when foodgrains stocks are exhausted. Foodgrains are then repaid alongwith interest @ 25 per cent to 50 per cent in grains or in manual labour.

Why Grain Banks?

The grain bank as a programme for food security, has the following objectives:

(i) to overcome food crises arising out of unforeseen calamities like famine, drought, *etc.*

(ii) to ensure availability of essential food items to remove areas where supply gets cut off during the rainy season.

(iii) to meet the seed requirements of individual farmers during time of sowing.

(iv) to harness the buffer stock as a community resource fund for the cause of community development initiatives in coming years.

(v) to reduce rural indebtendness particularly among poor tribals as 80 per cent of their income is spent on food.

The paddy or ragi or maize is contributed after harvests in December/January and stocked in one or two places in the village, in traditional golas built by the community. The grains are stored in an indigenous hut called 'Puda' made of intertwined paddy straw or bamboo with cow-dung, neem leaves and sticks with local/traditional methods so as to ensure that the grain banks are free from pests or rodents. The grain is usually stored from December/January to June after which there is no stock as the entire grain stock is lent and then replenished with interest @ 25 per cent to 50 per cent in grain. Those who cannnot repay, are given an opportunity to pay for foodgrains at cost and repayment terms are also lengthened over 2 years. If no repayment is done within the extended period, no grains are lent again as that family is permanently debarred. The grain gola was maintained by the village headman. A number of NGO's have set up grain banks in their area of operations in Orissa, due to a number of starvation deaths occuring every year. But the operation of these grain banks vary from village to village. The Orissa State Government has also promoted some grain banks as Orissa & some other States have been implementing the Scheme for establishment of Village Grain Banks in tribal villages, since 1996–97. The grain banks set up in the tribal districts of Koraput, Kalahandi Rayagada, Kandhamal & Sundergarh, provide a safeguard against fall in nutrition standards of tribal people living in remote rural areas. The grain bank is perceived as an insurance to prevent the possibility of farmers committing suicide due to abject poverty. A minimum availability of foodgrains is assured for the very poor rural people living in dire financial straits.

Grain Banks and MSSRF Initiative

The grain bank concept has recently been revived and sponsored by the M.S. Swaminathan Research Foundation (MSSRF). The proposal is based on the estimate that one tonne of wheat or rice is sufficient for a family of five for a year. About 25,000 grain banks are to be set up all over the country with priority being given for remote areas with poor communications and as hill and desert areas, a stock of 200 tonnes of wheat or rice or other locally acceptable grain like ragi (finger millet), jowar (sorghum), bajra (pearl millet) and maize are proposed to be established at poverty-struck villages. It is proposed that 5 million tonnes of foodgrains from the central stocks (estimated at 65 million tonnes) could be diverted for the setting-up of grain banks as also continued govt. support. The grain banks are expected to be successful in States with political will and social infrastructure, as they will be linked to the rural godowns scheme and are expected to function under the overall umbrella of the Gram Sabha and operated by local self help groups. This is to ensure their relevance to local conditions in addition to incurring low transaction costs. Before taking up the construction of grain banks, it would be necessary to evaluate the existing models for sustainability as it would be difficult to expect the Central/State Governments to be saddled with operational expenses in addition to one-time construction costs and costs of initial stocking of foodgrains. Before setting up grain banks on a large scale, it has to be ensured that the concept of grain banks should be set up on the basis of best practices followed and should not be based on the flawed concept of continuing govt. financial support, after the project is set up.

GRAIN BANK MODELS: A REVIEW

The traditional 'grain gola' model and the MSSRF model details have been mentioned earlier. But for a sustainable and stable grain bank operating model, a review of the various models available should be taken up. While the traditional tribal grain gola meets the requirements of a tribal village of about 50 families only and is run by the tribal village headman who is answerable to nobody, the MSSRF model assures that continued state funding support will continue. While the tribal model is too small to take care of the needs of a huge area which is prone to drought induced disaster and hunger, the MSSRF model is dependent on Government largesse and given the precarious finance of State Government, is not at all sustainable. The operational review of a few grain banks operating successfully in various parts of the country, need to be studied, for replicability and sustainability.

Care and Vaks, Chaatna block, Bankura, West Bengal

These grain banks are based on Rabindranath Tagore's idea of a 'Dharma Gola' at Santiniketan. Each household in the area of operations are encouraged to save a fistful of grain everyday while cooking and the accumulated grain is stored in the village to be utilised for community feeding during emergencies (flood/draught). At times, accumulated grain is sold off to provide the villagers with cash loans when needed for medical expenses and emergencies. Grains are also used for supplementary nutrition in areas where the child welfare projects are not implemented. Formation of the grain bank requires active community mobilisation especially among the women and is done through Self Help Groups (SHGs). This project enables sustainable nutrition and timely help to needy members and food security in times of distress.

The most active grain bank in the area is in Meghakata village run by 20 active members. Every 15 days, some of the SHG members go to every household and collect 1 kg of grain per household from whatever the members have saved on a daily basis. This ensures that 20 kg of grains are collected every fortnight. Most of the grains are stored in the grain bank while some grains are sold and the amounts are kept with the group leader. This amount serves as ready cash and is granted as loans to group members whenever needed in emergencies. The grain that is retained in the grain bank is lent out to the group members either in kind or after converting it into cash for emergencies. The group leader maintains records of all transactions of the grain bank. Many grain banks do not operate throughout the year but so only during the food-scarce months of June-September (monsoons). Due to continued droughts, some grain banks have stopped operations because of labour migrations as the SHG members prefer to take ready cash rather than grains. Some grain banks in high income areas are being used only for purposes for sowing operations and grains are not used for food purposes.

BRAC, SAGORIB & Private Firms, Bangladesh

Grain banks store rice, pulses and potatoes are stored in the godowns for the farmers who have to pay fees. Farmers can take a loan, amounting to 50 per cent to 75 per cent (variable) of the total value of rice or pulses on hypothecation basis and the interest charged is 15 per cent to 20 per cent per annum. Farmers repay the loan in one instalment alongwith interest, after the off-season sales when prices rise or may repay in several instalments as negotiated with the grain bank while receiving the loans. For potatoes, interest rates are slightly higher and farmers can sell their potatoes to the bank at prevailing market rates. The farmers are greatly benefitted from such banks which are organised only on commercial lines and without any subsidy.

Youth for Action (NGO) Model, Karnataka

Grain banks are established for access to essential grains namely rice and jowar for deserving families and these are established in the villages where low-cost granaries have been established. Members contribute 1–2 kg of grains per member *with matching contribution* from the project funds. The grain is rotated among the members on interest basis and records are duly maintained by the Sangham members. During non-agricultural seasons or when wage earners are unable to earn food due to illness, grain from the grain bank comes to their rescue, providing essential food security for the village people. Grain bank committees are also formed with the involvement of the NGO volunteers.

Agragramee (Action Aid) Model, Koraput, Orissa

From June to September, during the monsoon season, the tribal people cannot earn from wages/minor forest produce/wood, and the agricultural produce from fields is also exhausted. During the 'hunger' period, tribals borrow heavily from money lenders for meeting food requirements. Moneylenders are usually local traders, lending at various rates with security being mortgage of land or pawning of jewellery. The moneylender has also to be pleased by offering liquor and/or meat before the loan is given. Returns also include terms of labour for marriages or other ceremonies of individual families. Non repayment of loans leads to bondage thus sealing the only productive resource of the tribal poor, *i.e.*, labour. This increases the dependency relationship on the moneylender as all economic channels are blocked.

The concept of grain bank is derived from the traditional grain gola concept with active community participation to grain community acceptance and has been operating in Koraput since 1983. Since 1993, UNICEF/State Government support has been made available. Grain banks are operationalised in a village with a single and equal contribution of grains by all families during harvest period, with a matching contribution from the NGO, for motivating the community and for building up corpus of grains. The collected grain is stored in a bamboo dudi (stored bin) lined with cowdung to prevent attacks from pests and rodents. Each village has 1-2 dudis with safety of grains being a collective responsibility of the community though the family on whose land the dudi stands, plays an important role. Each village has a Panthi Committee with 7 members (4 male and 3 female) for taking decisions and are either selected or elected. Bye-laws framed by the NGO are followed by the Committee. Grain banks are usually operated twice a year during harvest times when members repay dues and during monsoon months when grain disbursement is made. The Panthi Committee decides on each family's entitlement depending upon family size, need, grains availability, *etc.* If the storage position is comfortable, the distribution is based on household needs otherwise it is divided equally among all families. All transactions are in kind and borrowers are expected to repay the borrowed money with interest in kind, with flexibility in types of grains repaid. All grain banks started with ragi, the stable food of the tribal people but paddy and sanwan (local millets) are also accepted, if the family does not have enough ragi. Repayment is not based on market value of the grain but on the quantity that has to be returned. The Committee President ensures that all transactions are recorded by the educated members of the community and if these are not available, people from other villages are invited to carry out the task (school teachers or relatives) and they are provided with one meal as honorarium. The NGO has no inputs except for the initial capacity-building facilitation and matching grain contribution for the 'gola'. The programme is largely community-managed, addressing the key issue of hunger and instils confidence in the community.

Established committees are confident of independent maintenance of the grain bank and maintain surpluses even during the 'hunger period' in monsoons. The options before the Panthic Committees having considerable surpluses, are:

(*i*) selling surplus grain and investing the money for capital purchases (such as land) for the community benefit.

(ii) selling the surplus and dividing the profit equally among all the member families.

(iii) lending surplus grain on interest basis (25 per cent to 50 per cent) to non-members from other villages during the hunger periods.

(iv) Adding more 'dudies' (storage bins) to the grain bank and keeping the grain aside for emergencies or natural calamities that do not occur every year.

The interesting lessons from the villages where the grain banks were set up, reveal that where collective farming is practised by the tribal community, the grain banks are easier to set up at harvest times. Interest rate on grain rent is usually 50 per cent. Though borrowing is regular during initial years, this has reduced over the years as many families are increasingly becoming food-secure even during the monsoon months. Panthic committees sometimes meet thrice a year. In the first meeting, repayments and requests for loans are considered while distribution of grain takes place in the second meeting. The third meeting (not regularly held) is for distribution of surplus grain or for deciding on loan requests from external borrowers.

Repayment is usually 100 per cent and there are virtually no cases of defaults from members. In case of default, grain is lent for a maximum period of 2 years after default. If the borrowers fail to repay by the third year, the lending is completely stopped. This continues till full repayment is made by the borrowers. For external borrowers who default, coercive methods of collection are resorted to.

The grain dudies are maintained in separate houses while the responsibility for the safety of grain, lies with the individual household. There are no additional benefits for the family maintaining dudies and this also ensures that the grain bank is not a centralised affair.

These grain banks are expected to continue till all families in the village become food secure especially during the 'hunger' months from June to September.

State Sponsored Grain Banks–M.P., A.P. & Orissa

Since 1997, some State Governments have taken steps to set up grain banks in the remote drought prone or areas with poor communication. In Orissa, some grain banks were set up in tribal areas in 1997 but there is little data available about their operations. The Government or development agency bears the cost of food and the cost of works. In A.P. where the model grain banks were set up, an experiment at decentralisation of grain procurement operations has been done by linking grain banks to the public distribution system. Concerned NGOs procure grain from the AP Government for on-lending to the villagers. This not only cuts down transaction, storage and administrative costs to the PDS but also ensures better out-reach and better quality of grain being distributed. In MP, the programme was started in 1998 focussing on tribal villages in 5 districts. After formation of

Chattisgarh, only two districts in M.P. and have 366 villages under the grain bank programme in Jhabua & Dhindari district. Four more tribal belts are being covered 2001–02, to be managed by 7–15 SHGs. Maharashtra has also launched several cash dependent grain banks but the repayments have been as low as 2–4 per cent. NGOs have also attempted promoting of grain banks in the State but due to high gestation the programme has been paralysed.

Karjat Model, Maharashtra

All decisions are taken by elected managing committee of 5 members and loan transaction are in grain with 25 per cent interest and fixed repayment time. The bank becomes self-sufficient in 4 years and later on a buffer stock is created against future food shortages and offered to neighbouring villages as a rotating loan. This spreads food security across a constantly growing chain of villages. The emergence of a local leadership is encouraged by giving clear responsibilities for administrative, accounting and management responsibilities for operating the bank. Villages provide financial and logistical support. The functional tools of the grain bank are based on volume-based measures called 'fari' which are easy to use and hard to steal. Participation rules are laid down in the villages and are flexible. In eight years, the concept has spread to 80 villages in the tribal block of Karjat with 2000 tribal families. 48 grain banks are now-self-sufficient and run independently by the villages themselves.

CONCLUSION

To address the persistent problem of hunger and malnutrition especially in tribal villages in India, the Central/State Governments are proposing to set up national level grain banks to eliminate poverty-include hunger by 2007. These community grain banks could be set up in two phases. The first phase would be to set up grain banks in tribal villages which are assisted in the initial stages by Government aid in the form of grains and NGO assistance in formulating the policies while the villagers pool surpluses and run the grain banks on their own. An economic model is set up at Annexure 15.1.

Later on, based on the success of the model, grain banks can be set up to take the burden of the PDS and even utilise the grain for Food for Work programmes. Already MP & AP have taken the initiative to run village-based grain banks by local women and self-help groups through micro-credit financing. It would be better to have flexible grain banks which are sustainable and self-managed rather than to set them up with fixed ideas about their size, scope of operations and continuous interference by either NGOs or Governments. Grain banks operated on self-help principles by the villagers, have the best chance for food security for our villages.

ANNEXURE 15.1

Food Security for a Tribal Village—Grain Gola Economics

(i)	Individual tribal person requires	:	400 gm of cereals per day
(ii)	Average size of tribal family	:	5 persons
(iii)	Size of tribal village	:	50 huts
(iv)	Average tribal family requirement of foodgrains per day	:	2 Kg
(v)	Cereals required for tribal village per day	:	1000 Kg
(vi)	Hunger period or lean period from July to September	:	100 days
(vii)	Total grain gola storage capacity needed 100 × 1000	:	1,00,000 Kg
(viii)	Average cost of grain per Kg at market price (rice/jowar/ragi/bajra/maize)	:	Rs. 5.70
(ix)	Initial cost of grain stocked in 2 Golas in village	:	Rs. 5,70,000
(x)	Cost of 2 Grain Gola (bamboo and traditional) including own labour	:	Rs. 10,000

Grain Bank to become self-sustaining in 4–5 years depending upon 25 per cent rate of interest payable in grains.

CHAPTER XVI

LAMPS: Brighter Days Ahead for Tribals

INTRODUCTION

For about 25 years after Independence, the Primary Agricultural Credit Societies (PACS) were established all over the country to meet credit requirements of the tribal community. But, the intricacies of tribal credit system led to the realisation that the requirements of tribals were not being met by the traditional PACS, and specialised tribal cooperative societies combining various functions the Large Sized Adivasi Multipurpose Societies (LAMPS) were set up. There is a need to review the operational inadequacies and the problems of LAMPS in Orissa and offer practical solutions for strengthening the LAMPS all over the country so as to meet the genuine requirements of tribals. It is felt that instead of prescribing yet another specialised institution, effort should be made to identify various reasons for non-performance of the LAMPS. There is a need to revitalise the LAMPS on the basis of emerging requirements and therefore, identifiy constraints. LAMPS should be given a fair chance to effectively meet the requirements of the tribals. An integrated approach for strengthening LAMPS and reducing exploitation can serve tribal interests in Orissa.

After 1947, cooperative societies were assigned the role of furthering socio-economic activities in rural areas due to the agrarian base. While these service cooperative societies lent cash and inputs to the tribal exploitation of tribal farmers by traders, middlemen did not cease due to the absence of strong marketing/procurement agencies and surplus agricultural produce continued to be sold at low prices. The PACS had limited role in relating to disbursal of agricultural credit (cash and inputs) for land improvement (including irrigation) and allied purposes as also procurement of surplus produce by linking credit with marketing and distribution of consumer articles including on barter. The State Government provided package assistance such as *(i)* share capital assistance, *(ii)* risk fund contribution, *(iii)* price fluctuation compensation, *(iv)* managerial subsidy, *etc.* These were expected to strengthen the cooperative structure and make them viable. In tribal areas, the PACS failed to make any impact, due to the following reasons:

(i) The PACS were meant to provide traditional credit support to farmers while in tribal areas the land was mostly unirrigated, and unscientific farming practices were practised thus rendering traditional credit business unviable.

(ii) Erratic monsoons and drought conditions resulted in reduced loan recovery. In view of minimum loan collection stipulations for eligibility of fresh finance, sale proceeds of marketing and consumer business was siphoned off for loan repayment due to pressure from the DCCBs, resulting in non-availability of funds for procurement/marketing of consumer operations, in tribal PACS.

(iii) As the tribal PACS were located in inaccessible places, the RCMAS and Consumer Federation did not meet their requirements, resulting in drying up of marketing and consumer business.

(iv) While officially the PACS discontinued procurement/marketing operations, many Chief Executive Officers (Secretaries) continued to procure SAP/MFP in a private capacity by giving cash advances or consumer goods on 'barter-trade'. These Secretaries ran private trading operations using society funds and flouted rules for procurement and evaded taxes. Tribal exploitation continued due to inaccessibility and poor monitoring.

(v) The management of PACS in tribal areas was dominated by non-tribals and vested interests who did not have any stake in empowering the tribals. In most cases, the President and other office-bearers of PACS were non-tribals, belonging to either money-lenders or traders who exploited the tribals.

THE NEED FOR SPECIALISED COOPERATIVES FOR TRIBALS

The Fifth Five Year Plan emphasised reorganisation of cooperatives in tribal sub-plan areas to act as centres of tribal economic activities. To avoid regional imbalances and to free the tribals from the grip of money-lenders/traders, the 'service cooperative societies' were reorganised to serve tribal needs. The Bawa Committee, 1971, recommended that Large-Sized Adivasi Multipurpose Cooperative Societies (LAMPS) should be set up by amalgamating service cooperative societies in tribal areas, to give more emphasis to procurement of minor forest produce and surplus agricultural produce and to provide long term loans and consumption loans so as to undertake consumer business including supply and sales. In 1975–76, the reorganisation of LAMPS was taken up and 43 LAMPS were set up, covering large tribal areas. There are now 223 LAMPS in 16 districts covering 1410 gram panchayats and 118 tribal blocks. Factors responsible for setting up of the LAMPS included viability on the basis of population and potentials as well as compact area of operations from the communications point of view. In vast areas, branches of LAMPS were also opened. 46 are block level LAMPS, while 177 LAMPS are of smaller size. Only 193 are functional today while the other 30 are non-functional. 52 of these LAMPS are doing well while the others are incurring losses. Most of the LAMPS were housed in one of the buildings/godowns of the Service Cooperative Societies (SCS) and the other SCS in the area of operations were converted into branches or procurement/sales outlets. The recommended staff at the branch of the LAMPS include the Managing Director, an Accountant-cum-Branch Manager, one storekeeper-cum-salesman and one peon-cum-watchman. Most of the employees of the existing service cooperative societies instead of being retrenched, were absorbed in LAMPS due to political pressure, court orders, intervention of Labour Department, or on humanitarian considerations. Thus, the viability of the LAMPS was doomed from inception itself due to excess staffing.

As per Government of India guidelines, the MD of the LAMPS was the key person to achieve the desired goal of the LAMPS and officers of ARCS rank with missionary zeal were to be posted for the sensitive posts of MDs of LAMPS. But in practice, unwanted ARCS were posted in one or two LAMPS while officers of SARCS rank were deputed to other LAMPS. In the tribal areas which did not have infrastructural facilities or amenities, most SARCS were also not willing to work under adverse conditions without special incentives. Gradually, the SARCS were also withdrawn and today Inspectors of Cooperative Societies or CCB employees are now functioning as Managing Directors of LAMPS, providing poor quality leadership.

Functions of LAMPS

The LAMPS were re-designed as multipurpose societies and could take up only economic activity. 100 per cent of the tribal population were expected to be enrolled as members. Of the Committee of Management, non-tribal. consumption credit was to be given to the tribals and no land-mortgage was insisted upon as tribals had either no land or no record of rights. Loans could be given against personal sureties and tribal members were automatically 'A' class members while non-tribals were 'B' class members and only 5 per cent share contribution was demanded as against 10 per cent for others. Concessions were offered on long-term loan interest rates with longer repayment periods. Short-term and medium-term loans were given for agricultural and allied activities and also for handicrafts and cottage industries without mortgages. The block level LAMPS were expected to disburse at least Rs. 10 lakh per year while smaller LAMPS were to disburse Rs. 5 lakh.

Various Government agencies like ITDA, DRDA, *etc.*, also provided financial assistance for share capital contributions upto Rs. 40 per member so as to enable loan limits upto 20 times and also gave risk-fund contributions to effect possible loans. Minimum collection stipulations were also dropped. For the first time, consumption credit upto Rs. 250 was provided, repayable in 1–3 years, for medical expenses and social needs against personal surety only to those tribals selling SAP/MFP to the LAMPS, and an interest rebate of 2 per cent was also given on loan repayments. LAMPS were also appointed as collection agents for Surplus Agricultural Produce (SAP) and Minor Forest Produce (MFP) on behalf of the Tribal Development Cooperative Corporation (TDCC) which was the sole lease-holder along with the Orissa Forest Development Corporation (OFDC).

All LAMPS branches at growth centres were to sell essential commodities and other consumer goods as also purchase SAP/MFP under the traditional barter system. LAMPS had to purchase goods only from TDCC which was also expected to close down its procurement centres/consumer sales outlets which it never did and offered unhealthy competition to the LAMPS. And where TDCC distribution was weak, LAMPS did not get consumer articles to sell, which weakened the LAMPS considerably. LAMPS were also expected to sell agricultural inputs like seeds, fertilisers, raw materials for tribals engaged in cottage industries and handicraft activities besides small agricultural implements as the agents of the Orissa Agro-Industries Corporation. LAMPS having good potential were encouraged to open agro-service centres and small processing units like oilcrushers, huller units, *etc.*, which could be hired on nominal charges by tribals. Certain operational data of LAMPS in the country, are set out at Annexure 16.1.

The Realities of LAMPS in Orissa

Only 52 LAMPS are making profits out of 223 (1993–94 data) and 30 are non-functional. The total membership is 9.03 lakh, of which 5.13 lakh are tribals, out of a total tribal population of 70 lakh. The number of borrowing members has been decreasing as it can be seen from the following Table:

Table 16.1
Decrease in Borrowing Members of LAMPS

Sl. No.	*Year*	*Percentage of borrowing members to total members*	*Remarks*
1.	1980–81	30	—
2.	1986–87	12	Debt-relief Scheme
3.	1989–90	3	Debt-relief Scheme
4.	1994–95	6	—

Source: RCS, Bhubaneswar, Orissa.

The mini-bank scheme has shown very good performance during the last two years and deposits have increased sharply. The increased aggressiveness in deposits mobilisation reflects the LAMPS ability to change and function more efficiently. The lending operations and also recovery performance have not shown good results as under:

Table 16.2
Details of LAMPS Operation

Sl. No.	*Year*	*Amount of loans disbursed*	*Recovery (percentage)*
1.	1981–82	1865	60
2.	1989–90	303	5
3.	1994–95	1579	35

Source: RCS, Bhubaneswar, Orissa.

The procurement of SAP/MFP by LAMPS has never been encouraging and has been restricted to the undivided Koraput and Mayurbhanj districts, mainly due to lack of coordination among LAMPS, TDCC and the Forest Department. This has benefited only the private traders at the expense of the helpless and innocent tribals who depend on forest produce for sustenance. Consumer business is poor with an average business is only Rs. 4 lakh per year. Unless a business turnover of each LAMPS is not achieved up to Rs. 30 Lakh per year is achieved, the sale of mixed commodities including textiles, *etc.*, break-even business is not possible. A recent study by AFC of LAMPS in Orissa in 1996 has opined that the tangible net worth, capital funds and net working capital are negative in most LAMPS and there is no provision being made for bad debts. Even financial statements are not prepared in time and audit is in arrears for 2/3 years in some LAMPS. In most LAMPS, the committee members and staff are not present most of the time and this is one of the reasons for the poor operating results. No agro-processing of Minor Forest Produce (MFP) is being done and private traders continue to proliferate and squeeze the tribals. There is a need for financial restructuring of LAMPS so as to make them self-supporting and viable institutions which are able to meet the tribal requirements. The transportation charges for carrying goods from the purchasing centres to the inaccessible and remote tribal areas, has affected the profitability/viability of LAMPS. The transportation subsidy for PDS and for OSCMF (Orissa State Cooperative Marketing Federation) supplied goods like fertilisers, seeds, *etc.*, are inadequate. The LAMPS have an uneconomic margin by way of commission after meeting all charges for processing various materials rendering all procurement/sales activities as unviable. Another major gap in profitable operations is due to the TDCC's unwillingness to appoint LAMPS as agents for procurement of SAP/MFP and in fact, private traders are appointed as sub-agents. Thus, LAMPS do not provide essential services and hence, the tribals do not depend on

LAMPS. The share capital and managerial assistance provided to LAMPS is inadequate and there is a need to restructure the share capital contribution of LAMPS members. The staffing pattern of LAMPS is not uniform and deputationists from CCBs, TDCC and Cooperation Department have differing pay structures which affect LAMPS viabilities and also staff morale and efficiency. Due to weak financial condition, LAMPS are unable to invest in purchase of fertilisers for meeting the tribal farmers' requirements. Some LAMPS are even unable to meet the salaries of staff members. The official working hours of LAMPS are also often inconvenient to tribals and hence business suffers.

Profitability and Break-even Levels of LAMPS

Out of 223 LAMPS spread over in different districts of the State, 210 LAMPS are considered to be viable and 13 are potentially viable as per the assessment by the Cooperation Department. As reported in the earlier paragraphs, there are 9,03,000 members in all the LAMPS, out of which 5,13,000 members belong to STs and 1,31,000 belong to SCs. The total paid-up share capital of LAMPS was Rs. 9.64 crore as on 31 March 1994. The reserves of the LAMPS by way of apportionment of profits, made during the year as well as reserves in other forms amounted to Rs. 6.51 crore. The total deposit of the LAMPS is Rs. 4.23 crore and the borrowings made from the higher agencies amounted to Rs. 23.56 crore. The working capital base of the LAMPS has aggregated to Rs. 60.95 crore. The total number of borrowers of LAMPS is estimated to be at 65,000. The loan outstanding as on 30 June 1994 of the LAMPS has been estimated at Rs. 20.84 crore and the entire loan amount has been given to agricultural operations for ST communities. As per the latest report available on cooperative statistics, 52 LAMPS have been found in profit, the total amount of profit making LAMPS is Rs. 20 lakh whereas 171 LAMPS have incurred losses aggregating to Rs. 3.46 crore. In a study on the functioning of LAMPS and role of nationalised banks, made by AFC, most of the LAMPS have yet to attain break-even level of business, *e.g.*, in case of financial analysis carried out in respect of certain major LAMPS like Balliguda, Karanjia, Kamormunda, Patna, G. Udayagiri it has been found that the net worth of these LAMPS are on the positive side with a range of Rs. 0.56 lakh to as high as Rs. 10.03 lakh and all the LAMPS as mentioned above are having profits, though marginal as on 31 March 1994.

However, the low business turnover has impeded the functioning of LAMPS to a large extent. The average business turnover is as low as Rs.3 lakh per year. Moreover, the cost of management in the LAMPS is found to be disproportionate to the volume of business. This needs an analysis in detail, *e.g.*, the ratio of cost of management to the gross income. The details of 4 LAMPS which have been taken for study are given as under:

Table 16.3
Analysis of LAMPS Cost

Name of the LAMPS	*Cost of management to gross income (per cent)*
Balliguda	8.94
Karanjia	16.92
Kumarmunda	4.53
Patna	18.59

Source: RCS, Bhubaneswar, Orissa.

Diversification of Activities of LAMPS

As a part of diversification of various activities of LAMPS, some of the important activities like processing units in regard to agricultural produce, especially fruits and other vegetables like tomatoes and mushrooms can be given encouragement in the State.

The Regional Research Laboratory, Bhubaneswar, is equipped with technical know-how regarding extraction of essential oils from aromatic grasses, plants and spices. This technology can be utilised by LAMPS through higher cooperative agencies under the MFP scheme.

The processing is essential to add value to the MFP to benefit tribal people who are primarily gatherers of such items. Incidentally, most of the products can be processed at the primary stage right in the houses of tribal people. Very simple and less expensive decorticators are available for different seeds, tamarind products, sal seeds, mahua seeds. These activities are ideal for value-addition which fetches great benefits to the tribals. Therefore, the LAMPS should diversify their activities in extending financial support to the target scheme of the population for these activities. The production of kusumi lac has also good scope in this State. The production of lac can be given encouragement in 3 specific districts of the State, *i.e.*, Keonjhar, Koraput and Kalahandi. However, the lac cultivation is spread over in 9 districts of the State and out of them Keonjhar and Sundargarh are specially identified as districts for lac cultivation. These activities can be promoted with financial assistance from LAMPS.

Revitalisation of LAMPS

The LAMPS have been set up with wide-ranging objectives to enable the tribal members to be self-sufficient and also to empower them so as to enable them to survive in a hostile world. To enable the complete involvement of the tribals with the LAMPS, there has to be restructuring of the LAMPS, both financially and organisationally in order to enable them to achieve the goals of tribal empowerment and financial stability. The manpower development and training needs of LAMPS have to be met by on-site training programmes as the tribals rarely prefer leaving their area of operations. The OSCB has already prepared a draft MoU for LAMPS and PACS to be signed by the DCCBs and PACS/LAMPS so that their functioning is rendered viable and profitable. Certain practical suggestions for strengthening LAMPS have been made in Annexure 16.2 which will go a long way in empowering the tribals. These suggestions have been made on the basis of various studies and need to be implemented on an urgent basis. However, there are a few more suggestions for economic upliftment of the tribals using the credit-oriented process as a lever of development:

(i) The LAMPS operating in tribal areas need persons who must be sympathetic to the tribals and their way of life. Postings in tribal areas are generally not preferred by most officials. So reward system for working in tribal areas, like in the form of weightage in promotion, educational allowance for children, additional health and LFC facilities, extra remuneration, *etc.*, will be a desirable step to induce quality staff. A majority of the branches have no vehicular facility for mobility of the staff. Motorcycles or cycles should be provided to these branches on a priority basis for the mobility of the staff.

(ii) Lack of entrepreneurship/awareness is found to be one of the main reasons for the economic backwardness of the tribals. The bank branches in coordination with the developmental departments of the State Government/NGOs should, therefore, undertake entrepreneurship development/awareness programmes and also provide adequate finance so that the tribals could undertake investment ventures for their economic benefits. The banks may form Farmers' Clubs in the tribal areas with financial support available from NABARD under its Vikas Volunteer Vahini programme to preach the principles of development through credit in order to ensure proper utilisation of loans and satisfactory recovery thereof.

(iii) The security-oriented lending approach of the banks is a hindrance in flow of adequate credit to the tribal areas. The commercial banks insist on security, two to three times of the loan assistance provided. While the present security norms merits further relaxation by RBI, a system may be developed by the State Government to provide guarantee for payment of interest and repayment of principal by the tribal borrowers, particularly for the tribals who do not possess the requisite ownership to land. The land records of the tribals also should be set right so that they can avail of loans from the banks, wherever necessary, against land mortgage.

The timing of provision of tribal credit is also an important factor. In Orissa, the tribals observe a festival called 'Nuakhai' sometime around August-September of the year when new clothes, new household items, *etc.*, have to be purchased as also feasts have to be organised. As the harvest season is only in January/February, it would not be possible for banks to lend money against the future produce, for the festival requirements. So, the tribals are forced to depend on traders/middlemen/agents who loan small amounts of money to the tribals against future produce/sales. Thus, the middlemen/agents/traders are able to purchase produce at very low rates due to the tribals' indebtedness. In tribal areas, the crop production loan may have three components, *viz.*,

(i) production component in cash (30 per cent)
(ii) kind component (seeds, fertilisers, pesticides, agricultural components) (40 per cent)
(iii) marketing/consumption component in cash (30 per cent) for meeting festival/social obligations.

This will enable the tribal farmers to escape from the clutches of the traders/agents/moneylenders who are now able to exploit the tribals year after year. The third 'cash' component would be given as and when required by the tribal farmers for festival/consumption purpose, under relaxed conditions.

(i) Self-Help Groups with linkages with the financing banks may be encouraged among the tribals. This innovative credit dispensation system not only reduces the transaction costs of the banks and borrowers, but also enables leadership development, meets emerging credit requirements of the members and ensures recovery of loans. The 100 per cent refinance facility available from NABARD for financing of SHGs may be availed of by the banks.

(ii) The Sri Lanka experiment, known as Community Credit Facilitators (CCFs) Scheme, may be adopted in the tribal areas. The scheme has enabled the people in Sri Lanka to obtain loan facilities conveniently at reasonable rates of interest through the Community Credit Facilitators who are appointed by the banks for routing bank loans through them. As the tribals are more inclined to deal with a person whom they know well rather than with banks which create a transaction cost for them in travelling, filling up forms, providing collateral security and loss of man-hours, the CCF scheme could be ideally implemented in tribal areas of the State. It would be desirable to implement the scheme on a pilot basis in one or two tribal blocks of the State first and replicate the same subsequently, based on the results.

(iii) The procurement activities of the line organisations needs improvement to save the tribals from exploitation by the traders, middlemen, *etc.* The LAMPS, TDCC and other agencies should operate with cooperation and coordination among themselves. There should be healthy functional linkage and coordination among the LAMPS, TDCC, OSCMF and other apex organisations in the State as also with National Level Federations like TRIFED and NAFED.

As per the decision of the Government, it should be ensured that LAMPS function as agents for procurement of SAP and MFP in all tribal sub-plan areas on commission basis. Funds for the purpose may, therefore, be placed with LAMPS well in advance. The State Cooperative Marketing Federation/Tribal Development Cooperative Corporation may ensure marketing of the produce collected by the LAMPS on priority basis. The LAMPS too, on the other hand, should properly utilise the funds given for procurement without diverting the same for meeting their administrative expenditure.

The credit support available from NABARD for development of lac cultivation and collection and marketing of minor forest produce has not been availed by the OSCB. As these are primarily meant for the tribals, the OSCB may take advantage of the facility.

(iv) The tribals are still found in the exploitative clutches of the traders, middlemen and money-lenders and sell their produce at prices dictated by them. Due to poor finances, the TDCC and OSCMF are unable to procure the entire MFP collected/SAP produced by the tribals and make timely payment thereon. Both the cooperative agencies are running under losses for the last several years. The State Government should make a detailed study of the functioning of these two premier agencies in procurement and marketing of tribal produce and initiate suitable measures for re-establishing their effectiveness. Processing units should be set up in tribal areas taking into consideration the quantum of procurement and demand in the market. This will not only create additional employment opportunities for the tribals but also add value to the produce to fetch a better price for the tribals. These processing units may be set up by LAMPS/OSCMF/TDCC and other tribal development organisations.

PERSPECTIVES

The economic activities of the tribals have to be linked to the restructuring of the LAMPS as a first step towards the tribal people's participation in their own empowerment, if they are not to be permanently sidelined in the economic liberalisation process which has been set up by the Government without a social safety net for the neglected and deprived people. An integrated approach is needed if the tribal people of Orissa are to claim their rightful place in the State's economy. A vast chunk of the tribal population in Orissa are living in remote and hilly areas. The natural isolation has deprived them of the fruits of development on the one hand and on the other, they are far behind the mainstream on social, cultural and economic fronts. Their problems are mainly due to ignorance, illiteracy, rigid adherence to traditional faiths, poverty, adverse terrain and lack of communication. All these factors encouraged the traders/middlemen to exploit the tribals. What is surprising is that despite the frauds perpetuated by unscrupulous traders/middlemen in purchasing their goods at very low prices and charging higher rates for the goods sold to them and cheating in weights, the tribals continue to fall an easy prey for these middlemen. A majority of the tribal households sell their produce to the traders/middlemen and also buy their essential requirements from them and remain indebted to them. Even after reorganisation of the cooperative societies from 1975-78, creation of various institutions to serve them, initiation of several stringent measures by the State Government in promulgating several Acts and Rules and enforcing them rigidly, exploitation could not be checked as a result of which the tribal economy is being marginalised. A piecemeal approach will fetch no results while an integrated approach to develop and sustain the tribal economy essential. Development should not be imposed on them. The need for result-oriented NGOs to take up work in these areas, is the need of the hour.

ANNEXURE 16.1

Operational Data on LAMPS (As at end December 1995)

	Membership Categories	*Population*
1.	Total Number of LAMPS	3,352
	(*i*) viable	2,027
	(*ii*) potentially viable	1,044
	(*iii*) dorment	76
	(*iv*) defunct	10
2.	Total Number of Borrowers	14,48,000
	(*i*) of which SC	1,92,000
	(*ii*) of which ST	7,13,000
3.	Membership Details of LAMPS	
	(*i*) SC members	4,93,000
	(*ii*) ST members	29,29,000
	(*iii*) small farmers	16,96,000
	(*iv*) marginal farmers	6,82,000
	(*v*) rural artisans	2,02,000
	Total	48,00,000
4.	Total share capital of 3,352 LAMPS is Rs. 79.79 lakh, of which Government share is Rs. 28.40 lakh.	
5.	Profitability of LAMPS	Total
	(*i*) LAMPS in profit–1324	11,75,000
	(*ii*) LAMPS in losses–1380	10,54,000
	(*iii*) Break-Even LAMPS–120	

ANNEXURE 16.2

LAMPS in Orissa: Some Recommendations

To strengthen the functioning of LAMPS in Orissa, the following recommendations may be given effect:

1. The large area of operations of LAMPS had made them ineffective in meeting the demands of the tribals. Task force comprising DRCS/Secretary, DCCB/PO, ITDA belonging to respective districts and select representatives of LAMPS may therefore be constituted to suggest the service area, volume/mix of business, margin, staffing pattern, *etc.*, for a viable and effective LAMPS. No direct or indirect recruitment may be permitted till the LAMPS are reorganised and staffing norms prescribed.
2. The pay and allowances of the staff may be made commensurate with the business level and provide for minimum salary. Incentive Schemes may be introduced for enhancing business level and recovery performance.
3. Although it is the responsibility of LAMPS to arrange for loan recovery drives, the support and intervention of State Government agencies are inevitable in view of the adverse climate for recovery. The following steps need to be initiated to improve recovery climate/recoveries, which holds the key for viability:
   - *(a)* The loan procedures and policies should be revamped to avoid delays in disbursement.
   - *(b)* Defaults should be studied on a case-by-case basis and strategies evolved for recovery.
   - *(c)* Recovery targets should be fixed and the recovery performance be carefully monitored and appropriate remedial steps be taken for achieving the target.
   - *(d)* The State Government shall not interfere in the recovery process except in declaring *'Annewari'* for rephasing/rescheduling of loan instalments in natural calamities, *etc.*, as per guidelines in vogue.
4. An awareness shall be brought about the credit discipline and it should be made part of all training programmes for officials. They should be exposed to training on recovery ethics, discipline and imperatives.
5. The LAMPS staff may be vested with adequate powers to execute the EP cases.
6. A uniform service code may be developed and implemented at the earliest
7. Imbalances may be avoided by strengthening recovery and passing on the same to the DCCBs.
8. Audits of Accounts should be streamlined and made up-to-date. An Audit Calendar be prepared for strict compliance. Special audit and inspection of records without prior intimation be introduced to take up the vigilance function.
9. Management Information System needs to be established/revamped to meet the requirement of emerging challenges. An expert in the field be identified and appointed to work out appropriate Management Information System and Accounting System (preferably computer-based).
10. As a result of PDS, the LAMPS are incurring small losses each year when only the revenue receipts and expenditures are taken into consideration.

But when the cost of capital is also added, average annual erosion of funds is to the tune of Rs. 880 for Ganjam and Rs. 723 for Dhenkanal district after accommodating consumer subsidies received by CSs.

11. Imposition of flat margins (Rs. 15 per bag) in case of all commodities except kerosene puts far-flung and inaccessible LAMPS, at a loss.
12. Most of the LAMPS deal only in sugar and kerosene. Wheat, rice or palmolein are seldom dealt with.
13. Most of the LAMPS have reported that there is always a shortage of 2–5 kg per bag in the case of sugar at the time of taking the deliveries from wholesalers. The latter refuse weighing prior to purchase.
14. Transportation of commodities from the godown of wholesalers to retailing shops is the responsibility of retailers. It involves huge costs to them as transportation facilities in rural areas are inadequate.
15. Supply of commodities by wholesalers is also irregular. Different commodities are supplied at different times with an average of nearly three times per month. LAMPS thus have to pay more on transportation.
16. The following are the measures suggested for profitability of PDS operations of LAMPS;
    - *(i)* Supply to retail centres may be made the responsibility of wholesalers.
    - *(ii)* LAMPS may be permitted to open PDS accounts with CCBs and pay by cheques for the supplies.
    - *(iii)* Licensing procedures for PDS operations may be simplified. It need not require annual renewal for LAMPS.
    - *(iv)* Margins for sugar transactions may be increased to 28 paise per kg.
    - *(v)* Supply may be streamlined.
    - *(vi)* Margin in case of wheat and rice may be increased to Rs. 20 per bag.
    - *(vii)* LAMPS located at block headquarters may be encouraged to take up wholesale activities for PDS.
17. Human Resources Development in LAMPS needs the attention of policy-makers. Practical training and orientation courses may be imparted to the staff as well as directors of LAMPS. Cost consciousness may be emphasised.
18. The role of procurement of SAP and MFP and distribution of agricultural inputs as well as essential consumer goods and area-specific innovative functions need to be greatly increased. The provision of essential consumer goods operations need to be greatly increased in view of the potential profits available.
19. As regards the deposit-tapping functions, the commission allowed to LAMPS by CCBs may be raised to 2 per cent and 4 per cent for recurring and fixed deposits respectively.
20. During formation of LAMPS, they have inherited some bad and irrecoverable loans due to excess financing over the repaying capacity of members in most of the cases. As a result, the LAMPS are facing the problem of overdues and bad debts. The loss arising out of bad debts need be shared by all the members of three tier credit structure, *i.e.*, LAMPS, Central Banks and State Cooperative Banks at the ratio of 60 : 20 : 20.
21. The fixation of target for financing different schemes by the Government at the state level and its implementation at the district level by compulsion through the pressure of District Collector, DRCS and other district level officers, sometimes leads to bad finance and often goes to wrong persons.

Before fixing targets, the needs of the members should be ascertained and proper identification of beneficiary/loanee should be made at the leval of the LAMPS to avoid wrong financing and misutilisation.

22. Consumption loan must be given to meet the consumption needs of tribals in off-seasons when they need it most, as an advance for purchase of minor forest produce. However, soon after the collection of MFP, LAMPS personnel should approach them for procurement of MFP, so that the consumption loan advance for MFP will be collected. By this method, linking of credit with the marketing can be implemented and the tribals will not be compelled to go to unscrupulous traders and money-lenders.
23. Credit should be available to the LAMPS at the right time before commencement of *rabi* and *kharif* seasons.
24. In order to increase the working capital of LAMPS, Government of Orissa may be requested to contribute more share capital, besides working capital loan at concessional rate of interest.
25. In order to ensure better involvement of the Directors and Presidents, some incentive scheme should be worked out.
26. To tap the SAP and MFP of the tribal members, it is necessary to provide consumption loans to them at the time of their need preferably in shape of daily necessities instead of cash.
27. Marketing of new items like oil-seeds, Sabai grass, pulses, *etc.*, may be exclusively given to the LAMPS.
28. Soft loans should be extended to LAMPS by State Government in the form of working capital to carry on fertiliser business of PDS business.
29. No private agent should be allowed to undertake procurement operations of SAP and MFP in tribal areas.
30. Market price is to be fixed selling the goods. Absence of sales centres at the district level sometimes creates barriers for LAMPS. District level tribal societies may be organised to meet the need.
31. The margin available for procurement of SAP and MFP to LAMPS is considered to be much less in comparison to the expenditure involved in it. The margin should be considerable so as to strengthen the LAMPS.
32. All the LAMPS should be allowed to undertake independent procurement of SAP and MFP preferably as a lease holder. Therefore, it is suggested that Government or NCDC should provide funds to the LAMPS at a concessional rate to take up the business.
33. Small-scale processing units like powdering of turmeric and chilly and sal leaf, lac processing units should be set up in selected LAMPS with financial assistance from NCDC.
34. The margin fixed for LAMPS on fertiliser business are much less as compared to the OSCMF. Therefore, more commission is to be given in order to minimise losses.
35. The transportation charges on fertiliser available to LAMPS is not sufficient to meet the cost. It should be increased suitably.
36. Consumer business is very much affected due to paucity of funds. Therefore, adequate funds from State Government or NCDC, centrally-sponsored scheme may be provided to rehabilitate the weaker LAMPS.
37. The civil supplies authority should ensure timely release of stocks from storage agents and extend door delivery facilities at the retail outlet points.

38. The stock should be supplied considering the regional variation of demand in order to prevent unnecessary stock piling in certain items and scanty supply in certain other items.
39. Prudent fund management is necessary for restricting the diversion of funds from consumer section; fresh financial assistance may be given to the societies for increasing their credit business.
40. Government land should be made available to the cooperatives free of cost or at a nominal price preferably in the vicinity of the local market to open sales centres and give better facilities to consumers.
41. For the distribution of consumer goods by the LAMPS at various branches, mini delivery vans or tempos be supplied to the LAMPS to ensure transportation.
42. Clearance sale of slow moving stock, writing off of damaged stock may be made at half-yearly intervals and the power for all items be vested in the Board Management.
43. Well-trained personnel both in maintaining accounts and undertaking expansion of business shall be appointed in the LAMPS with appropriate pay scale.

CHAPTER XVII

Tribal Self Help Groups

INTRODUCTION

Unlike many countries which have implemented Self Help Groups (SHGs) after the mid-seventies, as a part of the formal credit delivery system, India has been experimenting since the 1960s with very flexible systems, giving a lot of freedom to the non-governmental organisations (NGOs) to set up SHGs based on various models. SHGs are mostly informal groups of people where members pool their savings and re-lend in the group on rotational basis, depending upon need for consumption, production or investment needs. The SHGs have a common perception of need and improvise in collective decisions and actions. Many such groups are formed around specific production activities to promote savings among members and use the pooled common resources to meet emerging credit needs of members. Where funds generation is low in the initial phases due to low savings capacities, these are supplemented by external resources by NGOs. Thus, SHGs have been able to provide rudimentary banking services to the members on a cost-effective basis and meet urgent credit requirements in time which ensures almost cent per cent repayment of loans. Based on local requirements, SHGs have evolved their own characteristics of functioning as under :

(i) The Groups usually create a common fund by contributing their small savings on a regular basis.

(ii) SHGs evolve flexible systems of operations, often with the help of NGOs and manage common pooled resources in a democratic manner.

(*iii*) Loan requests are considered by groups in periodic meetings with competing claims on limited resources, being settled by consensus as regards greater need.

(*iv*) Loaning is mainly on the basis of mutual need and trust with minimum documentation and without any tangible security.

(*v*) The loan amounts are small, frequent and for short durations, and are mainly for unconventional purposes.

(*vi*) Rates of interest vary from group to group, depending upon the purpose of loan, and is often higher than that of banks but lower than that of money-lenders.

(*vii*) At periodical meetings besides collecting money, emerging rural, social and economic issues are discussed.

(*viii*) Defaults are rare due to group pressures and intimate knowledge of the end-use of credit as also the borrowers' economic resources.

SHGs IN ORISSA

India has about 1,50,000 credit outlets in the rural institutional sector including cooperatives and the disbursements made by the banks for agricultural purposes during 1996–97 amounted to Rs. 28,187 crore. Inspite of this, rural people depend on money-lenders for all consumption purposes. Even for production it is estimated that rural credit institutions supply only 12–13 per cent of the actual credit requirements with the rest being met from other sources, like friends and relatives, traders, money lenders and landlords. With land reforms being a forgotten issue, gross capital formation in agriculture has also been falling. Banks are unable to meet rural credit requirements due to various organisational inadequacies and the large poor population (estimated at around 240 crore) have little or no access to rural credit due to the following reasons.

(*i*) Attitude of banks in view of rising NPAs and poor loan recovery rates.

(*ii*) Attitude of borrowers in being wilful defaulters.

(*iii*) Prevalence of illiteracy.

(*iv*) High level of indebtedness due to natural calamities

(*v*) Non-availability of consumption credit.

(*vi*) Time taken to sanction rural loans (1 month to 18 months)

(*vii*) High loan transaction costs for both the poor rural borrowers and the rural banks.

With the help of some banks and a few committed NGOs, the number of SHGs in Orissa have been rising steadily as under:

Table 17.1
SHGs in Orissa and India

	1992–93	*1993–94*	*1994–95*	*1995–96*	*1996–97*
SHGs in India	255	620	2,122	4,600	8,000
SHGs in Orissa	—	180	203	461	753
Women's SHGs in Orissa	—	180	201	459	703

Source: NABARD, RO, Bhubaneswar.

Though there has been a tradition of thrift and mutual help in the villages, pooled cash savings in SHGs is an alien concept in Orissa. However, in some villages, the concept of grain 'goals' in tribal villages (at times of drought) and 'Kothas' or village funds, has been prevalent. The linkage process which has been emphasised by NABARD since 1992, has been centered around the following broad concepts:

(i) Savings first, no credit without savings.
(ii) Savings as partial collateral
(iii) Bank loans to the SHGs for on-lending to members
(iv) Income generation programmes to be popularised along with SHG concepts.
(v) Credit decisions for on-lending to be the prerogative of SHG members.
(vi) Interest rates and other terms and conditions for loans to be left to SHG members to decide.
(vii) Joint liability as a substitute for physical collateral.
(viii) Ratio between savings and credit contingent upon credit worthiness and could increase over a period due to good repayment record.
(ix) Small loans to begin with and then slowly based on repayment performance and needs, may graduate to higher credit amounts.

While the SHG linkage has the capacity to develop into an alternative credit delivery system, the problem is that of finding an adequate number of committed bankers and NGOs to carry forward this programme. Inspite of the blessings of RBI and the initiative taken by NABARD on an all-India basis, the progress in the formation of SHGs has not been encouraging. The status of banks/NGOs involved in the SHG programme since 1992–93 is as under :

Table 17.2
NGOs and SHGs in Orissa

Funding agencies	*Orissa*	*All-India*
No. of Banks	28	300
No. of banks linked with NGOs/SHGs	7	15
No. of NGOs	5,817	23,780
No. of NGOs involved in RD/Thrift	105	1,999
NGOs linked with banks in SHG formation	9	87

Source: NABARD, RO, Bhubaneswar.

The banks have been apathetic to SHG linkage concepts partly because the linkage concepts have yet to percolate down to the branch level with each bank having its own guidelines. Also, SHG lending is not perceived as normal lending activity but is treated as a concessional dispensation while most bankers distrust lending to the poor and also NGOs due to the poor credibility of the existing poverty alleviation programmes and poor interaction of NGOs with banks. On their part, NGOs also distrust banks and their bureaucratic procedures and most NGOs are not interested in thrift-based programmes as they depend upon foreign funding on very generous terms and without much interference. Many NGOs feel that expert manpower is needed for maintaining thrift-based savings especially accounts maintenance but the major problem is that of linkage with banks due to the suspicious attitude of bankers as they are handling the money of other people.

SUCCESS STORIES OF A FEW TRIBAL SHGs IN ORISSA

(i) Less Dependence on Money-lenders — Kalahandi/Bolangir

Usuary in its most deplorable form exists where the lender tries to coerce the borrower into a dependency-relationship from which the borrower cannot escape. Rural money-lenders charge interest @ 10 per cent per month (Lal Bangla in Sambalpur) or the Charni Kalantar (in Bolangir and Kalahandi) charge 25 per cent per month. The NGOs have been able to organise SHGs comprising of women in these areas and inculcate habits of thrift and income-generation activities. Loans have been utilised for growing crops, blacksmithy work, making of hill brooms, trading and business, collection of sal leaves, tailoring *etc.* Repayment among these women SHGs is 100 per cent. These groups have also taken up community development like adult education, fair price shops, construction of village roads, mini-medicine banks, community grain centres. No lien on the deposits of the groups have been taken in respect of loans advanced to the SHGs by the Bolangir and Kalahandi Anchalik Gramin Banks.

(ii) Food Security — Koraput

The tribals of Koraput had set up centuries-old grain banks in their villages where villages put in grain in times of harvest and withdrew grain when absolutely needed. But setting up of credit cooperatives forced the closure of these grain-banks. Under the active guidance of Ankuran, SHGs have re-established grain banks as a hedge against starvation deaths in tribal areas in most villages of Narayampatna in Rayagada district.

(iii) Village Savings — Dhenkanal

Jahnitala in Dhenkanal District is a small village with nil-overdues. All 93 borrowers have repaid their loan instalments to Canara Bank. The village has a common fund with all households making deposits and needy persons take and repay loans within a year @ 25 per cent per annum and as the interest amount adds to the fund, borrowers do not mind the additional interest. About 50 years back, the village elders took up forest plantation on common village wastelands and today the forests are over 40 years old and guarded at village expense. Another interesting innovation is that all houses in the village must be represented during all village meetings and a fine of 99 paise is imposed for non-attendance. The difficulties in gathering exactly 99 paise ensures that no household is unrepresented in the village meetings. Since 1947, no single police case has been registered in the village and no political meetings or smoking or drinking is permitted in the village. A model village indeed!

(iv) Stopping Tribal Exploitation — Kalahandi

The poor tribals of the Rampur of Kalahandi District are exposed to Cerebral Malaria and to starvation for 4 months in a year, apart from being exploited by moneylenders, middlemen and businessmen. Their main income is from shifting cultivation and collection of minor forest produce. Antodaya has been assisting these tribals and 800 tribal women have formed 35 SHGs with small savings. KAG has given an amount of Rs. 30,000 on loan to help them to evade from the clutches of money lender during the festive season and this helped the tribals to avoid selling the forest/agricultural produce to the moneylender traders, at nominal prices. The NGO has also helped the tribals to break the trader monopoly on hill-brooms and instead of Rs. 3 per Kg, the tribals now secure Rs. 15 per Kg which has helped them pay their loans in time. Various production activities such as leaf-plate stitching, bee-keeping and agarbathi making have also been taken up.

(v) Banker Vs. Money-lender — Kalahandi

In most of the tribal areas in Kalahandi, borrowing for consumption purposes against the pledge of standing crops is a common practice. Such borrowing is particularly heavy when it is undertaken for celebrating festivals or discharging religious responsibilities after the death of a family member. The trader-moneylender who advances the loan usually charges very high interest rates, sometimes even beyond 100 per cent on an annualised basis. Usually, the interest charged is not explicit but is implicitly contained in the difference between the market price of the produce and the sale price to the trader-moneylender. This system, called by various names such as "palemode" in the tribal parts of Thane district is one of the mechanisms by which the surplus generating capacity of the poor tribals gets eroded. A reduction in poverty among tribals will be achieved even if such usurious activities are eliminated.

The Gram-Vikas Development Society (GDS) operating in the Kalahandi district of Orissa has attempted an intervention in precisely such a situation. The GDS finances village committees to step into the shoes of the moneylender-trader. The village committees and the GDS together finance the consumption needs of the farmers against the pledge of the farmers' produce and also undertake trading of the produce after harvesting. The interest rates charged by the village committees on the consumption loans are usually much above the rates charged by the banks. The GDS makes a profit in the trading activity by selling produce in the competitive market. The profit made is distributed back to the village committees and the members. Since the trade is handled by the Village Committees and the GDS, the full recovery of the previous consumption loans is ensured. Interestingly, the GDS generates part of the finance for this activity by drawing trade credit at commercial interest rates from the banks operating in that area.

OPERATIONAL PROBLEMS OF SHGs IN ORISSA

The emergence of Self-Help Groups as a supplementary credit channel and its evolution from a pilot project to a business opportunity for the banks is a departure from traditional banking practices. This has necessitated constant review of the functioning of SHGs and assessment of their strength and weaknesses.

The flexibility provided in operation and linkage process has encouraged and helped the groups/NGOs/banks to evolve procedures and patterns suitable to their needs. This needs to be continued. At the same time standardisation may be attempted only in areas where flexibility has been misinterpreted or where imposition or rigidity is a necessity.

A study of all the Self-Help Groups, NGOs and Banks where the credit linkage had been established upto March 1995 was taken up in mid-1996. All the existing models of linkage has been covered. In all 8 NGOs, 11 banks and 14 SHGs were covered during the study covering almost the entire State. Structured questionnaires were used for collection of data besides field studies on the basis of interviews and through non-participative observation at SHG level.

The major findings of the study are summarised below:

(i) The repayment performance of the loans of SHGs *vis-a-vis* those under IRDP and the branch's overall recovery performance were compared. It was observed that the average recovery percentage of the branches visited in respect of IRDP, SHGs and branch as a whole were 36 per cent, 88 per cent and 71 per cent respectively.

(ii) An attempt has been made to assess the initial costs incurred by the NGOs in promotion and linkage of SHGs, and the source from which the same is met. It was mentioned by the NGOs that when the number of groups are comparatively more, the initial costs incurred are less due to economics of scale.

(iii) The study team attempted to evaluate the transaction costs incurred by banks for linking SHGs with bank credit. Similarly, the transaction costs for SHGs *vis-a-vis* other loans was also studied. Most of the bankers were of the view that the transaction costs for SHGs were low compared to those for small loans by banks especially when the linkage was through an NGO.

(iv) The record keeping and accounting procedures maintained at the SHG and NGO level varied depending upon the involvement of NGO, level of awareness of members *etc.* There is no need to impose a common system for the sake of uniformity.

(v) Documentation for sanction of loans and securities collected at the bank's level while providing credit linkages has brought out

certain interesting observations. The number of such documents varied from bank to bank (4 to 11). While many banks kept the savings of the groups in fixed deposits as lien, a few preferred to keep the same in savings bank deposits and two banks did not keep any lien at all on the group deposits.

(vi) The rules and regulations formulated and adopted by the SHGs for smooth operations varied from SHG to SHG. There were a plethora of guidelines regarding group discipline, savings discipline and credit discipline among the groups.

(vii) The choice of SHG members is limited to a few activities because the amount of loan is small in the initial years of linkage programme concerned. At a few places group activities have been pursued with bank credit support and in most of the cases there is provision for consumption loans for members. The repayment period was short in view of low level of operations to accommodate more members availing credit.

(viii) The groups were found to take conscious decisions regarding utilisation of earned interest. While in most cases the interest earned is ploughed back to the seed money of the group, there were a few instances where the same was utilised for common welfare activity.

(ix) The study team came across a few successful instances of conflict resolution and role of peer pressure which need to be documented, for the very practical approach taken in ensuring that the SHG remains in continuous operations. In some groups, SHGs debarred members who had availed of IRDP/DRI loans from banks but had not repaid them while in others, members paid off small amounts of bank loans remaining unpaid for some time, before SHGs were constituted. In many instances, members forced repayment of SHG dues from recalcitrant members while in some cases, SHGs expelled persons who were of doubtful integrity and could not be relied upon to repay loans. The amount of money lent and the interest rates charged by the SHG, were subject to intense negotiation and justification of need by members. The desire to ensure that the SHG continues its operations, was reflected in the mature decision making process.

(x) The study team also made a survey of the group decisions regarding amount of savings, frequency of savings and the source of savings and concluded that most SHGs had a mastery over financial intricacies and could manage lending decisions effectively.

(xi) The income generated out of small ventures undertaken by SHG members varied depending upon the activity undertaken and the manufacture/marketing skills of the individual SHG member.

(xii) The membership size of the groups varied from group to group. However, it was observed that except two groups, others never

considered the membership size as causing any problem to the functioning of the group.

(xiii) The rate of interest charged for consumption and production varied from group to group ranging between 10 per cent to 36 per cent.

(xiv) The study team also explored the possibility or otherwise of rotation in leadership to maintain the democratic character of the group. The majority opinion is that the SHGs should decide the matter.

(xv) The tribal women were more easily motivated to save rather than the tribal men and the women and their savings on better food and nutrition for the children and family, while men preferred to waste money on gambling, cock-fighting and drinking. The tribal SHG responded better to the volunteers from tribal dominated NGOs.

NEED FOR SHGs

The thrift-based SHGs have proved that given flexible conditions, the poor can also save significant amounts. But thrift groups alone will not be able to help its members unless a loaning programme is also set up for enhancing their income-generating capacity. The UAA, Ganjam example reveals poor loan allocations capability if there is no bank linkage programme. But the other SHGs which had a slender resource base, utilised the bank loans to augment lending capacity which could help more members by way of loans and enhance their income-generation capacities. After about 3–5 years of building up SHG funds corpus, the NGO could withdraw and set up new SHGs.

Thus, the concessional funds from NABARD in the initial years would be useful for SHGs to augment their funds and to stabilise the funds resource base of the SHGs. However, there is no indiscriminate showering of funds for SHGs, given the hostile environment for SHG linkage, even after 8 years of having the SHG bank linkage programme.

Banks are wary of giving excess credit especially when they are very conscious about non-performing assets (NPAs) and preparing a 'healthy' balance sheet. The availability of concessional funds would enable the SHGs to build up their financial resources base faster and help inculcate the principles of self-help as the corpus of SHG funds is built up over 3–5 years. The SHG would be able to generate more funds and rely on members rather than on cheap bank funds. The banks would also find this system of lending convenient as the recovery rates exceed 90 per cent in most cases and the transaction costs are lowered while priority sector lending is carried out as per targets set by Reserve Bank of India. The SHG linkage programme cannot be replicated without using NABARD refinance as the volume of funds is low. For Orissa, only an amount of Rs. 22.57 lakh has been given as NABARD refinance for 404 SHGs as on 30 September 1995 (over 3 years) revealing that per SHG refinance is only Rs. 5,615 with each SHG comprising an average of about 20 members. The availability of concessional refinance has been targeted towards banks so as to popularise the SHG linkage programme and make it more attractive to banks which otherwise generally treat NGOs with suspicion. The use of refinance is part of NABARD's strategy of healthy NGO-bank linkage to bring about integrated rural development with "people's" participation. No concessional funding is being contemplated under the NABARD bank linkage scheme. Refinance is available at the same rate as is available to banks for normal development purposes. The issue of all NABARD refinance being concessional and the need for refinance when the process of economic liberalisation is being implemented, is beyond the scope of this paper. However, SHGs/NGOs should not be discriminated against by imposing higher refinance rates when other sections are being given concessional refinance for development purposes. External funds do not dilute self-help concept for NGOs but refinance certainly helps in forging healthy linkages between banks and NGOs for more involvement in other rural development processes. Taking into account the various factors stated earlier, we conclude that if linkages between SHG-Members, banks and NGOs are usefully built up, there will be reduction of transaction costs for both banks and borrowers, better loan recovery and mobilisation of deposits at low costs and will not merely add one more tier in the complex rural credit delivery system or dilute the principles of self-help as no subsidy is included at all. In the initial stages, as banks and NGOs are both wary of each other, RBI/NABARD intervention is necessary to enable SHGs to sustain/expand their operations and over a period 3–5 years, they will be able to stabilise their operations and build up a healthy resources base. It is still too early to say if banks can provide funds from their internal resources (without recourse to NABARD refinance). However, it may be stated that many NGOs prefer not to have recourse to funds from banks with a lot of problems in arranging linkages. Such a short-sighted approach does not augur well for the future of these NGOs. Many NGOs have been suspicious about the performance of banks inspite of the need to augment SHG resources, and have firmly resisted the bank linkage programme of NABARD. Thus, NABARD intervention to reduce mutual suspicions and encourage a healthy working relationship should continue. This will not dilute the principle of self-help as no concessions/subsidies have been envisaged in the linkage programme. But the sad truth is that due to the non-availability of a number of good NGOs which have a diversity of activities and for whom the bank linkage programme is one of many developmental activities, the SHGs can only be an efficient supplement to the credit delivery system rather than form an alternative credit delivery system. There are certain advantages in the NABARD-SHG linkage programme.

No subsidy is contemplated and the SHG is free to charge higher rate of interest ranging from 18 per cent to 36 per cent per year. The bank charges a lower rate of interest (9.5 per cent) and a 3 per cent margin is available to the NGO to meet their transaction costs. No concessional lending to the SHG borrower is contemplated in the scheme as it would dilute the 'self-help' process and provide only temporary crutches to the poor to lean on. One of the findings of a study (ODA-PHEP Study — "Credit for Fisherfolk"–June 1995) states. "There are a few NGOs who have started saving and credit programmes among marine fishing fold through the SHGs. For lending they rely mainly on mobilisation of savings. But the amounts being very small, credit based solely on the savings of the community is not adequate to meet the requirements, particularly for assets". Thus, the need for SHG-NGO-bank linkage under NABARD refinance support and guidance, continues to be felt. For ensuring that the tribal people can access credit easily, the formation of SHGs in exclusively tribal villages, with tribal volunteers/facilitators, and credit uplinking facilities from commercial banks and NABARD refinance, is a step in the right direction.

CONCLUSION

The SHG concept helps members to develop both economic and social strength with the collateral substitute positively influencing the SHG resources with members meeting their contingent liabilities without resorting to money-lenders. The uplinking finance facility to banks with NABARD refinance, enables quick availability of financial resources when needed and the collective funds management capabilities of the SHG members encourages the bankers to lend funds at minimal risk. Repeated interaction between bank officials and tribal group members helps in developing mutual trust and confidence using group presence, strength, assistance and persuasion as collateral substitutes without any tangible security for availing of loans from banks. Financing through tribal SHGs has proved to be an effective supplement to the institutional credit delivery system. The transactions with tribal borrowers are reduced while credit availability in time, is enhanced. Another important point is that the banks too reduce loan administrative costs and recovery of loans is almost 100 per cent. Thus the use of group presence and moral/social security as collateral substitutes indirectly contributes to the viability of the bank through reduced transaction costs and prompt repayment, thereby augmenting the resources for further lending.

CHAPTER XVIII

Consumption Credit for Tribal People

INTRODUCTION

A tribal family derives its income from a variety of sources like forest produce collection, subsistence farming, cultivation of commercial and food crops, horticultural and forest produce and from agricultural labour. The tribals are mainly dependent on the local money-lenders and petty traders for their credit needs incase of accidents, sickness, death in the family, *etc.* This is because of lack of any institutional credit for such needs and also, obtaining credit from the money-lender is a quick process. In emergencies, the response time of the credit given is the most important consideration. Even for needs like marriages, child birth, other religious ceremonies and festivals, the tribals are dependent on money-lenders because all these needs are classified as consumption needs and there is no institutional mechanism for meeting these needs. Thus, whatever income a tribal earns, he is forced to utilise most of it for repaying money-lenders. As his income is only marginally surplus, the tribals continue to be in bondage to the money-lender and the ultimate consequences of this bondage is selling away of meager land holdings, leasing of land to the money-lender in perpetuity or becoming bonded labourers.

The existing credit institutions (Cooperative and Rural Banks) provide credit only for cultivation expenses which is regarded as production credit. This leaves a wide gap in the credit requirements of the landless poor tribals and even among the tribal farmers, as there is no provision for unpredictable credit requirements. Normally, consumption credit is distinguished from agricultural credit but in a simple tribal economy which is an integrated whole, the consumption and productive requirements of credit cannot easily be separated even though they can be identified separately. For example, a tribal cultivator taking loan for agricultural purpose may suddenly use part of it to meet the expenditure on medicines for his family members. At times, it may also happen that he may be forced to use a part or whole of the money on a death ceremony which, in his opinion is more urgent and important. Therefore, the total credit requirement of the community in different seasons of the year has to be clearly identified with specific provisions to meet unforeseen expenditure. It would be more useful to categorise credit requirements based on the degree of predictability of the need rather than on norms of consumption and production credit. Some credit needs are predictable and others are highly unpredictable. This kind of categorisation is important because the institutional responses vary accordingly.

It is estimated that there are about 30,000 landless tribal families dependent on minor forest produce (MFP) collection, agricultural and forest labour in Andhra Pradesh. More than 75 per cent income of this category of tribals is derived from MFP collections and agricultural/forest labour. It is not possible to collect MFP throughout the year or earn from agricultural labour throughout the year. From June to October, there will not be any MFP collection and consequently the tribal will have no income during this lean period. He is driven to the money-lender or local trader for his needs and is forced to sell away MFP during the season to the money-lender at low prices. Therefore, there is a need to extricate him from the clutches of the money-lender or trader by giving timely credit assistance.

The Girijan Cooperative Corporation (GCC) in Andhra Pradesh with more than three decades of association with the tribal economy has expanded its activities in qualitative and quantitative terms. From two small societies in 1956 at G.L. Puram in Srikakulam District and Downur in Visakhapatnam District, it has expanded into a vast organisation covering the entire tribal areas of Andhra Pradesh. Out of a total tribal population of 30 lakh in AP, GCC caters to a population of 20 lakh tribals who are forest-based. GCC is an apex body of 31 Girijan Primary Societies. It has 31 branches, 8 divisions and 801 Domestic Requirement Depots covering the entire tribal areas. It is the only credit and marketing organisation for the tribal population living in interior forest areas of AP, providing the following services:

- *(a)* Procurement of MFP and agricultural produce from tribals and marketing.
- *(b)* Supply of domestic requirements, and
- *(c)* Credit.

The burden of overheads of staff and forest royalties is not passed on to the tribal while fixing the purchase price. The Government of AP provides budgetary support for meeting most of the expenditure on staff and forest rentals and, therefore, it has been possible to provide a fair and competitive price to the tribals collecting MFP compared to the prevailing market price. GCC is also the agency for implementing the public distribution system in the tribal areas.

CONSUMPTION LOAN PROGRAMME

In 1990–91 consumption loans to a tune of Rs. 25.99 lakh, benefiting over 6000 tribal families, were disbursed. In order to implement the programme in a systematic way, detailed discussions are held with tribals in almost all the tribal areas of the State and a series of instructions are given to the field functionaries duly modified from time to time to suit local conditions. Periodical meetings are conducted with the tribal participants and based on the feedback from these meetings, instructions are modified. Thus, a comprehensive credit programme is initiated for provision of credit to the tribal populations.

The organisation of the programme is broadly as follows:

The Domestic Requirements Depots (DRDs) located at the doorsteps of the tribals act as liaison between the tribals and the organisation. These depots are opened throughout the week and are manned by a salesman and supported by measurer-cum-watchman. Most of these functionaries are local tribal people. Before starting of the credit programmes, the gaps in geographical coverage of all these DRP are identified and sub-depots were started wherever required. While locating these sub-depots, it is ensured that they are geographically centrally located and also it is a place where tribals traditionally gather periodically for some social or economic activity. Moreover, identification of these places is done in consultation with the tribal people and experienced field functionaries. All these new depots are manned by local tribals sponsored by the tribal community and they are given all the responsibilities such as collection of MFP / AP, sale of DRDs, issue and collection of agricultural and consumption credit.

The elders of the village are associated in identification of the loanees and each one stands as guarantor for 6–10 loanees. The tribal elders constitute the Village Committee for each tribal habitation. The Village Committee is responsible for identification of needy tribals and are also responsible for the recovery of the loans. The Committee will identify and decide the credit limit for each tribal based on his needs and creditworthiness in terms of value of MFP brought by him and his earnings through other sources. The Committee also decides on the cash and kind components of the loan amount. The quantum of assistance is normally Rs. 500 for consumption loans, but for emergencies and life cycle ceremonies, the ceiling is enhanced to Rs. 2,000. The Village Committee which ensures proper recovery of the loan, gets a financial incentive for prompt recovery of dues.

The association of the tribal people has received immediate and very good response. This response was spontaneous in the sense that the tribals identified themselves with the programme. Moreover, the procedure for disbursement and collection of the loans is simplified, *i.e.*, most of the loans are given partly in kind and partly in cash while part of the MFP brought by them is accounted for, against the loan. The advantage from the tribal point of view is that it is based on the barter economy which the tribal is used to, without the exploitative elements.

The tribal participants of the programme are given passbook-cum-identity card called 'GIRICARD' in which entries of loans disbursed, repayments made, *etc.*, are entered by the salesmen of DRDs. Even though credit limits are fixed, Managers of the local Primaries of GCC have powers to enhance the limits in individual cases depending on the urgent requirements. Thus, the present system of loaning has all the advantages of private money-lenders and banking institutions, without the exploitative potential of the private money-lenders and none of the cumbersome procedures of banks.

Further, performing all the transactions at the doorsteps of the tribals, has reduced wastage of time and energy in going to markets located at a distance. Moreover, a tribal going to a distant market is singled out by the private merchants for exploitation whereas salesmen of DRDs in the tribal village have become part of the tribal social organisation. Therefore, this programme has received immediate acceptance from the tribal people.

Unit of Loan Assistance

The consumption loan is sanctioned to a maximum of Rs. 500 per family, except in emergencies where the ceiling is Rs. 2,000. The loan is sanctioned by the Divisional Manager as per list prepared by the Manager of the concerned Primary Society. The loans are issued partly in cash and partly in kind as required by the beneficiary. Recoveries can be effected through the MFP brought by the tribals. The tribal beneficiary can operate the limit of Rs. 500 sanctioned to him as cash credit account during the period of one year for which it is sanctioned. The accounts are closed only at the end of the year and they are sanctioned fresh limits after lapse of 15 days only. Therefore, the amount given to each village is a kind of revolving fund for the villagers to meet the consumption credit requirements of the tribals of the village community. No interest is charged on loans in the year in which the loan is sanctioned, but an amount equal to 10 per cent of the limit sanctioned is collected towards thrift amount which forms a deposit in the name of the tribal.

Proposals of GCC

The landless tribals dependent on MFP collection require money for *(i)* lean period consumption, *(ii)* religious ceremonies like marriage, child birth, *etc.* and *(iii)* unforeseen expenditure.

(i) Lean Period Consumption and Festival Celebration. The lean season requirements are predictable. Therefore, the procedure for sanction of loans has to start in the month of March and the loans have to be sanctioned by end of May. The requirement per family can be put at Rs. 500. This may be given in both cash and kind and this amount is repayable by sale of MFP to GCC during the season starting from November. This amount is basically a revolving fund and after repayment of the amount the tribal will be eligible for a similar amount for purchase of cloths, utensils, *etc.*, on festive occasions in the same year. This is normally done during Sankranti, *i.e.*, January. This amount will also be repaid through MFP procurement. Thus, the tribal will rotate credit atleast twice in a year.

(ii) Religious Ceremonies. The tribal needs assistance but at short notice. Therefore, a simpler procedure for sanction has to be evolved. A certificate from village elders recommending the loan is insisted upon as this not only ensures moral obligation on the part of the community but also justifies the actual requirement of the tribals. The unit of assistance varies upto a maximum of Rs. 2,000 to be recovered in two years.

(iii) Unforeseen Expenditure. Consumption credit has to be provided to tribals to enable them to meet any unpredictable events like accidental disabilities while collecting MFP, sudden sickness, injuries due to attack by wild animals, deaths, *etc.* For these purposes, an imprest amount of Rs. 5,000 is created and kept with the GCC, DRD Salesman concerned. The salesman of GCC advances the amount required to the tribal based on the recommendation of the Village Committee. The Village Committee is responsible for recommending the loan and also for the recovery.

The Forest Department is liable to pay for injuries/deaths due to attack by wild animals. But there is a lot of procedural delay in sanctioning compensation and the tribal people cannot afford to wait. To avoid this delay, they are given an advance from the above imprest amount and can lodge a claim on the Forest Department through GCC. GCC will then take up the matter with the Forest Department and claims the compensation. After recovering the advance, the balance amount will be paid to the tribal person. GCC plans to insure all MFP-collectors against accidents and deaths due to other causes. The tribal people can claim the amount from the GCC salesman as an advance from this imprest amount and the amount will be repaid after GCC claims it from the insurance company. As far as chronic sickness is concerned, every ITDA has a provision under "Impact Money" to facilitate treatment of chronic sickness. After drawing the amount from GCC salesman, the tribal will make a claim to ITDA through GCC and the amount drawn from GCC will be reimbursed after the impact money from ITDA is sanctioned.

Since 1990–91, NABARD has recognised GCC as a Cooperative Central Bank for the purpose of routing short term agricultural loans to the tribals through the primary network of GCC. GCC has obtained refinance from

NABARD on the loans advanced by it since Kharif 1990. The amount required for consumption cannot be given as grant by NABARD which also does not sanction refinance for consumption loans provided by GCC.

The important point in consumption loaning is close supervision and intensive monitoring of the loanees. This process is both internal, *i.e.*, the tribal loanee himself and the Village Committee, and external, *i.e.*, supervision exercised by the Salesman of GCC and the procurement staff. An amount of 5 per cent is required as service charge of which 2 per cent will be passed on to the Village Committee for ensuring 100 per cent recovery and 3 per cent will be towards expenditure by GCC in recovery of the loan. Thus, if GCC gets the amount at 5 per cent, the loanee will be charged 10 per cent interest.

Risk Fund

10 per cent of the loan amount is given as risk fund to cover bad debts. This normal pattern should not be made applicable for the backward tribal population in the State. The reason is that the tribal people living in hills and forest areas have greater risk of losing the produce due to the vagaries of nature. Therefore, the risk fund could be increased to 20 per cent in the case of tribal people in general and 30 per cent in case of primitive tribals.

PERSPECTIVES

Refinance from NABARD is not available for consumption loans. This needs to be reconsidered for tribal areas. There ought to be flexibility in norms for consumption loans. Increase of risk fund from 10 per cent to 20 per cent (30 per cent for primitive tribals); and building up of Village Corpus Fund over a period of time to reduce dependence on external agencies for consumption loaning, needs to be done. The objective here is that the Villages which do well in terms of recovery should get the un-utilised risk fund as a Corpus Fund to the Village. Thus, for each successful year of loaning and recovery, the corpus fund of the Village increases. Each year's loaning will be a mix of advance from the corpus fund and from GCC. Over a period of time, the Village Community should be able to manage the entire consumption loaning from its corpus fund only. The SHG experiment could be tried for tribal SHGs with minor modifications.

CHAPTER XIX

Tribal Credit Facilitators and Voluntary Agencies

INTRODUCTION

Like many low income countries, there exist two distinct credit delivery systems in Sri Lanka. The informal credit delivery system mainly consisting of money-lenders, traders, friends and relatives provides small but timely credit without any cumbersome procedural formalities. The rate of defaults (loan delinquency) is within tolerable limits, mainly because of effective supervision and informal relationship. However, due to the usurious motives and limited resource base, they could not meet fully, credit requirements particularly for developmental purposes. On the other hand, the institutional credit delivery system comprising Agriculture Service Centre, branches of commercial banks, Cooperative Rural Banks and Regional Rural Development Banks designed for retailing credit for rural development, could not succeed in supplanting money-lenders due to some inherent weaknesses in the system. The institutional credit delivery system suffers from *(a)* cumbersome procedural formalities causing inordinate delay in disbursement and inadequate financing, *(b)* higher loan delinquency particularly due to formal relationship between banker and borrower, *(c)* growing operational costs affecting the financial health of these credit institutions and above all *(d)* urban biases of branch managers.

THE SCHEME

In order to combine the best of both the systems, an experiment has been made in Sri Lanka. This experiment known as Community Credit

Facilitators Scheme has been designed to provide institutional credit through individuals or through local institutions outside the banking system. The scheme enables the people to obtain loan facilities conveniently at reasonable rates of interest through Credit Facilitators. Credit facilitators are appointed by banks for routing bank loans through them. Initially, there are three credit facilitators per block but it will be extended to have one credit facilitator per Gram Sewaka Division. The sponsoring banks provide loans to credit facilitators at a rate of interest of 18 per cent per annum for relending to rural masses at a rate of interest not exceeding 30 per cent per annum. While the prevailing rate of interest in informal rural financial market is in the range of 36 to 48 per cent per annum, the rate of interest charged by banks to their usual borrowers is between 18 to 24 per cent per annum. The scheme has been sponsored by two major public sector commercial banks of Sri Lanka, *viz.*, Bank of Ceylon and People's Bank and operated through their branches. Credit facilitators borrow from branches and function under them. Loans are obtained from credit facilitators by local people with or without offering any security. The rate of interest is, however, negotiable within the ceiling limit of 30 per cent per annum. However, the entire credit risk of lending to clients rests with credit facilitators. In the event of default by the client, sponsoring banks will not be a party to any legal action between credit facilitators and borrowers. While selecting a credit facilitator, the following eligibility conditions have been laid down in the scheme:

(i) He should be a person maintaining good track record with the bank.
(ii) He should be a permanent resident within his area of operation.
(iii) He should have the ability to ensure security for his cash holdings.
(iv) He should be in a position to provide acceptable collateral to the bank.
(v) He should not be defaulter of any previous borrowing from the bank or any other credit institutions.
(vi) He should be of integrity and possess an exemplary character.

Further, preference is given to those having,
(a) previous experience in informal lending in his locality
(b) ability to maintain simple accounts
(c) ability to command respect in his area of operation.

Loans are granted for any purpose that enhance socio-economic development in that area. However, special care has been taken in the scheme to grant loan for productive and developmental purposes. Loans for consumption purposes are discouraged as they generally pose problem of recovery. Loans are issued upto SL Rs. 5,000 per borrower depending upon the requirement and repaying capacity of the borrower. The scheme has a number of special advantages: *(a)* it facilitates quick and efficient financial assistance without any cumbersome formalities to the bottom line of population who are unable to conform to normal banking requirements, *(b)* financial requirements are met by persons familiar with and close to the borrower, *(c)* reduces additional expenses incurred by persons obtaining small loans, *(d)* reduces the higher rate of interest prevailing in the rural financial market, *(e)* reduces administrative expenses and optimises the limited bank resources.

A control system has been developed to have an effective control over the activities of credit facilitators. They have been advised to display a name board at the place of the business. The board should contain the name of the credit facilitators, current interest rate and name of sponsoring bank. They have been further advised to maintain simple record of financial dealings with borrowers. Simple monthly returns have also been devised to monitor the scheme. In this way, an endeavour has been made to establish a firm linkage between the formal and informal sectors of rural financial markets through the new breed of non-banking intermediaries.

Introduced in 1988, the scheme has made rapid progress both in number of Community Credit Facilitators and outstanding amount against them. As at the end of 1992, there were 3,589 Community Credit Facilitators on the roll of Bank of Ceylon as against only 47 Agricultural Service Centre Branches of the bank. Amount outstanding stood at SL Rs. 301 million at the end of 1992. People's Bank appointed 6,905 Community Credit Facilitators by the end of 1992 as against 938 outlets for rural credit. Advances outstanding amounted to SL Rs. 216 million at the end of 1992. As a result of sound knowledge of local conditions, the Community Credit Facilitators are in a better position to identify borrowers, disburse small loans, supervise such loans and recover them more effectively than sponsoring bank. An internal evaluation of the scheme by sponsoring banks has revealed the following shortcomings in the selection of Community Credit Facilitators: *(i)* 'higher authorities' had restricted the local bank manager's freedom to select the candidates freely and *(ii)* plan targets for appointment of Community Credit Facilitators had to be met, which further facilitated the inclusion of unwanted Community Credit Facilitators in the scheme. While confirming the findings of internal evaluation it was reported that villages were well-informed about the scheme by mass media and were instrumental in a proper implementation of the scheme. However, it has been reported that the money-lenders in Sri Lanka, have managed to pre-empt the scheme by giving benami loans to their own relatives and then using the bank funds for money-lending business with better margins.

Relevance for Tribal Areas

By and large, low income countries, particularly in Asia and Pacific region too have the same weaknesses in the credit delivery systems. The preponderance of small as well as scattered tribal villages or dwelling units is one of the important factors restricting further branch expansion programme in these countries. Reaching and serving thousands of small tribal borrowers in these scattered villages will be difficult if not impossible task particularly in view of the weak financial health of some of these credit institutions. Similarly, geographical as well as cultural and attitudinal gaps between borrowers and bankers will continue to hamper the recovery performance of banks. In order to overcome the weaknesses of the credit delivery system and help the rural poor obtain loan facilities conveniently at reasonable rates of interest, it would be advantageous to introduce the scheme at least on an experimental basis, in a few selected areas. Several studies on rural credit have revealed that borrowers are concerned more about timeliness and adequacy of loans rather than to interest cost.

Against this background, it will not be out of context to develop a supplementary credit delivery system for tribals which will be in a position to deliver credit quickly. Necessary modifications could be made in the scheme particularly relating to quantum of loans and rate of interest to suit local conditions. At the same time, suitable measures may be taken up for plugging loopholes in the selection process of Community Credit Facilitators to avoid what was experienced in Sri Lanka under the scheme. However, on successful completion of the experiment, the scheme can be extended in a phased manner in all the remote tribal villages in the country. The implementation of the scheme will not only generate additional employment opportunities, but will also make both informal as well as the formal credit delivery system more effective and efficient by introducing some element of competition. Further, there will be effective control on the informal rural credit market, particularly as regards rate of interest. It will also establish better linkages between the formal and informal rural financial markets. The scheme will help small tribal borrowers particularly in the remote areas to obtain timely credit for developmental and production purposes on the one hand and relieve banks from the difficult as well as loss-making proposition of financing small loans scattered over remote unbanked tribal centres on the other. The transaction cost of credit for tribal borrowers will be reduced on account of savings in expenditure.

Apart from interest on loans and insurance premium, the transaction costs of credit to borrowers include certain other expenses like travel for completing loan formalities, boarding expenses on the days of visit to branch and other offices, stationery charges, stamp duty, photograph charges, evaluation fees, underhand payments and opportunity cost of time involved to complete all required procedures. Cumbersome procedures adopted by formal lending agencies at times increase borrowers' transaction costs to levels that are much higher as compared to tribal borrowers' transaction cost for obtaining loan from informal sources. Ladman worked out transaction costs in case of Bolivia at $ 136 (forming about 4 per cent) for obtaining a loan of $ 3,695 from the Bolivian Agricultural Bank and $ 4 (forming about 1 per cent) for obtaining $ 480 from money-lenders.

A similar study by Zia-Ur-Ahmed in Bangladesh also revealed that the ratio of transaction cost to loan was as high as 22 per cent in case of borrowers of Bangladesh Krishi Bank as compared to 2 per cent in case of their counterparts borrowing from the informal sector. The study also pointed out that effective cost of credit was higher for small loans than for large loans in case of borrowers of Bangladesh Krishi Bank. This suggests that small borrowers would prefer to obtain credit from relatively less expensive informal market while the large borrowers would seek the cheaper formal credit. Indeed, dealing by informal lender within the small circle of persons in face-to-face arrangemenrts, not only greatly facilitates lending decisions, but also reduces borrowers' and lenders' transaction cost. Lenders' transaction costs relate to salary of the staff, office rent, TA and DA, stationery, supervision and recovery expenses. In case of informal sources of credit, the lenders' transacton costs are at times worked out to near-zero levels, whereas formal source of credit incur huge transaction costs depending upon type, incidence, size of loan amount, repayment period, *etc.* According to latest estimates, lenders' transaction costs vary between 6 per cent in case of commercial bank to about 7 per cent in case of RRBs in India. Smaller the size of loan amount, higher is the lenders' transaction costs. The introduction of this supplementary credit delivery system of Community Credit Facilitators, particularly to deal with small loans in unbanked tribal areas, would reduce both the tribal borrowers' costs and lenders' transaction costs substantially. Moreover, the service of Community Credit Facilitators can also be utilised by the sponsoring banks for supervising the end use of credit and monitoring recovery of loans of their large-sized borrowers in unbanked villages on a commission basis. In other words, the scheme will benefit both borrowers and bankers to a significant extent in terms of reduced transaction costs and better recovery performance. The development of such a credit delivery system will be an important step forward towards meeting the credit gaps in remote tribal areas and would go a long way in liberalisation of the market mechanism that determines the interest rate in rural financial markets in the informal sector and ensure easier credit availability for the tribal borrowers. However, the cost of training the tribal credit facilitators will be high initially but in the long run, will be beneficial to the institutional credit sector due to reduced transaction costs, better deposits and margins, proper loan utilisation and improved loan recovery rates. The tribal bank customer would be able to approach banks through a facilitator, initially till there is better understanding of each other. Such a step could also be useful in setting up Self Help Groups.

A Helping Hand

The colonial British administration systematically had sought to use forests for commercial/industrial use, unmindful of the fact that the tribal forest dwellers were totally dependent on forests for their food and survival. With tightening controls and forest laws and an insensitive forest bureaucracy, the tribal people have been deprived of access to forests and their usufructory rights too have been severely curtailed. This has crushed their economic independence and brought them into direct conflict with the Government machinery set up to conserve forests. While conceding the fact that forests are being cut down indiscriminately by tribals for the benefit of contractors, traders, *etc.*, and the fact that tribal people tend to keep away from non-tribal people, it is necessary to review the limitations of the government administrative machinery while dealing with the tribal people and the far-from-friendly relations between the tribal people and the forest officials. There is a need for effective intermediation between the forest dwellers and the official machinery.

The role is being filled in by voluntary organisations or non-government organisations (NGOs) and they are a crucial elements in bringing about change and development in the stagnant tribal society and economy. The development of a healthy interface between the tribal people and the rest of the world could be better managed by the an NGO. The staff attached to all NGOs are generally trained and sensitised to development issues but the staff of NGOs working with tribal people, have to be very alert to tribal susceptibilities and sensitivities. They need to be patient, observant and understand the tribal psyche. Consequently, though there is tremendous potential for NGOs if they choose to work in tribal areas, there are few NGOs which actually work with the tribal people, to begin the process of reflection among them about their precarious situation and inculcate the idea of finding localised solutions. These NGOs have been the catalysts of change among the tribal people and bring about development.

TYPES OF NGOs

There are NGOs and various schemes of the Central/State Governments providing incentives, subsidies and grants for various production/welfare measures. In addition, a large number of foreign organisations offer grants-in-aid through NGOs, for better utilisation. Since the Seventh Five Year Plan, there has been an emphatic attempt by the Government to involve NGOs in the micro-development efforts in view of the ability of the NGOs to build up sustainable systems with the active involvement of the local people. The proliferation of the local bureaucracy does not help in bringing about sustainable development at the grass-roots level and ensures that most of the funds meant for development, end up as salaries and office expenses of petty bureaucracy. But the recent proliferation of NGOs is also not a healthy sign. In tribal areas, it is common to find an NGO conducting diverse activities such as family planning, adult literacy, carpet-weaving and sericulture, not because they have intrinsic strengths in these fields of activity or have developed professional skills/expertise but for the receipt of grants and funds! The moment these activities are curtailed by the Government for want of funds, these NGOs will stop supporting the particular activity! This grant-based approach to development is destined to fail and is slowly being reduced to a farce. In addition, there are a large number of fly-by-night NGO operators who set up NGOs to siphon off funds; they develop links with petty Government officials and without any developmental activity, funds are siphoned off while the Government is blissfully unaware that the development remains on paper only. There are also many high-flying NGOs which had done good work in the past but are now resting on their laurels and their top 'executives' attend international seminars all over the world, get a lot of money from foreign donors/agencies and do only minimal work today. Such NGOs do not want even Government subsidies or funds as they are dollar-aided! In fact, there are so many NGOs which have earned a dubious reputation, that CAPART has over 10,000 NGOs in various States which are on the black-list and debarred from further funding. This does not deter the NGO operators from setting up new NGOs under a new banner and continuing their nefarious activities. Many State Governments have developed signs of NGO fatigue and are wary of dealing with NGOs. This may be due to the clout of NGOs in reducing the spoils/loss of government funds by exposing Government officials! But there are a number of dedicated NGOs in all States which have done excellent work like BAIF, Pune, Antodaya, Koraput, Gram-Vikas, Ganjam, *etc.* These excellent NGOs with very dedicated and expert staff, need to be encouraged.

NGOs which work in tribal areas, have to be very effective as these NGOs have to win the trust and affection of the tribal people before they can communicate effectively with the tribals, preferably in their own dialect. It would also help to have trusted local facilitators for replicating good work done by the NGO in other tribal villages. Some case studies of NGOs which work in tribal areas, would serve to highlight the good work being done by them, including innovative and replicable practices.

1. Spice Processing

The only NGO sponsored by a bank (SBI) in India, SAMANWITA, Kandhmahals, was set up with State Government's help and BAIF assistance, for better quality cattle availability through artificial insemination. Somehow this project did not take off even after all facilities were available. The NGO, however, continued to be aided by SBI and the State Government tried to take up sericulture, processing of Sabai grass and also turmeric processing besides health and welfare of tribal people, especially women and children. These sericulture activities were a flop but the other two activities were successful. Today, the NGO has started processing various other spices which are grown locally and packing them and selling them under their own brand name which is successful. The tribal men and women who work for Samanwita, do the processing and the marketing. SAMANWITA has also set up women SHGs in tribal villages and these are running successfully.

2. Non-timber Forest Produce

KIRDTI, an NGO organises tribals to collect various forest products, especially the mahua flower in April and May and which fetch low prices if sold then. The NGO has set up informal cooperatives which buy mahua from the individual tribal collectors with the money being provided by the NGO. The cooperative stores the flowers in the Mandaghera/Kothaghar (community hall) for a few months and sell these in September/October when the flowers fetch a more remunerative price, with profits ranging from 50 per cent to 100 per cent. The informal tribal cooperatives are managed by a President and Secretary. All those who contribute by selling flowers are members. Sesame seeds are also collected in a similar manner. During 1996, the NGO lent a sum of Rs.1.14 lakh to 15 NFTP societies.

3. Grain Banks

KIRDTI and Antodaya have organised a large number of grain banks in various villages in Orissa. The grain banks for paddy are managed by the male tribals and contain about 8–10 quintals of paddy. For 20 kg of paddy taken as seed, the borrower has to return 30 kg of paddy after harvest but if 20 kg of paddy is taken for food purposes, 25 kg of paddy has to be deposited after harvest. While the grain banks have been operational every year, the NGO provided an initial deposit of 1.5 quintals of paddy. There are big grain banks for a group of villages and have in stock over 270 quintals and receive about 13–28 quintals of paddy every year as interest. The grain banks for Sesame seeds are managed by the tribal women.

4. Water-harvesting

KIRDTI has taken up in Badhumiduda, Keonjhar, a unique land development scheme on 10-acre plots gifted to the villagers under the Indira Patta Schemes, by the State Government. Niger is grown as water is now available in the 17 water-harvesting structures constructed in 25 villages. With the help of an agricultural engineer, 1,858 days employment was created for the villagers and Rs. 75,000 was paid towards labour involved in land levelling and plot preparation. Today, the farmers are able to earn good money.

5. Pipeline Flow Irrigation System

PRADAN has assisted the Juang tribals of Bayanpandadhar in Keonjhar to secure water for their fields. A Water Harvesting Structure (WHS) was situated below the village. Hiring pumpsets and lifting water was too costly. Water was diverted from a natural stream in the mountains, stored in a concrete tank and then passed through an underground pipe to the tank and the over flow was sent to the fields. This system provided water for irrigating 8 acre in Rabi and 12 acre in Kharif.

6. Marketing of Agricultural Produce

CYSD in Orissa has built up 52 tribal SHGs in Saharapada, Keonjhar, with only women members. To avoid distress sale of paddy, non-timber forest produce, these SHGs purchase produce from the farmers/gatherers at a fair price, selling these at higher price after a few months. One SHG has also purchased a sewing machine from their funds (availing a loan from

CYSD) and has started a training-cum-production centre. Some SHGs are venturing into leaf-plate making through new machines. These products are being marketed by CYSD thereby avoiding middlemen who were offering very low prices earlier. Another SHG has taken up production of bamboo products such as baskets and broom-sticks.

7. Five percent Corner Pit for Irrigation

PRADAN has developed dryland paddy cultivation in tribal areas of Purulia district through 5 per cent corner water-pit concept and CYSD took a team of tribal farmers for an exposure visit and this method has been replicated in Saharapada block, Keonjhar, in 10 acre. HYV seeds, pesticides, fertilisers have been provided by the CYSD. The 5 per cent corner water pit is a method of storing rain water in hilly sloping lands by digging a deep pit in the corner of the plot. 20 per cent yield in increase of paddy is seen at a nominal expense of Rs. 1,500 only.

8. Assisting Fishermen

ANARDE, an NGO, has helped the fishermen of Khajurijuari village in Ghategaon, Keonjhar, who had individual ponds but no fishing net. The fishermen used to hire the net from a middlemen who charged 25 per cent of the catch as hire charges. The SHG of fishermen borrowed Rs. 5,000 from a bank and bought a new fishing net for their members, who use it as and when required.

CONCLUSION

The best help for tribals is self-help with NGOs lending a helping hand as and when required as State/Central Government officials rarely have the time to meet the needs and requirements of tribal people. More dedicated people are needed to work with tribal people by setting up NGOs which seek to empower the tribal people and set them up on their feet rather than seeking to corner them into a dependency relationship. Such NGOs can and do make a difference in tribal areas. The NGOs operating in tribal areas have a small operational base and little manpower depending upon operational strategies which are innovative, for results. They are highly sensitive to the needs of the tribals and they are trusted by the tribals. These NGOs have to look after the health aspects and also educational needs of tribal children and sometimes, adults. They are able to utilise local resources and knowledge for the tribal people's benefit but their financial and technical resources are very limited. If the tribal NGOs can network and empower the tribals to affirmative action with a view to reducing their poverty levels, then the traders and middlemen who have preyed on the tribal people, will disappear.

CHAPTER XX

Contractual Farming System for Tribal Farmers

INTRODUCTION

The agriculture sector comprises the largest private sector in the Indian economy with millions of farmers engaged in the most risky and uncertain of economic ventures. Since independence, agricultural policy has been to achieve dual objectives of self sufficiency in food grain production and also to make food grains available at affordable prices to millions of poor in the country, for which a myriad of controls on production, pricing transportation, processing, exports have been built, which also included subsidies and a complex web of cross subsidisation. Export restrictions have artificially kept the prices of agricultural commodities lower than the international prices (34 per cent low in case of paddy, 30 per cent for protein foods and 12 per cent for wheat). Moreover, these restrictions have become hindrances for private investment in agricultural development, at a time when the public investment is showing a downward trend (Proportion of Public sector investments in agriculture have declined from 33 per cent during 1981–82 to 23 per cent during 1990s). Unlike in China, economic reforms in India have not been preceded by rural reforms. Since 1978, the Chinese have concentrated on efficiency improvements with decentralisation of decision-making and market-oriented policies at the local level. The Chinese agricultural reforms till 1984 concentrated on four principle elements:

(*i*) On increased scope for production specialisation

(ii) Closer links between local productivity and rewards
(iii) Higher real output prices and
(iv) Dismantling of the commune system with long-term rights assigned for lands.

It may be noted that the economic and industrial growth in China has been spurred on by the strong growth recorded earlier in the agricultural sector. It is unfortunate that we have not learnt sufficient lessons from the Chinese experience and our vast agricultural sector has not been adequately touched by reforms. But the challenges the Indian Agriculture sector is now facing is stupendous, with the population growth projected at 1.1 billion by 2001 and 1.8 billion by 2050, when we need to boost our food grain production to around 500 million tonnes, while the 200 million tonnes barrier is yet to be overcome by 1997–98. The poor growth of agriculture is too low to sustain a GDP growth rate of 7 per cent per annum.

ECONOMIC REFORMS AND SCOPE FOR AGRICULTURAL INVESTMENTS

Economic reforms and liberalised trade has definitely improved the terms of trade for agriculture, but it continues to be 9.1 per cent against agricultural sector. The weakening of the Indian rupee *vis-à-vis* the dollar has certainly improved the agricultural export volumes as Indian agricultural exports are now more competitive in the export markets, but the devaluation of currencies of South East Asia has robbed us of this advantage. The opening up of Indian agriculture under GATT/WTO and the changes in world agricultural patterns, is likely to accelerate the process of correction in terms of trade for agricultural commodities.

Cost competitiveness and stepping up agricultural outputs are important factors if we are to take advantage of opportunities opened up by liberalisation. We must be able to step up investment in the agricultural sector and also build up simultaneously, the requisite rural infrastructure needed to support technological progress made. There is expected to be greater concentration of production in the non-grain products or non-traditional sectors such as horticulture, plantation crops, poultry, dairy, agro-processing which will not only have a huge market potential within the country but also abroad. The WTO agreement is expected to be favourable to developing economies because non-tariff barriers can be by-passed if we develop suitable technologies for production and also maintain exacting quality standards as per international norms like EEC standards, *etc.* However, export-led growth especially in agricultural commodities and preserved foods, is not immune from price fixing and dumping practices as also non-tariff barriers and hence it would be a better proposition to aim at creating a local market and aim surpluses for exports. To benefit from these new opportunities, the country has to take a number of measures and investment becomes a key factor for sustained growth in the desired sectors.

The country's food industry is growing at the rate 2.4 per cent which is much higher than that of the Power and Telecom sectors. The processed food available in India, as per the Mc Kinsey Report, is stupendous :

Table 20.1
Agro-processing Potential

[Amount in Rs. crore]

Products	*Amount*	*Products*	*Amount*
Frozen vegetables	350	Confectionery	6,500
Fresh vegetables	1,200	Tea & Coffee	7,400
Purees & Sauces	1,000	Bakery	10,000
Fruit drinks	2,000	Meat & Poultry	9,000
Cheese, ice-cream	4,700	Soft drinks	10,500
Sugar	2,400	Packaged atta	36,000
Oil	5,000	Pasteurized milk	27,000

Source: Mc Kinsey—FAIDA Report, 1998.

Branded products have gained consumer acceptance only in a few sections of the urban economy and in a few sections of the rural economy. However, the agricultural production system is very inefficient and about 20 per cent of the value of rural produce in India today, is allowed to rot due to inefficient distribution and poor infrastructure. A review of the food chain in India reveals that investments of over Rs. 1,40,000 crore are needed in the next 2–3 years in capital, skills and technology development, as under:

Corporate farming is beginning to make its presence felt in India, much of it riding Piggy-back on foreign direct investment in food processing. There is an increasing demand for corporatised agriculture especially after the CII-commissioned, Mc Kinsey FAIDA Report, 1998 which envisages by 2005, a minimum ot 10 farm sector companies with turnover in excess of Rs. 3,000 crore. Indian Agriculture require a transformation, if we are to tap these huge potentials and face the challenge of international competition at this critical juncture. The present paper looks into the present system of agriculture and feasibility of an alternative system with active corporate involvement.

TRADITIONAL AGRICULTURAL PRODUCTION SYSTEM

Inspite of the Green Revolution in the 1960's, agriculture production continues to be characterised by small land holdings, low productivity, dispersed production, under-serviced by banking system, low capital formation, unorganised marketing, poor linkage between producer and end user (processor), poor infrastructure and sub-optimal maintenance and use of common infrastructure (like irrigation, power, extension services *etc.*, specially when community/Govt. owned), which culminated into slow technology adoption and inefficient use of natural resources.

The traditional agricultural production system has a number of interacting components, which seek to maximise individual benefits in the market, which may not lead to overall efficiency.

This system has the following features, which constraint optimum use of resources and equitable distribution of profits among various participants in the agricultural production system.

(*a*) The individual farmer is constrained in terms of input supply, technology, timely credit, infrastructure, besides marketing support, which restricts optimum utilisation of available resources of Land, Capital and Man power and enhances risk.

(*b*) Rural banking is constrained with low business levels, dispersed clientele which adds to the overhead costs on sanction and monitoring and higher level of transaction cost both for banks and borrowers, than those prevalent in urban banking institutions. This is coupled with poor recoveries (around 50 per cent) which erodes the banks' capability to recycle the funds.

(*c*) Since the passage of Co-operative Societies Act, 1904, various producer's co-operative societies have emerged as poor man's companies in just about every endeavour of economic activity such as Water users' co-operatives, Milk producer's co-operatives, Oil seed producer's co-operatives, Salt producer's co-operatives, Fishermen's co-operatives, *etc.*, However, their success is limited to milk producer's co-operatives in Anand and replicated elsewhere, Sugar and Spinning mills, Housing co-operatives in Maharashtra. The goal of most producer's co-operatives are partially realised due to lack of sufficient managerial and financial strengths, poor leadership and marketing abilities and environmental constraint. These co-operative credit institutions formed on principles of co-operation and mutual help have also fallen prey to vested interests and lack of adequate financial and marketing strengths.

(*d*) Inadequate rural infrastructure and their sub-optimal utilisation due to lack of co-operative action/ co-ordination among the users and implementing Govt. agencies constrain the farmers in fully utilising the natural endowments. Uneconomic pricing of services like water suppy, electricity is adversely affecting the viability of the Govt. agencies implementing the infrastructure, which further erodes the investment in rural infrastructure.

(*e*) The number of intermediaries between the producer and consumer adds to the transaction cost and limit the profitability of the farmer, which also affects the production system.

Economic liberalisation has brought corporate sector into agriculture and agro-processing sectors and also exposed them to the international competition. Due to constraints discussed above, the traditional agricultural system is unable to cope with the quality, quantity, time scheduling and price optimisation requirement of the corporate processor. Thus Contractual Farming System (CFS) is emerging as an alternative production system.

A detailed study was made on CFS practices in Orissa and Maharashtra as practised by Private sugarcane factories (Ponni Sugars and Shakti Sugars), Farm forestry for production of pulp wood by Paper Industries (JK Corps, Mangalam Timbers), Tassar and mulberry sericulture (Orissa State Tassar and Silk Co-operative Society Ltd.), Fruits & Vegetables (Bilati Orissa Ltd., Keonjhar), Milk (OMFED), Groundnut oil (Oil Orissa), sunflower Oil (Marico industries), Spices (SAMANWITA, an NGO, Phulbani), Spice powder, weaning food from ragi, papad *etc.* by household women (Mahila Vikas Nigam, Bhubaneswar), Oil seed production (Western Orissa Oil growers Society). Objectives of the study is to understand dynamics of Contractual farming system being practised by various sectors and asses the benefits of the system, besides exploring the possibilities of integrating co-operative system with the Corporate sector. A summary of the finding are summarised below.

CONTRACTUAL FARMING SYSTEM

In the Contractual Farming System (CFS), the processor, who is a demand centre in the production system, organises the farmers (primary producers) into formal/informal groups and extend technical and managerial inputs for quick transfer and adoption of technologies, besides linking bank credit and marketing support to the producers. Common infrastructure like irrigation, quality planting materials, electricity *etc.* are also organised through channelling the resources both from banking sector and Govt. Production in CFS is as per a contract between processor, producer and the financier, hence the production system is called a contractual farming system. In a nutshell, contractual farming system is a comprehensive arrangement where full control is established on all factors of production and marketing linkages, thus making the production system a profitable and stable one. CFS combines the strengths of co-operative system and dynamism of private sector involvement and overcomes fluctuations of market forces. For the tribal farmer, a regular market is assured as also fairly stable prices and input support without the usurious money-lending trader, siphoning off huge profits at minimal risk.

The range of industries which can take up Contractual Farming System varies from processors (milk, fruit and vegetables, sugarcane, oil palm *etc.*) to marketers with a bit of value addition like grading, packaging (spices, oil seeds, dry fish *etc.*). Common features of these industries is their dependence for large quantities of agri-produce which is produced in a decentralised way or diseconomies of scale operate in their production. Contractual farming system has been adopted for products which are perishable *viz.* milk, fruits & vegetables *etc.*) or needs processing before consumption (Oil palm, Sericulture, Sugarcane *etc.*) Growing medicinal herbs for the local/export market is also a lucrative proposition for tribal farmers.

There are two basic types of CFS as under:

(a) Industry driven CFS for industries which are in need of large quantities of raw material like Sugar cane mills, paper mills, milk processing plants as these units will not be able to procure raw materials by themselves and hence they have to initiate the CFS process and support the production system with financial, technical, managerial and input support.

(b) Marketing driven CFS facilitate marketing arrangements such as sericulture societies, milk unions, cobblers co-operatives which are a result of Govt. initiative for creating infrastructure for supporting dispersed production systems and for marketing support with technical and managerial support by State Govt. agencies. (Operation flood for Milk Unions; Sericulture Dept for Sericulture project).

VARIATIONS IN CONTRACTUAL FARMING SYSTEM

Corporate Processing units promoted formal societies or co-operative unit when there is a need for creation of common infrastructure like irrigation *etc.* Sugarcane companies have promoted sugar cane growers/water users' societies in order to create common infrastructure facilities through group loans and the society managing the assets. In case of spices promoted by Samanwita, self help groups are promoted and through them the spices are collected and credit is dispensed. In case of oil palm, pulp wood the companies are dealing with individual farmers as there is no common infrastructure involved. In case of mulberry co-operative society, a federation structure is created with primary co-operative societies at district/block level which form into an Apex-co-operative society at State level as in Orissa State Tasar and Silk Co-operative Society Ltd. Primary Milk Producer's Societies at village level organise themselves into District Milk Unions, which in turn are federated into a state level OMFED (Orissa Milk Federation). Implicitly, there is not much difference in this group approach an agency or NGO. However, there is some qualitative differences between a corporate approach and an agency approach. In case of a corporate approach, the contract revolves round certain basic or hard economic negotiation on pure cost and benefit considerations.

Tribal farmers who are integrated into contractual farming system could thus function as individuals or as informal self-help groups (SHGs) or could be members of a formal societies. Individuals/ self help groups are not registered bodies and hence may not have access to concessional credit. However, when the production credit requirements are low or loans are partly production and partly consumption, SHGs would be a more flexible method of accessing bank credit through an NGO. This would be especially useful for tribal production groups or women's groups, in the initial stages. In case of societies, options available are either to register under Societies Act, 1936 or Co-operative Societies Act of respective States.

Role of Various Components of CFS

Processor/End-user

(*a*) Identification of suitable area and farmer groups having traditional experience based on technical and financial feasibility.
(*b*) Organising and motivating the farmers/ primary producers to take up production of specific crops/livestocks as per requirement.
(*c*) Training and skill up-gradation of the farmers for adoption of scientific production practices.
(*d*) Promotion of farmer groups (informal society/ co-operatives) for extending technological, managerial and financial inputs for running of the same.
(*e*) Identification and formulation of infrastructural projects on behalf of the members and co-ordination with Govt. and financial institutions for organising their implementation.
(*f*) Facilitating consolidated flow of various subsidies/concessions available under existing Govt. schemes.
(*g*) Arranging credit by extending corporate guarantees to the bank against loans to co-operatives through tripartite contractual agreements.
(*h*) Provision of seed capital/interim finance/ bridge loans , pending sanction at society level by banks.
(*i*) Marketing support to primary producers at a pre-negotiated prices and associated marketing facilities.

Financing Bank

(*a*) Reduction in loan appraisal and transaction costs for production loans as loan is sanctioned to society with proportional liability raised against each member.
(*b*) Appraisal, sanction and release of loans for common infrastructural facilities sanctioned to society with counter guarantee of corporate processor.
(*c*) Bank can monitor society's performance and reduce loan recovery and marketing costs.
(*d*) Simplifying documentation and procedures in extending loans to farmers as individuals/ as a group.
(*e*) Ensuring repayment of bank's dues by crediting sale proceeds to the individual farmer's accounts at bank.

Farmers' Co-operative Societies

(*a*) Organising the tribals for co-operative and collective action for the mutual benefit of its members.

(b) Implementation and maintenance of common infrastructural facilities
(c) Provide a legal framework to members against loan/subsidies *etc.* regarding procedures and documentation.
(d) Provide inputs, technical support for scientific production and facilitate marketing through pooling.
(e) Acts as single point contact for interaction with agencies like banks, Govt. and processors.
(f) Credit delivery to its members for production purposes.

ADVANTAGES OF CONTRACTUAL FARMING SYSTEM

Contractual Farming System offered various advantages for each of the components as under:

(a) *Speedy Adoption of New Technologies in Crop/Livestock Management as per the Processor's Requirement.* Several organisations have made serious attempt to adopt new crops/plantations/technology in the region. JK corp has encouraged tribals and small and marginal formers to grow commercial eucalyptus trees in the Koraput-Kalahandi region. Besides, Ponni Sugar Company assisted the tribals in adopting fertilisers, single node cutting in sugar cane plantation and SAMANWITA has also promoted new varieties in Turmeric and Ginger in Bolangir district.

(b) *Efficient Backward and Forward Linkages.* Industry is promoted CFS with financial and managerial strengths, along with forward and backward linkages like irrigation, input supply, marketing were provided timely and in an orderly manner. Industry served as a buffer for any lacunae in the system. (*e.g.*, import of quality animals by OMFED, bulk purchase of pumpsets, fertilisers by Shakti Sugars for the farmers). Marketing of their produce at a predetermined or pre-negotiated prices is assured. (Yearly fixation of prices in Sugarcane, minimum price announced by JK corps and scope for future negotiation based on the market prices; fixing of prices of milk based on the cost of production).

(c) *Easy Availability of Credit.* Credit requirements of the CFS are being organised on a collective basis and documentation and other cumbersome procedures are undertaken by Industry or Society. Small and Marginal farmers with limited credit worthiness are also covered under the schemes, which is hard to come by as an individuals (80 per cent of the members of the Farm forestry scheme of JK are small and marginal farmers, who are given concession on mortgage of land up to a loan amount of Rs. 20,000; small defaults/overdues of the sugarcane farmers are cleared by the company. In the initial years of CFS, the Sugar companies (Shakti sugars from City bank and OSCB) raised loans and extended to the farmers for infrastructure development and towards crop loans.)

(d) *Rise in Productivity.* In view of adoption of new technologies and provision of production linkages, productivity levels have increased under contractual farming system. (Productivity of Sugarcane increased from 15 T/ac at pre-contractual system to 25 T/ac in case of Shakti and Ponni sugar promoted CFS; Similarly, tomato yield increased from 7–8 T/ac to 20 T/ac with adoption of hybrids under CFS promoted by Bilati (Orissa) Ltd.

(e) *Project Implementation.* Project implementation like Lift Irrigation Projects was found to be speedy as the promoting company takes care of the project escalation and implementation. (Shakti and Ponni Sugars Promoted Irrigation Projects *vis-à-vis* Orissa Lift Irrigation Corporation). Operation of the infrastructure was also found to be better due to a dedicated electricity line /Diesel set provided in the project, which is not the case in OLIC implemented projects)

(f) *Bargaining Power.* Bargaining power of the primary producer increased because they are functioning like a group with common goals (Subsidy provided to Sugarcane cultivators for irrigation; price fixation for milk; bargaining power of the operation of the irrigation infrastructure owned by Govt.)

(g) *SHG and Micro-credit Innovations* lead to synergy and group/ individual benefits.

SYSTEMS OF CREDIT LINKAGES UNDER CFS

Under contractual farming, the following four types of credit linkages are noticed.

1. Financing to the individual tribal farmers for meeting his/her individual credit needs (JK corps in farm forestry scheme).
2. Financing to Society, where the documentation is between bank and society and society in turn enters into agreement with its members. (Shakti and Ponni Sugars)
3. Bulk financing to society, but the documentation is between bank and individual farmer, where the society facilitates the documentation procedures.
4. Bank lends to processor as indirect agriculture advance, which in turn finances to the member farmers. (Aska Sugar mills, Ganjam district, Orissa).

In case of financing to society or to the processor, the processor extends corporate guarantee, as the assets of the society are very limited to cover the liability.

Differences between individual financing and financing under contractual farming as noticed in sugar cane production system and farm forestry system are given in Annexures 20.1 and 20.2.

It is clear from Annexures 20.1 and 20.2 that, contractual accessibility facilitates easy flow of credit, share a part of the banks job, thus extending banks and reduce the time gap in availability of the loan. Through the legal contract, the dynamic market forces are moderated to a greater extent, which brings stability to the fluctuating agricultural production system. Besides these, the monitoring and supervision role of the bank in largely shared by the corporate body and this reduces the risk cost involved in individual financing.

Contractual farming system is bound legally by a tripartite agreement among bank, farmers and processor. Under this agreement, processor promises to extend technical and financial assistance to farmers by taking up a specified activity and agrees to purchase the produce at a predetermined price. Farmers agrees to adhere to the production schedules and supply the raw material to the processor. Banks agrees to extend the loan as per the terms and conditions agreed by all and the processor promises to credit the sale proceeds to the bank a/c of individual farmers thus the repayment of the bank loan is ensured.

As the CFS and Co-operatives operate with the same principles of co-operation and collective action, the advantages of CFS opens up opportunities for integrating the traditional co-operative sector with corporate sector, which is briefly analysed below.

A MODEL CFS FOR INTEGRATING CORPORATE SECTOR WITH CO-OPERATIVES

Background on Co-operative Credit Structure

The traditional co-operative structure is a three tier structure with PACS as grass roots organisations to link-up with District. Co-operative banks with an operational area encompassing one or a few districts, and an apex level State Co-operative Bank Ltd. In tribal areas, LAMPS (Large Area Multi-purpose Societies) have been formed with a purpose of extending credit to tribals besides providing them with inputs, consumable and marketing support. PACS and LAMPS have been formed with an objective to provide inputs and other backward linkages to its members besides production credit and at the same time to provide marketing support for the produce of its members. Regional Co-operative Marketing Societies (RCMS) have been formed to provide marketing support to co-operative credit structures, which are now almost defunct. Infrastructure for marketing, input supply, godowns for storage of inputs and produce, and processing facilities (oil mills, sugar mills *etc.*) have been created in the co-operative fold for providing support to the producer/ rural agricultural production system.

The rural credit structure in India, comprises of 100 commercial banks with about 36,000 rural and semi-urban branches, 196 Regional Rural Banks with a branch network of 14,500 branches, 28 State co-operative banks with 712 branches, 366 DCCBs (11,645 branches), and 90,783 PACS in short term co-operative credit and 20 SLDBs (with 1,060 branches) and 732 PLDBs (with 1,153 branches) in the long term co-operative credit structure, besides the end user's financial assistance as an advance to the producer. Under the liberalised economic situation, where profit has become the main motive of commercial banking system, co-operative credit system has emerged as the prime institutional agency in dispensation of rural credit with over 57 per cent of Short Term Credit and 29 per cent of Long Term Credit requirements being met by these agencies.

While NABARD provides refinance support to co-operatives and RRBs for ST credit and to all banks including commercial banks for LT credit, no refinance is provided for functional co-operatives, which increases the cost of credit for the members as credit is passed through PACS and commercial banks. This is presumably done so as to provide adequate business for the PACS which suffer from a low clientele and high operational costs.

Limitations

The cooperative credit structure in Orissa and elsewhere are constrained by their narrowing of roles, financial non-viability and political interference in their functioning, as under.

(a) Over the years, the co-operative credit structure has done away with the non-credit functions like input supply and marketing, which has resulted in narrowing of the cherished roles of the co-operatives .Viability studies of PACS undertaken in Orissa also revealed that the viability of the PACS would be improved, when they combine the credit functions with non-credit functions like marketing, input supply *etc.*

(b) Loan availing membership at PACS in many cases is as low as 10 per cent, and the enrolment process of membership also remained constant, hinting at book adjustments, year after year.

(c) Financial non-viability is due to rising overhead costs, with less than corresponding rise in business and poor recoveries. Due to political interference and lack of punitive action, the recovery is also poor, if the members dependency on the society is only credit. In the absence of control of the society on the repayment commitments and income of the members, wilful defaults have also gone up. Low levels of business and poor recoveries have made many a PACS financially non-viable.

(d) Response time of co-operative credit structure is very long and it takes about 4–6 months for actual cash disbursal. PACS prepare a base level credit plan and submits it to a branch of DCCB, who in turn forward it to DCCB HO. Loan committee of DCCB approves the credit limit for the PACS basing on the individual credit needs of the members. Basing on this sanction, members apply to PACS for loan and PACS forward the loan application to a branch of

DCCB, which provides the cash to the farmer. This process takes about 3–6 months and hence the credit doesn't serve the real purpose for which it is meant.

(e) Marketing of the produce collected by LAMPS/PACS in a professional way has been found to be the bottleneck in viability of LAMPS/PACS. Market being a competitive feature, where the decision making has to be quick and be able to take risks, co-operative structure is constrained by their elaborate procedures and rules. A private entity has all the flexibility and wherewithal to survive in the market, which is lacking with a co-operative structure. Failure of the co-operative structure to market the produce of the members is also resulting in wilful defaults.

(f) In view of the weaknesses at the Primary levels, there is an expansion in the roles of higher lending agencies like DCCB and SCB. DCCB and SCB are increasingly lending to areas/activities through their own branch network, thus making the role of primary agencies redundant or in other words, higher tiers of the co-operative credit structure are shouldering responsibility at the cost and with detriment to lower tiers.

As a result, the co-operative credit delivery system is not able to meet the genuine production/investment credit requirements of the farmers for undertaking high input agricultural activities. External credit support like NABARD refinance gets choked if there is a default at any level of the three tier credit structure, thus the primary members are deprived of credit.

(g) Co-operatives being a State subject and exploitation by political and vested interest, have been attributed to the ever mounting losses and revival of co-operative credit structure have yeilded little result. Co-operative credit structure is often interfered with lack of regular elections, superseding of the nominated boards and political interference in decision making. Lack of political will at macro level and lack of dynamic action within the co-operatives have resulted in this state of slumber in the reform process of co-operatives.

Opportunities

The SWOT analysis revealed that the co-operative credit structure has the strength of wider grassroots outreach while the corporate sector on the other hand have managerial and financial strength though having limitation of reaching a large number of small and marginal farmers for meeting their raw material requirement. Hence by complementing the strengths of co-operative and corporate, the agricultural production system becomes more efficient for mutual benefit.Contractual Farming System (CFS) provides a model for strengthening the co-operative credit structure and also for integrating the corporate sector and co-operatives for the mutual benefit.

In the existing system, contractual farming societies (registered under co-operative societies act) can be affiliated to District Co-operative Bank or Apex Co-operative Society. These societies can avail term loans for capital investment either from DCCB or Apex Society for infrastructure development. However, for their production and marketing credit requirement, the members have to depend on PACS/ Commercial Banks/ RRBs *etc.* Although legally, this dual institutional financing is possible, operationally it is difficult in implementation for reasons of administrative, documentation and political factors. This multi-agency approach dilutes the benefits of the contractual farming system towards a comprehensive system.

Integration of co-operatives and corporate sector can be by way of linking contractual farming systems with co-operative credit structure. CFS depending on the size of operation may be integrated with the co-operative credit structure at DCCB or SCB.

A contractual farming system with its operational area within a district can be linked with DCCB as a member at par with PACS (*e.g.*, Water users' co-operative societies promoted by Sugar companies). Here the CFS would be operating as a single tier structure.

In case of contractual farming system which is operating as two tier structure and operating in more than one district or state level, they can be integrated with SCB by giving society the status of DCCB (*e.g.*, Federation of Milk Societies or Apex society of Sericulture *etc.*)

Rationale

The mandate of the Co-operative Credit Structure and Contractual Farming Societies are the same as the society for the benefit of the member farmers by way of providing backward and forward linkages and credit support. Both PACS and CFS are operating at grassroots level with farmers as the members. Both the societies are governed by co-operative societies Act. CFS as such differ from the co-operative credit structure in terms of integrating the co-operative action with the corporate bodies for undertaking marketing and catalytic activities.

Thus a parallel could be drawn between Contractual Farming Societies and PACS for extending production credit from DCCB on concessional terms. Investment credit is already extended directly through Contractual Farming Societies and channelising the production credit to members of Contractual Farming Society for a specific crop/purpose is a logical extension.

It may however be argued that, PACS are operating in the same operational area and promoting other co-operative societies will eat into their business, hence production credit should continue to be extended through PACS. But this argument may not hold good in the present day context, when the co-operatives as such are competing with RRB/Commercial Banks in their service area. Of late, RBI is also liberal in extending relaxation in service areas, when a bank intend to finance in a contiguous area on a project basis. (State wide relaxation was given to SBI for financing eucalyptus promoted by JK Corp.). In addition, DCCB and Apex Co-operative Credit Societies are competing for making good financing, which otherwise should have been the prerogative of the PACS. NFS financing is increasingly done by DCCBs through their branch network. The present trend of integration of short term credit structure and Long term co-operative credit structure and less than optimum business levels at PACS levels may be an indication of a two tier co-operative credit structure in the coming years.

Hence it is suggested that the Contractual Farming Societies should be treated on par with PACS and extend both term loan and production credit for more effective use of credit. In fact, the success of these Contractual Farming Societies would trigger the business potentials under co-operative fold in rural areas, which would provide business to the traditional rural lending agencies.

Concessional credit available through the NABARD refinance channel deserves to be extended to Contractual Farming system, for rapid progress of same, besides improving their margins. The project approach to CFS through refinance from NABARD will improve the present scenario to a large extent.

POLICY CHANGES FOR CORPORATE CO-OPERATIVE INTEGRATION

Integration of the co-operatives and corporate sector can be achieved by two ways *i.e., (a)* integrating existing CFS with co-operatives at DCCB/OSCB level, *(b)* converting PACS/LAMPS into CFS. As the latter option needs initiative and willingness of the State Govt, the first option is assumed to be operationally viable.

The following changes are suggested.

Amendment of By-laws of Co-operatives

Presently by-laws of co-operatives permit financing corporates by taking them as nominated members. However amendments are required for extending credit to CFS on par with PACS for production credit. Present system allows cadre employees, Govt. employees, and employees of OSCB/DCCB to man PACS. Amendments are hence required for hiring professionals (from Company) in functioning of the Societies on contract basis. Provision for participation of the sponsoring processing company in management of the society is also required so that professional managerial experience could assist the co-operative system. Amendments are also required for allowing operations of CFS and PACS in the same service area.

Extending NABARD Refinance Support to CFS through DCCBs

Since the by-laws permit membership of CFS with DCCBs, extension of NABARD refinance [ST (SAO)] permit extension of credit to CFS on lines of PACS.

At present, lines of credit from NABARD are available to DCCBs for the purpose of marketing, weaver's credit, collection and marketing of Minor Forest Products, for onward lending to societies registered for specific purpose. However, production credit like ST (SAO) is the only line of credit which is exclusively routed through PACS. As a special case, production credit for fisheries (in land and marine) is available through societies formed for the specific purpose of fishermen.

On similar lines, NABARD may extend special lines of credit under ST (SAO), for specific crop production under contractual farming system.

Rationalisation of Voting Rights

Political interference could be curtailed by dividing the membership into active members with voting rights, (who are availing one or other services from society), and nominee members without voting rights. (In Orissa, 8–10 per cent of the total members are only reported to be availing services from the society, while the rest have been exploited for political uses).

Financial Viability

Other studies have revealed that the break even level of business for operational viability of PACS is Rs. 25 lakh for annum and only 5 per cent of the PACS have this levels of business. Hence, initially, only those of the contractual farming societies may be integrated with higher co-operative credit agencies, whose assured business levels would be Rs. 25 lakh.

Bulk Lending to SHGs

Bye-laws of the co-operatives at various levels may be amended to facilitate bulk lending to the SHGs, with refinance support from NABARD for the informal societies formed by corporate processor.

Interim Finance to Companies Promoting CFS

Companies promoting CFS through formation of societies may be provided interim finance pending formation of the society and documentation and the liability could be transferred to the society once the project is implemented. NABARD may consider refinancing the same.

PERSPECTIVES

Contractual Farming System has provided a framework for harnessing the benefits of co-operative system and corporate sector in agriculture. In the era of economic policy reform, every rupee invested is looked from the point of view of monetized returns to the society or the Government. Hence the Govt. supported investments in infrastructure for Agriculture and Rural Development, in not so developed States may not be immediate, unless the returns match the investment and leaves a sufficient surplus to further investment. Here, the role of co-operatives becomes all the more important for working as a pressure group for getting the due attention/ share in the Govt. funds for infrastructure development. A dynamic co-operative system is a pre-requisite, for which a change in out look is essential.

As the change in co-operative credit system has become torturous, Contractual Farming System needs integration with co-operative system, with the corporate sector acting as a pressure group for bringing changes in the co-operative credit structure. Professionalism of corporate sector and their need for quick response and huge credit needs would help co-operative credit structure to transform into viable entities. This optimism is basing on the reorientation of the bureaucracy under the liberalised economy to meets the needs of the corporate sector. The success of the co-operative credit structure in Western India is mostly due to their professional outlook and commercial orientation which can spread to other States through contractual farming system with link-up of the co-operatives and corporate sector. The best chance the tribal farmer can have for rapid modernisation of farming practices and ending the process of grinding poverty, is through the contractual farming system in areas of comparative advantage such as farm-forests, medicinal herbs, *etc.*

ANNEXURE 20.1

Differences between Contractual Farming Societies Registered under Different Acts

Items	*Registered under societies act, 1936*	*Registered under Orissa cooperative societies act, 1962*
Aims and Objectives	Socio-cultural upliftment, thrift and cooperative effort, agricultural development, common infrastructure development and maintenance; Land and water development, supply of inputs and marketing, arrange and advance loans for Short term and Long term purposes.	Own or hired agricultural implements, borrow to create infrastructure, thrift and self-help, common infrastructure development, land maintenance, land and water development, supply of inputs and marketing, arrange and advance loans for ST and LT purposes.
Governing Body	Consisting of 5 members each	11 Board of Directors directly elected by Governing Body. Equitable representation of SC/ST, Women, 3 Government representatives.
Share Capital/ Membership	Rs. 10 as membership.	A-class members: Minimum of 100 shares (@ Rs. 10 per share) per acre of command area under the project. B-class members (nominated Members): Of Rs. 5 per share, who have to join 'A' class members for execution of mortage bonds. C-class shares of Rs. 1,000 per share to be allotted to Government. Liability of members 10 times of the share capital.

Items	*Registered under societies act, 1936*	*Registered under Orissa cooperative societies act, 1962*
Formalities of formation, running of society.	Simple and as per Societies Act, 1936.	Governed by procedures and laws of Cooperative Societies Act.
Elections	Only nominated Board.	Elected Board. Initial few years exemption could be availed. In liew of elections registered cooperative society can have their membership.
Loaning	Can avail group loan/indirect agricultural loan and extend the same to members.	Can avail group loan on behalf of members.
Functioning	As per the wishes of the promoting company, who are in majority. During initial years, facilitates quick decision-making and implementation of projects. Members' voice is limited.	Democratic through elected board. During initial years, ignorance and individual interest may supersede group interest and delay implementation of projects. Control of the company is limited and indirect.

ANNEXURE 20.2

Differences between Individual Financing and Financing Societies under Contractual Farming System by Sugar Factories

S. No.	*Particulars*	*Individual financing*	*Society under contractual system*	*Remarks*
1.	Selection of enterpreneurs	By banker or individual approaches a bank or sponsored by Govt. agency for financing.	Processing company identifies the entrepreneurs, who become members of the cosiety.	Large numbers covered in a contiguous area.
2.	Selection of item of investment	Feasibility and individual choice individual investment.	Common infrastructure for the society as per the scheme promoted by the company. For individuals financed under the scheme, activity promoted by the processor as per the approved scheme.	High input intensive farming, with proven profitability.
3.	Credit worthiness	Individuals credit worthiness as assessed by the banker.	Not given much importance	A liberal view facilitates greater number of farmers getting access to bank credit.
4.	Documentation	Individuals enters into agreement with bank Deed of hypothecation agreement of term loan, deed of guarantee, time promissory note, deed of assignment *etc.*	Society enters in to agreement with bank as single entity. Society in turn enters in to agreement with member as per the proforma prescribed by bank. Society reassing the charge in favour of bank, which the farmers have assigned in its favour.	Simplified, which is the major bottleneck in rural financing. Cost of accessing documents also gets reduced with large number of farmers.
5.	Defaulters	Not eligible; No due certificates from all banks in the area are insisted.	Bank does not consider the default of the individual members of the society. If insisted up on, the processing company clears the dues if it is in small sums be recover from sale proceeds.	Defaulters get a second chance to access bank credit. Bank recovers a portion of bad loans.
6.	Service area	Financing is normally in the allocated service area only.	Although the members spread over many service areas, the cosiety service area is only considered.	Scheme is implemented by one bank in a contiguous area, thus the implementation becomes easy.
7.	Primary security	Hypothecation of the crop, assets, equitable mortgage of land for term loan above Rs. 15,000 for immovable property.	Reassignment of the hypothecation of assets created with loan. Corporate Guarantee of the processing company.	Company offers security, which is a major constraint in rural lending and acts as facilitator.
8.	Pre-sanction procedure	Pre-sanction visit for appraisal.	Project area is visited once with their expert team and all individuals may not be covered and depends on company's feed back.	Simplified/under taken by company, thus reducing banks overhead costs.

S. No.	*Particulars*	*Individual financing*	*Society under contractual system*	*Remarks*
9.	Disbursement	Loan disbursement in instalments as per progress and paid directly to the dealers.	Company spends the amount for implementation of the scheme, and gets reimbursement from bank as per the vouchers submitted. Company's a/c credited with the loan amount towards input supplied to farmers, based on their endorsement.	Speedy implementation due to flow of funds from company irrespective of the procedural delays at bank. Farmers donot have to go to many bankers for interin finance.
10.	Monitoring	Two visits for crop loan and half yearly visits for term loan, for end-use study.	Sample monitoring of the area and depends on the feedback from company.	Regular monitoring by company and the burden of bank reduced.
11.	Margin	Farmer invests margin money and rest is provided as loan.	In practice, the company pays for the margin stipulated on behalf of the members.	Company is subsidising farmers for speedy project implementation.
12.	Interest rate	Interest rate as per the different loan slabs.	Although the loan amount for society is at higher interest slab, interest rate is stipulated based on the amount per member. In case of difference, company bears the cost.	Interest rate of individuals is on favourable terms.
13.	Repayment	Individual deposits the sale proceeds towards repayment.	Company deposits the sale proceeds in individual farmer's a/c and bank recovers the instalment and the rest is credited to SB a/c.	Banks repayment is assured and wilful defaulters are minimised.
14.	Agreement on marketing	Does not exist.	A tripartite agreement among bank, farmers and factory for the marketing arrangements.	Organised marketing benefits the farmers and they have collective bargaining power also.
15.	Coverage per field officer	500 a/c including 150-200 Term Loan a/c.	A field officer can cover about 2000-2500 a/c under the society.	Overheads of banks reduced and improves banker's profitability.
16.	Interest burden during implementation, cost overruns	Adds burden to individuals.	Company subsidies the escalation, if any.	Individual's liability remains limited.

CHAPTER XXI

Forest Rejuvenation and Tribal Area Development

INTRODUCTION

The problems of people in tribal districts are typical in view of the vicious circle of poverty. Although the tribal regions are second to none in terms of natural resources endowment, lack of optimum utilisation of resources, inequality/skewed distribution of resources and increasing restrictions posed by Government on access to natural resources are the main causes of poverty in the tribal regions. This is compounded by the low level of skills and education, which is the bane of the backward tribal population. Land alienation coupled with skewed distribution of land due to poor implementation of land reform laws and ineffective laws protecting land ownership of tribal people are leading to further marginalisation of the tribal people. In addition, the traditional rights of tribals on forests and hill slopes used for shifting cultivation have been taken over during the land settlement and demarcation of Reserve Forests, without providing any alternative source of livelihood.

Developmental initiatives taken by Government since independence have not reached the targeted tribal people due to their inaccessibility, low density and dispersed population and low priority accorded by the polity. Investments in infrastructure, both physical and social, to tribal areas remained low *vis-a-vis* the developed areas of the country, either in terms of investment per capita or per-unit geographical area.

Utilisation of whatever infrastructure created in tribal areas remained underutilised (*e.g.*, a vast number of defunct irrigation projects) due to under-staffing of the Government agencies, which again is due to lack of sufficient educated manpower locally or their poor representation in the Government machinery. Lack of vibrant market mechanisms has also resulted in multi-tier structures, which compounded the problem of low returns to the people. Input supply and percolation of new technologies and entrepreneurship have not reached these areas for the same reasons attributed to poorly-developed market network.

Due to undulating terrain, rainfed nature of agriculture and abysmal extension work, the fruits of green revolution have bypassed tribal areas completely. The technologies promoted are capital intensive and dependent on external inputs and resources, which had no impact on the agriculture of the tribal regions. The traditional system of agriculture, which is suited to the rainfed low-input conditions of the region (irrigation systems of Mundas and Katas, multi-cropping systems in shifting cultivation, indigenous land and water conservation methods, *etc.*), neither have not been built upon nor could the new methods be adopted for want of funds and other resources.

Income from forest resources, which has been the main source of cash income and subsistence, is also being deprived due to alienation of traditional rights of tribals on forest produce, failure of the marketing agencies created for the purpose of market support and increased dependence of Government for revenue from the same resources. There is a clash of interest between the tribal poor and various Corporations of the Government which have been called upon to make profits. Electrical and telephone connections are rarely provided to remote tribal areas for want of economic viability, except in Himachal Pradesh.

Surplus income with the tribal people has thus remained negligible, leaving very little scope for local private capital formation in agricultural sector. Public investment in agriculture and infrastructure is too small to catalyse the agricultural economy of the region. In the absence of sufficient investments in either public/private sector, the scope of expanding development credit has been impaired. In addition, lack of capital and creditworthiness of the poor have adversely affected the credit absorption capacity of the region. Institutional credit linkages, most of which have been under Government-sponsored programmes, have been constrained by the poor recoveries, as the personal demands on the little surplus is too strong to repay the loans. This has led to poor financial position of rural financial institutions, which has further curtailed their lending capacity.

The tribal regions are characterised by endemic poverty, fragile ecology, primitive and subsistence economy, poor human development and infrastructural backwardness, in spite of being rich in natural resources. Kalahandi once known as rice bowl of Orissa, is now a byword for starvation deaths. Continuous neglect of the tribal regions and consequent backwardness would only encourage social unrest and resentment, which makes the region vulnerable to extremist activities.

BASIC APPROACH FOR FOREST DEVELOPMENT

The revival of the tribal economy and ensuring that tribal communities are firmly set on the path of sustainable development, is a challenging task. The focus should be on the tribal families, especially the women and the children, as the economic development should benefit the underprivileged. With their forests being stripped at a very fast rate, the tribal people are struggling to survive as neither formal plantation programmes nor legislative measures can save the forests or create new forests. It is only affirmative people-oriented action which can reverse the trend and revive the tribal economy. Relief and economic development measures for tribal people have been introduced as poverty alleviation programmes! Various Five Year Plans have tried to force the pace of tribal economic development and have ultimately failed. Misplaced concern for the 'disadvantaged' communities have not translated into viable plans for socio-economic development of the tribal people. The first two Five Year Plans introduced community development projects which did not target the tribal people. The Third Plan proposed multipurpose tribal development plans for areas with over 67 per cent concentration of tribal people. Five hundred Tribal Development Blocks were set up covering 40 per cent of the local population. In the Fourth Five Year Plan, special tribal development components such as Small Farmers Development Agency (SFDA), Drought Prone Area Programme (DPAP), *etc.*, were initiated. Special offices for tribal development with separate administrative set-ups were created. In all these plans, the Government realised that the tribal people were gaining little or no benefits and in the Fifth Five Year Plan, tribal sub-plans were prepared, *i.e.*, micro-planning approach rather than the 'one-size-fits-all' macro-economic planning.

The failure of 50 years of planned tribal economic development is all-too-apparent! Projects planned by bureaucrats with little knowledge of tribal needs and aspirations, were doomed to failure as 'top-down' models of development have always failed. The target-oriented approach resulted in creation of assets which were unviable and not always accessible, *viz.*, shops, schools, hospitals, *etc.* The schemes in fact benefited the non-tribal residents in the tribal areas due to their greater clout! Most programmes also followed the western mode of development and prescribed infrastructure which could not be handled by the tribal people. The 'one-step-at-a-time' principle was not followed!

The desired orientation and the technical skills were not available to the tribal people. An example is the land allocation scheme for tribals for loans for specific purposes. The tribal people have little understanding of the complicated legal procedures required for obtaining these assets. They also do not have the commercial expertise to make them financially viable! This makes them fall prey to the traders, money-lenders and petty Government officials who exploit them and divert the benefits to themselves. This has resulted in much loss of tribal land which by law, cannot be alienated.

If tribal economic development is to be a reality, then the forests have to be rejuvenated. If the forestry development model is followed, there is no relationship between the tribal community and the forests, as input-output considerations predominate. Slow-growing indigenous species will be replaced by fast-growing foreign species like eucalyptus which has a disastrous effect on other trees, shrubs, birds and animals. This capital-intensive process will alienate the tribal people and destroy much of what is left of their economy and sustenance. With the present low level skills, a tribal adult may not be easily employable in cities and factories even if they migrate. Thus, it is imperative that forests have to be rejuvenated on the community forest development model. Based on experiments conducted by Bharatiya Agro Industries Foundation in Gujarat and Maharashtra, Chattisgarh Bana Sevagram Parishad in Madhya Pradesh, Bhagavatulla Charitable Trust in Andhra Pradesh, MYRADA in Karnataka and Tamil Nadu, Gram Vikas in Karnataka and Orissa, the community-forest development model has been formulated.

Issues in Forest Development

The decision to plant various species of trees should be left to the tribal people as they alone can sustain the forests and guard them. This could be done under the supervision of an NGO with technical assistance from the Forest Department. Thus, technical support for the people's decisions would enable community participation in forest management rather than reducing the tribal people into daily-wage labourers for the Forest Department and implement strategies over which they have no control. It is interesting to note that tribal men prefer fruit and timber trees for the income-generating abilities while women want more fodder and fuel species apart from MFP varieties like mahua, mango and jack fruit. An illustrative list for Orissa is set out at Annexure 21.1. The species may vary from region to region depending upon the needs of the tribal communities. This creates a vested interest among tribals in reviving the forest and constructive dependence on forests. These forests must be an integral part of the tribal ecosystem which can be tapped on a sustainable basis without destroying the forests. Once the base for community-oriented forest-based economy is laid for sustainable development, there is a need for reformulating some basic concepts:

(i) Minor Forest Produce

This is the mainstay of the tribal economy along with subsistence agriculture. The right of the tribal people over the minor forest produce has been diluted due to the high-value now given to the minor forest produce rather than in the subsistence economy of yesteryears. The consumption pattern of tribals, due to exposure to radio/television, *etc.*, has undergone changes and there is now need of cash rather than the simple barter economy. The main source of cash income for the tribal people is minor forest produce which has been increasing with the diversification of their wants. Simultaneously, the value of minor forest produce has also appreciated in the outside markets. In some cases, there are situations of competing end-use like that for mahua flower. On the other hand, minor forest produce has also come to be looked upon as a source of revenue to the State with the introduction of royalty, the right of the tribal is being questioned or is being circumscribed strictly to *'bona fide domestic use'*. The price payable to the tribal is computed in terms of his labour input, sometimes even ignoring the 'cost' of transportation because of variation in distance. This renders collection of minor forest produce in the far-off areas, uneconomical.

This situation is a direct result of non-appreciation of change in the tribal economy. It is presumed that the tribals continue to live in a pre-monetised subsistence economy. The introduction of contractors in the working of forest has consolidated the ownership of the State on these resources; the tribals' right first came to be violated by these new elements, they were questioned subsequently and nullified finally. This situation has been corrected in some States by taking a policy decision to ensure full return of the minor forest produce to the tribal removing the incidence of royalty and sometimes even the operational costs. There is a consensus at the national level on this issue but it remains to be operationalised in the field. This single step will help the tribal economy substantially since it will give direct benefit to the individual tribal who is himself engaged in that economic activity. It is, therefore, necessary that the minor forest produce is not viewed as a source of State income but as an element which can be utilised to provide a sound economic-base to the tribal economy, particularly during the period of transition.

Once this concept is accepted, certain other aspects of minor forest produce will also need attention. So far, the tribals have been passive participants in the production of minor forest produce coming on the scene at the collection time. The existing potential of minor forest produce is sometimes over-exploited. There is no clearly-defined place for these items in the new forestry plantation programme. A positive policy should be evolved for this purpose with active participation of the tribal people so that they gradually become growers of minor forest produce rather than remaining merely collectors. This will help in bringing about a structural change in the economy over a period of time, balancing the interests of the tribal economy and the forest economy.

(ii) Limited Ownership and Right of Usufruct

The next crucial issue is that of divergent claims and differing perceptions about the ownership of forest resources. The Forest Department tends to view the tribal people as intruders and encroachers; the tribal people visualise the forest department and the contractor as competitors in the exploitation of forests, which they feel belong to them. The pressure on forest resources continues unabated, while little effort is made to take the tribal people into confidence and try to persuade them to become tenderers of trees and to take to scientific exploitation. Even in those areas where tribals found themselves as individual owners of sizeable forest wealth, no attempt has been made to induce scientific management. In due course, that valuable asset was lost, leaving the land without tree-cover.

It will be impossible to contain the pressure on the forest unless the tribals are encouraged to participate in the tree plantation and strengthening their economy. In this case, the objectives will have to be clearly defined. Today, conflict arises because there are only two mutually-exclusive situations, *viz.*, either there is a departmentally-managed forest in which even the rights are considered as burden, or in the alternative, the tribals somehow get hold of forest land, clear-fell it and take to cultivation irrespective of the quality of land or the yield which they may get. At the subsistence level of their economy, they are satisfied with whatever they can get from it and in their narrow arithmetical computation, they are net gainers. It is clear that the final objective of forest management has to be a better and extensive tree-cover despite commercialisation of forestry operations. The sub-marginal lands, which should be brought under tree cover even for restoring the ecological balance, are extensive. No effort of whatever dimension is too big if forest rejuvenation is to be achieved. Financial resources are not the only limiting factor. There has to be genuine involvement of the people. There is no reason why the tribals, who are part of forests and who can be easily take to plantation activity, should not be fully associated in this task. They can be brought into this programme by giving them limited ownership rights on the trees they help to grow with the condition that they will accept necessary technical advice for their maintenance and future use.

(iii) Casual Wage-Labour and Tribal Development

One of the important reasons for a comprehensive development programme, taking all aspects into consideration not emerging so far has been that mere provision of even casual wage employment in forestry operations has been treated as a measure of tribal development. This aspect needs to be analysed in some depth. It is true that a bulk of the investment in forestry programmes goes towards wage-labour. But here employment is largely casual and the individual tribal is not sure either the quantum of employment or its periodicity. Even accrual of additional income to the local community is subject to the overall labour position in the regions. In fact, it is incidental to the forestry development programme. It has no element for strengthening the tribal economy in the long run. Sometimes this approach is adopted even in plantation programmes taken up as a part of tribal development schemes; the tribal gets the minimal wage for the work done while the permanent asset becomes the property of the State!

The basic objective of a tribal development programme is to make each family economically viable with a clearly defined time frame. Therefore, a programme can be deemed to be a tribal development programme only if it strengthens the tribal economy on a permanent basis. The financial support of the State to the tribals, in this case, has to be used for converting their labour into assets which are under their own command.

(iv) Forest Labour

The next question is about the special position of forest labour in our national economic scene. Forestry is one of the few organised activities where labour is entirely casual and disorganised. It is an irony that a group of people, who consider themselves to be rightful owners of the entire resource-base in these areas, have almost no rights even when they are employed to work the same resources. In the forestry sector, on the other hand, as the State has emerged as an unquestioned owner of the resource-base and the participant labour is backward and largely dispersed, it has no benefit either as a participant in management or in getting a share in the value-addition arising from the new economic activity. In any scheme of working of forests, the local tribal community which provides the labour, should be accepted as a partner in the management and sharing of profits. If this concept is accepted, a healthy partnership can develop in the working and management of forestry resources in the tribal areas, tribal development and forestry development programmes reinforcing each other.

Restoring Forests

The future of the tribal people lies in restoring the degraded forest lands with appropriate technology and with the participation of the tribal people. The degraded forest lands have been caused by, extensive felling of trees by tribal people in collusion with contractors, char-coal making, over-grazing, firewood and fodder requirements of tribals and small timber felling for hunting. This is due to poverty of the tribal people which ultimately leads to environmental degradation and degradation of forest lands and this led to the tribal people resort to migration. Therefore it is necessary to address the tribal problems holistically.

The restoration of degraded forest land, ensures sustained employment round the year and improves the environment. The tribal people are able to secure employment both in the secondary and tertiary sectors at their doorsteps. About 500 forest-supported industries can be set up as per the Anthropological Survey of India. The gradual extinction of bamboo, dusdhi, khair and other trees have contributed to the extinction of a large number of local arts and crafts. The process of degradation varies from area to area and can never be the same everywhere. This means that diverse technology packages have to be drawn up for restoring the degraded forest lands. This leads us to the conclusion that micro-technology packages are required for restoring the forests in various areas. It must be remembered that till a century ago, these forests were productive as they were scientifically managed and they can be nurtured back into health. The appropriate technology package has to take into account the soil, water and climatic conditions as also the bio-mass quality.

The 'one-size-fits-all' policy for restoration of degraded forests is clearly not going to work. Another fake belief which needs to be laid to rest is the one which states that if man and his grazing animals leave the forests untouched, the forests will return to their primitive glory. This is against all known facts. A carefully-planned and implemented strategy alone can regenerate forests! Several preparatory exercises need to be undertaken such as:

(i) land evaluation and preparation of forest maps,
(ii) determination of rights, privileges, concessions and practices by the Revenue Department and the people needs to be intimated,
(iii) conflict resolution system, preferably by tribal/village councils,
(iv) land capability classification,
(v) ecological evaluation of existing vegetation and what could be planted,
(vi) grazing pressure and fire hazards, and
(vii) social evaluation of people's activities.

Restoration of degraded forest lands is not only re-establishing a tree coverage but also helping tribals in earning livlihood besides restoring flora and fauna and ecological balance.

The technology should be environmentally sound, socially acceptable by the tribal people and should lead to sustainable productivity. Other factors to be considered are:

(i) Progressively increasing production and productivity
(ii) Soil and moisture conservation and minimising water loss
(iii) Optimum use of land with dense planting
(iv) Locally available materials for mulching
(v) Cost-effective technologies.

The obvious answer is Community Based Forestry Programmes (CBFP) or Joint Forest Management (JFM) programmes as they are being implemented in India.

PROMOTING SUSTAINABLE FORESTS

If the tribal people are to be involved in forest protection and nurturing of forests, the process of promoting forests must be a tribal-friendly one and easily implementable by the local people and the NGOs. Collective action is possible for Joint Forest Management only if the tribal people are involved by the NGOs from the planning stages itself. The NGOs who are implementing the programme should have appropriate institutional capability and suitable operational procedures leading to successful implementation. The major factors are:

(i) Ensuring Tribal Participation and Action
(ii) Building up Tribal Capability
(iii) Improving Capacity Building of the Implementing Agencies.

These factors need to be studied in detail.

(i) Ensuring Tribal Participation and Action

This is an essential condition and requires much preparatory work if the tribal communities are to be involved from the planning stages and be involved in the entire exercise. The various factors involved are:

- (a) *Recognition of Rights.* The tribal people should have secure, stable and exclusive rights over the resources they are expected to nurture and guard. The extent of rights and their ramifications should be transparent and made known before the project is initiated.
- (b) *Responsibilities of Tribals.* The extent of involvement of various groups of tribals will vary from village to village and can vary from regulation of access to complete responsibility for resource use, regeneration and sustainable management. Responsibilities could also be shared between groups of tribals and NGOs, depending upon local conditions and capacity, benefits and costs, risks involved and the assistance provided.
- (c) *Linking Appropriate Rights and Responsibilities.* Instead of fixed options, it would be ideal to link responsibilities to the rights and duties performed by individual tribal groups as these can vary and will encourage communities to take greater responsibilities. The process is demand-driven and an effective control instrument.
- (d) *Market Motivation.* Tribal communities could benefit from project implementation depending upon the market factors such as market regulations, community rights, knowledge of marketing practices and technical aspects. NGOs or Government agencies should improve market effectiveness by developing market information systems, strengthening market regulations, enhancing marketing capability, building appropriate infrastructural and institutional supports and ensuring coordination among all agencies for market effectiveness.
- (e) *Incentives.* Regulated use could lead to immediate loss in product availability or cause disproportionate impact on marginal sections. This loss would have to be balanced in the short run, by additional incentives to make direct or indirect benefits from regulated use. The beneficial effects of the regulated use will become visible when local scarcity is avoided in the short term and the regenerated forests used in the long term.

(ii) Building up Tribal Capability

Once these preparatory works are taken up, the capacity and capability of the tribal people to handle the projects from the planning stages to successful implementation, has to be built up very carefully so that the tribal perception of project and its benefits to be clear.

(a) *Improving Organising Systems.* The formal implementation framework and procedural norms which will guide the operation of the forest regeneration project, has to be well-defined and structured. The organisation of tribal communities should be on the basis of social and territorial relationships rather than on political or administrative divisions.

(b) *Bond-strengthening.* Various ground-level realities should be taken into account, especially those which could weaken the united tribal community effort at regenerating the forests. Elite domination and social inequalities rooted in socio-economic traditions and other factors due to mode of operations of rural development programmes over the decades, could wreck the programme.

(c) *Broad-based Participation.* Equitable participation of the poorer and marginal sections including women, must participate in the project. Socio-economic factors should not come in the way of participation of the entire village/s, taking into account local factors.

(d) *Conflict Management Resolution.* As far as possible, all conflicts should be resolved locally and conflict resolution should be done by the tribal communities themselves.

(e) *Enforcing Regulatory Action.* The diverse regulatory mechanisms used by various tribal communities could be used as per local circumstances. The regulatory mechanisms which could lead to economically rational use of scarce resources, could be promoted through user fees and other such cost-inducing mechanisms.

(iii) Improving Capacity-Building of Implementing Agencies

The technological capabilities as also project implementation capacity of the implementing units like NGOs or Government organisations, have to be built up.

(a) *Appropriate Learning Environment.* Field-level decisions should be left to the implementing units as responsibility for implementation of the programme depends upon them. Tier-based responsibilities for resource management with overlapping responsibilities should be avoided and innovation and experimentation should be encouraged by gradually delegating decision-making powers, tolerating genuine mistakes and appreciating achievements as this will lead to growth of knowledge and skills within the organisation.

(b) *Developing Participatory Learning Skills.* A regular system of mutual sharing and learning and non-conventional organisations help in learning within the organisation, with appropriate vertical and horizontal linkages.

(c) *Collaborative Learning.* Collaboration between the core implementation function and specialised functions such as research, training, monitoring and policy-formulation is essential for forestry regeneration projects. Periodical monitoring and network building is necessary.

(d) *Competence Building.* Learner-centered programmes are more effective in building competency levels in these organisations with emphasis on experience-sharing, means of distant education and using training strategies to facilitate learning.

(e) *Motivating Better Performance.* Incentives for good performance are a must and sincere and consistent performance needs reinforcement by incentives and recognition. Monetary and other material benefits are the best encouragement.

Implementation of JFM or CBFP

The success of the Joint Forest Management (JFM) process depends upon:

(a) nature of available resources
(b) involvement and community strength
(c) Government policy and intervention.

The problem areas are:

(i) Poor management skills or traditions
(ii) Divisions in tribal society due to fractionalism, class or religion
(iii) Profitability of migration and mobility during stress conditions
(iv) Market forces integrating village and urban economies
(v) Dependency of poor on village elite and petty bureaucrats.

Table 21.1
Area under JFM

(sq. km.)

Sl. No.	*State/UT*	*Forest cover*	*Area under JFM*	*Percentage of forest cover*
1.	Madhya Pradesh	1,31,195	38,468	29.3
2.	Andhra Pradesh	43,290	15,243	35.2
3.	Orissa	46,941	11,098	23.6
4.	Bihar	26,524	7,192	27.1
5.	West Bengal	8,349	4,483	53.8
6.	Rajasthan	13,353	1,857	13.9
7.	Karnataka	32,403	814	2.5
8.	Gujarat	12,578	692	5.5
9.	Haryana	604	578	95.7
10.	Tamil Nadu	17,064	458	2.7
11.	Uttar Pradesh	33,994	189	0.6
12.	Jammu & Kashmir	20,440	141	0.7
13.	Himachal Pradesh	12,521	60	0.5
14.	Kerala	10,334	20	0.2
	Total	4,09,590	81,293	19.8

Source: Compiled from data available with Conservator of Forests, various States.

The area under JFM is too low and needs to be encouraged further.

Improving the Implementation Process

An extensive implementation process is needed with 10-15 tribal communities being looked after by a staff-member of the NGO/implementing unit. Efforts should be initiated in all clustered tribal communities and not only in selective areas which are easily approached by road. The process of project implementation has been divided into four phases and each phase divided into steps. Each phase has a distinct purpose and the move into the next phase is made only when the objective is achieved:

(i) Preparatory phase.
(ii) Mobilisation phase.
(iii) Formalisation phase.
(iv) Implementation phase.

Monitoring of implementation is taken up during the last phase and the regulatory systems have to be properly understood by the tribal people. The impact of these measures will be measured by the motivational levels of the implementing tribal communities. Besides community responses, it is necessary to monitor resource management.

(i) Preparatory Phase

Preliminary and basic data is collected and an assessment made of forest resource conditions, various pressures, local conditions and past efforts. Based on this data, a strategy for each community is decided.

(ii) Mobilisation Phase

In every tribal community, collective action is mobilised after a better understanding of local issues and problems. Forest degradation issues are discussed and the tribal people sensitised as regards their role, including women. Collective regulation is ensured and conflict management measures initiated.

(iii) Formalisation Phase

Formal agreements are prepared with the tribal communities for resource management. Appropriate goals, selection of forest regeneration methods and management options are set. Market support as also technical and management support is also given.

(iv) Implementation Phase

The tribal communities are provided appropriate resources as per the resource management agreement taking into account various incentives for successful implementation. An activity schedule is developed where responsibilities of the tribal communities and NGOs/government agencies are set out. Supply deficiences are made good through common or private property resources.

Various State Governments have implemented the Joint Forest Management system. A copy of the revised order of the Government of Rajasthan dated 10 May 1999, is set out at Annexure 21.2.

ANNEXURE 21.1

Community Forest Tree Species Identified

I. *Food*—Amla, Baheda, Barkali, Bela, Buro, Chahar, Danas, Dumer, Errin, Guava, Jackfruit, Jamun, Cashew, Kendu, Khajur, Kusum, Kuili, Leendee, Lime, Mahua, Mahal, Mango, Munga, Orange, Pijuli, Pipal, Sitaphal, Tamarind, Telet, Tulkali.

II. *Fodder*—Baba, Bamboo, Bansula, Bareda, Borkali, Borea, Buta, Ghatto, Khaiuse, Kilataka, Ombeda, Pipal, Rai, Subabul, Sial, Tasks.

III. *Fuel*—Amla, Baheda, Bija, Dhankra, Dhaura, Falsa, Hadan, Haldu, Jahaj, Jambo, Kashi Kakehua, Katechua, Kakla, Khaira, Kendu, Kenthual, Khaiuse, Kuss, Lee, Leondh, Mahua, Mango, Mode, Navrangi, Packo, Pagan, Piasal, Pirinji, Sal, Sanguan, Saragee, Saj, Sahaji, Siela, Siso, Sajana, Tagan.

IV. *Small Timber*—Asan, Bharma, Bija, Dhaura, Gambha, Hadan, Haldu, Jambhari, Kadam, Kaila, Karanja, Karuna, Kendu, Kha, Khair, Maisal, Mode, Piasal, Priya, Sahaj, Sangwan, Sal, Sishoo, Tagar, Teak.

V. *Housing*—Arjun, Bandhan, Bamboo, Bija, Bijasal, Chandan, Gamari, Hadan, Haldu, Jhapa-lana, Kashi, Kaso, Kerla, Khaiuso, Kuss, Kuruma, Lajore, Mahua, Mud, Neem, Packo, Piasala, Sal, Sagwan, Sahai, Sayan, Sena, Shaj, Siddha, Sisoo, Tagari, Tangiri.

VI. *Medicine*—Amla, Ambula, Amla, Araki, Arjun, Baheda, Barun, Batrasen, Beheeta, Bheru, Bhuhian, Chetralsori, Gamari, Garuda, Handa, Harida, Hawada, Kalia, Kha, Khumanda, Karajo, Kusum, Mahesinelu, Masanidula, Meena, Neem, Pamaize, Panain, Patalas, Pipal, Potela, Suwari.

VII. *Green Manure*—Asan, Babe, Bamboo, Bara, Charkunda, Sat Sial

VIII. *Other Needs*—Alia, Apple, Bamboo, Barnula, Barkali, Bora, Banjan, Bet, Bhahua, Bordi, Chinar, Charkunda, Kendu, Krishna, Neem, Pipal, Sial, Simuli, Sumari, Tetal, Timber.

ANNEXURE 21.2

Rajasthan Government Order

No. F-7(39)/Van/90 Dated: May 10, 1999

Subject: A scheme for mobilising support of village communities and voluntary agencies for rehabilitating barren and degraded forest lands.

India's National Forest Policy envisages participation of local people and non-governmental or voluntary agencies in protection and management of forests. This objective can be achieved by adopting a scheme of Joint Forest Management (JFM). To this effect, the state government had earlier issued the even numbered orders dated March 15, 1991 and March 20, 1997, which aimed at seeking participation of villagers and voluntary agencies in greening of barren and degraded forest lands. In order to get over the practical difficulties in implementation of the aforementioned orders, the government has decided to amend these orders as under, insofar as these relate to constitution and running of Village Forest Protection and Management Committees (VFPMCs) formed under Sections 28, 80 and 81 of the Rajasthan Forest Act, 1953.

The guidelines of JFM are based on the principle that the village communities are eager to participate in protection and management of forests and forest lands, because their livelihood directly depends upon proper management of these resources. These guidelines also propose many kinds of incentives to the VFPMCs. Such incentives include provision for share of the VFPMCs in the intermediate and final yield of forest produce from forest lands managed under joint efforts of the department and the local communities. In addition, the guidelines have been prepared so as to seek cooperation and participation of NGOs, cooperative societies and the *panchayat* in conservation and management of forest resources. Not only this, the department would welcome the cooperation of any other voluntary agency in protection and development of forests provided they do not wish to stake any claim from forest products. In fact, any contribution being offered, without any profit or share in lieu, should at once be accepted so that the JFM should become a wider effort at community level.

The guidelines are issued in the spirit that the practice of JFM should emerge as a public movement to protect and develop the forest resources of the state and that the forest department (FD) should accept every opportunity offered by such a movement.

The constitution and running of VFPMCs shall in future follow these guidelines;

1. *The Agency and Procedure for Work Execution*
   (*i*) In order to ensure active participation of the local communities, Tree Growers' Cooperative Societies (TGCSs) and VFPMCs will be entrusted with responsibilities of protection, development and management of a piece of degraded or barren forest land and other government wasteland that has been made available to the forest department for the purpose of management. All such lands will henceforth be referred to as 'forest lands' in the rest of this order. Where such VFPMCs or TGCSs do not exist, these will be constituted

by the department with the help of other NGOs and Voluntary agencies working in the area.

(ii) To the extent possible, it will be ensured that the piece of land so made available falls within the cadastral limits of a single village, so that the village will form a unit. The land shall be made available only to the committee or society constituted by the people of that village, or of a village located nearby. The committee or society will not have any or ownership rights on that land.

(iii) The committee or society will manage the piece of land in accordance with a prescribed management plan prepared by the local officers of the department in consultation with the members of the concerned committee or society through micro-planning process. Needs of the local people shall be taken into account while selecting species to be incorporated into such plans.

(iv) NGOs and VAs working in the area, will help in establishing and maintaining coordination between the committee/society and the departmental officers. The NGOs or VAs will only act as a catalyst to ensure sustainability of the JFM programme. They will not be entitled to any share in the produce from jointly-managed forest areas.

2. ***Constitution of VFPMCs***

(i) It shall be the endeavour of the department to constitute a VFPMC in each revenue village. Every family normally residing within the limits of that village and being entitled to the usufrust of natural resources falling within the boundary of that village shall have the right of being a member of the VFPMC.

(ii) As far as possible, there shall be a separate VFPMC for each village. However, under special circumstances—such as when a watershed area extends to two or more villages, or when a number of villages have traditionally been exercising rights on a given piece of land—a joint VFPMC of two or more villages can be formed. Similarly, in tribal areas the individual *phala* or *dhani* or in the command area of the Indira Gandhi *Nahar Pariyojana,* the individual *chak,* may form the basis of constitution of VFPMCs provided that all the people in the village agree, by consensus, to do so. In these orders the word 'village' will henceforth mean to include any of the aforementioned units.

3. ***Membership of VFPMC's***

(i) Two adult members, at least one of them being female, from each family residing within the revenue boundaries of the concerned village will be entitled to become members of the general body of the VFPMC. The Range Forest Officer or Forest Extension Officer (henceforth referred to as RFO) of the area will make a list of the willing persons with the help of the *panchayat* concerned or the NGOs or VAs active in the area. The RFO will invite, in written, the NGOs or VAs for help and cooperation. He will call a meeting of willing members, in which the quorum shall not be less than 40 per cent of the eligible persons in that village, and will obtain their consent for formation of the VFPMC. The RFO will then send the list of the members to the concerned Deputy Conservator of Forests or Divisional Forest Officer (henceforth referred to as DCF) who shall scrutinise and review the proposals and shall normally decide within

a period of three months whether to register the VFPMC or to reject it. In the scheduled tribal areas of the state, the VFPMC should be representative of the concerned gram sabha. In other words, the VFPMC should reflect stakes and opinions of all the people living within its jurisdiction.

(ii) The VFPMC shall prescribe on its own the procedure for removal or admission of old and new members, and whenever new members are admitted or existing ones are removed, it shall inform the DCF (the registering authority) of such changes, along with the list of removed and admitted, through the RFO concerned so as to enable the DCF to update his records.

4. ***Advisory Sub-Committee of Women***

(i) In addition to the VFPMC, each village shall have a *Women's Advisory Sub-committee* (WAS). It shall have not less than seven women from the village as its members who will, from among themselves, elect a chairperson. This subcommittee will contact the womenfolk of the village and present their problems in meetings of the executive of the VFPMC. The concerned Forester or Assistant Forester or Forest Guard (henceforth referred to as Forester) shall be responsible for ensuring that the WAS meets regularly to discuss women's problems and suggest solutions. He shall also present the decisions and recommendations of this subcommittee for consideration of the Executive. The Executive of the VFPMC shall give due consideration to the proposals of the subcommittee.

5. ***Constitution of Executive***

(i) The VFPMC shall elect, in a general body meeting (GBM) of its members, an Executive Committee (henceforth referred to as "the Executive") comprising of no more than 11 members. The required quorum for such a GBM shall be 40 per cent. The executive shall have at least one member each from the Scheduled Castes (SC) and Scheduled Tribes (ST) where the percentage of population of each of these groups is 10 per cent or more. Where the percentage of SC and ST populations combined is 15 per cent or less, at least one member from the SC or the ST shall be elected to the executive. The executive must have at least three women members. At least one member shall be elected from the landless. The RFO shall act as the election officer for election of the executive members.

(ii) The members of the executive shall elect, from among themselves, a Chairman, a Vice-Chairman and a Treasurer. In addition to the elected members of the executive, the *sarpanch* or *wardpanch* belonging to the village shall also be opted as a non-voting ex-officio member of the executive. The Forester shall be the ex-officio secretary of the executive but he shall not have voting power. The Chairperson of the WAS shall be a voting member of the Executive.

(iii) The executive may, of its own choice, opt a representative of an NGO or VA working in the area, as one of its non-voting members.

(iv) The tenure of the executive shall be of two years. It shall be reconstituted after expiry of its term. During reconstitution, it shall, have an elected member as its secretary in lieu of the Forester as its ex-officio secretary. The VFPMCs that have been constituted prior

shall be reconstituted under the provisions of this order. Even if an elected member is appointed as secretary of the executive, the Forester shall still be an ex-officio member of the executive.

6. ***Working of VFPMC***
   (i) *Meetings.* The VFPMC must hold at least two general body meetings in a year. The quorum for such meetings shall be 40 per cent. The Chairman or the Secretary may call a special meeting of the general body if it is so requested by at least one third of its members. The executive shall meet at least four times in a year, though more meetings can be held if so decided by the Chairman or the Secretary. The quorum for executive meetings shall be six members out of 11, at least one of them being a woman members. Special attention shall be paid to the suggestion made by women members in a meeting of the executive.
   (ii) *Duties of the Chairman and the Vice-Chairman.* The Chairman shall preside over the general body and executive meetings, and in his absence the Vice-Chairman shall discharge this duty. The Chairman shall also sign agreements and other documents on behalf of the VFPMC. In his absence the Vice-Chairman shall sign the documents. The Chairman and other members so nominated by the executive shall also act as representatives of the VFPMC and liaise with the various government departments and other institutions.
   (iii) *Duties of the Secretary.* The Secretary shall be responsible for convening meetings of the general body (at least two meetings in a year) and of the executive at least four meetings in a year). He shall record the proceedings of meetings and get these proceedings approved in subsequent meetings. He will also be responsible for handling paperwork and general correspondence of the VFPMC with the department, NGOs, and other agencies. He will help the VFPMC in drawing up microplans for development of pastures and other natural resources. He will also help establish liaison with other departments of the government. He will convene meetings of the Women's Advisory Sub-committee and record proceedings thereof and put up these proceedings in subsequent meetings of the executive.
   (iv) *Duties of the Treasurer.* He will maintain the accounts of the VFPMC and present these in meetings of the general body and the executive. The funds of the VFPMC shall be kept in a bank account in the nearest bank or post office. Whenever money is withdrawn from this account, after obtaining due authorisation of the executive, the Treasurer, the Secretary, and the Chairman shall jointly sign the cheque.
   (v) *Duties of the Sarpanch/Panch.* They shall help in maintaining liaison of the VFPMC with the *panchayat.*

7. ***Responsibilities of VFPMC***
   (i) The VFPMC shall work to protect forest and pasture lands which have been made available to it and raise plantations on such lands. This will be done after taking into account views of the people in general, and technical opinion of the departmental personnel, so that the *bonafide* needs of the people, such as of fodder, fuel and other non-timber forest produce, are met while conserving the resources for posterity.

(ii) The VFPMC shall evolve or prescribe or lay down rules for harvesting and sharing of forest produce, such as grass, leaves, fruits, lops, *etc.*, harvested from lands managed by it, including deciding amount of fee or levy to be charged, if any. Such rules shall be in agreement with the management plan adopted by it so that the harvesting of produce is sustainable.

(iii) The VFPMC shall strive to protect forests, forest lands, pasture lands, plantations and wildlife in its area of operation. It shall help protect such lands and resources from encroachment, grazing, lopping, theft of forest products, illicit mining and extraction, and forest fire, by informing and assisting the forest personnel.

(iv) The members of the VFPMC shall assist the forest personnel in arresting or prosecuting the offenders who damage or destroy forest plantations and forest resources. It shall prevent and help in preventing any act that is prohibited under the Rajasthan Forest Act 1953, the Wildlife (Protection) Act 1972, or rules made under any of these Acts.

(v) If any of the members of the VFPMC indulge in any act against the objectives of forest conservation or damage forests and plantations, the VFPMC, through its Executive or other members, shall inform the concerned RFO about such activities of such persons with a view to preventing these offences or prosecuting the offenders. The VFPMC shall ensure that none of its members misuse the benefits or conveniences offered by government. In case of such misuse, such persons can be punished with pecuniary fines in accordance with a procedure prescribed by the VFPMC in a consultative and consensual manner. Any fines received from such offenders shall be credited into the account of the VFPMC. In case of repeated misuses by a member, the VFPMC can expel such member on the basis of a majority decision of the Executive.

(vi) The VFPMC shall not be allowed to undertake any non-forestry activities in the forest land or wasteland made available to it. Activities such as agriculture, industry, residential construction, *etc.*, shall be totally prohibited.

(vii) The VFPMC shall prepare a plan for utilising the income received by it for replanting the existing area or raising a plantation on a new piece of land and/or for maintaining or improving the existing plantations or forest areas.

8. ***Responsibilities of the Departmental Officers***

(i) The DCFs in a district shall endeavour to constitute VFPMCs in as many villages as possible and nominate a departmental employee to act as secretary to each of these VFPMCs in their first constitution.

(ii) The officers and staff of the FD shall train the members of the VFPMCs in technical and managerial practices in raising of nurseries, tree planting, forest protection, biodiversity conservation, and maintenance of accounts and records. They shall help in improving skills of the members of the VFPMC so as to build their capacity for group action.

(iii) The departmental personnel shall extend active cooperation to the VFPMCs in protection of forests, selection of plantation sites and

microplanning for development of the forest resources falling within the jurisdiction of the VFPMC. The concerned DCF shall take into account the provisions of the Forest Conservation Act, 1980. The personnel of the department shall assist the VFPMC in implementing such management plans to the fullest.

(iv) Whenever the departmental personnel are informed, by the members of a VFPMC, of damage in plantations or forests, or possibility of such damage, they shall take immediate action in the matter.

(v) Cultural operations and harvesting operations in the areas under management of the VFPMC shall be carried out under supervision of the departmental officers or employees.

(vi) The DCF shall also be responsible to draft an action plan for raising a new plantation or protecting or maintaining existing plantations or forests with the investment of the funds earned by the VFPMC.

(vii) The department may allot funds or grants to a VFPMC for protection of the forest areas of plantations under its management, in which case the department itself shall not engage any cattle-guards for this purpose. The money allotted to the VFPMC for this purpose may also be spent on other developmental works in a village if the VFPMC has successfully ensured effective protection of the areas for which the grant was meant.

(viii) The departmental officers shall encourage the VFPMCs to undertake forestry developmental works under the *Janata Van Yojna* of the state governments. The VFPMC shall not be treated as a contractor while being entrusted with execution of these works.

(ix) The departmental officers or employees shall act as mediators in order to resolve conflicts and disputes, if any, arising in connection with the affairs of a VFPMC.

9. ***Responsibilities of NGOs or VAs***

(i) The NGOs or VAs in the area who are willing to play a role in the JFM programme of the state shall act to establish rapport and coordination between the VFPMC and the FD.

(ii) The NGOs or VAs shall act as a catalyst in formation of VFPMCs.

(iii) The NGOs or VAs shall assist in formulation of microplans and management plans.

(iv) The NGOs or VAs shall act to disseminate information among the general public about the policies and rules of the FD.

(v) The NGOs or VAs shall play the role of mediators in resolving disputes about sharing of forest produce among different sections of a VFPMC.

(vi) The NGOs or VAs shall be in touch with the villagers and shall convey problems and difficulties experienced by them to the departmental authorities.

10. ***The Joint Forest Management Plan***

(i) The Executive of the VFPMC shall prepare a Joint Forest Management Plan (JFM plan) in consultation with, and with the assistance of, the forest department's personnel, and the NGOs or VAs in the area. Such a plan shall be formulated in a participatory manner, ensuring participation of women and weaker sections of society, and shall be based on micro-planning. The plan shall take into account all the

important aspects of sustainable management of forest resources, such as sound silvicultural practices, effective soil and moisture conservation, and conservation of biodiversity.

(ii) The JFM plan so prepared by the Executive shall be placed before the general body of the VFPMC and discussed and approved therein. If any amendments or changes are recommended by the GBM, such changes shall be incorporated before the plan is approved by the DCF.

(iii) The approved plan shall form the basis of work to be executed in the land or forest area made available to the VFPMC for the purpose of management. Provisions of the working plan as regards that area shall remain suspended to that extent.

(iv) The above plan shall also incorporate provisions regarding sharing of produce and utilisation of generated funds. Such provisions shall be in accordance with the general spirit of this order.

(v) An agreement about management of the forest area made available to the VFPMC shall be executed between the DCF and the VFPMC. The format of this agreement shall be as enclosed with these orders.

11. Sharing of Produce from Forest Areas

1. *Produce Harvested Before Final Felling*

(i) The VFPMC shall be entitled to free nontimber forest produce harvested from the areas managed or protected by it. Such free produce shall include grass, leaves, *pala*, pods, fruits, flowers, seeds, dried or dead wood and branches, *munja, buhari, khas* and other produce to be removed in accordance with the provisions of the approved management plan. *Tendu* leaves and gum shall not form part of such free produce. The VFPMC shall frame rules for harvesting and sharing of these products and such rules may also provide for fees or levies which shall form a source of income to the VFPMC.

(ii) The following types of produce shall be available to the members of the VFPMC, only if the VFPMC has protected or managed the area after the agreement continuously for not less than five years.

(a) The produce removed from the area in course of cultural operations carried out in accordance with the prescriptions of the approved management plan, after deduction of the expenditure incurred by the department on the cultural operations.

(b) If the trees in the managed area are large enough to attract prescriptions of lopping laid down in the management plan, and the VFPMC decides to put such prescriptions into practice, the tree lops shall be available to the members of VFPMCs. Such lops should be distributed to the members on payment of a prescribed fee so that the VFPMC can earn some revenue from it.

(iii) All income earned out of the produce made available to the VFPMC shall be deposited in the account of the VFPMC.

2. *Produce at the Time of Final Felling*

(i) The crop in the managed areas shall be harvested on the basis of rotational felling or felling cycle as laid down in the approved management plan. Harvesting operations shall be carried out under supervision of the departmental officers. The felled produce, which

may consist of timber and bamboo, shall be divided into two categories.

(ii) In the first category will fall the tree logs, other than bamboo, having a girth (over bark) of 20 cm or less. This produce will be equally distributed as per recommendations of the VFPMC among its members under supervision of the forest officers.

(iii) In the second category will fall the tree logs with a girth (over bark) of more than 20 cm and all bamboo. This produce will be sold to the members of the VFPMCs at the rates prevalent in the market.

(iv) The produce which is surplus to the VFPMCs members' requirements, shall be auctioned in the open by the VFPMCs under supervision of the forest officers as per the FD's regulations. Alternatively, such produce may be sold to the general public on rates fixed according to the rules and regulations prevalent in the department.

3. *Division of Income*

(i) The income received from the intermediate yield or produce shall be used for the purpose of maintenance or protection of the forest area or plantation. Sometimes, this fund may also be used for small, contingent and urgent community works in the village.

(ii) Where a plantation has been raised by the VFPMCs and the expenses incurred on raising of that plantation have been met out of government funds, the income received from the final felling operation shall be divided into two equal parts. The first 50 per cent of its shall be deposited into the account of the VFPMCs and the remaining 50 per cent shall be remitted into the treasury as forest revenue. Of the amount credited into the VFPMCs account, 50 per cent shall be utilised in raising of new plantations on the same or different piece of land, or on maintenance and development of forests and existing plantations, and the remaining 50 per cent shall be utilised for other community development works as approved in GBM of the VFPMCs.

(iii) Where all expenses incurred on raising of a plantation have been borne by the VFPMCs itself, the income from the final felling operation shall be divided into two parts of 10 per cent and 90 per cent respectively. The first part (10 per cent) shall be credited into the treasury as forest revenue, and the second part (90 per cent) shall be credited into the account of the VFPMC. Of the amount credited into the VFPMCs account, 30 per cent shall be utilised for raising of new plantations on the same or different piece of land, or on maintenance and development of existing plantations or forest areas, and remaining 70 per cent shall be utilised for other works as approved in a GBM of the VFPMC.

(iv) Where the VFPMCs role has been limited to protection and management of a forest area only, the income received from the final felling operation shall be divided into two parts. The first 80 per cent of it shall be remitted into the treasury as forest revenue and the remaining 20 per cent shall be deposited into the VFPMC account. The VFPMC shall be free to use this money for any work as approved in its GBM.

(v) All the income which accrues to the VFPMC from time to time shall be deposited into its bank account. The VFPMC shall maintain

complete record of its income. All the record so maintained shall be open to the inspection of officers of the FD.

12. *Resolution of Disputes*
   (i) The Executive shall resolve disputes among the different members or groups of members of the VFPMC and where necessary it shall take assistance of the NGOs or VAs and the forest personnel working in the area. The decisions taken by a majority of members of the executive committee in the matter shall be final.
   (ii) Whenever there is a dispute between two or more VFPMCs or between a VFPMC and the *panchayat*, the RFO concerned shall act as a mediator or negotiator and help resolve such disputes or conflicts.
   (iii) In all such matters the appeal against decisions shall lie with the concerned DCF.

13. *Failure of a VFPMC to Act According to the Agreement*
   (i) A VFPMC shall have to sign an agreement with the department before a piece of forest land is made available to it for management or protection. If any member of the VFPMC acts in contravention of the provision contained in the agreement so signed, or in contravention of the guidelines generally laid down in this order, the VFPMC must with due process take action against such a member, including termination of his membership, and report the action taken to the DCF concerned.
   (ii) Whenever the VFPMC collectively violates any of the provisions of the signed agreement or the guidelines as generally laid down in this Order, the RFO concerned shall issue a notice to the VFPMC in the matter, calling for reasons why action should not be taken against it and advising it to stop such contravention in future. If despite having been served such notice twice, the VFPMC continues to fail to act in accordance with the provisions of the agreement, the RFO shall report the matter to the DCF concerned who shall enquire into the matter and take suitable steps to ensure compliance of the agreement by the VFPMC. If the VFPMC still continues to defy and fails to reform its attitude, the DCF shall be free to revoke the agreement. Consequent upon such revocation, the area entrusted to the VFPMC shall be taken over by the DCF who will arrange for its management as per the management plan.
   (iii) The VFPMC may, if it likes, appeal to the Conservator of Forests (CF) concerned in the matter of revocation by the DCF of the agreement. The decision of the CF in the matter shall be final and binding upon both the VFPMC and the department.

By Order

Sd/-

(S. Ahmed)

Secretary to the Government

Form of Agreement to be signed between a TSCS/VFPMC and the Department for development/Management of Forest Land

Signed this day .... of the month .... of the year .... between the Chairman of the Village Forest Protection & Management Committee .... (hereinafter known as the Committee) and the Deputy Conservator of Forests .... (hereinafter known as the Department) on behalf of the Governor of Rajasthan.

Whereas the following specified forest lands/government wastelands have been made available to the Committee for a period of .... years starting from date .... and ending on date .... for the purpose of managing/protecting/developing the said lands, namely:

1. District ....
2. Division ....
3. Range ....
4. Naka ....
5. Heat ....
6. Forest Block & Compartment/Khasra Nos. in case of wasteland other than forest land ....
7. Area (ha) ....
8. Boundaries:

   North ....

   South ....

   East ....

   West ....

The Committee shall work/manage the above lands in accordance with the provisions laid down in the government Order No. .... dated .... However, if the Committee fails to act in accordance with the provisions of the aforementioned order, action shall be taken against it according to Para 13 of the said order.

The Department in turn binds itself to act in accordance with the provisions of the aforementioned order.

Sd/	Sd/
On behalf of the Committee	On behalf of the Governor
Witness 1 ____________	Witness 1 ____________
____________	____________
____________	____________
Witness 2 ____________	Witness 2 ____________
____________	____________
____________	____________

CHAPTER XXII

Integrated Tribal Development: An Approach

SUMMING UP

Since 1947, various attempts to improve the lot of the tribal people, have met with very limited success. Despite Government efforts to aid the developmental projects, the lot of tribal areas and the tribal people have not changed. To ensure sustainable development and a healthy environment, the '4-A' approach of BAIF needs to be implemented:

(i) Anna (livelihood)
(ii) Akshar (literacy)
(iii) Arogya (health) and
(iv) Aacharan (moral values).

Thus increasing food production is as important as improving access to nutritious food at affordable costs. Production by masses deserves priority over mass production. Agricultural production techniques should be followed up by marketing and post-production activities, to ensure good returns for the tribal people. Development of entrepreneurship and empowerment of tribal women are very important tasks.

CAUSES FOR BACKWARDNESS

Majumdar and Madan in 'An Introduction to Social Anthropology' 1970 (Asian Publication House, Bombay) isolated 9 important economic traits among the tribal people, which are responsible for their dire economic status, as under:

(i) *Barter and exchange* is the basic economic relation rather than money which is used for dealing with non-tribal people. Banking outlets and credit from institutional sources are very rare. A more monetised economy is needed.

(ii) *Absence of Technology.* Poor quality of technology leads to insufficient, inadequate or even wasteful exploitation of natural resources and an economic surplus is rare in such a marginal economy.

(iii) *Poor Profit Motive.* Profit is not a motive which is replaced by a sense of duty and obligation, sharing and fellow-feeling.

(iv) *Cooperation.* The need for bonding, for cooperation and collective endeavour, is very strong among the tribal people.

(v) *Poor Innovation.* The rate of innovation, internal or induced, is very low and hence leads to poor progress.

(vi) *Market Forces Initiative.* The lack of competitiveness and monopoly or will to dominate, is absent and the nearest market is the weekly 'haat', where surpluses are sold and daily necessities are purchased.

(vii) *Poor Manufacturing Base.* The manufacture of consumer goods is common rather than capital goods and surplus is consumed rather than saved or is exchanged in trade.

(viii) *Specialisation.* This is based on specially acquired skills and technical activity and is virtually absent in tribal society except for gender-specific skills which are passed on from father to son or mother to daughter.

(ix) *Notion of Property.* Display of wealth for expenditure exists rather than accumulation of wealth in tribal societies. Ownership can be collective or individual.

These features of a primitive economy have led the tribal economy to relative backwardness when compared to the rural economy which is witnessing a boom and is speeding up. To bring about integrated development, some basic policy issues have to be tackled quickly.

BASIC ISSUES

Apart from enhanced public investment for development of agriculture and infrastructure in the region, certain policy initiatives are essential to ensure that the poor are benefitted from the development process. The poor are required to be empowered by way of land reforms, rationalising their access to natural resources and thereby enhancing their cash surplus and resulting in capital formation, which is essential for tribal involvement and participation in any development initiatives.

Specific policy measures suggested for integrated tribal development are:

1. Effective land reforms are needed for orderly agricultural development. In the hilly regions dominated by tribals, the

non-forest revenue lands affected by shifting cultivation, upto 30 per cent slope may be given to tribals on ownership basis.

2. Usufructory rights of the poor on common natural resources, viz., Tree Patta Scheme, preferential leasing of water bodies to local poor for fisheries, plantations of various crops taken up by Government Departments on Government lands can be handed over to local communities/individual poor households for management and maintenance.
3. Minor Forest Produce collection is a major source of income to the poorest in the region, which can be used as a targeted programme for increasing their income in the quickest possible time, with least leakage and with minimum investments. Government policy of maximising revenues from forest resources should be replaced with a policy of "treating minor forest produce collection by the poor as a means of their economic upliftment". For example, tendu leaf collectors in tribal regions earn on an average Rs. 1,500 per household from kendu leaf collection, while by sharing 50 per cent of the surplus going to Government as royalty to the tribal collectors, it could be doubled to Rs. 3,000 per household per annum.
4. Value-addition to minor forest products and agriculture products should be made mandatory at the primary and local level, which can at least triple the income at primary level and provides employment for 3–4 months during the lean season. Current policy on MFP discourages value-addition at primary level as they are leased out on monopoly basis (*e.g.*, allowing locals to make hill broom triples the income compared to selling the grass to Government organisations). Monopoly leasing of forest product should be replaced with a policy of encouraging local communities to collect, process and market, where the Government or Private agencies can provide market support.
5. As irrigation can provide a quick boost to the agricultural economy, emphasis should be on development of minor and medium irrigation and water harvesting structures (check dams, mundas and katas, diversion weirs, *etc.*) on a watershed basis. For effective use of irrigation infrastructure, their management should be delegated to the users through "Water Users' Societies", the Government playing the role of facilitator only (*e.g.*, Andhra Pradesh experiment).
6. Ground water exploitation in tribal regions is limited because of high frequency of failed wells due to the hard rocky soil. A comprehensive insurance policy on failed wells/bore wells is essential for exploitation of the ground water resources in tribal regions.
7. Livestock being the major source of draught power to the people in remote places, improvement of livestock for draught power

should be taken up on priority basis. Alternatively, dual purpose breeds need to be encouraged rather than the present policy of breed improvement for only milch animals.

8. Focus on small animal development (Goat, Sheep, Pigs, *etc.*) can yield quick income to the poor, in spite of the geographical limitations of the tribal regions, rather than the present focus on milch animals, which face the problem of marketing.
9. Watershed development as a strategy for soil and moisture conservation for increasing productivity of rainfed and hill agriculture has been implemented by Government machinery. Its sustainability and effectiveness are limited due to poor people's participation. Alternatively, KFW model of development successful in Maharashtra needs to be promoted, where usufructory rights on common resources is available to village committee.
10. Command Area Development in the newly-created irrigation commands including RIDF-funded projects, need to be taken on priority basis, lest the intended benefits are not realised.
11. Government should consider subsidising energisation cost of pumpsets in tribal regions by renewing REC funding or through alternate mechanism, which might defy the economic viability logic of the World Bank's recommendation to reduce subsidies. Better targetting of subsidies is needed.
12. Special Area Development projects need to be initiated in tribal regions, which have a unique competitive advantage (for example, cotton, maize, sunflower, spices, medicinal plants, off-season vegetables, citrus, *etc.*) Besides technology and input supply, these projects should ensure backward and forward linkages (Post-harvest technology, improved seeds, marketing *etc.*).
13. Low productivity constraint of various crops (due to non-use of fertilisers and pesticides) in tribal regions should be converted into advantage by promoting the same as "organically produced or green produce" with systematic exploitation of their export potentials.
14. Non-Farm Sector, including tiny and household sector, handlooms and handicrafts need focussed thrust in tribal regions which are highly labour-intensive and low in capital requirements. (handlooms, gem stone polishing, fruit and MFP processing, *etc.*)
15. Population being sparse and dispersed in tribal regions, providing social and commercial infrastructure may not be economically viable; hence consolidation of dwellings near irrigated areas, could be an alternative, depending on forest regeneration efforts.
16. Alternative models of development through involvement of corporate sector (contractual farming) needs to be explored. As contractual farming system involves transfer of technology, input supply with corporate intervention, Government assistance

available under various schemes implemented by various developmental departments should be channelised through a single window system in coordination with the promoters, *i.e.,* NGO, corporate body or the banks.

Special funds like "Technology Transfer Fund" and "Risk Fund" may be created to support the corporate sector in popularising the contractual farming system.

"Contractual Farming Societies (CFS)" being multipurpose societies promoted by corporates under Contractual Farming System, they should be treated as equivalent to PACS/LAMP in the area of operation and allowed to obtain credit from Cooperative Banks. CFS activities being specific to the activity taken up, overlapping of areas of operation of PACS/LAMP and CFS should be allowed, for which necessary amendment should be made in State Cooperative Acts.

17. Rural financial institutions operating in tribal districts are burdened with huge accumulated losses, inspite of the improvement shown during the last few years. Recapitalisation programmes of RRBs are constrained by non-release of funds from State Governments and Sponsor Banks. Cooperative institutions (CCBs, LAMPS and LDBs), whose reach to the poor is unparalleled by CBs or RRBs in tribal regions, need recapitalisation and restructuring on priority basis, with assistance from Central or State Governments.
18. Besides the various policy initiatives suggested, political will is the crucial element in development of tribal areas. Extremely poverty-stricken tribal areas need bold initiatives like special treatment for tribal people in Government recruitment, special educational institutions and redirecting of the public investment flow to tribal areas from comparatively more developed areas.
19. Education of tribal children is necessary if literacy rates among tribal people (17.8 per cent for men and 7.8 per cent among women) are to improve. School drop-out rates are high in spite of free education facilities including hostels, indicating that changes are required in the basic education policy. More vocational education courses are required.
20. Transportation and poor communication facilities (especially telephones) in almost all tribal areas, are very poor compared to the developed areas. The infrastructure is poor and needs to be improved upon.

INTEGRATED DEVELOPMENT: SOME SUGGESTIONS

The tribal family is a unit of both production and consumption and the tribal community is itself a large cooperative unit with families being economically interdependent. Distribution is generally by gift or ceremonial exchange.

A vast chunk of the tribal population of the country is living in remote and hilly areas. The natural isolation has deprived them of the fruits of development on the one hand and on the other, they are far behind the mainstream on social, cultural and economic fronts. Their problems are mainly due to ignorance, illiteracy, rigid adherence to traditional beliefs, poverty, adverse terrain and lack of communications. All these combine to encourage the traders/middlemen to exploit the tribals. What is surprising is that despite the frauds perpetuated by some unscrupulous traders/middlemen in purchasing their goods at very low prices and charging higher rates for the goods sold to them and cheating in weights, the tribals continue to fall an easy prey of these middlemen. A majority of the tribal households sell their produce to the known traders/middlemen and also buy their essential requirements from them and remain indebted to them. Even after reorganisation of the cooperative societies in 1971 and creation of various institutions to serve them, initiation of several stringent measures by the State Governments in promulgating several Acts and Rules and enforcing them rigidly, exploitation of tribals could not be checked as a result of which the tribal economy is being eroded.

The following suggestions are, therefore, offered for improving the conditions of the tribals. While the major initiatives should come from the State/Central Governments for creation of adequate infrastructural facilities, the financial institutions are required to gear up their credit functions in generating economic activity among the tribals.

ENFORCEMENT OF PROTECTIVE ACTS/REGULATIONS/RULES

(i) The investments in tribal areas, however well-planned and massive these may be, will only add to the miseries of the tribal people if they are not provided with proper protection umbrella. It is, therefore, strongly felt that the protective laws should be strictly implemented so as to ensure benefits of economic development to the tribals. The loopholes in the existing laws should be plugged forthwith and regulations of anti-exploitative nature strictly enforced in the field of land reforms, credit, bonded labour, trade, excise, forests, *etc.*

(ii) The lacunae and shortcomings in the Acts and Rules for "reservation of posts and services" for tribals should be removed and such enactments should be enforced rigidly. It should be made a cognisable offense to violate such rules.

(iii) For tribal migrants, a small amount of advance in the beginning will come in handy and guidance should be provided during the migration period, so that they do not fall into the clutches of the unscrupulous labour contractors. The provisions of the Inter State Migrant Workman (Regulation of Employment and Conditions of Service) Act, 1979, should be enforced strictly.

(iv) Liquor shops in tribal areas are the source of much nuisance, exploitation and are ruining the economic backbone of the tribals and hence, these should be closed.

A. Administrative Structure, Personnel Training, *etc.*

(i) The developmental blocks may be rationalised by reorganising them into smaller blocks with high percentage of tribal population. This may affect implementation of ITDPs for the benefit of the tribals. The thrust should be towards raising the socio-economic standard of each tribal family.

(ii) The Project Administrator in-charge of ITDA blocks should have full control over the blocks. He should have a definite standing in the district administrative hierarchy.

(iii) Administration of tribal areas should be comprehensive and unified, combining development, regulatory and public distribution system. Such combination of functions should be effected in the Project Administrators at the ITDA level and the block level as far as possible.

(iv) The quality of personnel is crucial to implementation of developmental programmes. Only suitable officers, *i.e.,* those having requisite aptitude, empathy and dedication should be posted in tribal areas. The recommendations of the Maheswar Prasad Committee on Administrative Arrangement and Personnel Policy in Tribal Areas should be implemented.

(v) The traditional tribal institutions for grain storage, settling disputes, *etc.,* should be revived and reinforced and made vehicles for tribal participation in development works.

B. Planning, Finance, Implementation & Evaluation

(i) The data base for tribal development planning should be strong and reliable and steps are, therefore, urgently necessary for preparing the same.

(ii) The developmental plans of the State Government should be integrated with the credit plans of the financial institutions. Credit will be productive only when it is matched with appropriate/adequate infrastructural facilities. As the financial institutions start preparing credit plans for the next year by October, the State Government may endeavour for advance planning and make the plan documents available to the former so that necessary credit projections/provisions could be made by them, in accordance with Government priorities and tribal requirements.

(iii) Constant dialogue and cooperation between the developmental agencies and the financial institutions, is a must for successful implementation of different income-generating programmes. The Government machinery should extend cooperation to the financial

institutions for scheme formulation/ implementation and recovery of loans.

(iv) The example of Gujarat Government on the issue of financial sanctions for a five-year period indicating annual phasing and assuring field agencies of availability of funds every year without having to wait for the annual formal sanctions, may be followed.

(v) A supplement to the State Budget for the tribal sub-plan, giving a clear picture of project-wise financial positions, would be helpful for coordinated planning and implementation.

(vi) The role of the Monitoring and Review Committees should be made effective. Periodic evaluation should be undertaken through independent bodies and the feedback utilised for policy formulation.

(vii) The process of planning has to be built up from below, funneling upwards, implying realistic integrated efforts. A realistic long-term perspective plan with clear-cut objectives is expected to bring about development of tribals.

C. Involvement of Voluntary Organisations

(i) Voluntary organisations with proven track records should be involved in development of the tribals. Their services could be utilised by ensuring active participation and involvement of the tribals in their welfare programmes and approaching tribal' problems and programmes from a closer perspective. Implementation of schemes of direct and indirect benefits to them and organisation of tribal voluntary workers and group leaders for social work, especially in primitive tribal areas where on account of inaccessibility and lack of communication facilities, the government programmes do not adequately reach the lowest level, could also be possible with the involvement of the voluntary organisations. Besides, the voluntary organisations may fare well in their efforts in providing training and upgrading the skills of the tribals, particularly of the women.

D. Rehabilitation of the Nomadic Tribes

(i) The hunters, gatherers and shifting cultivators who are nomadic should be suitably rehabilitated by setting up model forest villages. Medium-sized villages of 20 to 40 households with houses and homestead land, backyard land for horticultural plantation, land for settled cultivation and also for fuel-wood plantation and pasture may be set up.

The nomadic tribals may also be rehabilitated by undertaking commercial plantations with the help of their labour in forested or deforested government land as is being adopted in Gujarat and Tripura. The tribals may be paid monthly allowances/wages till the plantations provide stabilised yields and thereafter, the same may be handed over to them for their benefit. Further, to increase the income level of the tribals, some other activities which generate immediate income should be financed as the monthly allowances/wages may not be adequate for sustenance.

Floriculture in tribal regions can be promoted where special wild varieties with medicinal values are available. Development of sericulture and medicinal plants which would be well suited to the tribals, can also be taken up on a large scale basis.

E. Forest Policy

(i) The tribals have a symbiotic relationship with the forest and for a variety of their requirements including food, they depend on the forest. Mixed cropping instead of mono-cropping is, therefore, suggested with conferment of rights to the usufructs. Horticulture may be given priority as the tribal areas are suitable for it. Plantation of Arjun and Asan trees which would be the base for tassar silk-worm rearing should be attempted in addition to other plantations.

(ii) Minor Forest Produce (MFP) plays an important role in the tribal economy. The right of tribals for collection of all MFP should be conferred by the State Government with adequate buy-back arrangements for the purpose of processing and marketing. The Government-owned procurement and marketing agencies like TDCC, OSCMF, OFDC, UFP, TRIFED, NAFED should try to set up processing plants wherever needed for value-addition to the minor forest produce collected by the tribals for ensuring better remuneration and also opening up employment opportunities for the latter. A long term perspective plan for the development and marketing of such items with clear targets may be spelt out.

F. Development of Non-Farm Sector Activities

(i) Traditional tribal handicrafts and products of arts and crafts should be encouraged and markets provided. Steps should be taken to locate the vanishing tribal arts and crafts for revival, promotion and development.

(ii) Forest-based cottage, village and small industries, *i.e.*, honey extraction, lac culture, beedi leaves processing, tassar silk-worm culture, carpet-making, tamarind paste, wood-based industries, gums and resins, broom-stick manufacture, *etc.*, have good scope for development which may be encouraged as these can be easily handled by the tribal men and women. They can be suitably trained, provided with important tools, raw materials and marketing assistance.

G. Social Infrastructure

(i) The State Governments may provide adequate support for social infrastructure creation, particularly relating to education and

health. Lack of education and awareness is the primary reason for absence of entrepreneurship among the tribals. Education and awareness programmes should, therefore, receive adequate attention of the State Governments. A detailed study may be mounted by the State Governments to identify the bottlenecks for low literacy levels among the tribals and initiate drastic measures, based upon the study findings.

H. Transport, Communication and Electrification

(i) Lack of communication facilities is still a major problem in tribal areas which requires attention on a priority basis. Road development may be taken up accompanied by effective implementation of protective measures, lest it may help the exploitative forces to the detriment of tribal interests. Important administrative centres like the Tehsils and blocks should be made accessible as early as possible. Further, weekly haats/markets should also be connected with roads on a priority basis.

(ii) Electrification of tribal areas should qualify for special attention. Rural Electrification Corporation schemes may be implemented in tribal areas on a preferential basis.

I. Banking Development

(i) The Bawa Committee, recommended sanction of production and consumer credit to tribals by LAMPS on a larger scale so that the tribals should not be indebted to the traders and middlemen. The LAMPS should also play an effective role in marketing of the produce of the tribals. But the LAMPS have failed to function as expected as they are suffering from poor management, low resource base, low level of business, inadequate margins, *etc.* The LAMPS should be streamlined and strengthened to do away with the tribal exploitation in credit and marketing. The large areas covered by LAMPS, makes them less effective to meet the demands of the tribals. Their performance relating to supply of consumer goods and PDS is also far from satisfactory. Task Forces may be appointed to go into the details of the working of the LAMPS in various State and suggest measures for their revival at the earliest. Tribal people are not attuned to savings, due to the extremely low level of surplus generation from the sale of various agricultural and minor forest produce or from their labour or their handicrafts. Their primary concern is food security and thus their major savings are preferably in the form of *(i)* grain golas for storage of surplus foodgrains on an individual or community basis and *(ii)* in the form of scrub cattle which can be sold or butchered, as the need arises. Thus, the LAMPS have not been able to meet the demands of tribal savings. To encourage tribal savings in the form of money, there must be creation of sizeable surpluses which obviate the need

for food security in the form of grain or cattle and encourage the need for monetary savings.

(ii) The allocation of service areas for bank branches in tribal districts needs a fresh look. The bank branches are seen catering to the credit requirements of a large number of villages (more than 100) spread over a vast geographical area measuring even 300 sq. km. against the National average of about 70 sq. km. The average population served by some branches also exceeds the average of about 13,000 persons per branch. For tribal areas, smaller service areas with lower population criteria may be adopted so that the banking services in the form required for tribals, could be available expeditiously.

(iii) The staff strength of the branches operating in tribal areas needs persons who are sympathetic to the tribals and their way of life. Postings in tribal areas are generally not preferred by most officials. So, implementation of a system of rewards for working in tribal areas, in the form of weightage in promotion, educational allowance for the children, additional health and LFC facilities, extra remuneration, *etc.*, will be a desirable step to induce staff.

(iv) A majority of the branches have no vehicular facility for mobility of the staff. Motorcycles should be provided to these branches on a priority basis for the mobility of the staff.

(v) Lack of entrepreneurship/awareness is found to be one of the main reasons for the economic backwardness of the tribals. The bank branches in coordination with the developmental departments of the State Government/ NGOs should, therefore, undertake entrepreneurship development/ awareness programmes and also provide adequate finance so that the tribals could undertake investment ventures for their economic benefits. The banks may form Farmers' Clubs in the tribal areas with financial support available from NABARD under its Vikas Volunteer Vahini programme to preach the principles of development through credit in order to ensure proper utilisation of loans and satisfactory recovery thereof.

(vi) The security-oriented lending approach of the banks is a hindrance in flow of adequate credit to the tribal areas. The banks insist on security, two to three times of the loan assistance provided. While the present security norms merits further relaxation by RBI, banks, a system may be developed by the State Governments to provide guarantees for payment of interest and repayment of principal by the tribal borrowers, particularly for the tribals who do not possess the requisite ownership titles to land. The land records of the tribals also should be set right so that they can avail of loans from the banks, wherever necessary, against land mortgage.

The timing of provision of tribal credit is also an important factor. In Orissa, the tribals observe a festival called Nua Khai sometime around August–September of the year when new clothes, new household items, *etc.*, have to be purchased as also feasts have to be organised. As the harvest season is only in January/February, it would not be possible for banks to lend money against the future produce, for the festival requirements. So, the tribals are forced to depend on traders/middlemen/agents who loan small amounts of money to the tribals against future produce/sales. Thus, the middlemen/agents/traders are able to purchase produce at very low rates due to the tribals' indebtedness. In tribal areas, the crop production loan may have three components, *viz.*,

(*a*) production component in cash (30 per cent)
(*b*) kind component (seeds, fertilisers, pesticides, agricultural components) (40 per cent)
(*c*) marketing/consumption component in cash (30 per cent) for meeting festival/social obligations.

This will enable the tribal farmers to escape the clutches of the traders/ agents/money-lenders who would be able to exploit him year after year. The third 'cash' component would be given as and when required by the tribal farmers for festivals/consumption purpose, under relaxed conditions.

(*vii*) Self-Help Groups having linkages with financing banks, may be encouraged among the tribals, especially women. This innovative credit dispensation system not only reduces the transaction costs of the banks and borrowers, but also enables leadership development, tribal empowerment, meets emergent credit requirements of the members and ensures recovery of loans. The 100 per cent refinance facility available from NABARD for financing of SHGs may be availed of by the banks.

(*viii*) The Sri Lanka experiment known as Community Credit Facilitators (CCFs) Scheme may be adopted in the tribal areas. The scheme has enabled the people in Sri Lanka to obtain loan facilities conveniently at reasonable rates of interest through the Community Credit Facilitators who are appointed by the banks for routing bank loans through them. The tribals are more inclined to deal with a person whom they know well rather than with banks which create a transaction cost for them in travelling, filling up forms, providing collateral security and loss of manhours; the CCF scheme could be ideally implemented in tribal areas of the State.

It would be desirable to implement the scheme on a pilot basis in one or two tribal blocks of each State first and replicate the same subsequently, based upon the results.

J. Marketing Support

(*i*) The procurement activities of the line-organisations needs improvement to save the tribals from exploitation by the traders, middlemen, etc. The LAMPS, TDCC, GCC and other agencies should operate with cooperation and coordination among themselves. There should be healthy functional linkage and coordination among the LAMPS, TDCC, OSCMF and other apex organisations in the State as also with National Level Federations like TRIFED and NAFED.

(ii) As per the decision of the Government, it should be ensured that LAMPS function as agents for procurement of SAP and MFP in all tribal sub-plan areas on commission basis. Funds for the purpose may, therefore, be placed with LAMPS well in advance.

The State Cooperative Marketing Federations/Tribal Development Cooperative Corporations may ensure marketing of the produce collected by the LAMPS on priority basis. The LAMPS too, on the other hand, should properly utilise the funds given for procurement without diverting the same for meeting their administrative expenditures.

(iii) The credit support available from NABARD for development of lac cultivation and collection and marketing of minor forest produce has not been availed by the SCBs. As these are primarily meant for the tribals, the SCBs may take advantage of the facility.

(iv) The tribals are still found in the exploitative clutches of the traders, middlemen and money-lenders and sell their produce to them at prices dictated by the former. Due to poor finances, institutions such as the TDCC and OSCMF are unable to procure the entire MFP collected/SAP produced by the tribals and make timely payment thereof. Both the cooperative agencies are running on losses for the last several years. The State Governments should make a detailed study of the functioning of agencies engaged in procurement and marketing of tribal produce and initiate suitable measures for re-establishing their effectiveness.

(v) NABARD may consider the pilot scheme suggested by NAFED to improve procurement position of SAP/MFP at the grassroots level through LAMPS. Under the pilot scheme, NABARD has to finance direct to the LAMPS during the peak procurement period and NAFED will under a tie-up arrangement, ensure repayments to NABARD out of the sale proceeds of the items.

(vi) Processing units should be set up in tribal areas taking into consideration the quantum of procurement and demand in the market. This will not only create additional employment opportunities for the tribals but also add value to the produce and fetch a better price for the tribals. These processing units may be set up by LAMPS, NGOs and other tribal development organisations.

Prevention of Starvation deaths in Tribal Areas

Every year there are 'starvation' deaths in tribal areas *e.g.*, Kashipur in Koraput district, Orissa, Chandrapur district, Maharashtra, tribal areas of

Rajasthan and Madhya Pradesh & Andhra Pradesh. It has become so routine that many newspapers fail to report such deaths. Public awareness has been de-sensitised by such deaths and possibly do not bother about the precious lives of our tribal brothers and sisters.

The deaths according to the various State Governments are due to malnutrition of chronic diseases. Deaths could, also be caused due to eating of 'infected' mango kernels which may not have been properly dried in the summer and which are eaten as a grual for the carbohydrate/fat content. In order to survive for 2–3 months during monsoon when food is very scarce and it is not possible to go to the jungles in search of food such as yams, tubers, dead animals *etc.* Another reason for deaths is 'anthrax' and other cattle borne diseases as rotten or infected carecasses of dead cattle, are often eaten by tribal people when no other food is available.

It is obvious that rotting carcasses and infected mango kernels are eaten by tribal people not because they prefer such foods but because no other food is available to them. The 65 million tonnes of buffer foodgrains stock rotting in the FCI and other government godowns for the last 4–5 years, could obviously be put to better use than feeding the huge rats and worms that infest foodgrain godowns.

Many tribal societies (though not all of them) used to have a system of 'grain golas'. This was a primitive bamboo-woven enclosure for grains stocked in a central place in the tribal village and maintained by the entire community. Any tribal family in th village which had no grains left, could withdraw foodgrains measured by the fist-full. But at harvest time or if the family purchased grains, for every fist-ful of grain taken from the grain gola, two fist-fulls of grain had to be re-stocked in the grain golas. this was how primitive tribal societies warded off starvation deaths. Grain golas were never cheated of their dues and the grain stocks were always replenished as no tribal would ever dream of cheating and not retuning grains to the grain golas.

But in the late 1950's and early 1960's these grain golas were destroyed as a matter of policy to give way to the tribal cooperative societies which were supposed to meet all the tribal food, credit and marketing needs. Today, the tribal people are saddled with non-functioning/dyfunctional LAMPS and only a few grain golas survive.

The only way to prevent further loss of precious tribal lives is to set up grain golas in each tribal village with the tribal community contributing to creation of golas by way of 'shramdan' and a 'tiny fraction of the surplus foodgrains from the buffer stock of over 65 million tonnes, could be given free by the Central Government. The tribal people would themselves run the grain golas as they have done for centuries and these starvation deaths would be avoided. Also, grains would not rot away, in Government godowns but could be used in the grain golas which are the tribal peoples godowns. Starvation deaths need not occur and it would be a crime if the grain gola concept is not revived for tribal benefit.

Tribal economic development will be a reality if the desire for change is felt and is perceived as the need of the entire community. The desire for progress and enhancement of individual/collective status, has yet to be experienced, in the tribal context. The winds of change must be from within and should not be imposed by external forces whether they be NGOs, Governments or religious institutions. The tribal people should be enabled to work out their destiny, at their own pace. However, lack of progress or stagnation leads to decay in any society and the tribal society needs to guard against this.

Bibliography

Bose, N.K., Tribal Life in India, National Book Trust, Delhi, 1971.

Chakrabarti, M. & Mukherjee, D., Indian Tribes, Saraswati Library, Calcutta, 1971.

Danda, A.K., Tribal Economics and their Transformation, ICSSR, 1973.

Doshi, S.C., Emerging Tribal Image, Rawat Publications, Jaipur, 1997.

Edward, Jay, A Tribal Village in Middle India, Anthropological Survey of India, Calcutta, 1970.

Elwin, Verrier, A New Deal for Tribal India, Ministry of Home Affairs, Publications Division, New Delhi, 1963.

Fernandes, Walter, Geeta Menon and Philip Viegas, Forest, Environment and Tribal Economy, Indian Social Institute, New Delhi, 1988.

Ganguli, I.B., Economic Problems of the Jhumias of Tripura, Bookland, Calcutta, 1969.

Ghurye, G.S., The Scheduled Tribes, Popular Book Depot, Bombay, 1963.

Haimendorf, C.V.M. Fuser, Tribe Raj — Gonds in Adilabad, Macmillan, London, 1948.

Ledgier, Mary McDonald, Forest Tribes, BA CSA, London, 1991.

Majumder, D.N., Affairs of Tribes, Universal Publishers, Lucknow, 1953.

Mishra, A.K., A Small Step Forward, NABARD, Bhubaneswar, 1999.

Nadeem Hasnain, Tribal India Today, Manman Publications, New Delhi, 1991.

Rao, L. Murali Krishna, Marketing in Tribal Economy, Inter India Publications, New Delhi, 1952.

Rao, V.K.R.V., Social Change and Tribal Society, *Journal of Social Research*, Vol. IX, No. 2, September, 1966.

Rao, Venkat A., A Century of Tribal Politics, S. Chand, New Delhi, 1976.

Satyanaryan, M., Tribal Development in India: A Trend Report, Inter-India Publication, New Delhi, 1990.

Saxena, R.P., Tribal Economy in Central India, Calcutta, 1964.

Singh, Suresh K., Tribal Situation in India, Indian Institute of Anthropology, Simla, 1972.

Srinivas, M.N., Social Change in Modern India, Allied Publishers, Bombay, 1965.

Thakur, Devendra and Thakur, D.N. *Ed.*, Tribal Life in India–Vol. 3 (Tribal Life and Forests), Deep & Deep Publications, New Delhi, 1994.

UNO, Rural Development Administration in India, UNO.

Vidyarthi, L.P. & Ravi, B.K., The Tribal Culture of India, Concept Publishing Company, New Delhi, 1976.

Zafur, M., Policy for Planning and Development in Tribal Areas, NICD, Hyderabad, 1975.

Index